OLD ENGLISH PROSE AND VERSE

Old English Prose and Verse

AN ANNOTATED SELECTION
WITH INTRODUCTIONS AND
NOTES BY

Roger Fowler

LONDON

ROUTLEDGE AND KEGAN PAUL

NEW YORK: THE HUMANITIES PRESS

First published 1966
by Routledge & Kegan Paul Limited
Broadway House, 68–74 Carter Lane
London, E.C.4

Printed in Great Britain
by Richard Clay (The Chaucer Press) Ltd.
Bungay, Suffolk

CONTENTS

VERSE

I. HEROIC POETRY

II. RELIGIOUS EPIC

III. SHORT POEMS

IV. POETIC PARAPHRASE

PREFACE

IF THE STUDY OF OLD ENGLISH, the greatest survivor of our early Germanic literatures, is to be maintained, adequate materials for reading it are needed: grammars, dictionaries, collections of texts. All are, after a sort, available: but students' basic needs are, generally, supplied by old publications. Since the great days of Anglo-Saxon editing, especially, attitudes to the literature have changed, and the demands of its audience have become very different. The decline in philological specialisation, and the usual reduction in teaching time devoted to Old English, make it necessary to revise the balance of contents, and extend the apparatus, of beginners' selections of Old English texts.

This collection has two main objects: to provide enough, and the right sort of, texts for a complete elementary course; and to supply a full apparatus to assist in their study. Twenty complete or excerpted texts are included, giving representation of virtually every text of major literary interest. Verse predominates over prose, in acknowledgement of its obviously greater literary value in Old English, and it is hoped that the bulk of what is offered will be used, despite the temptation of elementary Old English courses to concentrate on the easier prose. Trivial curiosities such as Gnomic Verses and Charms are avoided (although the inclusion of some such things might have given a fairer picture of the range of surviving texts), as are pieces of purely linguistic or historical interest.

The critical and explanatory material represents the sort of aid for which I would have been grateful as a student, and which I as a teacher expect the text-book rather than the teacher to supply: I hope this has not made it too idiosyncratic. The short introductions to individual texts are designed to be informative rather than interpretative, indicating (where possible) something about date, authorship, manuscript situation, character and critical interest. The notes comment on people and places mentioned; explain allusions; assist in linguistic difficulties, sometimes offering paraphrases; draw attention to points of lexical interest; and cite and quote parallels. The bibliography is in two chief sections, recommending books and articles of a general nature and then works on specific texts. Items are recommended for throwing light on factual and literary matters, and specialised, advanced and (it is hoped) eccentric material is avoided. Two main aims govern the glossary: completeness in the listing of different forms and adequacy of cross-reference. Fuller explanation of the working of the glossary is given in a note at its head.

Editing this volume has been a complex task, and its scope must have given occasion for many errors of judgement, fact or technique. A great many things have been put right on the advice of several individuals. Chief among these are Mrs Margaret 'Espinasse, J. Norton-Smith, and R. F. Lawrence, of the University of Hull, who between them read most of the introductory material and notes. My wife provided invaluable assistance by checking the text in typescript and proof. If errors remain, I must be blamed for prematurely convincing these people and myself that the job was complete.

ROGER FOWLER

University of East Anglia

ABBREVIATIONS

ME	Middle English
Mod.E.	Modern English
MS(S)	Manuscript(s)
OE	Old English
ON	Old Norse
OS	Old Saxon
CBEL	*Cambridge Bibliography of English Literature*
EETS	Early English Text Society
EHR	*English Historical Review*
ELH	*Journal of English Literary History*
JEGP	*Journal of English and Germanic Philology*
MLN	*Modern Language Notes*
MLR	*Modern Language Review*
MPh	*Modern Philology*
PBA	*Proceedings of the British Association*
PMLA	*Publications of the Modern Language Association of America*
PQ	*Philological Quarterly*
RES (n.s.)	*Review of English Studies* (new series)
SP	*Studies in Philology*
TPS	*Transactions of the Philological Society*
TRHS	*Transactions of the Royal Historical Society*

* Denotes a reconstructed, unrecorded, form of a word.

For abbreviations of grammatical terms see headnote to Glossary.

PROSE

I. THE ANGLO-SAXON CHRONICLE

The Anglo-Saxon Chronicle is the chief continuous narrative prose work in Old English, and the most valuable single written source for the history of the period. Its origin is usually traced to the Easter Tables—tables used by priests to calculate the date of Easter in any particular year. These had a left-hand column with the date of each year written on a separate line, a number of other vertical columns and a wide margin on the right. It was the practice to write a short note of an event of one year in the margin opposite the date; not in order to provide a historical record, but merely to identify individual years. Such a set of annals is found in one manuscript, Cotton Caligula A. xv, of which a part is reproduced by Professor Garmonsway (*The Anglo-Saxon Chronicle*, pp. xxiv–xxv). A relic of this system may be seen in the Parker MS, in which the scribe first wrote the year-numbers, one year to a line, in a continuous column for several pages, with the result that some longer annals spread over several years, causing faults in the chronology.

The *Chronicle* as we now have it—much developed from the original primitive annals—exists in seven chief manuscripts. We print from two of these: those containing the Parker and Peterborough chronicles, early and later versions respectively. The Peterborough chronicle (MS Laud Misc. 636) was written in the twelfth century; it is a copy of a Canterbury chronicle to 1121, and was later continued to 1154. The Parker manuscript (Corpus Christi College, Cambridge, MS 173) is the most important of the seven, because it is the earliest (late ninth-eleventh centuries) and thus nearest to the original, and sheds some light on the material from which it and the other versions were compiled. The extant manuscripts are in fairly close agreement to about 890, and diverge after that date; the Parker version is written in one hand to almost the end of 891. These facts suggest that all the versions are derived from (lost) copies of an earlier compilation which were made about this date. It is commonly believed that King Alfred had a hand in the compilation and circulation of the *Chronicle* at this time; this would be consistent with the policy and known practice of his literary programme (cf. extract 4): note the West Saxon character of the entries; the few verbal parallels with Alfred's *Orosius*; the references to Winchester, Alfred's 'capital'; the emphasis on his achievements against the Danes. Hodgkin gives the evidence for Alfred's hand in the work; Stenton has argued against this (see Bibliography for references). It seems reasonable to call this an 'Alfredian' or 'West Saxon' chronicle: the stimulus may well have come under Alfred's rule, but the exact place and circumstances of composition are difficult to establish.

1. THE FEUD OF CYNEWULF AND CYNEHEARD

THIS NARRATIVE of what amounts to a grim vendetta has often been praised and anthologised. It is one of the longest of the earlier entries of the *Chronicle*, and is a completely developed short story. The chronicler, with a clear perception of cause-and-effect relationship, puts together events thirty years apart. (Cynewulf's death occurred in 786, and the annal, starting with his accession, is incorrectly dated 755 for 757.) The chain of events starts with a political action, the deposition of Sigebryht; but after this the narrative consists of a string of personal acts of vengeance, in which even the lowest members of a household participate. This is the story of several stages of a feud reminiscent of the family feuding in the Icelandic sagas.

This episode is often referred to as a source of evidence for Anglo-Saxon social history: evidence that (as we see also in the *Battle of Maldon*) the *comitatus* system and ideals were actually important in Anglo-Saxon society. Chief among these ideals are those concerning the relationship between retainer and lord, and the duty of the retainer to avenge his lord or seek death; the tie of allegiance greater than the tie of kinship; the refusal of bribes. With the *Battle of Maldon*, the Cynewulf and Cyneheard episode gives full illustration of the operation of the *comitatus* system late in Germanic heroic society, and so is valuable to the historian. Perhaps of greater interest to the student of Old English literature is the completeness with which the motives of the protagonists are presented. There is every sign that Anglo-Saxon writers were interested in people's reactions to events; this fact, which is evidenced fully in *Beowulf*, the *Battle of Maldon* and the highly subjective elegiac poems, has been in the past obscured by critics who merely quarried these works for documentation of historical theses. In this extract motivation is given at almost every stage: the murder of Sigebryht is not just an event, but is presented as a deliberate act of vengeance; in the final encounter the attitudes of both sides are given fully; at the end, even the reason why one survivor was spared is given.

The full investigation of motivation marks this extract off from other parts of the Alfredian *Chronicle*. It stands out also because of the completeness and lucidity of the narrative. It is self-contained and self-explanatory, the reasons for each stage of the story being given. There is variety in the method of narration: direct narration, reported speech, direct speech. These qualities justify its inclusion in an anthology as an example of the excellence the *Chronicle* can achieve as narrative prose, although it is hardly typical of the normal technique of the *Chronicle*.

Some commentators have been so struck by the outstanding character of this extract that they have been unwilling to accept it as a piece originally written down as part of the *Chronicle* (because its quality, supposedly, differentiates it from ordinary chronicle writing) and have postulated more 'literary' originals on which it might have been based. Suggestions have been that it is based on a poem relating a heroic encounter, in the manner of *Maldon* or *Brunanburh*; or that it stems from a prose saga orally transmitted. Wright suggests that it 'must have taken form quite soon after the happening itself and continued in oral circulation until it was written into an annalistic series, which was incorporated in the *Chronicle* in its present form in the time of Alfred'. He calls it a 'saga' and cites the example of the Icelandic sagas. Magoun, however, argues that the political interest of the events was great enough to justify extended treatment by the chronicler: he stresses (perhaps too much) the historical and heroic achievement of Osric in quelling an abortive putsch by Cyneheard.

755 [757] Her Cynewulf benam Sigebryht his rices ond West-Seaxna wiotan for unryhtum dædum, buton Hamtunscire; ond he hæfde þa oþ he ofslog þone aldormon þe him lengest wunode. Ond hiene þa Cynewulf on Andred adræfde, ond he þær wunade oþþæt hiene an swan ofstang æt Pryfetes flodan; ond he wræc þone aldormon Cum- 5
bran.

Ond se Cynewulf oft miclum gefeohtum feaht uuiþ Bretwalum; ond ymb xxxi wintra þæs þe he rice hæfde, he wolde adræfan anne æþeling se was Cyneheard haten; ond se Cyneheard wæs þæs Sige- bryhtes broþur. Ond þa geascode he þone cyning lytle werode on 10 wifcyþþe on Merantune, ond hine þær berad ond þone bur utan beeode ær hine þa men onfunden þe mid þam kyninge wærun. Ond þa ongeat se cyning þæt, ond he on þa duru eode, ond þa unheanlice hine werede oþ he on þone æþeling locude, ond þa ut ræsde on hine ond hine miclum gewundode. Ond hie alle on þone cyning wærun 15 feohtende oþþæt hie hine ofslægenne hæfdon. Ond þa on þæs wifes gebærum onfundon þæs cyninges þegnas þa unstilnesse, ond þa þider urnon, swa hwelc swa þonne gearo wearþ ond radost. Ond hiera se æþeling gehwelcum feoh ond feorh gebead; ond hiera nænig hit geþicgean nolde. Ac hie simle feohtende wæran oþ hie alle lægon 20 butan anum Bryttiscum gisle, ond se swiþe gewundad wæs.

Þa on morgenne gehierdun þæt þæs cyninges þegnas þe him beæf- tan wærun, þæt se cyning ofslægen wæs, þa ridon hie þider, ond his aldormon Osric, ond Wiferþ his þegn, ond þa men þe he beæftan him læfde ær; ond þone æþeling on þære byrig metton þær se cyning 25 ofslægen læg—ond þa gatu him to belocen hæfdon—ond þa þærto eodon. Ond þa gebead he him hiera agenne dom feos ond londes gif hie him þæs rices uþon, ond him cyþdon þæt hiera mægas him mid wæron, þa þe him from noldon. Ond þa cuædon hie þæt him nænig mæg leofra nære þonne hiera hlaford, ond hie næfre his banan folgian 30 noldon, ond þa budon hie hiera mægum þæt hie gesunde from eodon. Ond hie cuædon þæt tæt ilce hiera geferum geboden wære þe ær mid þam cyninge wærun; þa cuædon hie þæt hie hie þæs ne onmunden 'þon ma þe eowre geferan þe mid þam cyninge ofslægene wærun.'

33. *hie hie:* the second *hie* has been inserted above the line.

35 Ond hie þa ymb þa gatu feohtende wæron oþþæt hie þærinne fulgon
ond þone æþeling ofslogon ond þa men þe him mid wærun, alle
butan anum: se wæs þæs aldormonnes godsunu, ond he his feorh
generede; ond þeah he wæs oft gewundad.

2. ALFRED'S WARS WITH THE DANES

THIS EXTRACT narrates one of the most terrible onslaughts of the Danes on
England. It records how the Danes, starved out of France, overran the
country for several years in a series of campaigns which oppressed large
areas of England; suffered several defeats (Farnham, Benfleet, for example)
and yet were almost always a move ahead of the English; and in the end
left because they reaped no real advantage. The initiative was almost
always with the invaders, who were able to move quickly, harass the English in several places at once, and recover after defeat. The English pursued
the Danes; when they caught up with them (usually when the Danes were
fortified within their objective) victory often went to the *fyrd*. But the
length of the struggle suggests that there were no really crushing defeats.
The strategies and detailed moves of both sides are of interest: the successful diversion by the Danelaw invaders which allowed the remains of the
great army to escape from Thorney Island; Alfred's clever damming of the
River Lea; the Danes' reliance on sudden moves across country; the
destruction of the crops at Chester; Alfred's design for a fleet, which met
with mixed fortune; his reliance on the truce with Hæsten, and the latter's
treachery.

The literary interest in this passage must be in the chronicler's success
or failure to present intelligibly an extremely complex narrative of simultaneous campaigns by several protagonists in a large geographical setting,
over a period of time. We are, of course, at a disadvantage: there are
difficulties for us which would not have troubled a contemporary—the
identification of place-names, for example. It must be admitted that there
is some confusion, especially in regard to the truce with Hæsten and the
movements of the two Danish armies in the early stages. Hodgkin calls it
an 'animated but tangled story'. It is animated in the sense that we have a
good impression of the vigour of the campaigns, perhaps of the English
feeling that the Danes were striking unexpected blows from all sides. I do
not sense the 'glowing patriotism' that Hodgkin detects: the chronicler is
fair in giving the initiative constantly to the Danes and in not overplaying
the contribution of Alfred to the English successes.

A summary of the movements may be useful:

1. Great army arrives at the Lympne from France and encamps at
Appledore. Hæsten, with a smaller force, takes up position at Milton
Royal. Danelaw people co-operate with the invaders.

2. Alfred establishes himself between the armies and makes peace with
Hæsten, who moves off to the north of the Thames. Later we hear that
he entrenches himself at Benfleet, breaks the truce and plunders the
countryside.

6

3. The great army, with much booty, makes a break to try to join Hæsten; defeated by Edward at Farnham, driven north up Colne and besieged on Thorney Island.

4. Alfred, going to relieve the besieging division when their supplies run out, has to move west to counter two attacks in the West Country. The Danes keep Alfred busy in the west by raids along the coast: the great army escapes and goes to Hæsten's camp at Benfleet.

5. Edward, Æthelred and the Londoners defeat the great army at Benfleet. The survivors join up with Hæsten, and both armies are established at Shoebury.

6. (a) First of three raids in a north-west direction; Danes defeated at Buttington.

(b) Second raid; Danes starved out of Chester, return through Northumbria and East Anglia, and set themselves up on Mersea.

(c) Third raid; Danes reach Bridgenorth, but disperse the next year: some return to the Continent.

7. Alfred's naval battle finally quells the Danes marauding on the south coast, in a rather untidy action.

893 [892] Her on þysum geare for se micla here, þe we gefyrn ymbe spræcon, eft of þæm eastrice westweard to Bunnan, ond þær wurdon gescipode, swa þæt hie asettan him on anne siþ ofer mid horsum mid ealle, ond þa comon up on Limene muþan mid ccl hunde scipa. Se muþa is on easteweardre Cent æt þæs miclan wuda eastende þe we 5 Andred hatað. Se wudu is eastlang ond westlang hundtwelftiges mila lang oþþe lengra, ond þritiges mila brad. Seo ea þe we ær ymbe spræcon lið ut of þæm wealda. On þa ea hi tugon up hiora scipu oþ þone weald iiii mila fram þæm muþan uteweardum, ond þær abræcon an geweorc inne on þæm fenne; sæton feawa cirlisce men on, ond 10 wæs samworht.

Þa sona æfter þæm com Hæsten mid lxxx scipa up on Temese muðan ond worhte him geweorc æt Middeltune, ond se oþer here æt Apuldre.

894 [893] On þys geare, þæt wæs ymb twelf monað þæs þe hie on 15 þæm eastrice geweorc geworht hæfdon, Norþhymbre ond East-Engle hæfdon Ælffrede cyninge aþas geseald, ond East-Engle foregisla ui; ond þeh, ofer þa treowa, swa oft swa þa oþre hergas mid ealle herige ut foron, þonne foron hie oþþe mid oþþe on heora healfe an. Þa gegaderade Ælfred cyning his fierd ond for þæt he gewicode betwuh 20 þæm twam hergum, þær þær he niehst rymet hæfde for wudufæstenne

1. 892: MS *Anno dcccxciii;* but an extra *i* has been added by mistake to the annals 892–928.　　　　　　　　　5. *miclan:* MS *miclam.*

10. *inne on þæm fenne:* some other MSS read *fæstenne,* and most editors adopt this reading. I follow Smith in restoring the MS reading.

19. *an:* Smith and other editors read *on* and emend to *healfe. Ond þa . . .* But *an* appears to be the MS reading.

B　　　　　　　　　　　　7

ond for wæterfæstenne, swa þæt he mehte ægþerne geræcan gif hie
ænigne feld secan wolden. Þa foron hie siþþan æfter þæm wealda
hloþum ond flocradum bi swa hwaþerre efes swa hit þonne fierdleas
25 wæs; ond him mon eac mid oþrum floccum sohte mæstra daga ælce,
oþþe on niht, ge of þære fierde ge eac of þæm burgum. Hæfde se
cyning his fierd on tu tonumen, swa þæt hie wæron simle healfe æt
ham, healfe ute, butan þæm monnum þe þa burga healdan scolden.
Ne com se here oftor eall ute of þæm setum þonne tuwwa: oþre siþe
30 þa hie ærest to londe comon, ær sio fierd gesamnod wære, oþre siþe
þa hie of þæm setum faran woldon.

Þa hie gefengon micle herehyð ond þa woldon ferian norþweardes
ofer Temese in on East-Seaxe ongean þa scipu, þa forrad sio fierd hie
foran ond him wið gefeaht æt Fearnhamme, ond þone here gefliemde
35 ond þa herehyþa ahreddon, ond hie flugon ofer Temese buton ælcum
forda, þa up be Colne on anne iggað. Þa besæt sio fierd hie þær utan
þa hwile þe hie þær lengest mete hæfdon. Ac hi hæfdon þa heora
stemn gesetenne ond hiora mete genotudne, ond wæs se cyng þa
þiderweardes on fære mid þære scire þe mid him fierdedon. Þa he þa
40 wæs þiderweardes ond sio oþeru fierd wæs hamweardes, ond ða
Deniscan sæton þær behindan, forþæm hiora cyning wæs gewundod
on þæm gefeohte, þæt hi hine ne mehton ferian, þa gegaderedon þa þe
in Norþhymbrum bugeað ond on East-Englum sum hund scipa ond
foron suð ymbutan ond sum feowertig scipa norþ ymbutan, ond
45 ymbsæton an geweorc on Defnascire be þære Norþsæ; ond þa þe
suð ymbutan foron ymbsæton Exancester. Þa se cyng þæt hierde, þa
wende he hine west wið Exanceastres mid ealre þære fierde buton
swiþe gewaldenum dæle easteweardes þæs folces.

Þa foron forð oþþe hie comon to Lundenbyrg, ond þa mid þæm
50 burgwarum ond þæm fultume þe him westan com foron east to
Beamfleote. Wæs Hæsten þa þær cumen mid his herge þe ær æt
Middeltune sæt, ond eac se micla here wæs þa þær tocumen þe ær on
Limene muþan sæt æt Apuldre. Hæfde Hæsten ær geworht þæt
geweorc æt Beamfleote, ond wæs þa ut afaren on hergaþ; ond wæs se
55 micla here æt ham. Þa foron hie to ond gefliemdon þone here, ond
þæt geweorc abræcon, ond genamon eal þæt þær binnan wæs, ge on feo
ge on wifum ge eac on bearnum, ond brohton eall in to Lundenbyrig;
ond þa scipu eall oððe tobræcon oþþe forbærndon oþþe to Lundenbyrig brohton oþþe to Hrofesceastre. Ond Hæstenes wif ond his suna
60 twegen mon brohte to þæm cyninge, ond he hi him eft ageaf, forþæm
þe hiora wæs oþer his godsunu, oþer Æðeredes ealdormonnes. Hæfdon
hi hiora onfangen ær Hæsten to Beamfleote come, ond he him hæfde

---

28. *burga*: *a* inserted above.   39. *scire*: *ci* over an erasure.
62. *hæfde*: above the line.

8

geseald gislas ond aðas, ond se cyng him eac wel feoh sealde, ond eac
swa þa he þone cniht agef ond þæt wif. Ac sona swa hie to Beamfleote
comon ond þæt geweorc geworct wæs, swa hergode he on his rice   65
þone ilcan ende þe Æþered his cumpæder healdan sceolde, ond eft
oþre siþe he wæs on hergað gelend on þæt ilce rice þa þa mon his
geweorc abræc.

Þa se cyning hine þa west wende mid þære fierde wið Exancestres,
swa ic ær sæde, ond se here þa burg beseten hæfde, þa he þær to   70
gefaren wæs, þa eodon hie to hiora scipum. Þa he þa wið þone here
þær wæst abisgod wæs, ond þa hergas wæron þa gegaderode begen
to Sceobyrig on East-Seaxum ond þær geweorc worhtun, foron begen
ætgædere up be Temese; ond him com micel eaca to, ægþer ge of
East-Englum ge of Norþhymbrum. Foron þa up be Temese oþþæt   75
hie gedydon æt Sæferne, þa up be Sæferne. Þa gegaderode Æþered
ealdormon ond Æþelm ealdorman ond Æþelnoþ ealdorman ond þa
cinges þegnas þe þa æt ham æt þæm geweorcum wæron, of ælcre
byrig be eastan Pedredan, ge be westan Sealwuda ge be eastan, ge
eac be norþan Temese ond be westan Sæfern, ge eac sum dæl þæs   80
Norðwealcynnes. Þa hie þa ealle gegaderode wæron, þa offoron hie
þone here hindan æt Buttingtune on Sæferne staþe, ond hine þær
utan besæton on ælce healfe on anum fæstenne. Þa hie ða fela wucena
sæton on twa healfe þære é, ond se cyng wæs west on Defnum wiþ
þone sciphere, þa wæron hie mid metelieste gewægde, ond hæfdon   85
micelne dæl þara horsa freten ond þa oþre wæron hungre acwolen, þa
eodon hie ut to ðæm monnum þe on easthealfe þære é wicodon, ond
him wiþ gefuhton, ond þa Cristnan hæfdon sige. Ond þær wearð
Ordheh cyninges þegn ofslægen ond eac monige oþre cyninges þegnas
ofslægen; ond se dæl þe þær aweg com wurdon on fleame generede.   90

Þa hie on East-Seaxe comon to hiora geweorce ond to hiora scipum,
þa gegaderade sio laf eft of East-Englum ond of Norðhymbrum
micelne here onforan winter ond befæston hira wif ond hira scipu ond
hira feoh on East-Englum, ond foron anstreces dæges ond nihtes
þæt hie gedydon on anre westre ceastre on Wirhealum, seo is Lega-   95
ceaster gehaten. Þa ne mehte seo fird hie na hindan offaran ær hie
wæron inne on þæm geweorce; besæton þeah þæt geweorc utan sume
twegen dagas ond genamon ceapes eall þæt þær buton wæs, ond þa
men ofslogon þe hie foran forridan mehton butan geweorce, ond þæt
corn eall forbærndon ond mid hira horsum fretton on ælcre efenehðe.   100
Ond þæt wæs ymb twelf monað þæs þe hie ær hider ofer sæ comon.

---

64. *Beamfleote:* MS *bleam fleote.*
65. *geworct:* t added above line; *on* added above line in another hand.
84. *þære é:* MS *þæré*; *wæs west:* MS *wæst*, with *wes* above *t.*
89. *þegnas:* as added above by another scribe.

895 [894] Ond þa sona æfter þæm on ðys gere for se here of Wirheale
in on Norðwealas, forþæm hie ðær sittan ne mehton; þæt wæs forðy
þe hie wæron benumene ægðer ge þæs ceapes ge þæs cornes, ðe hie
105 gehergod hæfdon. Þa hie ða eft ut of Norðwealum wendon mid þære
herehyðe þe hie ðær genumen hæfdon, þa foron hie ofer Norðhymbra
lond ond East-Engla, swa swa seo fird hie geræcan ne mehte, oþþæt
hie comon on East-Seaxna lond easteweard on an igland þæt is ute on
þære sæ, þæt is Meresig haten. Ond þa se here eft hamweard wende
110 þe Exanceaster beseten hæfde, þa hergodon hie up on Suð-Seaxum
neah Cisseceastre, ond þa burgware hie gefliemdon ond hira monig
hund ofslogon ond hira scipu sumu genamon.

Ða þy ilcan gere onforan winter þa Deniscan þe on Meresige
sæton tugon hira scipu up on Temese ond þa up on Lygan. Þæt wæs
115 ymb twa ger þæs þe hie hider ofer sæ comon.

896 [895] On þy ilcan gere worhte se foresprecena here geweorc be
Lygan, xx mila bufan Lundenbyrig. Þa þæs on sumera foron micel
dæl þara burgwara, ond eac swa oþres folces, þæt hie gedydon æt
þara Deniscana geweorce, ond þær wurdon gefliemde, ond sume
120 feower cyninges þegnas ofslægene. Þa þæs on hærfeste þa wicode se
cyng on neaweste þære byrig þa hwile þe hie hira corn gerypon, þæt
þa Deniscan him ne mehton þæs ripes forwiernan. Þa sume dæge rad
se cyng up bi þære eæ ond gehawade hwær mon mehte þa ea forwyrcan, þæt hie ne mehton þa scipu ut brengan. Ond hie ða swa dydon:
125 worhton ða tu geweorc on twa healfe þære eas. Þa hie ða þæt geweorc
furþum ongunnen hæfdon, ond þærto gewicod hæfdon, þa onget se
here þæt hie ne mehton þa scipu ut brengan. Þa forleton hie hie, ond
eodon ofer land þæt hie gedydon æt Cwatbrycge be Sæfern, ond þær
gewerc worhton. Þa rad seo fird west æfter þæm herige, ond þa men
130 of Lundenbyrig gefetedon þa scipu, ond þa ealle þe hie alædan ne
mehton tobræcon, ond þa þe þær stælwyrðe wæron binnan Lundenbyrig gebrohton. Ond þa Deniscan hæfdon hira wif befæst innan
East-Engle ær hie ut of þæm geweorce foron. Þa sæton hie þone winter
æt Cwatbrycge. Þæt wæs ymb þreo ger þæs þe hie on Limene
135 muðan comon hider ofer sæ.

897 [896] Ða þæs on sumera on ðysum gere tofor se here, sum on
East-Engle, sum on Norðhymbre, ond þa þe feohlease wæron him
þær scipu begeton ond suð ofer sæ foron to Sigene. Næfde se here,
Godes þonces, Angelcyn ealles forswiðe gebrocod. Ac hie wæron
140 micle swiþor gebrocede on þæm þrim gearum mid ceapes cwilde ond
monna, ealles swiþost mid þæm þæt manige þara selestena cynges
þena þe þær on londe wæron forðferdon on þæm þrim gearum: þara

10

wæs sum Swiðulf biscop on Hrofesceastre, ond Ceolmund ealdormon
on Cent, ond Beorhtulf ealdormon on East-Seaxum, ond Wulfred
ealdormon on Hamtunscire, ond Ealhheard biscop æt Dorceceastre,   145
ond Eadulf cynges þegn on Suð-Seaxum, ond Beornulf wicgerefa on
Winteceastre, ond Ecgulf cynges horsþegn, ond manige eac him, þeh
ic ða geðungnestan nemde.

Þy ilcan geare drehton þa hergas on East-Englum ond on Norðhymbrum West-Seaxna lond swiðe be þæm suðstæðe mid stælhergum,   150
ealre swiþust mid ðæm æscum þe hie fela geara ær timbredon. Þa
het Ælfred cyng timbran langscipu ongen ða æscas; þa wæron fulneah
tu swa lang swa þa oðru; sume hæfdon lx ara, sume ma; þa wæron
ægðer ge swiftran ge unwealtran ge eac hieran þonne þa oðru. Næron
nawðer ne on Fresisc gescæpene ne on Denisc, bute swa him selfum   155
ðuhte þæt hie nytwyrðoste beon meahten. Þa æt sumum cirre þæs
ilcan geares comon þær sex scipu to Wiht ond þær micel yfel gedydon,
ægðer ge on Defenum ge welhwær be ðæm særiman. Þa het se cyng
faran mid nigonum to þara niwena scipa ond forforon him þone muðan foran on utermere. Þa foron hie mid þrim scipum ut ongen hie,   160
ond þreo stodon æt ufeweardum þæm muðan on drygum; wæron þa
men uppe on londe of agane. Þa gefengon hie þara þreora scipa tu
æt ðæm muðan uteweardum, ond þa men ofslogon; ond þæt an oðwand: on þæm wæron eac þa men ofslægene buton fifum; þa comon
forðy onweg ðe ðara oþerra scipu asæton. Þa wurdon eac swiðe   165
uneðelice aseten; þreo asæton on ða healfe þæs deopes ðe ða Deniscan
scipu aseten wæron, ond þa oðru eall on oþre healfe, þæt hira ne
mehte nan to oðrum. Ac ða þæt wæter wæs ahebbad fela furlanga
from þæm scipum, þa eodon ða Deniscan from þæm þrim scipum
to þæm oðrum þrim þe on hira healfe beebbade wæron, ond hie þa   170
þær gefuhton. Þær wearð ofslægen Lucumon cynges gerefa, ond
Wulfheard Friesa, ond Æbbe Friesa, ond Æðelhere Friesa, ond
Æðelferð cynges geneat, ond ealra monna Fresiscra ond Engliscra
lxii, ond þara Deniscena cxx. Þa com þæm Deniscum scipum þeh ær
flod to, ær þa Cristnan mehten hira ut ascufan, ond hie forðy ut   175
oðreowon. Þa wæron hie to þæm gesargode þæt hie ne mehton Suð-
Seaxna lond utan berowan, ac hira þær tu sæ on lond wearp, ond þa
men mon lædde to Winteceastre to þæm cynge, ond he hie ðær ahon
het. Ond þa men comon on East-Engle þe on þæm anum scipe wæron,
swiðe forwundode. Þy ilcan sumera forwearð nolæs þonne xx scipa   180
mid monnum mid ealle, be þæm suðriman.

146. *wicgerefa:* MS *wicgefera.*   170. *hie:* added above.
175. *ascufan: f* altered from *t.*

3. A PORTRAIT OF WILLIAM THE CONQUEROR

THIS IS THE MOST FAMOUS fully developed description of an individual in Old English, and has impressed readers by the immediacy suggested by ll. 12–13: 'we will write of him just as we, who have looked upon him and once dwelt at his court, saw him'. The author claims impartiality and direct knowledge, and appears to give a balanced account in a lucid and stylish manner. A closer examination slightly takes the edge off our admiration, because we see that most of William's described attributes are merely those features which manifested themselves in his dealings with his subjects— naturally, but making a limited description of character. Again, though the chronicler claims to set down both good and evil things about William, he dwells on the harshness of William's character; the good features are either side-products of his sternness or just public gestures.

The passage is usually quoted from l. 10, and little attention is paid to the homiletic material at the end and in ll. 1–9 here and just before this extract. Miss Clark says that the virtues of the passage are 'homiletic rather than historiographical'. The framework of homiletic comment at beginning and end makes it clear that this is not just a descriptive character-study. The rhetoric and the conventional references to the fall of the great suggest that the author means what he says at the end, and particularly that we are not to emulate William's sins. Nevertheless, the *Portrait of William* is a convincing portrait of a man, because it is lucid, confidently written, factual and dispassionate.

The doggerel poem is of some interest as, unlike the few other poems in the *Chronicle*, it departs almost completely from Old English poetic conventions in employing rhyme and lines (half-lines?) of greatly varying length, and dispensing almost completely with alliteration. Apart from the rhyme, it is reminiscent of the rhythmical prose of Ælfric and Wulfstan; it shares with them the characteristic of two strong stresses in the shorter lines.

Two other portraits of William, giving somewhat different pictures, should be compared with the English chronicler's account: those of an unknown monk of Caen and of Ordericus Vitalis, translated as extracts 6 and 7 of *English Historical Documents*, vol. II.

[1087] Hwæt mæg ic teollan? Se scearpa deað þe ne forlet ne rice menn ne heane, seo hine genam. He swealt on Normandige on þone nextan dæg æfter Natiuitas Sancte Marie, and man bebyrgede hine on Caþum æt Sancte Stephanes mynstre; ærer he hit arærde and

5   syððan mænifealdlice gegodade. Eala, hu leas and hu unwrest is þysses middaneardes wela! Se þe wæs ærur rice cyng and maniges landes hlaford, he næfde þa ealles landes buton seofon fotmæl; and se þe wæs hwilon gescrid mid golde and mid gimmum, he læg þa ofer-wrogen mid moldan. . . .

Gif hwa gewilnigeð to gewitane hu gedon mann he wæs, oððe   10
hwilcne wurðscipe he hæfde, oððe hu fela lande he wære hlaford,
ðonne wille we be him awritan swa swa we hine ageaton ðe him on
locodan and oðre hwile on his hirede wunedon. Se cyng Willelm
þe we embe specað wæs swiðe wis man, and swiðe rice, and wurð-
fulre and strengere þonne ænig his foregenga wære. He wæs milde   15
þam godum mannum þe God lufedon, and ofer eall gemett stearc
þam mannum þe wiðcwædon his willan. On ðam ilcan steode þe God
him geuðe þet he moste Engleland gegan, he arerde mære mynster
and munecas þær gesætte and hit wæll gegodade. On his dagan wæs
þet mære mynster on Cantwarbyrig getymbrad, and eac swiðe manig   20
oðer ofer eall Englaland. Eac þis land wæs swiðe afylled mid munecan,
and þa leofodan heora lif æfter Sanctes Benedictus regule. And se
Cristendom wæs swilc on his dæge þet ælc man hwæt his hade to
belumpe folgade se þe wolde. Eac he wæs swyðe wurðful. Þriwa he
bær his cynehelm ælce geare swa oft swa he wæs on Engelande: on   25
Eastron he hine bær on Winceastre, on Pentecosten on Westmynstre,
on Midewintre on Gleaweceastre; and þænne wæron mid him ealle
þa rice men ofer eall Englaland, arcebiscopas and leodbiscopas, abbodas and eorlas, þegnas and cnihtas.

Swilce he wæs eac swyðe stearc man and ræðe, swa þet man ne   30
dorste nan þing ongean his willan don. He hæfde eorlas on his
bendum þe dydan ongean his willan; biscopas he sætte of heora
biscoprice, and abbodas of heora abbotrice, and þægnas on cweartern. And æt nextan he ne sparode his agene broðor, Odo het: he wæs
swiðe rice biscop on Normandige—on Baius wæs his biscopstol—   35
and wæs manna fyrmest toeacan þam cynge; and he hæfde eorldom
on Englelande, and þonne se cyng wæs on Normandige, þonne wæs
he mægester on þisum lande—and hine he sætte on cweartern.

Betwyx oðrum þingum nis na to forgytane þet gode frið þe he
macode on þisan lande, swa þet an man þe himsylf aht wære mihte   40
faran ofer his rice, mid his bosum full goldes, ungederad. And nan
man ne dorste slean oðerne man, næfde he næfre swa mycel yfel
gedon wið þone oðerne. And gif hwilc carlman hæmde wið wimman
hire unðances, sona he forleas þa limu þe he mid pleagode.

He rixade ofer Englæland, and hit mid his geapscipe swa þurh-   45
smeade þet næs an hid landes innan Englælande þet he nyste hwa heo
hæfde, oððe hwæs heo wurð wæs, and syððan on his gewrit gesætt.
Brytland him wæs on gewealde, and he þærinne casteles gewrohte
and þet manncynn mid ealle gewealde. Swilce eac Scotland he him
underþædde for his mycele strengþe. Normandige þet land wæs his   50
gecynde; and ofer þone eorldom þe Mans is gehaten he rixade. And

10. gewilnigeð: MS ge wilniged.   37. wæs: not in MS.

13

gif he moste þa gyt twa gear libban, he hæfde Yrlande mid his werscipe gewunnon and wiðutan ælcon wæpnon.

    Witodlice on his timan hæfdon men mycel geswinc and swiðe
55 manige teonan:

        Castelas he let wyrcean,
        and earme men swiðe swencean.
        Se cyng wæs swa swiðe stearc,
        and benam of his underþeoddan manig marc
60   goldes, and ma hundred punda seolfres.
        Ðet he nam be wihte,
        and mid mycelan unrihte
        of his landleode,
        for littelre neode.
65   He wæs on gitsunge befeallan,
        and grædinæsse he lufode mid ealle.
        He sætte mycel deorfrið,
        and he lægde laga þærwið
        þet swa hwa swa sloge heort oððe hinde,
70   þet hine man sceolde blendian.
        He forbead þa heortas,
        swylce eac þa baras.
        Swa swiðe he lufode þa headeor
        swilce he wære heora fæder.
75   Eac he sætte be þam haran
        þet hi mosten freo faran.
        His rice men hit mændon,
        and þa earme men hit beceorodan;
        ac he wæs swa stið
80   þet he ne rohte heora eallra nið.
        Ac hi moston mid ealle þes cynges wille folgian
        gif hi woldon libban oððe land habban,
        land oððe eahta,
        oððe wel his sehta.
85   Walawa, þet ænig man
        sceolde modigan swa,
        hine sylf upp ahebban
        and ofer ealle men tellan.
        Se ælmihtiga God cyþæ his saule mildheortnisse,
90   and do him his synna forgifenesse!

Ðas þing we habbað be him gewritene, ægðer ge gode ge yfele, þet
þa godan men niman æfter þeora godnesse, and forleon mid ealle
yfelnesse, and gan on ðone weg þe us lett to heofonan rice.

---

59. *manig marc:* MS *man manig marc.*   64. *littelre:* MS *littere.*
73. *he:* added above.   79. *wæs:* not in MS.   90. *his:* added above.

II. ALFREDIAN PROSE

4. ALFRED'S PREFACE TO THE PASTORAL CARE

AS THIS FAMOUS *Preface* TELLS, Alfred's problems as virtual King of England were not merely the military ones of defence of the kingdom against the Danes. He was faced with internal problems, of which the one which concerned him principally was the degeneracy and illiteracy of both laity and clergy. In the later years of his reign he turned from his military exploits to a programme of ecclesiastical and educational reform.

As a reformer of the Church, his achievement was less that that of his successors, especially the Benedictine reformers of the later tenth century. But his problem was a huge one. In this *Preface* he conveys well the extent to which ecclesiastical learning and morale had declined from the earlier greatness of Bede's Northumbria. His remedies were the importation of scholars from the Continent, the reform and establishment of religious houses, and an educational programme, described in the *Preface*, in which he himself gave the lead. During the last fifteen years of his life, between and after campaigns against the Danes, he learned Latin with the help of those people named in the *Preface*. He then translated—with how much help from his tutors it is impossible to say—several works *ðe niedbeðearfosta sien eallum mannum to wiotonne* from Latin into Old English, and had other scholars engage in translation, make copies, rewrite and revive the *Chronicle*. We must marvel at this literary achievement at the end of so full a life, and recognise Alfred's very personal contribution to the founding of English prose.

Besides the *Chronicle*, the chief products of Alfred's school were translations of Gregory's *Pastoral Care*, of his *Dialogues* (translated by Wærferth, Bishop of Worcester), of Bede's *Ecclesiastical History*, Orosius' *History*, Augustine's *Soliloquies* and the *Consolation of Philosophy* by Boethius. The translations are not 'literal'; expansions and explanations are inserted to suit the translation to the time. The translation of Orosius includes our extract 6, an interpolation by Alfred; that of Bede (which is not certainly by Alfred himself) extract 5.

The *Pastoral Care*, or *Regulae Pastoralis Liber*, was completed by Gregory the Great in 591, the year in which he became pope. A manual for ecclesiastics, it was written in response to Archbishop John of Ravenna's censure of Gregory for his reluctance to take up the pontificate; it became one of the great books of the Middle Ages, and was a natural choice for Alfred's first translation. Professor Potter (*Transactions of the Philological Society*, 1947, pp. 114-15) comments on a sentence from Gregory:

Leadership is the art of arts, or, as the Roman Gregory preferred to express it, *ars est artium regimen animarum*, the art of arts is the rule of souls, to which assertion the King of the West Saxons gave a characteristic turn when he boldly interpreted this as 'the craft of teaching is the craft of all crafts', *se cræft ðæs lareowdomes bið cræft ealra cræfta*. King Alfred's purpose was immediate: his aim was practical. He was directly concerned not so much with that universal activity, the governance of souls, as with that pressing necessity, the advancement of learning. Above all things he would bring home to the bishops their responsibility as *lareowas* or *lare þeowas*, learning's servants.

The completed translation presumably had many copies made of it, and a preface added, incorporating the name of the recipient and the plea for co-operation with Alfred's plans. The copy from which our text is printed was intended for Bishop Wærferth of Worcester, one of Alfred's chief helpers. The manuscript, now Hatton 20 in the Bodleian Library, is particularly important among Old English manuscripts as it is a contemporary one. The *Preface* in this copy has suffered a good deal of mutilation, with frequent erasures, alterations and additions. I have followed Sweet's editorial practice in restoring the original readings where possible. In the MS ðætte has often been changed to ðæt; -ie- has been replaced by the later West Saxon -y-; -æ has been altered to -e.

Ælfred kyning hateð gretan Wærferð biscep his wordum luflice ond freondlice; ond ðe cyðan hate ðæt me com swiðe oft on gemynd hwelce wiotan iu wæron giond Angelcynn, ægðer ge godcundra hada ge woruldcundra; ond hu gesæliglica tida ða wæron giond Angelcynn; 5 ond hu ða kyningas ðe ðone onwald hæfdon ðæs folces Gode ond his ærendwrecum hiersumedon; ond hie ægðer ge hiora sibbe ge hiora siodo ge hiora onweald innanbordes gehioldon, ond eac ut hiora eðel gerymdon; ond hu him ða speow ægðer ge mid wige ge mid wisdome; ond eac ða godcundan hadas hu giorne hie wæron ægðer ge ymb lare 10 ge ymb liornunga, ge ymb ealle ða ðiowotdomas ðe hie Gode don scoldon; ond hu man utanbordes wisdom ond lare hieder on lond sohte, ond hu we hie nu sceoldon ute begietan, gif we hie habban sceoldon. Swæ clæne hio wæs oðfeallenu on Angelcynne ðæt swiðe feawa wæron behionan Humbre ðe hiora ðeninga cuðen under- 15 stondan on Englisc, oððe furðum an ærendgewrit of Lædene on Englisc areccean; ond ic wene ðætte noht monige begiondan Humbre næren. Swæ feawa hiora wæron ðæt ic furðum anne anlepne ne

4. *woruldcundra:* 1st *d* inserted above.
5. *folces:* after and above is *on ðam dagum* in another hand.
6. *hiersumedon:* MS (emended) *hyrsumedon.*
7. *innanbordes:* after and above is *wel* in another hand.
10. *don:* inserted above.   12. 1st *hie:* MS (emended) *hy.*
13. *Swæ:* MS (emended) *swa.*   16. *ðætte: te* erased.
17. *Swæ:* MS (emended) *swa.*

mæg geðencean be suðan Temese ða ða ic to rice feng. Gode ælmihtigum sie ðonc ðætte we nu ænigne onstal habbað lareowa. Ond forðon
ic ðe bebiode ðæt ðu do swæ ic geliefe ðæt ðu wille, ðæt ðu ðe ðissa   20
woruldðinga to ðæm geæmetige swæ ðu oftost mæge, ðæt ðu ðone
wisdom ðe ðe God sealde ðær ðær ðu hiene befæstan mæge, befæste.
Geðenc hwelce witu us ða becomon for ðisse worulde, ða ða we hit
nohwæðer ne selfe ne lufodon ne eac oðrum monnum ne lefdon:
ðone naman ænne we lufodon ðætte we Cristne wæren, ond swiðe   25
feawe ða ðeawas.

Ða ic ða ðis eall gemunde, ða gemunde ic eac hu ic geseah, ær
ðæm ðe hit eall forhergod wære ond forbærned, hu ða ciricean giond
eall Angelcynn stodon maðma ond boca gefyldæ, ond eac micel
menigeo Godes ðiowa: ond ða swiðe lytle fiorme ðara boca wiston,   30
forðæm ðe hie hiora nanwuht ongiotan ne meahton, forðæm ðe hie
næron on hiora agen geðiode awritene. Swelce hie cwæden: 'Ure
ieldran, ða ðe ðas stowa ær hioldon, hie lufodon wisdom ond ðurh
ðone hie begeaton welan ond us læfdon. Her mon mæg giet gesion
hiora swæð; ac we him ne cunnon æfter spyrigean, ond forðæm we   35
habbað nu ægðer forlæten ge ðone welan ge ðone wisdom, forðæm
ðe we noldon to ðæm spore mid ure mode onlutan.'

Ða ic ða ðis eall gemunde, ða wundrade ic swiðe swiðe ðara godena
wiotona ðe giu wæron giond Angelcynn, ond ða bec eallæ be fullan
geliornod hæfdon, ðæt hie hiora ða nænne dæl noldon on hiora agen   40
geðiode wendan. Ac ic ða sona eft me selfum andwyrde ond cwæð: 'Hie
ne wendon ðætte æfre menn sceolden swæ reccelease weorðan ond
sio lar swæ oðfeallan; for ðære wilnunga hie hit forleton, ond woldon
ðæt her ðy mara wisdom on londe wære ðy we ma geðeoda cuðon.'
Ða gemunde ic hu sio æ wæs ærest on Ebriscgeðiode funden, ond   45
eft, ða hie Creacas geliornodon, ða wendon hie hie on hiora agen
geðiode ealle, ond eac ealle oðre bec; ond eft Lædenware swæ same,
siððan hie hie geliornodon, hie hie wendon ealla ðurh wise wealh-

---

19. *ðætte: te* erased.   20. *swæ:* MS (emended) *swa.*

25. *lufodon:* the other MSS have *hæfdon*; *ðætte: te* partially erased.

26. *feawe:* 2nd *e* erased and replaced by *a.*

29. *gefyldæ:* the first part of the digraph has been partially erased.

30. *menigeo: i* supplied above.

31. 2nd *forðæm:* above is inserted *ond þæt wæs*; 2nd *hie: y* written over *ie* erased.

32. *cwæden: o* has been written over *e* still clearly visible.

33. *ieldran: y* written over *ie* barely erased.

42. *ðætte: e* erased; *reccelease:* 1st *c* erased.

43. *swæ: swyðe* added above this word, which has been altered to *swa*; *hie:* MS (emended) *hy.*

45. *Ebrisc-: e* written above between *r* and *i.*

46. *Creacas:* altered to *Greccas.*

47. 2nd *ealle* crossed out and *mænige* above in another hand; *swæ:* MS (emended) *swa.*   48. *ealla:* final *a,* apparently, erased.

stodas on hiora agen geðiode. Ond eac ealla oðræ Cristnæ ðioda
50 sumne dæl hiora on hiora agen geðiode wendon. Forðy me ðyncð
betre, gif iow swa ðyncð, ðæt we eac sumæ bec, ða ðe niedbeðearfosta
sien eallum monnum to wiotonne, ðæt we ða on ðæt geðiode wenden
ðe we ealle gecnawen mægen, ond gedon, swæ we swiðe eaðe magon
mid Godes fultume, gif we ða stilnesse habbað, ðætte eall sio gioguð
55 ðe nu is on Angelcynne friora monna, ðara ðe ða speda hæbben ðæt
hie ðæm befeolan mægen, sien to liornunga oðfæste, ða hwile ðe hie
to nanre oðerre note ne mægen, oð ðone first ðe hie wel cunnen
Englisc gewrit arædan; læra mon siððan furður on Lædengeðiode ða
ðe mon furður læran wille, ond to hieran hade don wille.

60   Ða ic ða gemunde hu sio lar Lædengeðiodes ær ðissum afeallen
wæs giond Angelcynn, ond ðeah monige cuðon Englisc gewrit arædan, ða ongan ic on gemang oðrum mislicum ond manigfealdum bis-
gum ðisses kynerices ða boc wendan on Englisc ðe is genemned on
Læden Pastoralis, ond on Englisc Hierdeboc, hwilum word be worde,
65 hwilum andgit of andgite, swæ swæ ic hie geliornode æt Plegmunde
minum ærcebiscepe ond æt Assere minum biscepe ond æt Grimbolde
minum mæsseprioste, ond æt Iohanne minum mæssepreoste. Siððan
ic hie ða geliornod hæfde, swæ swæ ic hie forstod, ond swæ ic hie
andgitfullicost areccean meahte, ic hie on Englisc awende; ond to
70 ælcum biscepstole on minum rice wille ane onsendan; ond on ælcre
bið an æstel, se bið on fiftegum mancessan. Ond ic bebiode on Godes
naman ðæt nan mon ðone æstel from ðære bec ne do, ne ða boc
from ðæm mynstre: uncuð hu longe ðær swa gelærede biscepas sien,
swæ swæ nu, Gode ðonc, welhwær siendon; forðy ic wolde ðætte
75 hie ealneg æt ðære stowe wæren, buton se biscep hie mid him habban
wille, oððe hio hwær to læne sie, oððe hwa oðre biwrite.

5. BEDE'S ACCOUNT OF THE POET CÆDMON

THIS EXTRACT links three of the most notable early Englishmen: Bede,
King Alfred and Cædmon.

Bede, 'the first modern historian', lived from 673 to 735, spending most
of his life in Jarrow monastery. The founder of Wearmouth and Jarrow,

49. *ealla*: crossed out; *oðræ Cristnæ*: *æ* in each case partly defaced to give *e*.
51. *betre*: *eac* above in another hand; *sumæ*: *æ* turned into *e*.
53. *swæ*: MS (emended) *swa*.
54. *ðætte*: *te* erased.
65. *andgite*: *e* inserted above, between *i* and *t*; *swæ swæ*: MS (emended) *swa swa*.
68. *swæ swæ*: MS (emended) *swa swa*; *forstod*: crossed out and *betst understandon cuðe* in the margin; *swæ*: MS (emended) *swa*.
71. *mancessan*: final *n* perhaps added later.
74. *swæ swæ*: MS (emended) *swa swa*; *welhwær*: *ge* prefixed above in another hand; *ðætte*: *te* erased.

Benedict Biscop, did his utmost to create a centre of scholarship: Bede was
the greatest product of this school. He was a prolific writer, scientific in
his careful collection of facts and fair in drawing inferences from them. His
Ecclesiastical History of the English People, completed in 731, is his most
famous work. It is an essential source-book for the modern historian of the
Anglo-Saxon period, and was already regarded as a great book by the end
of this period. Besides the Latin versions, there are six complete, excerpted
or fragmentary Old English translations: we print from the early eleventh-
century Corpus Christi College, Oxford, MS 279. King Alfred comes into
the picture in connection with the authorship of the translation. His exact
contribution is a matter of doubt. External evidence is unavailable, and
stylistic investigation appears to prove little except that there are stylistic
differences among the group of Alfredian translations that make it unlikely that they are all the work of one man. One can only say cautiously
that the Bede translation is 'Alfredian'.

Cædmon is the only Anglo-Saxon poet of whom we have any detailed
knowledge. Unfortunately, Bede's description of him is all we know, and
the nine-line poem found here (Bede himself gives a Latin paraphrase)
comprises his total attested poetic works. Cædmon was a secular farmhand
working on the monastery of Strenæshalc (probably modern Whitby)
during the rule of Abbess Hild (658–80). We cannot date the beginning of
his writing career more precisely than that, nor determine anything else
about the dates of his birth or death.

He was an unlettered poet, and, as Magoun (art. cit. in Bibliography) has
demonstrated, his *Hymn* consists of a sequence of formulae, constructed
exactly as an orally composed poem may be expected to be. He is closer to
the Conversion and to the period of oral composition than any other
Christian poet we know of, and the question arises whether Cædmon impressed his contemporaries less by his miraculous inspiration (a personal
transformation) than by his suddenly discovered ability to put native
Germanic poetic conventions to the service of Christianity (a transformation of poetry). One cannot be sure; but Bede tells us of Cædmon's influence, and it is natural to view him as a remembered pioneer in the adaptation of native techniques to Christian themes. The impact made by Cædmon is reflected in the large number of copies of the poem—seventeen—
which survive, dating from half a century after his death (the Moore MS,
A.D. 737). Unfortunately, nothing else survives which can reliably be attributed to him. Junius, struck by the similarity of the contents of what is
now Bodleian MS Junius XI to Bede's list of his works, suggested that the
manuscript was a collection of his poems: indeed, it is still often referred to
as 'the Cædmon MS'. However, few scholars today would venture to attribute to Cædmon anything extant except the *Hymn*: but we recognise his
importance in the history of Old English poetry by using the term 'Cædmonian' to characterise poetry in his vein—poetry on a Christian theme
dense with the poetic devices of the pre-Christian period.

[In the footnotes, readings identified by T are MS Tanner 10.]

On þysse abbudissan mynstre wæs sum broðor synderlice mid godcundre gyfe gemæred and geweorþad, forþon he gewunade gerisenlice
leoð wyrcean þa þe to æfestnesse and to arfæstnesse belumpon; swa
þætte, swa hwæt swa he of godcundum stafum þurh boceras geleor-
5   nade, þæt he æfter medmiclum fæce in scopgereorde mid þa mæstan
swetnesse and inbryrdnesse geglencde and in Engliscgereorde wel
geworht forðbrohte. And for his leoðsongum monigra monna mod
oft to worolde forhohnesse and to geþeodnesse þæs heofonlican lifes
onbærnde wæron. And eac swylce monige oðre æfter him in
10   Ongelþeode ongunnon æfæste leoð wyrcan, ac nænig hwæþere him
þæt gelice don meahte. Forþon he nalæs from monnum ne þurh mon
gelæred wæs ðæt he þone leoðcræft geleornade, ac he wæs godcundlice
gefultumod, and þurh Godes gyfe þone songcræft onfeng. And he
forþon næfre noht leasunge ne idles leoþes wyrcan meahte, ac efne
15   þa an þa þe to æfæstnesse belumpon and his þa æfestan tungan
gedafenode singan.

Wæs he se mon on weoruldhade geseted oð ða tide þe he wæs
gelyfedre yldo, and he næfre ænig leoð geleornade. And he forþon
oft in gebeorscipe, þonne þær wæs blisse intinga gedemed þæt hie
20   ealle sceolden þurh endebyrdnesse be hearpan singan, ðonne he
geseah þa hearpan him nealæcan, þonne aras he for scome from þæm
symble, and ham eode to his huse. Þa he þæt þa sumre tide dyde
þæt he forlet þæt hus þæs gebeorscipes, and ut wæs gongende to neata
scypene, þara heord him wæs þære nihte beboden, ða he þa þær in
25   gelimplicre tide his limo on reste gesette and onslæpte, þa stod him
sum mon æt þurh swefn, and hine halette and grette and hine be his
naman nemde: 'Cædmon, sing me hwæthwegu.' Þa andswarode he
and cwæð: 'Ne con ic noht singan, and ic forþon of þyssum gebeorscipe ut eode, and hider gewat, forþon ic noht cuðe.' Eft he cwæð
30   se ðe mid him sprecende wæs: 'Hwæðere þu meaht me singan.'
Cwæð he: 'Hwæt sceal ic singan?' Cwæð he: 'Sing me frumsceaft.'
Þa he þa þas andsware onfeng, ða ongan he sona singan in herenesse
Godes scyppendes, þa fers and þa word þe he næfre ne gehyrde, þara
endebyrdnes þis is:

2. *gemæred:* 1st *e* inserted above.
6. *inbryrdnesse:* MS *inbrydnesse; geglencde: c* above; *wel geworht* T; MS *welgehwær.*
13. *þone:* MS *þonne* with first *n* erased.
15. *to:* inserted above.
18. *yldo: y* over an erasure of two letters.
19. *gebeorscipe: r* above.
20. *sceolden: n* above.
23. *forlet: t* over an erasure of two or three letters; *þæt:* MS *þa.*
25. *gelimplicre:* MS. *gelimplice; onslæpte: t* above.
27. *Cædmon:* MS *cedmon; hwæthwegu:* MS *æthwegu;* T *hwæthwugu.*
34. *endebyrdnes:* second *n* above.

Nu we sculan herian   heofonrices Weard,   35
Metodes mihte   and his modgeþonc,
weorc Wuldorfæder;   swa he wundra gehwæs,
ece Dryhten,   ord onstealde.
He ærest gesceop   eorðan bearnum
heofon to hrofe,   halig Scyppend;   40
ða middongeard   moncynnes Weard,
ece Dryhten,   æfter teode
firum foldan,   Frea ælmihtig.

Ða aras he from þæm slæpe, and eall þa þe he slæpende song fæste in
gemynde hæfde, and þæm wordum sona monig word in þæt ylce   45
gemet Gode wyrþes songes togeþeodde. Þa com he on marne to þam
tungerefan, se þe his ealdormon wæs, sæde him hwylce gyfe he
onfeng. And he hine sona to þære abbudyssan gelædde, and hire þæt
cyðde and sægde. Ða het heo gesomnian ealle þa gelærdestan men
and þa leorneras, and him andweardum het secgan þæt swefn and   50
þæt leoð singan, þætte ealra heora dome gecoren wære hwæt oðð e
hwonon þæt cumen wære. Þa wæs him eallum gesegen swa swa hit
wæs, þæt him wære from Dryhtne sylfum heofonlic gifu forgyfen.
Ða rehton hie him and sægdon sum halig spel and godcundre lare
word; bebudon him þa, gif he mihte, þæt he him sum sunge, and in   55
swinsunge leoðsonges þæt gehwyrfde. Ða he þa hæfde þa wisan
onfangene, þa eode he ham to his huse, and com eft on morgen and
þy betstan leoðe geglenged him asong and ageaf þæt him beboden
wæs.

Ða ongan seo abbudysse clyppan and lufian þa Godes gyfe in þæm   60
men, and heo hine þa monode and lærde þæt he weoroldhad forlete,
and munuchade onfenge: and he þæt wel þafode. And heo hine in
þæt mynster onfeng mid his godum, and hine geþeodde to gesom-
nunge þara Godes þeowa, and het hine læran þæt getæl þæs halgan
stæres and spelles. And he eall þa he in gehernesse geleornian mihte,   65
mid hine gemyngade, and swa swa clæne neten eodorcende in þæt
sweteste leoð gehwyrfde, and his song and his leoð wæron swa
wynsum to gehyrenne, ðæt þa sylfan his lareowas æt his muðe

---

35. *we:* above the line.   37. *weorc:* so T; MS *wera.*   38. *ord:* MS *oor^d*; T *or.*
39. *bearnum:* two letters erased after this word.
42. *teode:* a letter erased between *o* and *d.*   43. *foldan:* *n* above.
45. *monig:* *n* above.   46. *togeþeodde:* second *d* above.
47. *his:* *h* above.   53. *gyfu:* altered from *gyfo.*
55. *gif he:* MS *gife* with *h* above; *and:* above the line. 55–6 *in swinsunge* T; omitted
MS.
56. *gehwyrfde: wyrfde* written over an erasure.
60. *clyppan:* second *p* inserted above.
67. *gehwyrfde:* *y* above.   68. *gehyrenne: ge* above.

writon and leornodon. Song he ærest be middangeardes gesceape
70 and be fruman moncynnes, and eal þæt stær Genesis (þæt is seo
æreste Moises boc), and eft be utgonge Israela folces of Egypta
londe, and be ingonge þæs gehatlondes, and be oðrum monigum
spellum þæs halgan gewrites canones boca, and be Cristes mennisc-
nesse and be his þrowunge, and be his upastignesse on heofonas,
75 and bi þæs Halgan Gastes cyme, and þara Apostola lare; and eft bi
þam ege þæs toweardan domes, and be fyrhto þæs tintreglican wites,
and be swetnesse þæs heofonlican rices he monig leoþ geweorhte;
and swylce eac oþer monig be þam godcundum fremsumnessum and
domum he geworhte. On eallum þam he geornlice gymde þæt he men
80 atuge fram synna lufan and mandæda, and to lufan and to geornfull-
nesse awehte godra dæda; forþon he wæs se mon swiðe æfæst, and
regollicum þeodscypum eaðmodlice underþeoded. And wið ðam þa
ðe on oþre wisan don woldon he wæs mid wylme micelre ellenwod-
nesse onbærned, and he forþon fægere ende his lif betynde and
85 geendade.

6. THE VOYAGES OF OHTHERE AND WULFSTAN

ONE OF THE ALFREDIAN TRANSLATIONS commonly attributed to Alfred
himself rather than to his helpers is that of the *Histories against the Pagans*
or *World History*, by Paulus Orosius, a Spaniard writing in the early fifth
century. This was a universal history from the Creation to A.D. 407;
polemic in its intention (to demonstrate that mankind's sufferings before
Christ were greater than those after), but taken as an authoritative historical work in the early Middle Ages.

Whereas the West Saxon version of the *Pastoral Care* (less probably
by Alfred himself) is a fairly close translation (*word be worde*), that of
Orosius is more of a free paraphrase and adaptation. The propagandist
purpose has gone, and much of the content of the book which would have
been of little interest to the English has been omitted. The rendering of
what remains (about one-fifth of the original) is *andgit of andgite*: the sense,
rather than the verbal form of the Latin, determines the language of the
translation. Latin idioms are infrequent. Sweet comments (*Pastoral Care*
p. xl):

> In the detailed narratives of Alfred's campaigns and sea-fights the
> style [of the *Chronicle*] assumes a different aspect: without losing the
> force and simplicity of the earlier pieces, it becomes refined and polished
> to a high degree, and yet shows no traces of foreign influence. Accord-
> ingly, in the Orosius, the only translation of Alfred's which from the
> similarity of its subject admits of a direct comparison, we find almost
> exactly the same language and style as in the contemporary historical
> pieces of the Chronicle.

70. *eal: l* above.
73. *canones:* MS *cano es*, with an erasure.

72. *þæs: s* above.
76. *tintreglican: lic* above.

Although the overall length of Orosius has been considerably shortened, numerous original additions have been made. Chief among these are the lengthy sections describing the geography of Germania and the travels of Ohthere and Wulfstan. Sweet's remarks, implying a fluent and uncomplex style, are well applied to the account of the adventures of these two mariners. This can reasonably be supposed to be Alfred's natural style, although it is very different from that of the formal *Preface to the Pastoral Care* with its heavy subordination. It is to be noted that Alfred uses two different methods for reporting the stories of these two travellers. Ohthere's story is told indirectly with a liberal use of the formula *he cwæð/sæde þæt* . . .; the pronouns *we, us* are used in the account of Wulfstan's voyage, and almost the whole gives the impression of being in direct speech: I have therefore used quotation marks to show this.

Alfred's reasons for incorporating this fairly lengthy pair of narratives into his translation—taking them down almost from the mouths of the travellers, it may seem—deserve consideration. They obviously have an appeal simply as travellers' tales—especially Wulfstan's account of the Esthonians; and Ohthere's northern voyage was an adventure, a voyage of discovery, a feat: so the stories invite admiration in both senses of the word. But Alfred was most probably interested chiefly in supplying deficiencies in Orosius' geography of the north, an area of some considerable interest to him as a great king extending his knowledge of the customs of other nations, more particularly those of his Scandinavian adversaries. Ohthere and Wulfstan not only tell of their voyages but are also careful to add plenty of comment on the customs, economy and international relations of the peoples whose lands they passed. We may presume that Alfred was interested in those things not only for the light they threw on the contemporary state of the north but also because he learned something of the lands of his ancestors. It is not entirely a foreign and exotic region that the travellers describe, for, as Ohthere observes, 'In these countries dwelt the Angles, before they came here to this land.'

[Lines 1–35 of our text are taken from the tenth-century MS British Museum, Additional 47967 (the 'Tollemache' or 'Lauderdale' Ororius, designated 'L'). One quire is missing here, although the deficiency is made up by a copy of Junius' transcript of MS Cotton Tiberius B. i ('C'), from which the remainder of the extract is taken.]

Ohthere sæde his hlaforde, Ælfrede cyninge, þæt he ealra Norðmonna norþmest bude. He cwæð þæt he bude on þæm lande norþweardum wiþ þa Westsæ. He sæde þeah þæt þæt land sie swiþe lang norþ þonan; ac hit is eal weste, buton on feawum stowum styccemælum wiciað Finnas, on huntoðe on wintra ond on sumera on fiscaþe be   5
þære sæ.

He sæde þæt he æt sumum cirre wolde fandian hu longe þæt land norþryhte læge, oþþe hwæðer ænig mon be norðan þæm westenne

3. *þæt þæt:* so C; L *þæt.*

bude. Þa for he norþryhte be þæm lande: let him ealne weg þæt weste
10 land on ðæt steorbord, ond þa widsæ on ðæt bæcbord þrie dagas.
Þa wæs he swa feor norþ swa þa hwælhuntan firrest faraþ. Þa for he
þagiet norþryhte swa feor swa he meahte on þæm oþrum þrim dagum
gesiglan. Þa beag þæt land þær eastryhte, oþþe seo sæ in on ðæt lond,
he nysse hwæðer; buton he wisse ðæt he ðær bad westanwindes ond
15 hwon norþan, ond siglde ða east be lande swa swa he meahte on
feower dagum gesiglan. Þa sceolde he ðær bidan ryhtnorþanwindes,
forðæm þæt land beag þær suþryhte, oþþe seo sæ in on ðæt land, he
nysse hwæþer. Þa siglde he þonan suðryhte be lande swa swa he
mehte on fif dagum gesiglan. Ða læg þær an micel ea up in on þæt
20 land. Þa cirdon hie up in on ða ea, forþæm hie ne dorston forþ bi
þære ea siglan for unfriþe; forþæm ðæt land wæs eall gebun on oþre
healfe þære eas. Ne mette he ær nan gebun land siþþan he from his
agnum ham for, ac him wæs ealne weg weste land on þæt steorbord,
butan fiscerum ond fugelerum ond huntum, ond þæt wæron eall
25 Finnas; ond him wæs a widsæ on ðæt bæcbord. Þa Beormas hæfdon
swiþe wel gebud hira land; ac hie ne dorston þær on cuman. Ac þara
Terfinna land wæs eal weste, buton ðær huntan gewicodon, oþþe
fisceras, oþþe fugeleras.

Fela spella him sædon þa Beormas, ægþer ge of hiera agnum lande
30 ge of þæm landum þe ymb hie utan wæron; ac he nyste hwæt þæs
soþes wæs, forþæm he hit self ne geseah. Þa Finnas, him þuhte, ond
þa Beormas spræcon neah an geþeode. Swiþost he for ðider, toeacan
þæs landes sceawunge, for þæm horschwælum, forðæm hie habbað
swiþe æþele ban on hiora toþum—þa teð hie brohton sume þæm
35 cyninge—ond hiora hyd bið swiðe god to sciprapum. Se hwæl bið
micle læssa þonne oðre hwalas: ne bið he lengra ðonne syfan elna
lang. Ac on his agnum lande is se betsta hwælhuntað: þa beoð eahta
and feowertiges elna lange, and þa mæstan fiftiges elna lange. Þara
he sæde þæt he syxa sum ofsloge syxtig on twam dagum.

40 He was swyðe spedig man on þæm æhtum þe heora speda on beoð,
þæt is, on wildrum. He hæfde þagyt, ða he þone cyningc sohte, tamra
deora unbebohtra syx hund. Þa deor hi hatað 'hranas'; þara wæron
syx stælhranas; ða beoð swyðe dyre mid Finnum, forðæm hy foð þa
wildan hranas mid. He wæs mid þæm fyrstum mannum on þæm
45 lande. Næfde he þeah ma ðonne twentig hryðera, and twentig sceapa,
and twentig swyna, and þæt lytle þæt he erede, he erede mid horsan.
Ac hyra ar is mæst on þæm gafole þe ða Finnas him gyldað. Þæt

---

15. *ða:* C *þanon.* 20. *ða:* followed by an erasure, probably of *m.*
25. *Beormas:* first stroke of *m* erased. 27. *ðær:* inserted above in L.
28. *fugeleras: er* added above in L. 29. *Beormas:* last stroke of *m* erased.
32. *Beormas:* first stroke of *m* erased. 35. *hyd:* L breaks off after this word.

gafol bið on deora fellum, and on fugela feðerum, and hwales bane, and on þæm sciprapum, þe beoð of hwæles hyde geworht and of seoles. Æghwilc gylt be hys gebyrdum: se byrdesta sceall gyldan   50
fyftyne mearðes fell, and fif hranes, and an beran fel, and tyn ambra feðra, and berenne kyrtel oððe yterenne, and twegen sciprapas; ægþer sy syxtig elna lang, oþer sy of hwæles hyde geworht, oþer of sioles.

He sæde ðæt Norðmanna land wære swyþe lang and swyðe smæl.   55
Eal þæt his man aþer oððe ettan oððe erian mæg, þæt lið wið ða sæ; and þæt is þeah on sumum stowum swyðe cludig; and licgað wilde moras wið eastan and wið uppon emnlange þæm bynum lande. On þæm morum eardiað Finnas. And þæt byne land is easteweard bradost, and symle swa norðor swa smælre. Eastewerd hit mæg bion   60
syxtig mila brad, oþþe hwene brædre; and middeweard þritig oððe bradre; and norðeweard he cwæð, þær hit smalost wære, þæt hit mihte beon þreora mila brad to þæm more; and se mor syðþan, on sumum stowum, swa brad swa man mæg on twam wucum oferferan; and on sumum stowum swa brad swa man mæg on syx dagum   65
oferferan. Ðonne is toemnes þæm lande suðeweardum, on oðre healfe þæs mores, Sweoland, oþ þæt land norðeweard; and toemnes þæm lande norðeweardum, Cwena land. Þa Cwenas hergiað hwilum on ða Norðmen ofer ðone mor, hwilum þa Norðmen on hy. And þær sint swiðe micle meras fersce geond þa moras; and berað þa Cwenas   70
hyra scypu ofer land on ða meras, and þanon hergiað on ða Norðmen; hy habbað swyðe lytle scypa and swyðe leohte.

Ohthere sæde þæt sio scir hatte Halgoland þe he on bude. He cwæð þæt nan man ne bude be norðan him. Þonne is an port on suðeweardum þæm lande, þone man hæt Sciringes heal. Þyder he   75
cwæð þæt man ne mihte geseglian on anum monðe, gyf man on niht wicode, and ælce dæge hæfde ambyrne wind; and ealle ða hwile he sceal seglian be lande. And on þæt steorbord him bið ærest Iraland, and þonne ða igland þe synd betux Iralande and þissum lande. Þonne is þis land oð he cymð to Scirincges heale, and ealne weg on   80
þæt bæcbord Norðweg. Wið suðan þone Sciringes heal fylð swyðe mycel sæ up in on ðæt lond; seo is bradre þonne ænig man ofer seon mæge. And is Gotland on oðre healfe ongean, and siððan Sillende. Seo sæ lið mænig hund mila up in on þæt land. And of Sciringes heale he cwæð þæt he seglode on fif dagan to þæm porte þe mon hæt æt   85
Hæþum; se stent betuh Winedum, and Seaxum, and Angle, and hyrð in on Dene. Ða he þiderweard seglode fram Sciringes heale, þa wæs him on þæt bæcbord Denamearc, and on þæt steorbord widsæ þry dagas. And þa, twegen dagas ær he to Hæþum come, him wæs on

75. þone: C þonne.   83. siððan: C siðða.

90 þæt steorbord Gotland, and Sillende, and iglanda fela. On þæm landum eardodon Engle, ær hi hider on land coman. And hym wæs ða twegen dagas on ðæt bæcbord þa igland þe in on Denemearce hyrað.

Wulfstan sæde þæt he gefore of Hæðum, þæt he wære on Truso on
95 syfan dagum and nihtum, þæt þæt scip wæs ealne weg yrnende under segle. Weonoðland him wæs on steorbord, and on bæcbord him wæs Langaland, and Læland, and Falster, and Sconeg: and þas land eall hyrað to Denemearcan. 'And þonne Burgenda land wæs us on bæcbord, and þa habbað him sylf cyning. Þonne æfter Burgenda land
100 wæron us þas land, þa synd hatene ærest Blecingaeg, and Meore, and Eowland, and Gotland on bæcbord, and þas land hyrað to Sweon. And Weonodland wæs us ealne weg on steorbord oð Wislemuðan. Seo Wisle is swyðe mycel ea, and hio tolið Witland and Weonodland; and þæt Witland belimpeð to Estum. And seo Wisle lið ut of
105 Weonodlande, and lið in Estmere; and se Estmere is huru fiftene mila brad. Þonne cymeð Ilfing eastan in Estmere of ðæm mere ðe Truso standeð in staðe, and cumað ut samod in Estmere, Ilfing eastan of Estlande, and Wisle suðan of Winodlande. And þonne benimð Wisle Ilfing hire naman, and ligeð of þæm mere west and norð on sæ; forðy
110 hit man hæt Wislemuða.

Þæt Estland is swyðe mycel, and þær bið swyðe manig burh, and on ælcere byrig bið cyningc. And þær bið swyðe mycel hunig, and fiscað; and se cyning and þa ricostan men drincað myran meolc, and þa unspedigan and þa þeowan drincað medo. Þær bið swyðe mycel
115 gewinn betweonan him. And ne bið ðær nænig ealo gebrowen mid Estum, ac þær bið medo genoh. And þær is mid Estum ðeaw, þonne þær bið man dead, þæt he lið inne unforbærned mid his magum and freondum monað, ge hwilum twegen; and þa kyningas, and þa oðre heahðungene men, swa micle lencg swa hi maran speda habbað,
120 hwilum healf gear þæt hi beoð unforbærned, and licgað bufan eorðan on hyra husum. And ealle þa hwile þe þæt lic bið inne, þær sceal beon gedrync and plega, oð ðone dæg þe hi hine forbærnað. Þonne þy ylcan dæge þe hi hine to þæm ade beran wyllað, þonne todælað hi his feoh, þæt þær to lafe bið æfter þæm gedrynce and þæm
125 plegan, on fif oððe syx, hwylum on ma, swa swa þæs feos andefn bið. Alecgað hit ðonne forhwæga on anre mile þone mæstan dæl fram þæm tune, þonne oðerne, ðonne þæne þriddan, oþþe hyt eall aled bið on þære anre mile; and sceall beon se læsta dæl nyhst þæm tune ðe se deada man on lið. Ðonne sceolon beon gesamnode ealle ða
130 menn ðe swyftoste hors habbað on þæm lande, forhwæga on fif

108, 111. *Estland(e)*: C *Eastland(e)*.
123. *dæge: e* added in another hand; *þe:* not in MS.

milum oððe on syx milum fram þæm feo. Þonne ærnað hy ealle
toweard þæm feo; ðonne cymeð se man se þæt swiftoste hors hafað
to þæm ærestan dæle and to þæm mæstan, and swa ælc æfter oðrum,
oþ hit bið eall genumen; and se nimð þone læstan dæl se nyhst þæm
tune þæt feoh geærneð. And þonne rideð ælc hys weges mid ðan feo,   135
and hyt motan habban eall; and forðy þær beoð þa swiftan hors
ungefoge dyre. And þonne hys gestreon beoð þus eall aspended,
þonne byrð man hine ut, and forbærneð mid his wæpnum and
hrægle. And swiðost ealle hys speda hy forspendað mid þan langan
legere þæs deadan mannes inne, and þæs þe hy be þæm wegum   140
alecgað, þe ða fremdan to ærnað, and nimað. And þæt is mid Estum
þeaw þæt þær sceal ælces geðeodes man beon forbærned; and gyf
þar man an ban findeð unforbærned, hi hit sceolan miclum gebetan.
And þær is mid Estum an mægð þæt hi magon cyle gewyrcan: and
þy þær licgað þa deadan men swa lange and ne fuliað, þæt hy wyrcað   145
þone cyle him on. And þeah man asette twegen fætels full ealað oððe
wæteres, hy gedoð þæt ægþer bið oferfroren, sam hit sy sumor sam
winter.'

132. *swiftoste:* C *swifte.*   144. *Estum:* C *Eastum.*
146. *him:* C *hine.*   147. *ægþer:* C *oþer.*

III. ROMANCE

7. APOLLONIUS OF TYRE

THE POPULARITY of the Apollonius legend in the Middle Ages is well attested by the very large number of versions still surviving. Its ultimate source appears to have been a lost Greek romance; the closest we can come to this source is a Latin version of about the fifth century which must be presumed to lie behind the existing manuscripts in Latin. There is a very large number of these manuscripts, and among them considerable textual differences, making it difficult to decide what form of the Latin version provided the basis of the Old English translation. No single MS corresponds exactly; Goolden prints a Latin text reconstructed from a large sample of the MSS, designed to parallel closely the Old English.

The Old English translation, first of many English translations and adaptations, consists of two substantial fragments, amounting to about half the story, in an eleventh-century manuscript. This, Corpus Christi College, Cambridge, MS 201, contains chiefly laws secular and ecclesiastical, and sermons, and is connected with the homilist Wulfstan. *Apollonius* sits uneasily in this manuscript, and in fact is unparalleled as an Old English secular prose romance.

An extract is offered here because of this uniqueness. The same justification may be given for the inclusion of *The Phoenix*: both illustrate facets of Old English literature which are poorly documented in surviving manuscripts and which are overshadowed through the preponderance of heroic and didactic material. In *Apollonius* (as in parts of Alfred's translations) we find evidence of interest in a society other than heroic Germanic or medieval Christian, and in narrative themes other than those typified by heroic legends or saints' lives. Romantic situations are handled competently: the fortuitous circumstances bringing the lovers together, their separation, their reunion after years of adventure. The personalities involved in the story are nicely drawn: the boasting perfidy of Antiochus; Apollonius' just mixture of realism (fleeing from Antiochus), generosity (his rewards to the citizens of Tarsus for harbouring him, and his kind treatment of all who aided him), nobility (his behaviour at the court of Arcestrates), and his modesty in the face of Arcestrate's compliments and her declared love for him; Arcestrate's generous and tolerant treatment of Apollonius, his daughter's perseverance and constancy in her love for the hero. Details are keenly observed: Apollonius' blushing, the suitors' foolishness, the courtiers' reaction to Arcestrate's and Apollonius' harping.

The full story, briefly, is this: Apollonius, a young prince of Tyre,

28

suitor to the daughter of the tyrant Antiochus, incurs the wrath of Antiochus when, through solving a riddle, he uncovers the king's incest with his daughter. Antiochus condemns him, so he flees from Tyre to escape. After certain adventures he is shipwrecked at Cyrene, losing all his belongings and followers. He obtains King Arcestrates' favour by pleasing him at a game, and is invited to a banquet, clothed and feasted by the king. At this point our extract begins . . . Apollonius marries the daughter, Arcestrate, who subsequently appears to die in childbirth. Finally, there is the expected reunion of the romance genre, with Apollonius at last discovering the revivified Arcestrate and their daughter Thasia, each after her separate adventures.

Mid þi ðe se cyning þas word gecwæð, ða færinga þar eode in ðæs cynges iunge dohtor and cyste hyre fæder and ða ymbsittendan. Þa heo becom to Apollonio, þa gewænde heo ongean to hire fæder and cwæð: 'Ðu goda cyningc and min se leofesta fæder, hwæt is þes iunga man þe ongean ðe on swa wurðlicum setle sit mid sarlicum andwlitan? 5 Nat ic hwæt he besorgað.' Ða cwæð se cyningc: 'Leofe dohtor, þes iunga man is forliden, and he gecwemde me manna betst on ðam plegan, forðam ic hine gelaðode to ðysum urum gebeorscipe. Nat ic hwæt he is, ne hwanon he is; ac gif ðu wille witan hwæt he sy, axsa hine, forðam þe gedafenað þæt þu wite.' Ða eode þæt mæden to 10 Apollonio and mid forwandigendre spræce cwæð: 'Ðeah ðu stille sy and unrot, þeah ic þine æðelborennesse on ðe geseo. Nu þonne gif ðe to hefig ne þince, sege me þinne naman and þin gelymp arece me.' Ða cwæð Apollonius: 'Gif ðu for neode axsast æfter minum namon, ic secge þe ic hine forleas on sæ. Gif ðu wilt mine æðelborennesse 15 witan, wite ðu þæt ic hig forlet on Tharsum.' Ðæt mæden cwæð: 'Sege me gewislicor, þæt ic hit mæge understandan.'

Apollonius þa soðlice hyre arehte ealle his gelymp, and æt þare spræcan ende him feollon tearas of ðam eagum. Mid þy þe se cyngc þæt geseah, he bewænde hine ða to ðare dohtor and cwæð: 'Leofe 20 dohtor, þu gesingodest; mid þy þe þu woldest witan his naman and his gelimp, þu hafast nu geedniwod his ealde sar. Ac ic bidde þe þæt þu gife him swa hwæt swa ðu wille.' Ða ða þæt mæden gehirde þæt hire wæs alyfed fram hire fæder þæt heo ær hyre silf gedon wolde, ða cwæð heo to Apollonio: 'Apolloni, soðlice þu eart ure. Forlæt þine 25 murcnunge, and nu ic mines fæder leafe habbe, ic gedo ðe weligne.' Apollonius hire þæs þancode, and se cyngc blissode on his dohtor welwillendnesse and hyre to cwæð: 'Leofe dohtor, hat feccan þine

1. *þar:* above the line. 2. *iunge:* above the line. 6. *Leofe:* MS *leofa.*
10. *þu wite:* about a fifth of the line, including part of the *w* of *wite,* erased between these two words.
11. *stille:* MS *stilli.* 20. *Leofe:* MS *leofa.* 28. *Leofe:* MS *leofa.*

hearpan and gecig ðe to þinum frynd, and afirsa fram þam iungan his
30 sarnesse.' Ða eode heo ut and het feccan hire hearpan, and sona swa
heo hearpian ongan, heo mid winsumum sange gemængde þare
hearpan sweg. Ða ongunnon ealle þa men hi herian on hyre swegcræft,
and Apollonius ana swigode. Ða cwæð se cyninge: 'Apolloni, nu ðu
dest yfele, forðam þe ealle men heriað mine dohtor on hyre swegcræfte,
35 and þu ana hi swigende tælst.' Apollonius cwæð: 'Eala ðu goda
cyngc, gif ðu me gelifst, ic secge þæt ic ongite þæt soðlice þin dohtor
gefeol on swegcræft, ac heo næfð hine na wel geleornod. Ac hat me
nu sillan þa hearpan; þonne wast þu þæt þu nu git nast.' Arcestrates
se cyning cwæð: 'Apolloni, ic oncnawe soðlice þæt þu eart on eallum
40 þingum wel gelæred.' Ða het se cyng sillan Apollonige þa hearpan.
Apollonius þa ut eode and hine scridde, and sette ænne cynehelm
uppon his heafod and nam þa hearpan on his hand, and in eode and
swa stod þæt se cyngc and ealle þa ymbsittendan wendon þæt he nære
Apollonius ac þæt he wære Apollines, ðara hæðenra god. Ða wearð
45 stilnes and swige geworden innon ðare healle. And Apollonius his
hearpenægl genam, and he þa hearpestrengas mid cræfte astirian
ongan and þare hearpan sweg mid winsumum sange gemængde. And
se cyngc silf and ealle þe þar andwearde wæron micelre stæfne
cliopodon and hine heredon. Æfter þisum forlet Apollonius þa
50 hearpan, and plegode and fela fægera þinga þar forð teah þe þam
folce ungecnawen wæs and ungewunelic, and heom eallum þearle
licode ælc þara þinga ðe he forð teah.

Soðlice mid þy þe þæs cynges dohtor geseah þæt Apollonius on
eallum godum cræftum swa wel wæs getogen, þa gefeol hyre mod on
55 his lufe. Ða æfter þæs beorscipes geendunge cwæð þæt mæden to
ðam cynge: 'Leofa fæder, þu lyfdest me litle ær þæt ic moste gifan
Apollonio swa hwæt swa ic wolde of þinum goldhorde.' Arcestrates
se cyng cwæð to hyre: 'Gif him swa hwæt swa ðu wille.' Heo ða
swiðe bliðe ut eode and cwæð: 'Lareow Apolloni, ic gife þe be mines
60 fæder leafe twa hund punda goldes and feower hund punda gewihte
seolfres and þone mæstan dæl deorwurðan reafes and twentig ðeowa
manna.' And heo þa þus cwæð to ðam þeowum mannum: 'Berað
þas þingc mid eow þe ic behet Apollonio minum lareowe, and lecgað
innon bure beforan minum freondum.' Þis wearð þa þus gedon æfter
65 þare cwene hæse, and ealle þa men hire gife heredon ðe hig gesawon.
Ða soðlice geendode þe gebeorscipe, and þa men ealle arison and

---

31. *hearpian:* MS *heapian*; *gemængde:* MS *gemægnde.*
38. 2nd *nu:* in MS this follows the 1st *þu.*   47. *gemængde:* MS *gemægnde.*
50. *plegode:* after *plegod* the rest of the line (about a third) has been erased; *þar:* above the line.
51. *ungecnawen:* MS *ungecnawe.*   59. *swiðe:* MS *sweoðe.*
60. *gewihte:* after this word a letter has been erased.

gretton þone cyngc and ða cwene, and bædon hig gesunde beon, and
ham gewændon. Eac swilce Apollonius cwæð: 'Ðu goda cyngc and
earmra gemiltsigend, and þu cwen, lare lufigend, beon ge gesunde.'
He beseah eac to ðam þeowum mannum þe þæt mæden him forgifen   70
hæfde, and heom cwæð to: 'Nimað þas þing mid eow þe me seo cwen
forgeaf, and gan we secan ure gesthus þæt we magon us gerestan.' Ða
adred þæt mæden þæt heo næfre eft Apollonium ne gesawe swa raðe
swa heo wolde, and eode þa to hire fæder and cwæð: 'Ðu goda
cyningc, licað ðe wel þæt Apollonius, þe þurh us todæg gegodod is,   75
þus heonon fare, and cuman yfele men and bereafian hine?' Se cyngc
cwæð: 'Wel þu cwæde. Hat him findan hwar he hine mæge wurðlicost
gerestan.' Ða dide þæt mæden swa hyre beboden wæs, and Apollonius
onfeng þare wununge ðe hym getæht wæs and ðar in eode, Gode
þancigende ðe him ne forwyrnde cynelices wurðscipes and frofres.   80
   Ac þæt mæden hæfde unstille niht, mid þare lufe onæled þara
worda and sanga þe heo gehyrde æt Apollonige, and na leng heo ne
gebad ðonne hit dæg wæs, ac eode sona swa hit leoht wæs and gesæt
beforan hire fæder bedde. Ða cwæð se cyngc: 'Leofe dohtor, for hwi
eart ðu þus ærwacol?' Ðæt mæden cwæð: 'Me awehton þa gecneord-   85
nessan þe ic girstandæg gehyrde. Nu bidde ic ðe forðam þæt þu
befæste me urum cuman Apollonige to lare.' Ða wearð se cyningc
þearle geblissod, and het feccan Apollonium and him to cwæð: 'Min
dohtor girnð þæt heo mote leornian æt ðe ða gesæligan lare ðe þu
canst; and gif ðu wilt þisum þingum gehyrsum beon, ic swerige ðe   90
þurh mines rices mægna þæt swa hwæt swa ðu on sæ forlure ic ðe on
lande gestaðelige.' Ða ða Apollonius þæt gehyrde, he onfengc þam
mædenne to lare and hire tæhte swa wel swa he silf geleornode.
   Hyt gelamp ða æfter þisum binnon feawum tidum þæt Arcestrates
se cyngc heold Apollonius hand on handa, and eodon swa ut on ðare   95
ceastre stræte. Þa æt nyhstan comon ðar gan ongean hy þry gelærede
weras and æþelborene, þa lange ær girndon þæs cyninges dohtor. Hi
ða ealle þry togædere anre stæfne gretton þone cyngc. Ða smercode
se cyng, and heom to beseah and þus cwæð: 'Hwæt is þæt þæt ge me
anre stæfne gretton?' Ða andswerode heora an and cwæð: 'We bædon 100
gefirn þynre dohtor, and þu us oftrædlice mid elcunge geswænctest.
Forðam we comon hider todæg þus togædere. We syndon þyne
ceastergewaran, of æðelum gebyrdum geborene. Nu bidde we þe
þæt þu geceose þe ænne of us þrym hwilcne þu wille þe to aðume
habban.' Ða cwæð se cyngc: 'Nabbe ge na godne timan aredodne.   105
Min dohtor is nu swiðe bisy ymbe hyre leornunga; ac þe læs þe ic eow

78. *gerestan:* ge above line.   84. *Leofe:* MS *leofa.*
91. *mines:* m over an erasure.   101. *elcunge:* g written over a c.
106. *nu:* above the line.

a leng slæce, awritað eowre naman on gewrite and hire morgengife; þonne asænde ic þa gewrita minre dohtor, þæt heo sylf geceose hwilcne eowerne heo wille.' Ða didon ða cnihtas swa, and se cyngc

110 nam ða gewrita and geinseglode hi mid his ringe and sealde Apollonio, þus cweðende: 'Nim nu, lareow Apolloni, swa hit þe ne mislicyge, and bryng þinum lærincgmædene.'

Ða nam Apollonius þa gewrita and eode to ðare cynelican healle. Mid þam þe þæt mæden geseah Apollonium, þa cwæð heo: 'Lareow,

115 hwi gæst ðu ana?' Apollonius cwæð: 'Hlæfdige, næs git yfel wif, nim ðas gewrita ðe þin fæder þe sænde, and ræd.' Ðæt mæden nam and rædde þara þreora cnihta naman, ac heo ne funde na þone naman þaron þe heo wolde. Ða heo þa gewrita oferræd hæfde, ða beseah heo to Apollonio and cwæð: 'Lareow, ne ofþingð hit ðe gif ic þus wer

120 geceose?' Apollonius cwæð: 'Na, ac ic blissige swiðor ðæt þu miht ðurh ða lare, þe þu æt me underfenge, þe silf on gewrite gecyðan hwilcne heora þu wille. Min willa is þæt þu ðe wer geceose þar ðu silf wille.' Þæt mæden cwæð: 'Eala lareow, gif ðu me lufodest, þu hit besorgodest.' Æfter þisum wordum heo mid modes anrædnesse

125 awrat oðer gewrit, and þæt geinseglode and sealde Apollonio. Apollonius hit þa ut bær on ða stræte and sealde þam cynge. Ðæt gewrit wæs þus gewriten: 'Þu goda cyngc and min se leofesta fæder, nu þin mildheortnesse me leafe sealde þæt ic silf moste ceosan hwilcne wer ic wolde, ic secge ðe to soðan þone forlidenan man ic

130 wille; and gif ðu wundrige þæt swa scamfæst fæmne swa unforwandi-gendlice ðas word awrat, þonne wite þu þæt ic hæbbe þurh weax aboden, ðe nane scame ne can, þæt ic silf ðe for scame secgan ne mihte.'

Ða ða se cyningc hæfde þæt gewrit oferræd, þa niste he hwilcne

135 forlidene heo nemde. Beseah ða to ðam þrim cnihtum and cwæð: 'Hwilc eower is forliden?' Ða cwæð heora an, se hatte Ardalius: 'Ic eom forliden.' Se oðer him andwirde and cwæð: 'Swiga ðu! Adl þe fornime þæt þu ne beo hal ne gesund! Mid me þu boccræft leornodest, and ðu næfre buton þare ceastre geate fram me ne come. Hwar gefore ðu

140 forlidennesse?' Mid ði þe se cyngc ne mihte findan hwilc heora forliden wære, he beseah to Apollonio and cwæð: 'Nim ðu, Apolloni, þis gewrit, and ræd hit. Eaðe mæg gewurðan þæt þu wite þæt ic nat, ðu ðe þar andweard wære.' Ða nam Apollonius þæt gewrit and rædde, and sona swa he ongeat þæt he gelufod wæs fram ðam mædene, his

145 andwlita eal areodode. Ða se cyngc þæt geseah, þa nam he Apollonies hand and hine hwon fram þam cnihtum gewænde, and cwæð: 'Wast þu þone forlidenan man?' Apollonius cwæð: 'Ðu goda cyning, gif þin

107. *a:* above the line.
123. *Eala:* second *a* apparently over a partly erased *l*.

willa bið, ic hine wat.' Ða geseah se cyngc þæt Apollonius mid rosan rude wæs eal oferbræded, þa ongeat he þone cwyde, and þus cwæð to him: 'Blissa, blissa, Apolloni, forðam þe min dohtor gewilnað   150 þæs ðe min willa is. Ne mæg soðlice on þillicon þingon nan þinc gewurðan buton Godes willan.'

150. *Blissa:* MS *blisa.*

IV. HOMILIES

8. THE END OF THE WORLD

The Blickling Homilies is the title given by Morris, their first editor (EETS, 1874), to a collection of homilies in a manuscript formerly at Blickling Hall, Norfolk, and now in the John H. Scheide Library, Princeton, New Jersey. The date 971 on one page does not necessarily help us to date the homilies precisely; the manuscript is of the late tenth–early eleventh century, and the homilies are the direct antecedents of Ælfric's and Wulfstan's works in that genre.

J. W. Bright's *Anglo-Saxon Reader* printed the whole of the tenth homily (in Morris' numbering), but it is less of a favourite anthology-piece than most of the contents of the present selection. An extract is given here in acknowledgement of the importance of the homily genre in Old English and (if we follow Chambers' argument in *The Continuity of English Prose*) for the subsequent history of English prose: for the development of a prose style capable of flexibility for argument and of rhetoric for persuasion. The high point in sermon-writing in Old English comes with the homilies of Ælfric and Wulfstan, and this Blickling Homily illustrates the genre without the individuality of these two writers. The theme of this extract is practically the same as that of the *Sermo Lupi*: the sins of the world, and the need for reform before judgement. Like Wulfstan, the author of this homily begins with a condemnation of contemporary life; but he proceeds straight to admonition of reforms, omitting Wulfstan's argument that present evils are caused by visitation by Antichrist in punishment of men's sins. The Blickling author adds a conventional expression of the theme of mutability, with an exhortation to despise the world: here is the traditional theological background for the references to mutability in *The Wanderer* and *The Seafarer*. Some of the standard phraseology accompanying this theme—for example, the *ubi sunt* formula and the exhortation *ne beo to* + adjective—found here in its most stereotyped form is adapted in these poems. In this pair of poems and the homily we can study the interchange of stylistic and thematic influences between Old English genres, and in Wulfstan and Ælfric we see another borrowing, that of the two-stress rhythmical unit.

Magon we þonne nu geseon and oncnawan and swiþe gearelice ongeotan þæt þisses middangeardes ende swiþe neah is, and manige frecnessa æteowde and manna wohdæda and wonessa swiþe gemonig-

34

fealdode. And we fram dæge to oþrum geaxiað ungecyndelico witu
and ungecynelice deaþas geond þeodland to mannum cumene. And 5
we oft ongytaþ þæt ariseþ þeod wiþ þeode, and ungelimplico gefeoht
on wolicum dædum. And we gehyraþ oft secggan gelome worldricra
manna deaþ þe heora lif mannum leof wære, and þuhte fæger and
wlitig heora lif and wynsumlic. Swa we eac geaxiað mislice adla on
manegum stowum middangeardes, and hungras wexende. And manig 10
yfel we geaxiaþ her on life gelomlician and wæstmian, and nænig god
awunigende and ealle worldlicu þing swiþe synlicu. And colaþ to
swiþe seo lufu þe we to urum Hælende habban sceoldan, and þa
godan weorc we anforlætaþ þe we for ure saule hæle began sceoldan.

Þas tacno þyslico syndon þe ic nu hwile big sægde be þisse worlde 15
earfoþnessum and fræcnessum, swa Crist sylfa his geongrum sægde,
þæt þas þing ealle geweorþan sceoldan ær þisse worlde ende. Uton
we nu efstan ealle mægene godra weorca and geornfulle beon Godes
miltsa, nu we ongeotan magon þæt þis nealæcþ worlde forwyrde;
forþon ic myngige and manige manna gehwylcne þæt he his agene 20
dæda georne smeage, þæt he her on worlde for Gode rihtlice lifge,
and on gesyhþe þæs hehstan Cyninges. Syn we rummode þearfendum
mannum and earmum ælmesgeorne, swa us God sylfa bebead þæt
we soþe sibbe heoldan, and geþwærnesse us betweonan habban. And
þa men þe bearn habban læran hie þam rihtne þeodscipe, and him 25
tæcean lifes weg and rihtne gang to heofonum; and gif hie on ænigum
dæle wolice libban heora lif, syn hie þonne sona from heora wonessum
onwende, and fram heora unrihtum oncyrron; þæt we þurh þæt ealle
Gode lician, swa hit eallum geleaffullum folcum beboden standeþ,
næs na þam anum þe Gode sylfum underþeodde syndon mid myclum 30
hadum—biscopas and cyningas and mæssepreostas and heahdiaconas
—ac eac soþlice hit is beboden subdiaconum and munecum, and is
eallum mannum nedþearf and nytlic þæt hie heora fulwihthadas wel
gehealdan.

Ne beo nænig man her on worldrice on his geþohte to modig, ne 35
on his lichoman to strang, ne niþa to georn, ne bealwes to beald, ne
bregda to full, ne inwit to leof, ne wrohtas to webgenne, ne searo to
renigenne. Ne þearf þæs nan man wenan þæt his lichama mote oþþe
mæge þa synbyrþenna on eorþscrafe gebetan; ah he þær on moldan
gemolsnaþ and þær wyrde bideþ, hwonne se ælmihtiga God wille 40
þisse worlde ende gewyricean: and þonne he his byrnsweord getyhþ
and þas world ealle þurhslyhþ, and þa lichoman þurhsceoteð, and

---

4. *we:* *e* above.   9. *geaxiað:* second *a* above.   26. *tæcean:* *e* above.
32. *is:* inserted above.   33. *wel:* *l* above.   38. *þearf:* *r* above.
39. *mæge:* MS *mᵐ* *ge:* at least four letters erased, and *æ* inserted above; *eorþscrafe:*
above.

þysne middangeard tocleofeð, and þa deadan up astandaþ. Biþ þonne
se flæschoma ascyred swa glæs; ne mæg ðæs unrihtes beon awiht
45 bedigled. Forðon we habbaþ nedþearfe þæt we to lange ne fylgeon
inwitweorcum, ac we sceolan us geearnian þa siblecan wæra Godes
and manna, and þone rihtan geleafan fæste staðelian on urum
heortum þæt he ðær wunian mæge and mote, and þær growan and
blowan. And we sceolan andettan þa soþan geleaffulnesse on urne
50 Drihten Hælende Crist, and on his ðone acendan Suna and on ðone
Halgan Gast, se is efnece Fæder and Sunu. And we sceolan gehyhtan
on Godes þa gehalgodan cyricean and on ða rihtegelefedan, and we
sceolan gelyfan synna forlætnessa and lichoman æristes on domos dæg.
And we sceolan gelefan on þæt ece lif and on þæt heofonlice rice þæt
55 is gehaten eallum þe nu syndan godes wyrhtan. Þis is se rihta geleafa
þe æghwylcum men gebyreð þæt he wel gehealde and gelæste; forðon
þe nan wyrhta ne mæg god weorc wyrcean for Gode buton lufon and
geleafan. And us is mycel nedþearf þæt we us sylfe geðencean and
gemunan and þonne geornost, þonne we gehyron Godes bec us
60 beforan reccean and rædan, and godspell secggean, and his wuldor-
þrymmas mannum cyþan. Vton we þonne georne teolian þæt we
æfter þon ðe beteran syn and þe selran for ðære lare ðe we oft
gehyrdon.

Eala, men ða leofostan, hwæt, we sceolan geðencean þæt we ne
65 lufian to swyþe þæt þæt we forlæton sceolan, ne þæt huru ne forlætan
to swiþe þæt we ecelice habban sceolan. Geseo we nu forgeorne þæt
nænig man on worlde to ðæs mycelne welan nafað, ne to ðon modelico
gestreon her on worlde þæt se on medmycclum fyrste to ende ne
cume, and þæt eall forlæteð þæt him ær her on worlde wynsumlic
70 wæs and leofost to agenne and to hæbbenne; and se man næfre to
ðon leof ne bið his nehmagum and his worldfreondum, ne heora nan
hine to þæs swiþe ne lufað þæt he sona syþþan ne sy onscungend,
seoþþan se lichoma and se gast gedælde beoþ, and þincð his neawist
laþlico and unfæger. Nis þæt nan wundor; hwæt biþ hit la elles buton
75 flæsc seoððan se ecea dæl ofbiþ, þæt is seo sawl? Hwæt biþ la elles
seo laf buton wyrma mete? Hwær beoþ þonne his welan and his
wista? Hwær beoð þonne his wlencea and his anmedlan? Hwær beoþ
þonne his idlan gescyrplan? Hwær beoþ ðonne þa glengeas and þa
mycclan gegyrelan þe he þone lichoman ær mid frætwode? Hwær
80 cumaþ þonne his willan and his fyrenlustas ðe he her on worlde
beeode? Hwæt, he þonne sceal mid his saule anre Gode ælmihtigum
riht agyldan ealles þæs þe he her on worlde to wommum gefremede.

9. WULFSTAN'S ADDRESS TO THE ENGLISH

WULFSTAN was Bishop of London 996–1002 and then Bishop of Worcester 1002–16 and Archbishop of York from 1002 until his death (May 28, 1023). He was the most prominent statesman and ecclesiastic in the reigns of Ethelred and Cnut, and his multifarious activities are reflected in the range of his written works. He compiled, or was the chief compiler of, the later laws of Ethelred, and probably the first two legal codes issued in Cnut's reign. He is also credited with a number of short, specialised secular codes. Besides these secular laws, he wrote three codes of mainly ecclesiastical interest: the *Institutes of Polity*, a comprehensive document dealing with the duties and conduct of all classes of society, and more especially the clergy; the so-called *Canons of Edgar*, a set of rules directed chiefly towards the secular clergy; and the *Northumbrian Priests' Law*, an adaptation of the *Canons* for the northern diocese. He is best known for his large collection of highly rhetorical homilies, of which this *Sermo Lupi ad Anglos* is the most famous.

Besides assisting in the affairs of state and producing a body of eloquent and scholarly work, he was active in Church reform and in the promotion of scholarship. He followed in the tradition of St. Dunstan in enforcing the reform of the clergy; many of his written works reveal his reforming zeal and the anger he poured on degenerate priests. That he encouraged scholarship can be inferred from the existence of a large number of manuscripts connected with him. His scriptorium was occupied in compiling collections of the works of the most important liturgical and canonical writers, to provide convenient reference books for contemporary churchmen. Meanwhile, copies of his own works were being made, and, later, these were incorporated in the collections, thus making comprehensive libraries of sources and new writings. His activities in the field of manuscript compilation seemed to have been more thorough than Alfred's. We know that one of Alfred's translations was meant to be copied out many times and distributed to each of the bishoprics; Wulfstan not only had manuscripts of his own writings duplicated (and, it appears, circulated) but also established an extremely productive 'central library' and scriptorium.

Wulfstan is obviously a figure of some considerable historical interest; but he is known above all as a stylist. Professor Bethurum has demonstrated (in her introduction to *The Homilies of Wulfstan*) how thoroughly he followed the teachings of the rhetoricians in his exploitation of all the varieties of style, and of the figures of thought and sound. He also has his own set of stylistic devices, which are so individual that their detection has been often used as a basis for attributions of authorship.

His prose is, like some of Ælfric's and like Old English poetry, regularly rhythmical. As Professor McIntosh pointed out, his prose consists of 'a continuous series of two-stress phrases' much like the half-lines of Old English verse, and varied in their stress-patterns in somewhat similar ways. Examples may be taken from any part of the text: *ðeos wórold is on*

ófste, dwélode to swýpe, ýfel æfter óðrum, éalles to swýpe. The homilist, like
the political speaker, breaks his text up into short phrases and articulates
each forcefully. Wulfstan differs from Ælfric and from the poetry in his
use of alliteration relative to the 'half-line'. A few of the rhythmical units
are linked in pairs by alliteration; a few have their stressed syllables al-
literating. There is nothing like the consistent linking of half-lines into
full lines that we find in the poetry and in Ælfric's *Lives of the Saints.*
Another device which is evidently used for oratorical force is the intensify-
ing adverb; this also is linked to the rhythmical pattern. Wulfstan has a
set of favourite adverbs from which he selects under two rhythmical circumstances. A single word, such as *swyþe, georne, wide,* can be used to fill
out a unit and at the same time enforce its meaning: *and gehynede swyþe,
swyðe gedrehtan.* Or an adverbial phrase may occupy a whole unit; again,
Wulfstan has a much-used stock of such phrases: *ealles to gelome, inne and
ute, ealles to swyþe.* Rhythmically measured prose obviously lends itself
to parallelism, balance and antithesis. Examples are everywhere, and need
not be quoted here. Two final points concern his vocabulary. He is famed
for his choice of striking and emotionally charged words, many of them
compounds peculiar to his writings; his reputation in this respect comes
from the *Sermo Lupi* as much as any of his works, for the vocabulary of this
homily is both large and striking. And in this homily also we find another of
Wulfstan's devices, the accumulation of words, often the powerful ones
just mentioned, into long lists which give an effect of energy and crescendo.

Much of the phrasing of the *Sermo Lupi* is derived from, or parallels,
Wulfstan's other sermons and non-homiletic works: this is understandable,
as it deals with topics with which he was habitually concerned. But the
Sermo Lupi is, like all good sermons, a topical work. It is an attack of
contemporary sins, comprehensive and yet detailed in its reference. Social
and ecclesiastical sins and sinners are catalogued and harangued at length.
Wulfstan argues that the Danish invasions, which were afflicting the
country and leading to virtual anarchy, were a punishment for sin. We
would rather say that the sins Wulfstan condemns were symptoms of an
anarchic and disoriented society living under great stress. The *Sermo,*
though not factually precise, provides a vivid picture of the state of the
nation around A.D. 1000 which gives background and significance to the
more restrained and factual narrative of the *Chronicle.*

[The *Sermo Lupi* exists in five manuscripts which contain copies differing
in wording and in length. The present edition reproduces one of the
longer versions, from what is probably the earliest of the manuscripts,
British Museum, Cotton Nero A. i.]

Leofan men, gecnawað þæt soð is: ðeos worold is on ofste, and hit
nealæcð þam ende, and þy hit is on worolde aa swa leng swa wyrse,
and swa hit sceal nyde for folces synnan ær Antecristes tocyme
yfelian swyþe; and huru hit wyrð þænne egeslic and grimlic wide on
5   worolde. Understandað eac georne þæt deofol þas þeode nu fela

geara dwelode to swyþe, and þæt lytle getreowþa wæran mid mannum,
þeah hy wel spæcan, and unrihta to fela ricsode on lande. And næs a
fela manna þe smeade ymbe þa bote swa georne swa man scolde, ac
dæghwamlice man ihte yfel æfter oðrum, and unriht rærde and
unlaga manege ealles to wide gynd ealle þas þeode. And we eac   10
forþam habbað fela byrsta and bysmara gebiden, and gif we ænige
bote gebidan scylan, þonne mote we þæs to Gode ernian bet þonne
we ær þysan dydan. Forþam mid miclan earnungan we geearnedan
þa yrmða þe us on sittað, and mid swyþe micelan earnungan we þa
bote motan æt Gode geræcan, gif hit sceal heonanforð godiende   15
weorðan. La hwæt, we witan ful georne þæt to miclan bryce sceal
micel bot nyde, and to miclan bryne wæter unlytel, gif man þæt fyr
sceal to ahte acwencan. And micel is nydþearf manna gehwilcum þæt
he Godes lage gyme heonanforð georne, and Godes gerihta mid rihte
gelæste. On hæþenum þeodum ne dear man forhealdan lytel ne micel   20
þæs þe gelagod is to gedwolgoda weorðunge—and we forhealdað
æghwær Godes gerihta ealles to gelome. And ne dear man gewanian
on hæþenum þeodum inne ne ute ænig þæra þinga þe gedwolgodan
broht bið and to lacum betæht bið—and we habbað Godes hus inne
and ute clæne berypte. And Godes þeowas syndan mæþe and munde   25
gewelhwær bedælde; and gedwolgoda þenan ne dear man misbeodan
on ænige wisan mid hæþenum leodum, swa swa man Godes þeowum
nu deð to wide, þær Cristene scoldan Godes lage healdan and Godes
þeowas griðian.

Ac soð is þæt ic secge, þearf is þære bote, forþam Godes gerihta   30
wanedan to lange innan þysse þeode on æghwylcan ænde, and
folclaga wyrsedan ealles to swyþe, and halignessa syndan to griðlease
wide, and Godes hus syndan to clæne berypte ealdra gerihta and
innan bestrypte ælcra gerisena; and wydewan syndan fornydde on
unriht to ceorle, and to mænege foryrmde and gehynede swyþe; and   35
earme men syndan sare beswicene and hreowlice besyrwde and ut of
þysan earde wide gesealde, swyþe unforworhte, fremdum to gewealde;
and cradolcild geþeowede þurh wælhreowe unlaga for lytelre þyfþe
wide gynd þas þeode, and freoriht fornumene and þrælriht genyrwde
and ælmæsriht gewanode; and, hrædest is to cweþenne, Godes laga   40
laðe and lara forsawene. And þæs we habbað ealle þurh Godes yrre
bysmor gelome, gecnawe se þe cunne; and se byrst wyrð gemæne,
þeh man swa ne wene, eallre þysse þeode, butan God beorge.

Forþam hit is on us eallum swutol and gesene þæt we ær þysan

7. _spæcan:_ MS _swæcan._   20. _dear:_ MS _der_ with _a_ added above.
22. _dear:_ MS _der_ with _a_ added above.   28. _deð:_ altered from _dæð._
41. _forsawene:_ MS originally had a second _n._
42. _bysmor:_ MS _bysmora_ with _a_ erased; the first _se_ has been added above the line.
43. _eallre:_ MS has _re_ added later.

D   39

45 oftor bræcan þonne we bettan, and þy is þysse þeode fela onsæge.
Ne dohte hit nu lange inne ne ute, ac wæs here and hunger, bryne
and blodgyte, on gewelhwylcan ende oft and gelome. And us stalu
and cwalu, stric and steorfa, orfcwealm and uncoþu, hol and hete and
rypera reaflac derede swyþe þearle, and us ungylda swyðe gedrehtan,
50 and us unwedera foroft weoldan unwæstma. Forþam on þysan earde
wæs, swa hit þincan mæg, nu fela geara unrihta fela and tealte
getrywða æghwær mid mannum. Ne bearh nu foroft gesib gesibban
þe ma þe fremdan, ne fæder his bearne, ne hwilum bearn his agenum
fæder, ne broþor oþrum; ne ure ænig his lif ne fadode swa swa he
55 scolde, ne gehadode regollice, ne læwede lahlice. Ac worhtan lust
us to lage ealles to gelome, and naþor ne heoldan ne lare ne lage
Godes ne manna swa swa we scoldan. Ne ænig wið oþerne getrywlice
þohte swa rihte swa he scolde, ac mæst ælc swicode and oþrum derede
wordes and dæde; and huru unrihtlice mæst ælc oþerne æftan heaweþ
60 mid sceandlican onscytan, do mare gif he mæge. Forþam her syn on
lande ungetrywþa micle for Gode and for worolde, and eac her syn
on earde on mistlice wisan hlafordswican manege. And ealra mæst
hlafordswice se bið on worolde þæt man his hlafordes saule beswice;
and ful micel hlafordswice eac bið on worolde þæt man his hlaford of
65 life forræde, oððon of lande lifiendne drife; and ægþer is geworden
on þysan earde: Eadweard man forrædde and syððan acwealde and
æfter þam forbærnde, [and Æþelred man dræfde ut of his earde].
And godsibbas and godbearn to fela man forspilde wide gynd þas
þeode; and ealles to mænege halige stowa wide forwurdan þurh þæt
70 þe man sume men ær þam gelogode, swa man na ne scolde, gif man
on Godes griðe mæþe witan wolde. And cristenes folces to fela man
gesealde ut of þysan earde nu ealle hwile: and eal þæt is Gode lað,
gelyfe se þe wille. And scandlic is to specenne þæt geworden is to
wide, and egeslic is to witanne þæt oft doð to manege, þe dreogað þa
75 yrmþe, þæt sceotað togædere and ane cwenan gemænum ceape
bicgað gemæne, and wið þa ane fylþe adreogað, an æfter anum, and
ælc æfter oðrum, hundum geliccast, þe for fylþe ne scrifað, and
syððan wið weorðe syllað of lande feondum to gewealde Godes

46. *bryne:* something has been erased before this word.
49. The first *us* has been added above in this MS; the others have it in the text.
52. *getrywða:* MS *getryða.*
54. *ure:* MS has *u* above. *ne (fadode):* ne not in MS; supplied from other MSS.
62–3. *And . . . beswice:* these words repeated almost verbatim and then crossed out.
63. *hlafordswice:* h added above line.
67. *and . . . earde:* supplied from another MS.
73. After *wille,* the MS has *Eac we . . . gewearð* (as ll. 79–80), but this has later been deleted by a line encircling it.
75. *yrmþe:* some letters erased after this.

gesceafte and his agenne ceap, þe he deore gebohte. Eac we witan
georne hwær seo yrmð gewearð þæt fæder gesealde bearn wið weorþe,   80
and bearn his modor, and broþor sealde oþerne fremdum to gewealde:
and eal þæt syndan micle and egeslice dæda, understande se þe wille.
And gyt hit is mare and eac mænigfealdre þæt dereð þysse þeode:
mænige synd forsworene and swyþe forlogene, and wed synd
tobrocene oft and gelome; and þæt is gesyne on þysse þeode þæt us   85
Godes yrre hetelice on sit, gecnawe se þe cunne.

And la, hu mæg mare scamu þurh Godes yrre mannum gelimpan
þonne us deð gelome for agenum gewyrhtum? Ðeh þræla hwylc
hlaforde æthleape and of cristendome to wicinge weorþe, and hit
æfter þam eft geweorþe þæt wæpngewrixl weorðe gemæne þegene   90
and þræle, gif þræl þæne þegen fullice afylle, licge ægylde ealre his
mægðe; and gif se þegen þæne þræl þe he ær ahte fullice afylle, gylde
þegengylde. Ful earhlice laga and scandlice nydgyld þurh Godes
yrre us syn gemæne, understande se þe cunne; and fela ungelimpa
gelimpð þysse þeode oft and gelome. Ne dohte hit nu lange inne ne   95
ute, ac wæs here and hete on gewelhwilcan ende oft and gelome; and
Engle nu lange eal sigelease and to swyþe geyrigde þurh Godes yrre;
and flotmen swa strange þurh Godes þafunge þæt oft on gefeohte an
feseð tyne, and hwilum læs, hwilum ma, eal for urum synnum. And
oft tyne oððe twelfe, ælc æfter oþrum, scendað to bysmore þæs   100
þegenes cwenan, and hwilum his dohtor oððe nydmagan, þær he on
locað, þe læt hine sylfne rancne and ricne and genoh godne ær þæt
gewurde. And oft þræl þæne þegen þe ær wæs his hlaford cnyt swyþe
fæste and wyrcð him to þræle þurh Godes yrre. Wala þære yrmðe and
wala þære woroldscame þe nu habbað Engle, eal þurh Godes yrre!   105
Oft twegen sæmæn, oððe þry hwilum, drifað þa drafe cristenra
manna fram sæ to sæ, ut þurh þas þeode, gewelede togædere, us
eallum to woroldscame, gif we on eornost ænige cuþon ariht understandan; ac ealne þæne bysmor þe we oft þoliað we gyldað mid
weorðscipe þam þe us scendað: we him gyldað singallice, and hy us   110
hynað dæghwamlice. Hy hergiað and hy bærnað, rypað and reafiað
and to scipe lædað; and la, hwæt is ænig oðer on eallum þam gelimpum
butan Godes yrre ofer þas þeode swutol and gesæne?

Nis eac nan wundor þeah us mislimpe, forþam we witan ful georne
þæt nu fela geara mænn na ne rohtan foroft hwæt hy worhtan wordes   115

---

84. *synd: n* added above, *ð* erased after *d*.
86. *gecnawe:* MS *gecnewe.*   88. *hwylc:* MS *wylc.*
89. *æthleape:* MS *æthlepe* with *a* written above; *wicinge:* a letter has been erased
before *c*.
97. *geyrigde:* MS *geyrgde* with *i* written above.
107. *togædere: re* added above.   108. *woroldscame:* MS *wolodscame.*
111. *hergiað: i* written above.

41

oððe dæde; ac wearð þes þeodscipe, swa hit þincan mæg, swyþe forsyngod þurh mænigfealde synna and þurh fela misdæda: þurh morðdæda and þurh mandæda, þurh gitsunga and þurh gifernessa, þurh stala and þurh strudunga, þurh mannsylena and þurh hæþene 120 unsida, þurh swicdomas and þurh searacræftas, þurh lahbrycas and þurh æswicas, þurh mægræsas and þurh manslyhtas, þurh hadbrycas and þurh æwbrycas, þurh siblegeru and þurh mistlice forligru. And eac syndan wide, swa we ær cwædan, þurh aðbricas and þurh wed- brycas and þurh mistlice leasunga forloren and forlogen ma þonne 125 scolde; and freolsbrycas and fæstenbrycas wide geworhte oft and gelome. And eac her syn on earde apostatan abroþene and cyrichatan hetole and leodhatan grimme ealles to manege, and oferhogan wide godcundra rihtlaga and cristenra þeawa, and hocorwyrde dysige æghwær on þeode oftost on þa þing þe Godes bodan beodaþ, and 130 swyþost on þa þing þe æfre to Godes lage gebyriað mid rihte. And þy is nu geworden wide and side to ful yfelan gewunan þæt menn swyþor scamað nu for goddædan þonne for misdædan, forþam to oft man mid hocere goddæda hyrweð and godfyrhte lehtreð ealles to swyþe, and swyþost man tæleð and mid olle gegreteð ealles to gelome 135 þa þe riht lufiað and Godes ege habbað be ænigum dæle. And þurh þæt þe man swa deð þæt man eal hyrweð þæt man scolde heregian, and to forð laðet þæt man scolde lufian, þurh þæt man gebringeð ealles to manege on yfelan geþance and on undæde, swa þæt hy ne scamað na, þeh hy syngian swyðe and wið God sylfne forwyrcan hy 140 mid ealle, ac for idelan onscytan hy scamað þæt hy betan heora misdæda swa swa bec tæcan, gelice þam dwæsan þe for heora prytan lewe nellað beorgan ær hy na ne magan, þeh hy eal willan.

Her syndan þurh synleawa, swa hit þincan mæg, sare gelewede to manege on earde. Her syndan mannslagan and mægslagan and mæs- 145 serbanan and mynsterhatan, and her syndan mansworan and mor- þorwyrhtan, and her syndan myltestran and bearnmyrðran and fule forlegene horingas manege, and her syndan wiccan and wælcyrian, and her syndan ryperas and reaferas and woroldstruderas and, hrædest is to cweþenne, mana and misdæda ungerim ealra. And þæs 150 us ne scamað na, ac us scamað swyþe þæt we bote aginnan swa swa bec tæcan, and þæt is gesyne on þysse earman forsyngodan þeode.

123. First *þurh:* MS *þur.*
126. *syn on:* originally *synd* was written, then the *d* changed to *o.*
127. *manege: ne* written above. 129. Second *on:* MS *of.*
140–1. *heora misdæda:* MS *heo* with *re misdæda* in margin.
141. Some letters erased after *swa swa.* 146. *myltestran: r* added above
147. *manege:* a letter erased after this word; *wælcyrian: e* erased after *c.*
148. *woroldstruderas:* MS *worolstruderas.*
150. *aginnan:* corrected from *agunnan.*

Eala, micel magan manege gyt hertoeacan eaþe beþencan þæs þe an
man ne mehte on hrædinge asmeagan, hu earmlice hit gefaren is nu
ealle hwile wide gynd þas þeode. And smeage huru georne gehwa hine
sylfne and þæs na ne latige ealles to lange. Ac la, on Godes naman,   155
utan don swa us neod is, beorgan us sylfum swa we geornost magan,
þe læs we ætgædere ealle forweorðan.

An þeodwita wæs on Brytta tidum, Gildas hatte, se awrat be heora
misdædum, hu hy mid heora synnum swa oferlice swyþe God ge-
græmedan þæt he let æt nyhstan Engla here heora eard gewinnan and   160
Brytta dugeþe fordon mid ealle. And þæt wæs geworden, þæs þe he
sæde, þurh ricra reaflac and þurh gitsunge wohgestreona, þurh leode
unlaga and þurh wohdomas, þurh biscopa asolcennesse and þurh
lyðre yrhðe Godes bydela, þe soþes geswugedan ealles to gelome and
clumedan mid ceaflum þær hy scoldan clypian. Þurh fulne eac folces   165
gælsan and þurh oferfylla and mænigfealde synna heora eard hy forworhtan and selfe hy forwurdan. Ac wutan don swa us þearf is, warnian
us be swilcan; and soþ is þæt ic secge, wyrsan dæda we witan mid
Englum þonne we mid Bryttan ahwar gehyrdan; and þy us is þearf
micel þæt we us beþencan and wið God sylfne þingian georne. And   170
utan don swa us þearf is, gebugan to rihte, and be suman dæle unriht
forlætan, and betan swyþe georne þæt we ær bræcan; and utan God
lufian and Godes lagum fylgean, and gelæstan swyþe georne þæt þæt
we behetan þa we fulluht underfengan, oððon þa þe æt fulluhte ure
forespecan wæran; and utan word and weorc rihtlice fadian, and ure   175
ingeþanc clænsian georne, and að and wed wærlice healdan, and sume
getrywða habban us betweonan butan uncræftan; and utan gelome
understandan þone miclan dom þe we ealle to sculon, and beorgan
us georne wið þone weallendum bryne helle wites, and geearnian us
þa mærþa and þa myrhða þe God hæfð gegearwod þam þe his willan   180
on worolde gewyrcað. God ure helpe. Amen.

10. ÆLFRIC'S LIFE OF KING OSWALD

ÆLFRIC, the most polished of Old English prose writers, was a contemporary of Wulfstan. He was born about 955, and spent his youth at the Benedictine monastery at Winchester; in 987 or shortly after he went to the
recently founded monastery at Cernel (Cerne Abbas in Dorset), but stayed
only a brief period before returning to Winchester; in 1005 he was made
the first abbot at Eynsham, Oxfordshire, where he presumably remained
until his death some time after 1020.

152. *manege: ne* added above.   161. *fordon:* MS *fordom; þæs* added above.
163. *biscopa* corrected from *biscopas.*   168. *wyrsan: s* added above.
170. *wið:* added above the line.   175. *word* corrected from *weord.*
178. *miclan:* MS *miclam.*   180. First *þa* added above the line.

43

Like Wulfstan, he was a prolific writer with a wide range of interests. His purpose and achievement in Christian scholarship and education were similar to those of Alfred, whom he mentions in the Preface to his second set of homilies:

> Then it occurred to my mind, I trust through God's grace, that I would turn this book from the Latin language into the English tongue; not from confidence of great learning, but because I have seen and heard of much error in many English books, which unlearned men, through their simplicity, have esteemed as great wisdom: and I regretted that they knew not nor had not the evangelical doctrines among their writings, those men only excepted who knew Latin, and those books excepted which King Alfred wisely turned from Latin into English, which are to be had . . .

Ælfric's chief works are two series of homilies: the *Catholic Homilies*, his first work, consisting of two sets of liturgical homilies designed for specific occasions in the ecclesiastical calendar; and the *Lives of the Saints*, written somewhat later, but before his move to Eynsham. The *Life of King Oswald* is taken from the second collection. Besides these homilies and certain minor religious works and biblical translations, he wrote a Latin *Grammar* and *Glossary*, an educational dialogue, the *Colloquy*, which has an Old English gloss of some interest, a translation of Bede's *De Temporibus Anni*, five *Pastoral Letters*, one in Old English to Bishop Wulfsige of Sherbourne and two, in both Old English and Latin versions, to Wulfstan. These letters indicate something of Ælfric's scholarship and authority. He was obviously a man of wide learning and was respected for it by his superiors. He spoke authoritatively on liturgical points, on which he gave guidance to Archbishop Wulfstan.

Like Wulfstan, he was a stylist; but his rhetoric is gentler and his style smoother. Many of his homilies, and the *Lives* predominantly, are 'metrical', as Wulfstan's are: we find the same sequence of two-stress rhythmical units, often breaking up the grammar into short phrases. Alliteration is more common than in Wulfstan, and is often used to bind two rhythmical units together like the 'half-lines' of Old English verse. Skeat prints the *Lives* as verse, in long lines without the caesura. The opening lines of our extract arranged in this way will illustrate the metrical organisation, which falls short of the regularity of Old English verse but has an obvious relation to it:

Æfter ðan ðe Augustinus to Engla lande becom,
wæs sum æðele cyning, Oswold gehaten,
on Norðhymbra lande, gelyfed swyþe on God.
Se ferde on his iugoðe fram freondum and magum
to Scotlande on sæ, and þær sona wearð gefullod,
and his geferan samod þe mid him siþedon.
Betwux þam wearð ofslagen Eadwine his eam,
Norðhymbra cynincg, on Crist gelyfed,
fram Brytta cyninge, Ceadwalla geciged,

and twegen his æftergengan binnan twam gearum;
and se Ceadwalla sloh and to sceame tucode
þa Norðhymbra leode æfter heora hlafordes fylle,
oþþæt Oswold se eadiga his yfelnesse adwæscte.

Æfter ðan ðe Augustinus to Engla lande becom, wæs sum æðele
cyning, Oswold gehaten, on Norðhymbra lande, gelyfed swyþe on
God. Se ferde on his iugoðe fram freondum and magum to Scotlande
on sæ, and þær sona wearð gefullod, and his geferan samod þe mid
him siþedon. Betwux þam wearð ofslagen Eadwine his eam, Norð-   5
hymbra cynincg, on Crist gelyfed, fram Brytta cyninge, Ceadwalla
geciged, and twegen his æftergengan binnan twam gearum; and se
Ceadwalla sloh and to sceame tucode þa Norðhymbran leode æfter
heora hlafordes fylle, oþþæt Oswold se eadiga his yfelnesse adwæscte.
Oswold him com to, and him cenlice wið feaht mid lytlum werode, ac   10
his geleafa hine getrymde, and Crist him gefylste to his feonda slege.
Oswold þa aærde ane rode sona Gode to wurðmynte ær þan þe he to
ðam gewinne come, and clypode to his geferum: 'Uton feallan to
ðære rode, and þone Ælmihtigan biddan þæt he us ahredde wið þone
modigan feond þe us afyllan wile. God sylf wat geare þæt we winnað   15
rihtlice wið þysne reðan cyning to ahredenne ure leode.' Hi feollon þa
ealle mid Oswolde on gebedum; and syþþan on oðerne mergen eodon
to þam gefeohte, and gewunnon þær sige swa swa se Eallwealdend
heom uðe for Oswoldes geleafan; and aledon heora fynd, þone modigan
Cedwallan mid his micclan werode, þe wende þæt him ne mihte nan   20
werod wiðstandan.

Seo ylce rod siððan þe Oswold þær aærde on wurðmynte þær stod.
And wurdon fela gehælde untrumra manna and eac swilce nytena
þurh ða ylcan rode, swa swa us rehte Beda. Sum man feoll on ise
þæt his earm tobærst, and læg þa on bedde gebrocod forðearle,   25
oðþæt man him fette of ðære foresædan rode sumne dæl þæs meoses
þe heo mid beweaxen wæs, and se adliga sona on slæpe wearð gehæled
on ðære ylcan nihte þurh Oswoldes geearnungum. Seo stow is gehaten 'Heofonfeld' on Englisc, wið ðone langan weall þe þa
Romaniscan worhtan, þær þær Oswold oferwann þone wælhreowan   30
cynincg. And þær wearð siþþan aæred swiðe mære cyrce Gode to
wurðmynte, þe wunað a on ecnysse.

Hwæt ða Oswold ongann embe Godes willan to smeagenne, sona
swa he rices geweold, and wolde gebigan his leoda to geleafan and to
þam lifigendan Gode. Sende ða to Scotlande, þær se geleafa wæs ða,   35
and bæd ða heafodmenn þæt hi his benum getiþodon, and him sumne
lareow sendon, þe his leoda mihte to Gode geweman; and him wearð

---

4. *gefullod*: MS originally *fullod*.   6. *Ceadwalla*: altered from *cedwalla*.
8. *Ceadwalla*: altered from *cedwalla*.

þæs getiþod. Hi sendon þa sona þam gesæligan cyninge sumne
arwurðne bisceop, Aidan gehaten. Se wæs mæres lifes man on munu-
40 clicre drohtnunge, and he ealle woruldcara awearp fram his heortan,
nanes þinges wilnigende butan Godes willan. Swa hwæt swa him
becom of þæs cyninges gifum oððe ricra manna, þæt he hraðe dælde
þearfum and wædlum mid welwillendum mode.

Hwæt ða Oswold cyning his cymes fægnode, and hine arwurðlice
45 underfeng his folce to ðearfe, þæt heora geleafa wurde awend eft to
Gode fram þam wiþersæce þe hi to gewende wæron. Hit gelamp þa
swa þæt se geleaffula cyning gerehte his witan on heora agenum
gereorde þæs bisceopes bodunge mid bliþum mode, and wæs his
wealhstod; forþan þe he wel cuþe Scyttysc, and se bisceop Aidan ne
50 mihte gebigan his spræce to Norðhymbriscum gereorde swa hraþe
þa git. Se biscop þa ferde bodigende geond eall Norðhymbra land
geleafan and fulluht, and þa leode gebigde to Godes geleafan, and
him wel gebysnode mid weorcum symle, and sylf swa leofode swa
swa he lærde oðre. He lufode forhæfednysse and halige rædinge, and
55 iunge men teah georne mid lare, swa þæt ealle his geferan þe mid
him eodon sceoldon sealmas leornian oððe sume rædinge, swa hwider
swa hi ferdon þam folce bodigende. Seldon he wolde ridan, ac siðode
on his fotum, and munuclice leofode betwux ðam læwedan folce
mid mycelre gesceadwisnysse and soþum mægnum.

60 Þa wearð se cynincg Oswold swiðe ælmesgeorn and eadmod on
þeawum and on eallum þingum cystig, and man ahrærde cyrcan on
his rice geond eall and mynsterlice gesetnyssa mid micelre geornful-
nysse. Hit gelamp on sumne sæl þæt hi sæton ætgædere, Oswold and
Aidan, on þam halgan easterdæge; þa bær man þam cyninge cynelice
65 þenunga on anum sylfrenan disce; and sona þa inn eode an þæs
cyninges þegna þe his ælmyssan bewiste, and sæde þæt fela þearfan
sætan geond þa stræt gehwanon cumene to þæs cyninges ælmyssan.
Þa sende se cyning sona þam þearfum þone sylfrenan disc mid sande
mid ealle, and het toceorfan þone disc, and syllan þam þearfum heora
70 ælcum his dæl, and man dyde ða swa. Þa genam Aidanus se æðela
bisceop þæs cyninges swyþran hand mid swiðlicre blysse, and clypode
mid geleafan, þus cwæðende him to: 'Ne forrotige on brosnunge þeos
gebletsode swyðre hand.' And him eac swa geeode, swa swa Aidanus
him bæd, þæt his swiðre hand is gesundful oð þis.

75 Oswoldes cynerice wearð gerymed þa swyðe, swa þæt feower
þeoda hine underfengon to hlaforde—Peohtas, and Bryttas, Scottas,
and Angle—swa swa se ælmihtiga God hi geanlæhte to ðam for
Oswoldes geearnungum þe hine æfre wurðode. He fulworhte on

---

51. *land:* MS *lande.*   62. *gesetnyssa: a* altered from *e.*
73. *hand:* added above the line.

Eferwic þæt ænlice mynster þe his mæg Eadwine ær begunnon hæfde. And he swanc for heofonan rice mid singalum gebedum swiþor þonne 80 he hogode hu he geheolde on worulde þa hwilwendlican geþincðu, þe he hwonlice lufode. He wolde æfter uhtsange oftost hine gebiddan, and on cyrcan standan on syndrigum gebedum of sunnan upgange mid swyðlicre onbryrdnysse; and swa hwær swa he wæs he wurðode æfre God upawendum handbredum wið þæs heofones weard. 85

On þam ylcan timan com eac sum bisceop fram Romebyrig, Birinus gehaten, to Westsexena kyninge, Cynegyls gehaten, se wæs ða git hæðen and eall Westsexena land. Birinus witodlice gewende fram Rome be ðæs papan ræde þe ða on Rome wæs, and behet þæt he wolde Godes willan gefremman, and bodian þam hæþenum þæs 90 Hælendes naman and þone soðan geleafan on fyrlenum landum. Þa becom he to Westseaxan, þe wæs ða gyt hæþen, and gebigde þone cynincg Kynegyls to Gode, and ealle his leode to geleafan mid him. Hit gelamp þa swa þæt se geleaffulla Oswold, Norðhymbra cyning, wæs cumen to Cynegylse, and hine to fulluhte nam, fægen his gecyr- 95 rednysse. Þa geafon þa cynegas, Cynegyls and Oswold, þam halgan Birine him to bisceopstole þa burh Dorcanceaster, and he þærbinnan wunode Godes lof aræende and gerihtlæcende þæt folc mid lare to geleafan to langum fyrste, oðþæt he gesælig siþode to Criste. And his lic wearþ bebyrged on ðære ylcan byrig, oðþæt Hædde bisceop 100 eft his ban ferode to Wintanceastre, and mid wurðmynte gelogode binnan Ealdanmystre, þær man hine wurðað gyt.

Hwæt þa Oswold cyning his cynedom geheold hlisfullice for wo- rulde and mid micclum geleafan, and on eallum dædum his Drihten arwurðode, oð he ofslagen wearð for his folces ware on þam nigoðan 105 geare þe he rices geweold, þa þa he sylf wæs on ylde eahta and þrittig geara. Hit gewearð swa be þam þæt him wann on Penda, Myrcena cyning, þe æt his mæges slege ær, Eadwines cyninges, Ceadwallan fylste. And se Penda ne cuðe be Criste nan þincg, and eall Myrcena folc wæs ungefullod þa git. Hi comon þa to gefeohte to Maserfelda 110 begen, and fengon togædere, oðþæt þær feollon þa Cristenan, and þa hæðenan genealæhton to þam halgan Oswolde. Þa geseah he geneale- can his lifes geendunge, and gebæd for his folc þe þær feallende sweolt, and betæhte heora sawla and hine sylfne Gode, and þus clypode on his fylle: 'God, gemiltsa urum sawlum!' Þa het se hæþena 115 cynincg his heafod ofaslean and his swiðran earm, and settan hi to myrcelse.

Þa æfter Oswoldes slege feng Oswig his broðor to Norðhymbra rice, and rad mid werode to þær his broðor heafod stod on stacan

<hr>

85. *þæs:* added above the line.
107. *geara:* altered from *geare.*

106. *geweold:* altered from *weold.*
108. *Ceadwallan:* altered from *cedwallan.*

120 gefæstnod, and genam þæt heafod and his swiðran hand and mid
arwurðnysse ferode to Lindisfarnea cyrcan. Þa wearð gefylled, swa
we her foresædon, þæt his swiðre hand wunað hal mid þam flæsce
butan ælcere brosnunge, swa se bisceop gecwæð. Se earm wearð geled
arwurðlice on scrine, of seolfre asmiþod, on Sancte Petres mynstre
125 binnan Bebbanbyrig be þære sæ strande, and lið þær swa andsund swa
he ofaslagen wæs. His broðor dohtor eft siððan on Myrcan wearð
cwen, and geaxode his ban, and gebrohte hi to Lindesige to Bardanige
mynstre, þe heo micclum lufode. Ac þa mynstermenn noldon for
menniscum gedwylde þone sanct underfon, ac man sloh an geteld
130 ofer þa halgan ban binnan þære licreste. Hwæt þa God geswutelode
þæt he halig sanct wæs, swa þæt heofonlic leoht ofer þæt geteld astreht
stod up to heofonum swilce healic sunnbeam ofer ealle ða niht; and
þa leoda beheoldon geond ealle þa scire swiðe wundrigende. Þa wurdon þa mynstermen micclum afyrhte, and bædon þæs on mergen þæt
135 hi moston þone sanct mid arwurðnysse underfon, þone þe hi ær
forsocon. Þa ðwoh man þa halgan ban, and bær into þære cyrcan
arwurðlice on scrine, and gelogodon hi upp.

[Ælfric describes various miracles attributed to Oswald.]

Nu cwæð se halga Beda, þe ðas boc gedihte, þæt hit nan wundor
nys þæt se halga cynincg untrumnysse gehæle, nu he on heofonum
140 leofað, forðan þe he wolde gehelpan, þa þa he her on life wæs, þearfum
and wannhalum, and him bigwiste syllan. Nu hæfð he þone wurðmynt on þære ecan worulde mid þam ælmihtigan Gode for his
godnysse. Eft se halga Cuðberht, þa þa he git cnapa wæs, geseah hu
Godes ænglas feredon Aidanes sawle þæs halgan bisceopes bliðe to
145 heofonum to þam ecan wuldre þe he on worulde geearnode. Þæs
halgan Oswoldes ban wurdon eft gebroht æfter manegum gearum
to Myrcena lande into Gleawceastre; and God þær geswutelode oft
feala wundra þurh þone halgan wer. Sy þæs wuldor þam ælmihtigan
Gode þe on ecnysse rixað a to worulde. Amen.

123. gecwæð: altered from cwæð.

VERSE

I. HEROIC POETRY

II. BEOWULF

Beowulf IS A POEM of 3,182 lines surviving in one manuscript, British Museum, Cotton Vitellius A. xv, written about A.D. 1000. In the manuscript there are also a fragment of the poem *Judith*, a homily and two other prose pieces, *The Marvels of the East* and *Alexander's Letter to Aristotle*. The manuscript was one of those to suffer in the Cottonian fire of 1731. It was not as severely damaged as some, but was badly scorched; the edges became brittle, and most pages have lost some characters from the ends of the lines. In 1787, before the manuscript became as badly damaged through crumbling as it is today, the Icelander G. J. Thorkelin made copies of it. One (Thorkelin B) is in his own hand, and another (Thorkelin A) is the work of a professional copyist. These transcripts are of great value in supplying letters now lost; but of course some damage had been done by the time Thorkelin made these copies.

Our text is late, and apparently written in a dialect (late or 'classical' West Saxon) different from that of the original. Scholars agree that the poem existed, in a form substantially like that of today, not less than two centuries earlier than the Cotton MS, and in one of the Anglian dialects. The exact date and place of origin are impossible to determine. A sort of *terminus ad quem* is the last decade of the eighth century: from this time (beginning with the sacking of Lindisfarne and Jarrow in 793–4) the ravages of the Danes in this country would have made a poem with the Danes so much in the foreground unacceptable. Our earlier limit is equally imprecise. There is internal (stylistic) evidence that the author of *Beowulf* was familiar with Cædmon and Cædmonian poetry (probably *Genesis A* and *Daniel*). We know only roughly the period of Cædmon's literary work (see introduction to Extract 5); but this allows us to place a *terminus a quo* for *Beowulf* around, but not much earlier than, the last quarter of the seventh century. So the poem may have been written any time between, say, 680 and 790—and these dates are arrived at on the vaguest of evidence. Place of origin is equally unclear. The poem is most probably Anglian, but not obviously either Northumbrian or Mercian. Bede's Northumbria would have provided the right cultural milieu; but the Mercia of Offa (757–96) has also been proposed.

To an earlier generation of critics even as cautious a 'dating' as this would have been unacceptable or at least pointless. Modern textual criticism seeks to determine the date of composition of the poem in substantially its present form; earlier Anglo-Saxonists enquired into the *genesis* of the poem—what lay behind the present text. They viewed the poem as an assemblage from a number of pre-existing heroic lays; or as a core of Germanic material with Christian layers superimposed, or fragments interpolated; as a depaganisation of a somehow 'purer' Germanic original. These speculations seem unreal today. We are disposed to accept the extant text as the basis for criticism; and indeed a view of the poem as a final patchwork of ill-assorted elements from different ages and sources can only inhibit criticism. So it is regarded as a poem written by a Christian who was cognisant with, and not unsympathetic to, the narrative themes and attitudes of folklore and of Germanic legend and history; and who was an expert practitioner in the native forms of poetic expression inherited from the oral period and given the sanction of religious use (that is to say, for that period, literary vogue) by Cædmon and his school.

On this basis criticism can begin: we can enquire what sort of poem it is, how it is articulated, what its author's intention was. How do we characterise it? Epic, elegy, entertainment, didactic poem, allegory, embodiment of myth? What is its narrative structure? What is the relationship between the simple scheme of three looming fabulous incidents and the mass of actions, of various degrees of historicity, merely alluded to? What principle of characterisation has given rise to the hero? Is he a type from Germanic or Christian ideology, or from the many parallel but textually unconnected popular narratives? What themes are embodied in the action and characterisation? Just how Christian have these pre-Christian 'events' been made? We see that, when *Beowulf* is no longer branded an imperfect (mixed, unfused) poem, it becomes a difficult one. Its shape may appear odd, and needs hypotheses such as 'balance' to justify it (the main episodes balanced against each other, or the centre balanced, in a different dimension, against the edges); it 'lacks steady advance' and we have to debate the necessity or otherwise for progression; its Christianity is pervasive in extent yet limited in character (no New Testament references); it mixes folktale, legend and historical event. Naturally, criticism has flourished: in this respect, *Beowulf* is a sort of *Hamlet*. The editor cannot possibly do justice to *Beowulf*-criticism in such a short space, so the reader is referred to the Bibliography.

The poem describes the three greatest heroic deeds (others are alluded to) of one towering but historically unauthenticated hero against a now dimly understood background of relations among the Scandinavian/Baltic kingdoms of the sixth century. The international scene is constantly touched on: by reminiscences of events which are analogous to or illuminate details of the main action; by prognostications of effects of the action; and simply as background or as narrative entertainment within our narrative. Beowulf, a noble Geat, subject of the historical king Hygelac, crosses the sea to the land of the Danes and delivers them of a marauding cannibalistic giant Grendel. In revenge, Grendel's mother raids Heorot, the Danes' royal hall, killing a favourite thane Æschere. Beowulf pursues her and kills her in a struggle in a cave below a mysterious lake. He is rewarded by the Danish king Hrothgar and returns home to Geatland. Later he is persuaded to take the throne and rules well for fifty years. Then a treasure-guarding dragon is disturbed and ravages the country until he is slain by Beowulf and his one loyal retainer, Wiglaf. Beowulf is killed in the fight, and the poem ends with a terrible prognostication of disaster but with the praises of Beowulf.

There is, then, little plot—it is not a biography or a continuous narrative. It is not difficult to excerpt from this poem, for the central incidents stand out. (Critics no longer agree with W. P. Ker's assertion that the things of trivial narrative interest—monster-slayings—unartistically occupy the centre of the poem.) All three of Beowulf's fights are included here, simply because they *are* in the foreground and are more compelling than other quotable passages (e.g. Beowulf's sea-journey, the burial of Scyld, the funeral of Beowulf, Hrothgar's 'sermon', the elegiac passages). Extract 1 covers the whole of Beowulf's fight with Grendel, and illustrates the completeness and conciseness of the described incidents: *Beowulf* is naturally digressive and episodic, but the more memorable episodes are skilfully constructed units. 2 contains a famous, and, for Old English, uniquely expansive and evocative, description of Grendel's mere and its surroundings. 3 narrates the fight with Grendel's mother. 4, the longest extract, is offered less for the narrative interest of the combat than for its dramatisation of the personal relationships of the heroic *comitatus* system; it bears close comparison with the rather less personal exposition of the theme of loyalty in *The Battle of Maldon*.

1. BEOWULF'S FIGHT WITH GRENDEL

Com on wanre niht	702
scriðan sceadugenga. Sceotend swæfon,	
þa þæt hornreced healdan scoldon,	
ealle buton anum. Þæt wæs yldum cuþ,	
þæt hie ne moste, þa Metod nolde,	5
se scynscaþa under sceadu bregdan;	
ac he wæccende wraþum on andan	
bad bolgenmod beadwa geþinges.	
Ða com of more under misthleoþum	710
Grendel gongan: Godes yrre bær.	10
Mynte se manscaða manna cynnes	
sumne besyrwan in sele þam hean.	
Wod under wolcnum to þæs þe he winreced,	
goldsele gumena, gearwost wisse	
fættum fahne. Ne wæs þæt forma sið	15
þæt he Hroþgares ham gesohte;	
næfre he on aldordagum ær ne siþðan	
heardran hæle, healðegnas fand!	

6. *scyncaþa*: MS *synscaþa*.

53

720 Com þa to recede   rinc siðian,
20 dreamum bedæled. Duru sona onarn,
    fyrbendum fæst, syþðan he hire folmum æthran;
    onbræd þa bealohydig, ða he gebolgen wæs,
    recedes muþan. Raþe æfter þon
    on fagne flor   feond treddode,
25 eode yrremod;   him of eagum stod
    ligge gelicost   leoht unfæger.
    Geseah he in recede   rinca manige,
    swefan sibbegedriht   samod ætgædere,
730 magorinca heap. Þa his mod ahlog;
30 mynte þæt he gedælde, ærþon dæg cwome,
    atol aglæca,   anra gehwylces
    lif wið lice,   þa him alumpen wæs
    wistfylle wen. Ne wæs þæt wyrd þa gen
    þæt he ma moste   manna cynnes
35 ðicgean ofer þa niht. Þryðswyð beheold
    mæg Higelaces,   hu se manscaða
    under færgripum   gefaran wolde.
    Ne þæt se aglæca   yldan þohte,
740 ac he gefeng hraðe   forman siðe
40 slæpendne rinc,   slat unwearnum,
    bat banlocan,   blod edrum dranc,
    synsnædum swealh;   sona hæfde
    unlyfigendes   eal gefeormod,
    fet ond folma. Forð near ætstop,
45 nam þa mid handa   higeþihtigne
    rinc on ræste,   ræhte ongean
    feond mid folme;   he onfeng hraþe
    inwitþancum   ond wið earm gesæt.
750 Sona þæt onfunde   fyrena hyrde
50 þæt he ne mette   middangeardes,
    eorþan sceata,   on elran men
    mundgripe maran;   he on mode wearð
    forht on ferhðe;   no þy ær fram meahte.
    Hyge wæs him hinfus;   wolde on heolster fleon,
55 secan deofla gedræg;   ne wæs his drohtoð þær
    swylce he on ealderdagum   ær gemette.
    Gemunde þa se goda,   mæg Higelaces,

21. *æthran:* MS . .*hran,* with *hr* barely legible and *n* apparently altered from *m.*
22. *he gebolgen:* MS .*e ge bolgen?*
46. *ræste:* an erasure of about five letters after this word.
51. *sceata:* MS *sceat/ta.*

54

æfenspræce,   uplang astod
ond him fæste wiðfeng;   fingras burston;   760
eoten wæs utweard,   eorl furþur stop.   60
Mynte se mæra,   þær he meahte swa,
widre gewindan   ond on weg þanon
fleon on fenhopu;   wiste his fingra geweald
on grames grapum.   Þæt wæs geocor sið
þæt se hearmscaþa   to Heorute ateah!   65
Dryhtsele dynede;   Denum eallum wearð,
ceasterbuendum,   cenra gehwylcum,
eorlum ealuscerwen.   Yrre wæron begen,
reþe renweardas.   Reced hlynsode.   770
Þa wæs wundor micel,   þæt se winsele   70
wiðhæfde heaþodeorum,   þæt he on hrusan ne feol,
fæger foldbold;   ac he þæs fæste wæs
innan ond utan   irenbendum
searoþoncum besmiþod.   Þær fram sylle abeag
medubenc monig,   mine gefræge,   75
golde geregnad,   þær þa graman wunnon.
Þæs ne wendon ær   witan Scyldinga
þæt hit a mid gemete   manna ænig
betlic ond banfag   tobrecan meahte,   780
listum tolucan,   nymþe liges fæþm   80
swulge on swaþule.   Sweg up astag
niwe geneahhe: Norð-Denum stod
atelic egesa,   anra gehwylcum
þara þe of wealle   wop gehyrdon,
gryreleoð galan   Godes andsacan,   85
sigeleasne sang,   sar wanigean
helle hæfton.   Heold hine fæste
se þe manna wæs   mægene strengest
on þæm dæge   þysses lifes.   790
Nolde eorla hleo   ænige þinga   90
þone cwealmcuman   cwicne forlætan,
ne his lifdagas   leoda ænigum
nytte tealde.   Þær genehost brægd
eorl Beowulfes   ealde lafe;
wolde freadrihtnes   feorh ealgian,   95

61. *þær:* MS defective in top corner of a page; Thorkelin A reads . .*ær*, B *hwær*
(Zupitza comments '*hw* with another ink, and crossed out in pencil', but this
cannot be seen in the facsimile).
   64. *þæt:* MS . .*he*, Thorkelin A *ræt he*, B *þæt he.*   79. *betlic:* MS *hetlic.*
   92. *ænigum: i* above.   95. *feorh:* after this word an erasure of about five letters.

mæres þeodnes,   ðær hie meahton swa.
Hie þæt ne wiston,   þa hie gewin drugon,
heardhicgende   hildemecgas,
800   ond on healfa gehwone   heawan þohton,
100   sawle secan: þone synscaðan
ænig ofer eorþan   irenna cyst,
guðbilla nan   gretan nolde;
ac he sigewæpnum   forsworen hæfde,
ecga gehwylcre.   Scolde his aldorgedal
105   on ðæm dæge   þysses lifes
earmlic wurðan,   ond se ellorgast
on feonda geweald   feor siðian.
Ða þæt onfunde   se þe fela æror
810   modes myrðe   manna cynne,
110   fyrene gefremede—he wæs fag wið God—
þæt him se lichoma   læstan nolde,
ac hine se modega   mæg Hygelaces
hæfde be honda;   wæs gehwæþer oðrum
lifigende lað.   Licsar gebad
115   atol æglæca;   him on eaxle wearð
syndolh sweotol,   seonowe onsprungon,
burston banlocan.   Beowulfe wearð
guðhreð gyfeþe;   scolde Grendel þonan
820   feorhseoc fleon   under fenhleoðu,
120   secean wynleas wic;   wiste þe geornor
þæt his aldres wæs   ende gegongen,
dogera dægrim.   Denum eallum wearð
æfter þam wælræse   willa gelumpen.
Hæfde þa gefælsod   se þe ær feorran com,
125   snotor ond swyðferhð,   sele Hroðgares,
genered wið niðe.   Nihtweorce gefeh,
ellenmærþum.   Hæfde East-Denum
Geatmecga leod   gilp gelæsted,
830   swylce oncyþðe   ealle gebette,
130   inwidsorge,   þe hie ær drugon
ond for þreanydum   þolian scoldon,
torn unlytel.   Þæt wæs tacen sweotol,
syþðan hildedeor   hond alegde,
earm ond eaxle — þær wæs eal geador
135   Grendles grape — under geapne hrof.

110. *wæs:* not in MS or Thorkelin.
135. *hrof:* MS *h.* . .; Thorkelin A . . . . . .; B *hr.* .

2. THE PURSUIT OF GRENDEL'S MOTHER

'Ic þæt londbuend,   leode mine,   *1345*
selerædende,   secgan hyrde,
þæt hie gesawon   swylce twegen
micle mearcstapan   moras healdan,
ellorgæstas.   Ðæra oðer wæs,   140
þæs þe hie gewislicost   gewitan meahton,   *1350*
idese onlicnæs;   oðer earmsceapen
on weres wæstmum   wræclastas træd,
næfne he wæs mara   þonne ænig man oðer;
þone on geardagum   Grendel nemdon   145
foldbuende;   no hie fæder cunnon,
hwæþer him ænig wæs   ær acenned
dyrnra gasta.   Hie dygel lond
warigeað, wulfhleoþu,   windige næssas,
frecne fengelad,   ðær fyrgenstream   150
under næssa genipu   niþer gewiteð,   *1360*
flod under foldan.   Nis þæt feor heonon
milgemearces,   þæt se mere standeð;
ofer þæm hongiað   hrinde bearwas;
wudu wyrtum fæst   wæter oferhelmað.   155
Þær mæg nihta gehwæm   niðwundor seon,
fyr on flode.   No þæs frod leofað
gumena bearna,   þæt þone grund wite.
Ðeah þe hæðstapa   hundum geswenced,
heorot hornum trum,   holtwudu sece,   160
feorran geflymed,   ær he feorh seleð,   *1370*
aldor on ofre,   ær he in wille,
hafelan hydan.   Nis þæt heoru stow!
Þonon yðgeblond   up astigeð
won to wolcnum,   þonne wind styreþ   165
lað gewidru,   oðþæt lyft drysmaþ,
roderas reotað.   Nu is se ræd gelang
eft æt þe anum.   Eard git ne const,
frecne stowe,   ðær þu findan miht
felasinnigne secg;   sec gif þu dyrre.   170
Ic þe þa fæhðe   feo leanige,   *1380*
ealdgestreonum,   swa ic ær dyde,

145. *nemdon:* Thorkelin A, B *nemdod.*   149. *windige:* so Thorkelin A; B *windig.*
153. *standeð:* MS *stanðeð.*   163. *hydan:* not in MS.
169. *findan:* MS *finda n* with a letter erased between *a* and *n.*
170. *felasinnigne:* MS *fela sinnigne*; most editors remove *fela* as the alliteration is
imperfect.

    wundnum golde,   gyf þu on weg cymest.'
    Beowulf maþelode,   bearn Ecgþeowes:
175 'Ne sorga, snotor guma.   Selre bið æghwæm
    þæt he his freond wrece,   þonne he fela murne.
    Ure æghwylc sceal   ende gebidan
    worolde lifes;   wyrce se þe mote
    domes ær deaþe;   þæt bið drihtguman
180 unlifgendum   æfter selest.
1390 Aris, rices weard,   uton hraþe feran,
    Grendles magan   gang sceawigan.
    Ic hit þe gehate: no he on helm losaþ,
    ne on foldan fæþm,   ne on fyrgenholt,
185 ne on gyfenes grund,   ga þær he wille.
    Ðys dogor þu   geþyld hafa
    weana gehwylces,   swa ic þe wene to.'
      Ahleop ða se gomela,   Gode þancode,
    mihtigan Drihtne,   þæs se man gespræc.
190 Þa wæs Hroðgare   hors gebæted,
1400 wicg wundenfeax.   Wisa fengel
    geatolic gende;   gumfeþa stop
    lindhæbbendra.   Lastas wæron
    æfter waldswaþum   wide gesyne,
195 gang ofer grundas,   þær heo gegnum for
    ofer myrcan mor,   magoþegna bær
    þone selestan   sawolleasne
    þara þe mid Hroðgare   ham eahtode.
    Ofereode þa   æþelinga bearn
200 steap stanhliðo,   stige nearwe,
1410 enge anpaðas,   uncuð gelad,
    neowle næssas,   nicorhusa fela;
    he feara sum   beforan gengde
    wisra monna   wong sceawian,
205 oþþæt he færinga   fyrgenbeamas
    ofer harne stan   hleonian funde,
    wynleasne wudu;   wæter under stod
    dreorig ond gedrefed.   Denum eallum wæs,
    winum Scyldinga,   weorce on mode
210 to geþolianne,   ðegne monegum,

173. *wundnum:* MS *wun dini* or *wun dmi.*
174. *Ecgþeowes:* Thorkelin A *ecgþeo æs,* B *Ecgþeo wes.*
177. *æghwylc:* MS *æghwyle?;* Thorkelin A *æghryle,* B *æghwylc.*
179. *drihtguman:* MS *driht gumen* with *e* dotted and *a* above.
182. *gang:* final *g* inserted above in a different hand.
192. *geatolic:* Thorkelin B *geato.*   195. *þær heo:* not in MS.

oncyð eorla gehwæm, syðþan Æscheres   *1420*
on þam holmclife hafelan metton.
Flod blode weol (folc to sægon),
hatan heolfre. Horn stundum song
fuslic fyrdleoð. Feþa eal gesæt.   215
Gesawon ða æfter wætere wyrmcynnes fela,
sellice sædracan sund cunnian,
swylce on næshleoðum nicras licgean,
ða on undernmæl oft bewitigað
sorhfulne sið on seglrade,   220
wyrmas ond wildeor. Hie on weg hruron   *1430*
bitere ond gebolgne; bearhtm ongeaton,
guðhorn galan. Sumne Geata leod
of flanbogan feores getwæfde,
yðgewinnes, þæt him on aldre stod   225
herestræl hearda; he on holme wæs
sundes þe sænra, ðe hyne swylt fornam.
Hræþe wearð on yðum mid eoferspreotum
heorohocyhtum hearde genearwod,
niða genæged, ond on næs togen,   230
wundorlic wægbora; weras sceawedon   *1440*
gryrelicne gist.

3. THE FIGHT WITH GRENDEL'S MOTHER

Æfter þæm wordum Weder-Geata leod   *1492*
efste mid elne, nalas ondsware
bidan wolde; brimwylm onfeng   235
hilderince. Ða wæs hwil dæges,
ær he þone grundwong ongytan mehte.
Sona þæt onfunde se ðe floda begong
heorogifre beheold hund missera,
grim ond grædig, þæt þær gumena sum   240
ælwihta eard ufan cunnode.   *1500*
Grap þa togeanes, guðrinc gefeng
atolan clommum; no þy ær in gescod
halan lice; hring utan ymbbearh,
þæt heo þone fyrdhom ðurhfon ne mihte,   245

215. *fyrdleoð*: MS . . . .*leoð*. Thorkelin A . . . . .*leod*, B *f.* . .*leod; gesæt:* MS *ge seah* with *eah* crossed out and *æt* above in the same hand.
229. *genearwod*: two letters erased between *ge* and *nearwod*.
234. *ondsware*: Thorkelin A *7sware*, B *andsware*.
236. *hilderince*: Thorkelin A *hib de rince*, B *hil de rince*.

  locene leoðosyrcan   laþan fingrum.
  Bær þa seo brimwylf, þa heo to botme com,
  hringa þengel to hofe sinum,
  swa he ne mihte, no he þæs modig wæs,
250 wæpna gewealdan; ac hine wundra þæs fela
1510 swencte on sunde, sædeor monig
  hildetuxum heresyrcan bræc,
  ehton aglæcan. Ða se eorl ongeat
  þæt he in niðsele nathwylcum wæs,
255 þær him nænig wæter wihte ne sceþede,
  ne him for hrofsele hrinan ne mehte
  færgripe flodes; fyrleoht geseah,
  blacne leoman beorhte scinan.
    Ongeat þa se goda grundwyrgenne,
260 merewif mihtig; mægenræs forgeaf
1520 hildebille, hond sweng ne ofteah,
  þæt hire on hafelan hringmæl agol
  grædig guðleoð. Ða se gist onfand
  þæt se beadoleoma bitan nolde,
265 aldre sceþðan, ac seo ecg geswac
  ðeodne æt þearfe; ðolode ær fela
  hondgemota, helm oft gescær,
  fæges fyrdhrægl; ða wæs forma sið
  deorum madme, þæt his dom alæg.
270 Eft wæs anræd, nalas elnes læt,
1530 mærða gemyndig mæg Hylaces.
  Wearp ða wundenmæl wrættum gebunden
  yrre oretta, þæt hit on eorðan læg,
  stið ond stylecg; strenge getruwode,
275 mundgripe mægenes. Swa sceal man don,
  þonne he æt guðe gegan þenceð
  longsumne lof; na ymb his life cearað.
  Gefeng þa be eaxle (nalas for fæhðe mearn)
  Guð-Geata leod Grendles modor;
280 brægd þa beadwe heard, þa he gebolgen wæs,
1540 feorhgeniðlan, þæt heo on flet gebeah.

---

246. *leoðosyrcan:* Thorkelin A *leoðo syrcan,* B *leodo syrcan.*
247. *brimwylf:* MS *brim wyl.*
249. *þæs:* MS *þæm.*   251. *swencte:* MS *swecte.*
254. *in:* not in MS.   258. *scinan:* Thorkelin A *sciman,* B *scinan.*
261. *hond:* MS *hord; sweng:* MS *swenge.*   263. *Ða:* Thorkelin A *da,* B *ða.*
266. *ðeodne:* Thorkelin A *ðeodne,* B *deoðne.*
272. *Wearp:* *r* above in the same hand; *wundenmæl:* MS *wundel mæg* with *g* crossed out and *l* above.

Heo him eft hraþe andlean forgeald
grimman grapum ond him togeanes feng;
oferwearp þa werigmod wigena strengest,
feþecempa, þæt he on fylle wearð.   285
Ofsæt þa þone selegyst, ond hyre seax geteah,
brad ond brunecg; wolde hyre bearn wrecan,
angan eaferan. Him on eaxle læg
breostnet broden; þæt gebearh feore,
wið ord ond wið ecge ingang forstod.   290
Hæfde ða forsiðod sunu Ecgþeowes   1550
under gynne grund, Geata cempa,
nemne him heaðobyrne helpe gefremede,
herenet hearde, ond halig God
geweold wigsigor; witig Drihten,   295
rodera Rædend, hit on ryht gesced
yðelice, syþðan he eft astod.
  Geseah ða on searwum sigeeadig bil,
ealdsweord eotenisc ecgum þyhtig,
wigena weorðmynd; þæt wæs wæpna cyst,   300
buton hit wæs mare ðonne ænig mon oðer   1560
to beadulace ætberan meahte,
god ond geatolic, giganta geweorc.
He gefeng þa fetelhilt, freca Scyldinga
hreoh ond heorogrim, hringmæl gebrægd,   305
aldres orwena, yrringa sloh,
þæt hire wið halse heard grapode,
banhringas bræc. Bil eal ðurhwod
fægne flæschoman; heo on flet gecrong.
Sweord wæs swatig; secg weorce gefeh.   310
  Lixte se leoma, leoht inne stod,   1570
efne swa of hefene hadre scineð
rodores candel. He æfter recede wlat.
Hwearf þa be wealle, wæpen hafenade
heard be hiltum Higelaces ðegn,   315
yrre ond anræd. Næs seo ecg fracod
hilderince, ac he hraþe wolde
Grendle forgyldan guðræsa fela
ðara þe he geworhte to West-Denum

282. *andlean:* MS *handlean.*
283. *togeanes: a* above in the same hand. 284. *oferwearp:* Thorkelin A *ofer wearf,*
B *ofer wearp.*
286. *seax:* MS *seaxe.* 287. *ond:* not in MS. 300. *wæs:* not in MS.
316. *Næs:* altered from *nes,* according to Zupitza by the same hand.
61

320   oftor micle   ðonne on ænne sið,
1580 þonne he Hroðgares   heorðgeneatas
        sloh on sweofote,   slæpende fræt
        folces Denigea   fyftyne men,
        ond oðer swylc   ut offerede,
325   laðlicu lac.   He him þæs lean forgeald,
        reþe cempa,   to ðæs þe he on ræste geseah
        guðwerigne   Grendel licgan,
        aldorleasne,   swa him ær gescod
        hild æt Heorote.   Hra wide sprong,
330   syþðan he æfter deaðe   drepe þrowade,
1590 heorosweng heardne,   ond hine þa heafde becearf.
         Sona þæt gesawon   snottre ceorlas,
        þa ðe mid Hroðgare   on holm wliton,
        þæt wæs yðgeblond   eal gemenged,
335   brim blode fah.   Blondenfeaxe,
        gomele ymb godne   ongeador spræcon,
        þæt hig þæs æðelinges   eft ne wendon,
        þæt he sigehreðig   secean come
        mærne þeoden;   þa ðæs monige gewearð
340   þæt hine seo brimwylf   abroten hæfde.
1600 Ða com non dæges.   Næs ofgeafon
        hwate Scyldingas;   gewat him ham þonon
        goldwine gumena.   Gistas setan
        modes seoce   ond on mere staredon;
345   wiston ond ne wendon   þæt hie heora winedrihten
        selfne gesawon.
                 Þa þæt sweord ongan
        æfter heaþoswate   hildegicelum,
        wigbil wanian;   þæt wæs wundra sum,
        þæt hit eal gemealt   ise gelicost,
350   ðonne forstes bend   Fæder onlæteð,
1610 onwindeð wælrapas,   se geweald hafað
        sæla ond mæla;   þæt is soð Metod.
        Ne nom he in þæm wicum,   Weder-Geata leod,
        maðmæhta ma,   þeh he þær monige geseah,
355   buton þone hafelan   ond þa hilt somod,
        since fage;   sweord ær gemealt,
        forbarn brodenmæl;   wæs þæt blod to þæs hat,
        ættren ellorgæst,   se þærinne swealt.

333. *wliton:* Thorkelin A *wliton*, B *wlitom.*
340. *abroten:* MS *abreoten.*   343. *setan:* MS *secan.*
358. *ellorgæst: or* altered from *en; inne:* Thorkelin A *mne*, B *inne.*

Sona wæs on sunde se þe ær æt sæcce gebad
wighryre wraðra, wæter up þurhdeaf. 360
Wæron yðgebland eal gefælsod, *1620*
eacne eardas, þa se ellorgæst
oflet lifdagas ond þas lænan gesceaft.

4. THE DEATH OF BEOWULF

Næs ða long to ðon *2591*
þæt ða aglæcean hy eft gemetton. 365
Hyrte hyne hordweard, hreðer æðme weoll,
niwan stefne; nearo ðrowode,
fyre befongen, se ðe ær folce weold.
Nealles him on heape handgesteallan,
æðelinga bearn, ymbe gestodon 370
hildecystum, ac hy on holt bugon,
ealdre burgan. Hiora in anum weoll
sefa wið sorgum; sibb æfre ne mæg *2600*
wiht onwendan þam ðe wel þenceð.
Wiglaf wæs haten, Weoxstanes sunu, 375
leoflic lindwiga, leod Scylfinga,
mæg Ælfheres; geseah his mondryhten
under heregriman hat þrowian.
Gemunde ða ða are, þe he him ær forgeaf,
wicstede weligne Wægmundinga, 380
folcrihta gehwylc, swa his fæder ahte;
ne mihte ða forhabban, hond rond gefeng,
geolwe linde, gomel swyrd geteah; *2610*
þæt wæs mid eldum Eanmundes laf,
suna Ohteres; þam æt sæcce wearð, 385
wræccan wineleasum, Weohstan bana
meces ecgum, ond his magum ætbær
brunfagne helm, hringde byrnan,
ealdsweord etonisc; þæt him Onela forgeaf,
his gædelinges guðgewædu, 390
fyrdsearo fuslic, no ymbe ða fæhðe spræc,
þeah ðe he his broðor bearn abredwade.
He frætwe geheold fela missera, *2620*

359. *sæcce:* one *c* added above the line.
365. *aglæcean:* MS originally *aglægcean* with the second *g* partly erased.
369. *handgesteallan:* MS *heand gesteallan.* 385. *Ohteres:* MS *ohtere.*
386. *wræccan:* MS now *wr,* Thorkelin A *wræcca,* B *vr. . .;* *Weohstan:* MS *weoh stanes.*

63

bill ond byrnan, oððæt his byre mihte
395 eorlscipe efnan swa his ærfæder;
geaf him ða mid Geatum guðgewæda,
æghwæs unrim, þa he of ealdre gewat
frod on forðweg. Þa wæs forma sið
geongan cempan, þæt he guðe ræs
400 mid his freodryhtne fremman sceolde.
Ne gemealt him se modsefa, ne his mæges laf
gewac æt wige; þæt se wyrm onfand,
2630 syððan hie togædre gegan hæfdon.
    Wiglaf maðelode, wordrihta fela
405 sægde gesiðum (him wæs sefa geomor):
'Ic ðæt mæl geman, þær we medu þegun,
þonne we geheton ussum hlaforde
in biorsele, ðe us ðas beagas geaf,
þæt we him ða guðgetawa gyldan woldon,
410 gif him þyslicu þearf gelumpe,
helmas ond heard sweord. Ðe he usic on herge geceas
to ðyssum siðfate sylfes willum,
2640 onmunde usic mærða, ond me þas maðmas geaf,
þe he usic garwigend gode tealde,
415 hwate helmberend, þeah ðe hlaford us
þis ellenweorc ana aðohte
to gefremmanne, folces hyrde,
forðam he manna mæst mærða gefremede,
dæda dollicra. Nu is se dæg cumen
420 þæt ure mandryhten mægenes behofað,
godra guðrinca; wutun gongan to,
helpan hildfruman, þenden hyt sy,
2650 gledegesa grim. God wat on mec
þæt me is micle leofre þæt minne lichaman
425 mid minne goldgyfan gled fæðmie.
Ne þynceð me gerysne þæt we rondas beren
eft to earde, nemne we æror mægen
fane gefyllan, feorh ealgian
Wedra ðeodnes. Ic wat geare
430 þæt næron ealdgewyrht, þæt he ana scyle
Geata duguðe gnorn þrowian,

401. *mæges:* MS *mægenes.*   402. *þæt:* MS *þa.*
405. *sefa: f* altered from *w.*   406. *mæl:* Thorkelin B . . . . .
407. *we geheton:* MS ..*geheton,* Thorkelin A *wegeton,* B *vigheton.*
419. *dæg:* above the line in the same hand.   425. *fæðmie:* MS *fæðmię.*
429. *geare:* Thorkelin A *geare,* B *gear.*
431. *Geata:* Thorkelin A *geaca,* B *geata.*

gesigan æt sæcce; urum sceal sweord ond helm,
byrne ond beaduscrud bam gemæne.' 2660
Wod þa þurh þone wælrec, wigheafolan bær
frean on fultum, fea worda cwæð: 435
'Leofa Biowulf, læst eall tela,
swa ðu on geoguðfeore geara gecwæde,
þæt ðu ne alæte be ðe lifigendum
dom gedreosan. Scealt nu dædum rof,
æðeling anhydig, ealle mægene 440
feorh ealgian; ic ðe fullæstu.'
Æfter ðam wordum wyrm yrre cwom,
atol intwitgæst oðre siðe 2670
fyrwylmum fah fionda niosian,
laðra manna. Ligyðum forborn 445
bord wið rond, byrne ne meahte
geongum garwigan geoce gefremman,
ac se maga geonga under his mæges scyld
elne geeode, þa his agen wæs
gledum forgrunden. Þa gen guðcyning 450
mærða gemunde, mægenstrengo sloh
hildebille, þæt hyt on heafolan stod
niþe genyded; Nægling forbærst, 2680
geswac æt sæcce sweord Biowulfes,
gomol ond grægmæl. Him þæt gifeðe ne wæs 455
þæt him irenna ecge mihton
helpan æt hilde; wæs sio hond to strong,
se ðe meca gehwane, mine gefræge,
swenge ofersohte, þonne he to sæcce bær
wæpen wundrum heard; næs him wihte ðe sel. 460
Þa wæs þeodsceaða þriddan siðe,
frecne fyrdraca, fæhða gemyndig,
ræsde on ðone rofan, þa him rum ageald, 2690
hat ond heaðogrim, heals ealne ymbefeng
biteran banum; he geblodegod wearð 465
sawuldriore, swat yðum weoll.

432. *sceal:* added in the margin by the same hand.
433. *beaduscrud:* MS *byrdu scrud.*
434. *wælrec:* MS *wælræc* with 2nd *æ* altered to *e.*
435. *cwæð:* Thorkelin A *cwæð,*B *cvæd.*
444. *fyrwylmum: l* altered from *r; niosian:* MS *nio. . . .,* Thorkelin A *mosum,* B
niosnan with three dots under *nan.*
448. *under:* Thorkelin A *under,* B *und.*
451. *mærða:* only *m* remains in MS; gaps in Thorkelin.
455. *wæs:* lost at edge of MS; gaps in Thorkelin A and B.
460. *wundrum:* MS *wundū.*

Ða ic æt þearfe gefrægn   þeodcyninges
andlongne eorl   ellen cyðan,
cræft ond cenðu,   swa him gecynde wæs.
470 Ne hedde he þæs heafolan,   ac sio hand gebarn
modiges mannes,   þær he his mæges healp,
þæt he þone niðgæst   nioðor hwene sloh,
2700 secg on searwum,   þæt ðæt sweord gedeaf,
fah ond fæted,   þæt ðæt fyr ongon
475 sweðrian syððan.   Þa gen sylf cyning
geweold his gewitte,   wællseaxe gebræd
biter ond beaduscearp,   þæt he on byrnan wæg;
forwrat Wedra helm   wyrm on middan.
Feond gefyldan   (ferh ellen wræc),
480 ond hi hyne þa begen   abroten hæfdon,
sibæðelingas.   Swylc sceolde secg wesan,
þegn æt ðearfe.
                              Þæt ðam þeodne wæs
2710 siðast sigehwile   sylfes dædum,
worlde geweorces.   Ða sio wund ongon,
485 þe him se eorðdraca   ær geworhte,
swelan ond swellan;   he þæt sona onfand
þæt him on breostum   bealoniðe weoll
attor on innan.   Þa se æðeling giong,
þæt he bi wealle   wishycgende
490 gesæt on sesse;   seah on enta geweorc,
hu ða stanbogan   stapulum fæste
ece eorðreced   innan healde.
2720 Hyne þa mid handa   heorodreorigne,
þeoden mærne,   þegn ungemete till,
495 winedryhten his   wætere gelafede
hilde sædne,   ond his helm onspeon.
Biowulf maþelode   (he ofer benne spræc,
wunde wælbleate;   wisse he gearwe
þæt he dæghwila   gedrogen hæfde,
500 eorðan wynne;   ða wæs eall sceacen
dogorgerimes,   deað ungemete neah):

467. *gefrægn:* not in MS.   471. *mæges:* MS *mægenes.*
476. *his:* followed by another *his,* partly erased.   483. *siðast:* MS *siðas.*
485. *eorðdraca:* Thorkelin A *eorð-,* B *eord-.*
487. *bealoniðe:* Thorkelin A *bealomð,* B *bealo niði.*
489. *wishycgende: w* altered from *s.*   492. *healde:* Thorkelin B *heald.*
495. *winedryhten:* Thorkelin A *wine dryhł,* B *winedryht.*
496. *helm:* Thorkelin A *helo,* B *heb.*   500. *wynne:* Thorkelin A *wym,* B *wyni.*
501. *dogorgerimes: s* added, perhaps by a different hand.

'Nu ic suna minum   syllan wolde
guðgewædu,   þær me gifeðe swa   *2730*
ænig yrfeweard   æfter wurde
lice gelenge.   Ic ðas leode heold   *505*
fiftig wintra;   næs se folccyning,
ymbesittendra   ænig ðara,
þe mec guðwinum   gretan dorste,
egesan ðeon.   Ic on earde bad
mælgesceafta,   heold min tela,   *510*
ne sohte searoniðas,   ne me swor fela
aða on unriht.   Ic ðæs ealles mæg,
feorhbennum seoc,   gefean habban;   *2740*
forðam me witan ne ðearf   Waldend fira
morðorbealo maga,   þonne min sceaceð   *515*
life of lice.   Nu ðu lungre geong
hord sceawian   under harne stan,
Wiglaf leofa,   nu se wyrm ligeð,
swefeð sare wund,   since bereafod.
Bio nu on ofoste,   þæt ic ærwelan,   *520*
goldæht ongite,   gearo sceawige
swegle searogimmas,   þæt ic ðy seft mæge
æfter maððumwelan   min alætan   *2750*
lif ond leodscipe,   þone ic longe heold.'
    Ða ic snude gefrægn   sunu Wihstanes   *525*
æfter wordcwydum   wundum dryhtne
hyran heaðosiocum,   hringnet beran,
brogdne beadusercean   under beorges hrof.
Geseah ða sigehreðig,   þa he bi sesse geong,
magoþegn modig,   maððumsigla fealo,   *530*
gold glitinian   grunde getenge,
wundur on wealle,   ond þæs wyrmes denn,
ealdes uhtflogan,   orcas stondan,   *2760*
fyrnmanna fatu,   feormendlease,
hyrstum behrorene;   þær wæs helm monig   *535*
eald ond omig,   earmbeaga fela
searwum gesæled.   Sinc eaðe mæg,
gold on grunde,   gumcynnes gehwone
oferhigian,   hyde se ðe wylle.
Swylce he siomian geseah   segn eallgylden   *540*
heah ofer horde,   hondwundra mæst,
gelocen leoðocræftum;   of ðam leoma stod,

528. *beadusercean:* 2nd *e* altered from *a*; *under:* MS *urder.*
538. *grunde:* Thorkelin A, B *grund.*   542. *leoma:* MS *leoman.*

2770 þæt he þone grundwong   ongitan meahte,
wræte giondwlitan.   Næs ðæs wyrmes þær
545 onsyn ænig,   ac hyne ecg fornam.
Ða ic on hlæwe gefrægn   hord reafian,
eald enta geweorc   anne mannan,
him on bearm hladon   bunan ond discas
sylfes dome;   segn eac genom,
550 beacna beorhtost.   Bill ær gescod
(ecg wæs iren)   ealdhlafordes
þam ðara maðma   mundbora wæs
2780 longe hwile,   ligegesan wæg
hatne for horde,   hioroweallende
555 middelnihtum,   oðþæt he morðre swealt.
    Ar wæs on ofoste,   eftsiðes georn,
frætwum gefyrðred;   hyne fyrwet bræc,
hwæðer collenferð   cwicne gemette
in ðam wongstede   Wedra þeoden
560 ellensiocne,   þær he hine ær forlet.
He ða mid þam maðmum   mærne þioden,
dryhten sinne,   driorigne fand
2790 ealdres æt ende;   he hine eft ongon
wæteres weorpan,   oðþæt wordes ord
565 breosthord þurhbræc.   * * *
gomel on giohðe   (gold sceawode):
'Ic ðara frætwa   Frean ealles ðanc,
Wuldurcyninge   wordum secge,
ecum Dryhtne,   þe ic her on starie,
570 þæs ðe ic moste   minum leodum
ær swyltdæge   swylc gestrynan.
Nu ic on maðma hord   mine bebohte
2800 frode feorhlege,   fremmað gena
leoda þearfe;   ne mæg ic her leng wesan.
575 Hatað heaðomære   hlæw gewyrcean
beorhtne æfter bæle   æt brimes nosan;
se scel to gemyndum   minum leodum
heah hlifian   on Hronesnæsse,
þæt hit sæliðend   syððan hatan
580 Biowulfes biorh,   ða ðe brentingas

544. *wræte:* MS *wræce.*
548. *hladon:* MS *hlod.* ., Thorkelin A *holdon,* B *hlodon.*
550. *Bill:* 2nd *l* added by another hand.
554. *horde:* originally *hogode,* but the *g* erased and the 2nd *o* altered to *r.*
565. A half-line omitted; no gap in MS.
566. *giohðe:* MS *giogoðe; sceawode: w* altered from *þ.*   572. *mine:* MS *minne.*

ofer floda genipu   feorran drifað.'
Dyde him of healse   hring gyldenne
þioden þristhydig,   þegne gesealde,   2810
geongum garwigan,   goldfahne helm,
beah ond byrnan,   het hyne brucan well: 585
'Þu eart endelaf   usses cynnes,
Wægmundinga;   ealle wyrd forsweop
mine magas   to metodsceafte,
eorlas on elne;   ic him æfter sceal.'
Þæt wæs þam gomelan   gingæste word   590
breostgehygdum,   æt he bæl cure,
hate heaðowylmas;   him of hræðre gewat
sawol secean   soðfæstra dom.   2820
    Ða wæs gegongen   guman unfrodum
earfoðlice,   þæt he on eorðan geseah   595
þone leofestan   lifes æt ende
bleate gebæran.   Bona swylce læg,
egeslic eorðdraca   ealdre bereafod,
bealwe gebæded.   Beahhordum leng
wyrm wohbogen   wealdan ne moste,   600
ac hine irenna   ecga fornamon,
hearde heaðoscearpe   homera lafe,
þæt se widfloga   wundum stille   2830
hreas on hrusan   hordærne neah.
Nalles æfter lyfte   lacende hwearf   605
middelnihtum,   maðmæhta wlonc
ansyn ywde,   ac he eorðan gefeoll
for ðæs hildfruman   hondgeweorce.
Huru þæt on lande   lyt manna ðah
mægenagendra,   mine gefræge,   610
þeah ðe he dæda gehwæs   dyrstig wære,
þæt he wið attorsceaðan   oreðe geræsde,
oððe hringsele   hondum styrede,   2840
gif he wæccende   weard onfunde
buon on beorge.   Biowulfe wearð   615
dryhtmaðma dæl   deaðe forgolden;
hæfde æghwæðer   ende gefered
lænan lifes.
                Næs ða lang to ðon,
þæt ða hildlatan   holt ofgefan,

587. *forsweop:* MS *for speof.*   592. *hræðre:* MS *hwæðre.*
594. *guman:* MS *gumū.*   601. *hine:* MS *him.*
602. *heaðoscearpe:* MS *he aðoscearde.* 617. *æghwæðer:* MS *æg hwæðre.*

620 tydre treowlogan   tyne ætsomne,
ða ne dorston ær   dareðum lacan
on hyra mandryhtnes   miclan þearfe;
2850 ac hy scamiende   scyldas bæran,
guðgewædu   þær se gomela læg;
625 wlitan on Wilaf.   He gewergad sæt,
feðecempa   frean eaxlum neah,
wehte hyne wætre;   him wiht ne speow.
Ne meahte he on eorðan,   ðeah he uðe wel,
on ðam frumgare   feorh gehealdan,
630 ne ðæs Wealdendes   wiht oncirran;
wolde dom Godes   dædum rædan
gumena gehwylcum,   swa he nu gen deð.
2860 Þa wæs æt ðam geongan   grim andswaru
eðbegete   þam ðe ær his elne forleas.
635 Wiglaf maðelode,   Weohstanes sunu,
sec sarigferð   (seah on unleofe):
'Þæt, la, mæg secgan   se ðe wyle soð specan,
þæt se mondryhten,   se eow ða maðmas geaf,
eoredgeatwe,   þe ge þær on standað,
640 þonne he on ealubence   oft gesealde
healsittendum   helm ond byrnan,
þeoden his þegnum,   swylce he þrydlicost
2870 ower feor oððe neah   findan meahte,
þæt he genunga   guðgewædu
645 wraðe forwurpe,   ða hyne wig beget.
Nealles folccyning   fyrdgesteallum
gylpan þorfte;   hwæðre him God uðe,
sigora Waldend,   þæt he hyne sylfne gewræc
ana mid ecge,   þa him wæs elnes þearf.
650 Ic him lifwraðe   lytle meahte
ætgifan æt guðe,   ond ongan swa þeah
ofer min gemet   mæges helpan;
2880 symle wæs þy sæmra,   þonne ic sweorde drep
ferhðgeniðlan,   fyr unswiðor
655 weoll of gewitte.   Wergendra to lyt
þrong ymbe þeoden,   þa hyne sio þrag becwom.
Nu sceal sincþego   ond swyrdgifu,

627. *speow:* MS *speop.*
633. *geongan:* MS *geongū*; *andswaru:* Thorkelin A 7 *swaru*, B *and swarn.*
654. *fyr unswiðor:* MS *fyrun swiðor*, with *u* possibly altered from *a.*
655. *Wergendra:* MS *fergen dra.*
657. *Nu:* MS *hu.*

eall eðelwyn eowrum cynne,
lufen alicgean; londrihtes mot
þære mægburge monna æghwylc 660
idel heweorfan, syððan æðelingas
feorran gefricgean fleam eowerne,
domleasan dæd. Deað bið sella 2890
eorla gehwylcum þonne edwitlif!'

658. *eowrum cynne:* written above an erasure, according to Zupitza of the same words.
663. *dæd:* MS *dæld.*   664. *edwitlif: d* inserted above.

12. THE BATTLE OF MALDON

THIS POEM IS an almost contemporary account of the defeat by an invading Viking army of the East Saxons on August 10, 991, and of the death of their commander, Byrhtnoth. The event is recorded in several versions of the *Chronicle:*

In this year Ipswich was harried, and very soon afterwards ealdorman Byrhtnoth was slain at Maldon. In this year it was decided for the first time to pay tribute to the Danes because of the great terror they inspired along the sea coast. On this first occasion it amounted to ten thousand pounds.

The Parker Chonicle under 993 has a different account, and mentions the great Olaf Tryggvason as leader of the invaders. But his presence at Maldon is by no means certain, and it seems probable that this was a very minor battle in a series of raids on the east coast.

The geography of the battle has been worked out by E. D. Laborde. It seems that the Vikings sailed up the estuary of the River Blackwater towards Maldon and established themselves on the island of Northey, below the town. The island is triangular, and is surrounded by marshy ground, with the Blackwater to the north and Southey Creek to the south. At the western point there is a causeway linking the island to the mainland: the *bricg* or *ford* mentioned in the poem. The channels surrounding Northey are tidal, so the causeway is exposed only at low tide. At high tide the Vikings could not cross to Byrhtnoth's army, which was drawn up opposite the island near the causeway (ll. 62–71). When the tide went out, Byrhtnoth was able to prevent the Vikings crossing the causeway (72–83). But then he acceded to their request to cross and join battle (84–95); in the subsequent fighting he was killed and the English defeated.

It might be difficult to understand why an insignificant defeat should be celebrated in a poem of the heroic genre. The answer is that this is not primarily a historical poem but a poem about the behaviour of men in battle. The narrative directs us towards individual actions and personal combats, ignoring the general movement of the battle; it introduces over twenty English warriors by name. Their actions are narrated not for the

F

purpose of historical record, but in celebration of their fulfilment of the heroic code. The personal relationships between these men and their chief, Byrhtnoth, and among them as a group, are at the forefront of the poem's interest; the active demonstrations of these relationships are subject to the judgement of the code.

Byrhtnoth, whose fame is recorded in documents other than *The Battle of Maldon*, must have been about 65 at the time of the battle; he was made ealdorman of Essex in 956, had authority in Northumbria as well as Essex and was apparently active in the more general affairs of the country and the Church. It is clear that he was noble by birth and well connected by marriage—some indication of the extent of his family's lands is given by his wife Ælflæd's will. It is understandable that such a man should have had a large and devoted company of retainers; the poem is about his own noble conduct and above all the loyalty of the men who were attached to him. The scheme of values is a simple one, and substantially that described by Tacitus and implicit in other Old English heroic poetry. The chief gives his men a home and rich material reward; in return, they pledge themselves to service to the death. *The Battle of Maldon* is concerned with the ultimate vow they made: to avenge their lord or seek their own death in battle (see ll. 220–3, 246–53, 289–93).

The Battle of Maldon is thus of interest as a skilful and convincing treatment of the heroic ideals as they operated in an actual historical situation (cf. *Cynewulf and Cyneheard*); it convinces us that these ideals were still fully alive at this very late period in the history of the Germanic peoples—even in England at a particularly disastrous stage of her history. Also of importance is the way the theme is handled: how far are the poetic conventions which accompanied the themes of heroism observed at the end of the Old English period? Laborde (*MLR* 1924) has gone some way to answering this question, illustrating those devices of the earlier poetry which are still used extensively: circumlocution, parallelism, repetition and synonymy. Kennings are relatively rare, and, according to Laborde, 'hackneyed and conventional'. Some features of versification are noteworthy. Miss Ashdown (*English and Norse Documents*, pp. 241–3) points out irregular alliterations and, more interesting, cross alliteration; rhyme also occurs.

Laborde sums up (*Byrhtnoth and Maldon*, p. 61):

> Most of the chief traits of Germanic style are present, though they are, as in every 'classical' age, subject to formula and rule. The use of variation in subject-matter, phrase, and word was fully retained and even refined, and poetic phraseology has reached a stage of the utmost conventionality. Yet it was redeemed by its simplicity, for it used few figurative expressions, avoided the ornament of poetic allusion, contained no passages of high poetic colouring and no picturesque descriptions of nature. And in its plain, though lofty, style is perhaps the high-water mark of Old English narrative verse.

[The poem once existed in MS Cotton Otho A. xii, ff. 57ʳ–62ᵛ. As early as 1696 it was defective at the beginning and end. The fragment was printed in 1726 by Thomas Hearne, from a transcript made by John Elphinston. In 1731 a fire in the Cottonian Library at Westminster destroyed the MS, and Hearne's edition remained the only authority for modern editions, including Laborde's and Ashdown's. In 1935 N. R. Ker discovered that Elphinston's transcript was part of the Bodleian MS Rawlinson B. 203, and Gordon's, Dobbie's and this edition are based on the transcript. This differs only slightly from Hearne's edition, but is preferred as being evidently a careful copy and one stage nearer the original manuscript.]

brocen wurde.

Het þa hyssa hwæne   hors forlætan,
feor afysan,   and forð gangan,
hicgan to handum   and to hige godum.
Þa þæt Offan mæg   ærest onfunde,   5
þæt se eorl nolde   yrhðo geþolian,
he let him þa of handon   leofne fleogan
hafoc wið þæs holtes,   and to þære hilde stop;
be þam man mihte oncnawan   þæt se cniht nolde
wacian æt þam wige,   þa he to wæpnum feng.   10
Eac him wolde Eadric   his ealdre gelæstan,
frean to gefeohte;   ongan þa forð beran
gar to guþe.   He hæfde god geþanc
þa hwile þe he mid handum   healdan mihte
bord and bradswurd;   beot he gelæste   15
þa he ætforan his frean   feohtan sceolde.
    Ða þær Byrhtnoð ongan   beornas trymian,
rad and rædde,   rincum tæhte
hu hi sceoldon standan   and þone stede healdan,
and bæd þæt hyra randas   rihte heoldon   20
fæste mid folman,   and ne forhtedon na.
Þa he hæfde þæt folc   fægere getrymmed,
he lihte þa mid leodon   þær him leofost wæs,
þær he his heorðwerod   holdost wiste.
    Þa stod on stæðe,   stiðlice clypode   25
wicinga ar,   wordum mælde,
se on beot abead   brimliþendra
ærænde to þam eorle,   þær he on ofre stod:
'Me sendon to þe   sæmen snelle,
heton ðe secgan   þæt þu most sendan raðe   30

4. *to hige*: E(lphinston) *t hige.*   5. *Þa*: E *þ.*   7. *leofne*: E *leofre.*
10. *wige*: E *w. . . .ge*; Gordon gives *wigge.*   20. *randas*: E *randan.*

beagas wið gebeorge;   and eow betere is
þæt ge þisne garræs   mid gafole forgyldon,
þonne we swa hearde   hilde dælon.
Ne þurfe we us spillan,   gif ge spedaþ to þam;
35   we willað wið þam golde   grið fæstnian.
Gyf þu þat gerædest,   þe her ricost eart,
þæt þu þine leoda   lysan wille,
syllan sæmannum   on hyra sylfra dom
feoh wið freode,   and niman frið æt us,
40   we willaþ mid þam sceattum   us to scype gangan,
on flot feran,   and eow friþes healdan.'
Byrhtnoð maþelode,   bord hafenode,
wand wacne æsc,   wordum mælde,
yrre and anræd   ageaf him andsware:
45   'Gehyrst þu, sælida,   hwæt þis folc segeð?
Hi willað eow to gafole   garas syllan,
ættrynne ord   and ealde swurd,
þa heregeatu   þe eow æt hilde ne deah.
Brimmanna boda,   abeod eft ongean,
50   sege þinum leodum   miccle laþre spell,
þæt her stynt unforcuð   eorl mid his werode,
þe wile gealgean   eþel þysne,
Æþelredes eard,   ealdres mines,
folc and foldan.   Feallan sceolon
55   hæþene æt hilde.   To heanlic me þinceð
þæt ge mid urum sceattum   to scype gangon
unbefohtene,   nu ge þus feor hider
on urne eard   in becomon.
Ne sceole ge swa softe   sinc gegangan;
60   us sceal ord and ecg   ær geseman,
grim guðplega,   ær we gofol syllon.'
Het þa bord beran,   beornas gangan,
þæt hi on þam easteðe   ealle stodon.
Ne mihte þær for wætere   werod to þam oðrum;
65   þær com flowende   flod æfter ebban,
lucon lagustreamas.   To lang hit him þuhte,
hwænne hi togædere   garas beron.
Hi þær Pantan stream   mid prasse bestodon,
Eastseaxena ord   and se æschere.
70   Ne mihte hyra ænig   oþrum derian,
buton hwa þurh flanes flyht   fyl gename.
Se flod ut gewat;   þa flotan stodon gearowe,

33. *þonne:* E *þon; hilde:* E . *.ulde.*   61. *we:* E *þe.*

74

wicinga fela,   wiges georne.
Het þa hæleða hleo   healdan þa bricge
wigan wigheardne,   se wæs haten Wulfstan,   75
cafne mid his cynne,   þæt wæs Ceolan sunu,
þe ðone forman man   mid his francan ofsceat
þe þær baldlicost   on þa bricge stop.
Þær stodon mid Wulfstane   wigan unforhte,
Ælfere and Maccus,   modige twegen,   80
þa noldon æt þam forda   fleam gewyrcan,
ac hi fæstlice   wið ða fynd weredon,
þa hwile þe hi wæpna   wealdan moston.
Þa hi þæt ongeaton   and georne gesawon
þæt hi þær bricgweardas   bitere fundon,   85
ongunnon lytegian þa   laðe gystas,
bædon þæt hi upgang   agan moston,
ofer þone ford faran,   feþan lædan.
Ða se eorl ongan   for his ofermode
alyfan landes to fela   laþere ðeode.   90
Ongan ceallian þa   ofer cald wæter
Byrhtelmes bearn   (beornas gehlyston):
'Nu eow is gerymed,   gað ricene to us,
guman to guþe.   God ana wat
hwa þære wælstowe   wealdan mote.'   95
    Wodon þa wælwulfas   (for wætere ne murnon),
wicinga werod,   west ofer Pantan,
ofer scir wæter   scyldas wegon,
lidmen to lande   linde bæron.
Þær ongean gramum   gearowe stodon   100
Byrhtnoð mid beornum;   he mid bordum het
wyrcan þone wihagan,   and þæt werod healdan
fæste wið feondum.   Þa wæs feohte neh,
tir æt getohte.   Wæs seo tid cumen
þæt þær fæge men   feallan sceoldon.   105
Þær wearð hream ahafen,   hremmas wundon,
earn æses georn;   wæs on eorþan cyrm.
Hi leton þa of folman   feolhearde speru,
gegrundene   garas fleogan;
bogan wæron bysige,   bord ord onfeng.   110
    Biter wæs se beaduræs,   beornas feollon
on gehwæðere hand,   hyssas lagon.
Wund wearð Wulfmær,   wælræste geceas,

87. *upgang:* E *upgangan.*   97. *west:* E *þest.*
103. *feohte:* E *fohte.*   113. *wearð:* E *weard.*

Byrhtnoðes mæg;   he mid billum wearð,
115 his swuster sunu,   swiðe forheawen.
Þær wearð wicingum   wiþerlean agyfen.
Gehyrde ic þæt Eadweard   anne sloge
swiðe mid his swurde,   swenges ne wyrnde,
þæt him æt fotum feoll   fæge cempa;
120 þæs him his ðeoden   þanc gesæde,
þam burþene,   þa he byre hæfde.
Swa stemnetton   stiðhicgende
hysas æt hilde,   hogodon georne
hwa þær mid orde   ærost mihte
125 on fægean men   feorh gewinnan,
wigan mid wæpnum;   wæl feol on eorðan.
Stodon stædefæste;   stihte hi Byrhtnoð,
bæd þæt hyssa gehwylc   hogode to wige
þe on Denon wolde   dom gefeohtan.
130 Wod þa wiges heard,   wæpen up ahof,
bord to gebeorge,   and wið þæs beornes stop.
Eode swa anræd   eorl to þam ceorle,
ægþer hyra oðrum   yfeles hogode.
Sende ða se særinc   suþerne gar,
135 þæt gewundod wearð   wigena hlaford;
he sceaf þa mid ðam scylde,   þæt se sceaft tobærst,
and þæt spere sprengde,   þæt hit sprang ongean.
Gegremod wearð se guðrinc;   he mid gare stang
wlancne wicing,   þe him þa wunde forgeaf.
140 Frod wæs se fyrdrinc;   he let his francan wadan
þurh ðæs hysses hals;   hand wisode
þæt he on þam færsceaðan   feorh geræhte.
Ða he oþerne   ofstlice sceat,
þæt seo byrne tobærst;   he wæs on breostum wund
145 þurh ða hringlocan,   him æt heortan stod
ætterne ord.   Se eorl wæs þe bliþra;
hloh þa modi man,   sæde Metode þanc
ðæs dægweorces   þe him Drihten forgeaf.
Forlet þa drenga sum   daroð of handa,
150 fleogan of folman,   þæt se to forð gewat
þurh ðone æþelan   Æþelredes þegen.
Him be healfe stod   hyse unweaxen,
cniht on gecampe,   se full caflice
bræd of þam beorne   blodigne gar,
155 Wulfstanes bearn,   Wulfmær se geonga,

116. *wearð: E wærd*

forlet forheardne   faran eft ongean;
ord in gewod,   þæt se on eorþan læg
þe his þeoden ær   þearle geræhte.
Eode þa gesyrwed   secg to þam eorle;
he wolde þæs beornes   beagas gefecgan,   160
reaf and hringas   and gerenod swurd.
Þa Byrhtnoð bræd   bill of sceðe,
brad and bruneccg,   and on þa byrnan sloh.
To raþe hine gelette   lidmanna sum,
þa he þæs eorles   earm amyrde.   165
Feoll þa to foldan   fealohilte swurd;
ne mihte he gehealdan   heardne mece,
wæpnes wealdan.   Þa gyt þæt word gecwæð
har hilderinc,   hyssas bylde,
bæd gangan forð   gode geferan.   170
Ne mihte þa on fotum leng   fæste gestandan;
he to heofenum wlat:
'Geþancie þe,   ðeoda Waldend,
ealra þæra wynna   þe ic on worulde gebad.
Nu ic ah, milde Metod,   mæste þearfe   175
þæt þu minum gaste   godes geunne,
þæt min sawul to ðe   siðian mote
on þin geweald,   Þeoden engla,
mid friþe ferian.   Ic eom frymdi to þe
þæt hi helsceaðan   hynan ne moton.'   180
    Ða hine heowon   hæðene scealcas,
and begen þa beornas   þe him big stodon;
Ælfnoð and Wulmær   begen lagon,
ða onemn hyra frean   feorh gesealdon.
    Hi bugon þa fram beaduwe   þe þær beon noldon.   185
Þær wearð Oddan bearn   ærest on fleame,
Godric fram guþe,   and þone godan forlet
þe him mænigne oft   mear gesealde;
he gehleop þone eoh   þe ahte his hlaford,
on þam gerædum   þe hit riht ne wæs,   190
and his broðru mid him   begen ærndon,
Godwine and Godwig,   guþe ne gymdon,
ac wendon fram þam wige   and þone wudu sohton,
flugon on þæt fæsten   and hyra feore burgon,

171. *gestandan:* E *ge stundan.*
173. *Geþancie:* E *ge þance.*   Several editors supply *ic.*
186. *wearð:* E *wurdon.*   191. *ærndon:* E *ærdon.*
192. *Godwine:* E *Godrine;* some editors emend to *Godrinc.*

77

195 and manna ma þonne hit ænig mæð wære,
gyf hi þa geearnunga ealle gemundon
þe he him to duguþe gedon hæfde.
Swa him Offa on dæg ær asæde
on þam meþelstede, þa he gemot hæfde,
200 þæt þær modelice manega spræcon
þe eft æt þearfe þolian noldon.
Þa wearð afeallen þæs folces ealdor,
Æþelredes eorl; ealle gesawon
heorðgeneatas þæt hyra heorra læg.
205 Þa ðær wendon forð wlance þegenas,
unearge men efston georne;
hi woldon þa ealle oðer twega,
lif forlætan oððe leofne gewrecan.
Swa hi bylde forð bearn Ælfrices,
210 wiga wintrum geong, wordum mælde,
Ælfwine þa cwæð; he on ellen spræc:
'Gemunaþ þa mæla þe we oft æt meodo spræcon,
þonne we on bence beot ahofon,
hæleð on healle, ymbe heard gewinn;
215 nu mæg cunnian hwa cene sy.
Ic wylle mine æþelo eallum gecyþan,
þæt ic wæs on Myrcon miccles cynnes;
wæs min ealda fæder Ealhelm haten,
wis ealdorman, woruldgesælig.
220 Ne sceolon me on þære þeode þegenas ætwitan
þæt ic of ðisse fyrde feran wille,
eard gesecan, nu min ealdor ligeð
forheawen æt hilde. Me is þæt hearma mæst;
he wæs ægðer min mæg and min hlaford.'
225 Þa he forð eode, fæhðe gemunde,
þæt he mid orde anne geræhte
flotan on þam folce, þæt se on foldan læg
forwegen mid his wæpne. Ongan þa winas manian,
frynd and geferan, þæt hi forð eodon.
230 Offa gemælde, æscholt asceoc:
'Hwæt! þu, Ælfwine, hafast ealle gemanode
þegenas to þearfe, nu ure þeoden lið,
eorl on eorðan. Us is eallum þearf
þæt ure æghwylc oþerne bylde
235 wigan to wige, þa hwile þe he wæpen mæge

201. þearfe: E þære.   208. forlætan: E for lætun.
212. Gemunaþ: E ge munu.   224. ægðer: E ægder.

78

habban and healdan,   heardne mece,
gar and god swurd.   Us Godric hæfð,
earh Oddan bearn,   ealle beswicene.
Wende þæs formoni man,   þa he on meare rad,
on wlancan þam wicge,   þæt wære hit ure hlaford;   240
forþan wearð her on felda   folc totwæmed,
scyldburh tobrocen.   Abreoðe his angin,
þæt he her swa manigne   man aflymde!'
  Leofsunu gemælde   and his linde ahof,
bord to gebeorge;   he þam beorne oncwæð: 245
'Ic þæt gehate,   þæt ic heonon nelle
fleon fotes trym,   ac wille furðor gan,
wrecan on gewinne   minne winedrihten.
Ne þurfon me embe Sturmere   stedefæste hælæð
wordum ætwitan,   nu min wine gecranc,   250
þæt ic hlafordleas   ham siðie,
wende fram wige,   ac me sceal wæpen niman,
ord and iren.'   He ful yrre wod,
feaht fæstlice,   fleam he forhogode.
Dunnere þa cwæð,   daroð acwehte,   255
unorne ceorl,   ofer eall clypode,
bæd þæt beorna gehwylc   Byrhtnoð wræce:
'Ne mæg na wandian   se þe wrecan þenceð
frean on folce,   ne for feore murnan.'
Þa hi forð eodon,   feores hi ne rohton;   260
ongunnon þa hiredmen   heardlice feohtan,
grame garberend,   and God bædon
þæt hi moston gewrecan   hyra winedrihten
and on hyra feondum   fyl gewyrcan.
Him se gysel ongan   geornlice fylstan;   265
he wæs on Norðhymbron   heardes cynnes,
Ecglafes bearn;   him wæs Æscferð nama.
He ne wandode na   æt þam wigplegan,
ac he fysde forð   flan genehe;
hwilon he on bord sceat,   hwilon beorn tæsde,   270
æfre embe stunde   he sealde sume wunde,
þa hwile ðe he wæpna   wealdan moste.
  Þa gyt on orde stod   Eadweard se langa,
gearo and geornful,   gylpwordum spræc
þæt he nolde fleogan   fotmæl landes,   275
ofer bæc bugan,   þa his betera leg.
He bræc þone bordweall   and wið þa beornas feaht,

257. wræce: E wręce.

79

oðþæt he his sincgyfan on þam sæmannum
wurðlice wrec, ær he on wæle læge.

280 Swa dyde Æþeric, æþele gefera,
fus and forðgeorn, feaht eornoste,
Sibyrhtes broðor and swiðe mænig oþer,
clufon cellod bord, cene hi weredon.
Bærst bordes lærig, and seo byrne sang

285 gryreleoða sum. Þa æt guðe sloh
Offa þone sælidan, þæt he on eorðan feoll,
and ðær Gaddes mæg grund gesohte.
Raðe wearð æt hilde Offa forheawen;
he hæfde ðeah geforþod þæt he his frean gehet,

290 swa he beotode ær wið his beahgifan
þæt hi sceoldon begen on burh ridan,
hale to hame, oððe on here crincgan,
on wælstowe wundum sweltan;
he læg ðegenlice ðeodne gehende.

295 Ða wearð borda gebræc. Brimmen wodon,
guðe gegremode; gar oft þurhwod
fæges feorhhus. Forð þa eode Wistan,
Þurstanes sunu, wið þas secgas feaht;
he wæs on geþrang hyra þreora bana,

300 ær him Wigelmes bearn on þam wæle læge.
Þær wæs stið gemot; stodon fæste
wigan on gewinne, wigend cruncon,
wundum werige. Wæl feol on eorþan.
Oswold and Eadwold ealle hwile,

305 begen þa gebroþru, beornas trymedon,
hyra winemagas wordon bædon
þæt hi þær æt ðearfe þolian sceoldon,
unwaclice wæpna neotan.
Byrhtwold maþelode, bord hafenode

310 (se wæs eald geneat), æsc acwehte;
he ful baldlice beornas lærde:
'Hige sceal þe heardra, heorte þe cenre,
mod sceal þe mare, þe ure mægen lytlað.
Her lið ure ealdor eall forheawen,

315 god on greote. A mæg gnornian
se ðe nu fram þis wigplegan wendan þenceð.
Ic eom frod feores; fram ic ne wille,
ac ic me be healfe minum hlaforde,

---

279. *læge*: E *lęge*.   292. *crincgan*: E *crintgan*.   297. *Forð þa*: E *forða*.
298. *sunu*: E *suna*.   300. *Wigelmes*: E *wigelines*.

be swa leofan men,   licgan þence.'
Swa hi Æþelgares bearn   ealle bylde,   320
Godric to guþe.   Oft he gar forlet,
wælspere windan   on þa wicingas,
swa he on þam folce   fyrmest eode,
heow and hynde,   oðþæt he on hilde gecranc.
Næs þæt na se Godric   þe ða guðe forbeah.   325

324. *oðþæt:* E *od þ.*   325. *guðe:* E *gude.*

II. RELIGIOUS EPIC

13. ANDREAS

THIS LONG RELIGIOUS EPIC from the Vercelli Book has as its ultimate source an extant Greek prose narrative of the deeds of St. Andrew and St. Matthew. It is believed, however, that the Old English poet worked from a lost Latin translation, not directly from the Greek; but there is no close relationship between the poem and the two other Old English and two Latin versions which exist.

Of greater interest is the relationship between *Andreas* and secular Old English epic poetry, specifically *Beowulf*. Although our knowledge of Old English epic is limited, we have enough evidence to allow us to characterise *Andreas* as a religious poem influenced by the conventions of secular heroic verse: the typical military diction, and the Germanicised personal relationships and standards of conduct. In the first extract, Matthew emphasises one aspect of his predicament when he is captured by the Mermedonians: his status as a homeless man (*eðelleas*) in a foreign land, persecuted by the *elþeodige*: a situation dreaded by the Wanderer (extract 16). In 164–72 Andrew's *þegnas* react with horror to God's suggestion that they should leave their master to go alone to Mermedonia. Their speech recalls the protestations of the retainers in *Maldon* and *Cynewulf and Cyneheard*, stressing the disgrace and misery of the *hlafordleas* man. They are Andrew's *comitatus*, sworn to follow him to the death. It is significant that these followers are called retainers (*þegnas*), not disciples (*leornungcnihtas*).

It has been argued not only that *Andreas* is the archetype of the religious narrative based on heroic epic but also that it is consciously modelled on *Beowulf*. This was the conclusion of Krapp (*Andreas*, pp. li–lviii) and Klaeber (*Beowulf*, p. cxi). The argument was founded on similarities of situations and narrative pattern in the two poems, and on a very large number of verbal parallels, cited by Krapp (pp. lvi–lvii and Notes, *passim*). L. J. Peters denies this relationship, and since our attention has been drawn by Magoun and Greenfield to the conventional, formulaic nature of Old English poetry we are inclined to set less store by verbal parallels. The safest conclusion is that the author of *Andreas* was familiar with, and probably consciously remembered, epics in the Germanic manner.

The other question which needs to be mentioned is that of the authorship of *Andreas*. It used to be suggested that *Andreas* is the work of Cynewulf, the only named poet of the period from whom we have any quantity of poetry. Two sorts of evidence have been offered. The first is that *The Fates of the Apostles*, which follows *Andreas* in the manuscript and ends

82

with Cynewulf's runic signature, is not a separate poem but the end of *Andreas*. Krapp challenged this position, and today we generally follow him in regarding *Andreas* and *The Fates of the Apostles* as two separate poems from distinct sources. The second line of reasoning is to connect *Andreas* with Cynewulf on the strength of similarity of style and phrasing to his signed poems. But the stylistic arguments against this assertion, though untidily conducted, have been more convincing than those for it. Schaar (pp. 98–104) summarises these arguments.

Kenneth Sisam (*Studies*, p. 10) ventures that '*Andreas* is at once cruder and more vigorous than the certain work of Cynewulf'. The extracts chosen here may illustrate this opinion. Any crudeness in the style is usually a result of inappropriately used heroic expressions; the vigour is attested by the descriptions of the storm and of Andrew's torture.

I. MATTHEW GOES TO MERMEDONIA, AND IS CAPTURED

Hwæt! We gefrunan   on fyrndagum
twelfe under tunglum   tireadige hæleð,
þeodnes þegnas.   No hira þrym alæg
camprædenne   þonne cumbol hneotan,
syððan hie gedældon   swa him Dryhten sylf,   5
heofona Heahcyning,   hlyt getæhte.
Þæt wæron mære   men ofer eorðan,
frome folctogan   ond fyrdhwate,
rofe rincas,   þonne rond ond hand
on herefelda   helm ealgodon,   10
on meotudwange.   Wæs hira Matheus sum,
se mid Iudeum ongan   godspell ærest
wordum writan   wundorcræfte.
Þam halig God   hlyt geteode
ut on þæt igland,   þær ænig þa git   15
ellþeodigra   eðles ne mihte
blædes brucan.   Oft him bonena hand
on herefelda   hearde gesceode.
Eal wæs þæt mearcland   morðre bewunden,
feondes facne,   folcstede gumena,   20
hæleða eðel.   Næs þær hlafes wist
werum on þam wonge,   ne wæteres drync
to bruconne,   ah hie blod ond fel,
fira flæschoman   feorrancumenra,
ðegon geond þa þeode.   Swelc wæs þeaw hira   25
þæt hie æghwylcne   ellðeodigra
dydan him to mose   meteþearfendum,

4. *camprædenne*: MS *cam rædenne*.   6. *hlyt*: MS *lyt*.

þara þe þæt ealand   utan sohte;
swylc wæs þæs folces   freoðoleas tacen,
30 unlædra eafoð,   þæt hie eagena gesihð,
hettend heorogrimme,   heafodgimmas,
agetton gealgmode   gara ordum.
Syððan him geblendan   bitere tosomne
dryas þurh dwolcræft   drync unheorne,
35 se onwende gewit,   wera ingeþanc,
heortan on hreðre;   hyge wæs oncyrred,
þæt hie ne murndan   æfter mandreame,
hæleþ heorogrædige,   ac hie hig ond gærs
for meteleaste   meðe gedrehte.
40 Þa wæs Matheus   to þære mæran byrig
cumen in þa ceastre.   Þær wæs cirm micel
geond Mermedonia,   manfulra hloð,
fordenera gedræg,   syþþan deofles þegnas
geascodon   æðelinges sið.
45 Eodon him þa togenes,   garum gehyrsted,
lungre under linde;   nalas late wæron
eorre æscberend   to þam orlege.
Hie þam halgan þær   handa gebundon
ond fæstnodon   feondes cræfte,
50 hæleð hellfuse,   ond his heafdes segl
abreoton mid billes ecge.   Hwæðre he in breostum þa git
herede in heortan   heofonrices weard,
þeah ðe he atres drync   atulne onfenge.
Eadig ond onmod,   he mid elne forð
55 wyrðode wordum   wuldres aldor,
heofonrices weard,   halgan stefne,
of carcerne;   him wæs Cristes lof
on fyrhðlocan   fæste bewunden.
He þa wepende   weregum tearum
60 his sigedryhten   sargan reorde
grette, gumena brego,   geomran stefne,
weoruda wilgeofan,   ond þus wordum cwæð:
'Hu me elþeodige   inwitwrasne
searonet seowað!   A ic symles wæs
65 on wega gehwam   willan þines
georn on mode;   nu ðurh geohða sceal
dæde fremman   swa þa dumban neat.

31. *hettend:* MS *hetted; heafodgimmas:* MS *heafod gimme.*
32. *agetton:* MS *ageton.*   33. *geblendan:* MS *geblondan.*   36. *on:* not in MS.
43. *þegnas;* MS *þegn,* ending a page.   64. *seowað:* MS *seoðað.*
84

Þu ana canst ealra gehygdo,
meotud mancynnes, mod in hreðre.
Gif þin willa sie, wuldres aldor,   70
þæt me wærlogan wæpna ecgum,
sweordum aswebban, ic beo sona gearu
to adreoganne þæt ðu, Drihten min,
engla eadgifa, eðelleasum,
dugeða dædfruma, deman wille.   75
Forgif me to are, ælmihtig God,
leoht on þissum life, þy læs ic lungre scyle,
ablended in burgum æfter billhete,
þurh hearmcwide heorugrædigra,
laðra leodsceaðena, leng þrowian   80
edwitspræce. Ic to anum þe,
middangeardes weard, mod staþolige,
fæste fyrhðlufan, ond þe, fæder engla,
beorht blædgifa, biddan wille
ðæt ðu me ne gescyrige mid scyldhetum,   85
werigum wrohtsmiðum, on þone wyrrestan,
dugoða demend, deað ofer eorðan.'
   Æfter þyssum wordum com wuldres tacen
halig of heofenum, swylce hadre segl,
to þam carcerne. Þær gecyðed wearð   90
þæt halig God helpe gefremede.
Ða wearð gehyred heofoncyninges stefn
wrætlic under wolcnum wordhleoðres sweg
mæres þeodnes; he his maguþegne
under hearmlocan hælo ond frofre   95
beadurofum abead beortan stefne:
   'Ic þe, Matheus, mine sylle
sybbe under swegle. Ne beo ðu on sefan to forht,
ne on mode ne murn; ic þe mid wunige
ond þe alyse of þyssum leoðubendum,   100
ond ealle þa menigo þe þe mid wuniað
on nearonedum. Þe is neorxnawang,
blæda beorhtost, boldwela fægrost,
hama hyhtlicost, halegum mihtum
torht ontyned, þær ðu tyres most   105
to widan feore, willan brucan.
Geþola þeoda þrea! Nis seo þrah micel
þæt þe wærlogan witebendum,

71. *wærlogan:* MS *wær lo gan,* with a second *l* erased after *o.*
99. *ne murn:* MS *ne ne murn.* 101. Second *þe:* inserted above.

synne ðurh searocræft, swencan motan.

110 Ic þe Andreas ædre onsende
to hleo ond to hroðre in þas hæðenan burg.
He ðe alyseð of þyssum leodhete.
Is to þære tide tælmet hwile
emne mid soðe seofon ond twentig

115 nihtgerimes, þæt ðu of nede most;
sorgum geswenced, sigore gewyrðod,
hweorfest of henðum in gehyld Godes.'

2. ANDREW'S SEA-JOURNEY TO MERMEDONIA

359 Gesæt him þa se halga holmwearde neah,
æðele be æðelum. Æfre ic ne hyrde

120 þon cymlicor ceol gehladenne
heahgestreonum. Hæleð in sæton,
þeodnas þrymfulle, þegnas wlitige.
Ða reordode rice þeoden,
ece ælmihtig; heht his engel gan,

125 mærne maguþegn, ond mete syllan,
frefran feasceafte ofer flodes wylm,
þæt hie þe eað mihton ofer yða geþring
drohtaþ adreogan.
Þa gedrefed wearð,

370 onhrered hwælmere. Hornfisc plegode,
130 glad geond garsecg, ond se græga mæw
wælgifre wand. Wedercandel swearc,
windas weoxon, wægas grundon,
streamas styredon, strengas gurron,
wædo gewætte. Wæteregsa stod

135 þreata þryðum. Þegnas wurdon
acolmode; ænig ne wende
þæt he lifgende land begete,
þara þe mid Andreas on eagorstream

380 ceol gesohte. Næs him cuð þa gyt
140 hwa þam sæflotan sund wisode.
Him þa se halga on holmwege
ofer argeblond, Andreas þa git,
þegn þeodenhold, þanc gesægde,
ricum ræsboran, þa he gereordod wæs:

145 'Ðe þissa swæsenda, soðfæst meotud,
lifes leohtfruma, lean forgilde,

126. *feasceafte*: MS *fea sceaftne.*

weoruda waldend, ond þe wist gife,
heofonlicne hlaf, swa ðu hyldo wið me
ofer firigendstream, freode, gecyðdest! 390
Nu synt geþreade þegnas mine, 150
geonge guðrincas. Garsecg hlymmeð,
geofon geotende. Grund is onhrered,
deope gedrefed, Duguð is geswenced,
modigra mægen myclum gebysgod.'
Him of holme oncwæð hæleða scyppend: 155
'Læt nu geferian flotan userne,
lid to lande ofer lagufæsten,
ond þonne gebidan beornas þine,
aras on earde, hwænne ðu eft cyme.' 400
Edre him þa eorlas agefan ondsware, 160
þegnas þrohthearde; þafigan ne woldon
ðæt hie forleton æt lides stefnan
leofne lareow ond him land curon:
'Hwider hweorfað we hlafordlease,
geomormode, gode orfeorme, 165
synnum wunde, gif we swicað þe?
We bioð laðe on landa gehwam,
folcum fracoðe, þonna fira bearn,
ellenrofe, æht besittaþ, 410
hwylc hira selost symle gelæste 170
hlaforde æt hilde, þonne hand ond rond
on beaduwange billum forgrunden
æt niðplegan nearu þrowedon.'

3. ANDREW IS CAPTURED AND TORTURED

Æfter þam wordum com werod unmæte, 1219
lyswe larsmeoðas, mid lindgecrode, 175
bolgenmode; bæron ut hræðe
ond þam halgan þær handa gebundon,
siþþan geypped wæs æðelinga wynn,
ond hie andweardne eagum meahton
gesion sigerofne. Þær wæs sec manig 180
on þam welwange wiges oflysted
leoda duguðe; lyt sorgodon
hwylc him þæt edlean æfter wurde.
Heton þa lædan ofer landsceare,

---

152. *geofon:* MS *heofon.*   153. *duguð:* MS *dugud.*
172. *forgrunden:* MS *fore grunden.*

1230 ðragmælum teon   torngeniðlan,
swa hie hit frecnost   findan meahton.
Drogon deormode   æfter dunscræfum,
ymb stanhleoðo   stærcedferþþe,
efne swa wide   swa wegas tolagon,
190 enta ærgeweorc,   innan burgum,
stræte stanfage.   Storm upp aras
æfter ceasterhofum,   cirm unlytel
hæðnes heriges.   Wæs þæs halgan lic
sarbennum soden,   swate bestemed,
1240 banhus abrocen;   blod yðum weoll
hatan heolfre.   Hæfde him on innan
ellen untweonde;   wæs þæt æðele mod
asundrad fram synnum,   þeah he sares swa feala
deopum dolgslegum   dreogan sceolde.
200 Swa wæs ealne dæg   oððæt æfen com
sigeltorht swungen;   sar eft gewod
ymb þæs beornes breost,   oðþæt beorht gewat
sunne swegeltorht   to sete glidan.
Læddan þa leode   laðne gewinnan
1250 to carcerne.   He wæs Criste swa þeah
leof on mode;   him wæs leoht sefa,
halig, heortan neh,   hige untyddre.
   Þa se halga wæs   under heolstorscuwan,
eorl ellenheard,   ondlange niht
210 searoþancum beseted.   Snaw eorðan band
wintergeworpum.   Weder coledon
heardum hægelscurum,   swylce hrim ond forst,
hare hildstapan,   hæleða eðel
lucon, leoda gesetu.   Land wæron freorig
1260 cealdum cylegicelum;   clang wæteres þrym
ofer eastreamas;   is brycgade
blæce brimrade.   Bliðheort wunode
eorl unforcuð,   elnes gemyndig,
þrist ond þrohtheard   in þreanedum
220 wintercealdan niht.   No on gewitte blon,
acol for þy egesan,   þæs þe he ær ongann,
þæt he a domlicost   Dryhten herede,
weorðade wordum,   oððæt wuldres gim
heofontorht onhlad.   Ða com hæleða þreat
1270 to ðære dimman ding,   duguð unlytel,

196. *hatan heolfre:* MS *hat of heolfre.*
197. *untweonde:* MS *untweodne.*   208. *Þa:* MS *A* with *S* erased before.

88

wadan wælgifre   weorodes brehtme.
Heton ut hræðe   æðeling lædan
in wraðra geweald,   wærfæstne hæleð.
Ða wæs eft swa ær   ondlangne dæg
swungen sarslegum.   Swat yðum weoll   230
þurh bancofan,   blodlifrum swealg,
hatan heolfre.   Hra weorces ne sann,
wundum werig.

14. GENESIS B

Genesis IS A POEM of 2,936 lines found in MS Junius XI in the Bodleian Library: a manuscript which, on the evidence of Bede's story of Cædmon, was once believed to be a collection of Cædmon's works.

As early as 1826 it had been suggested (by W. D. Conybeare) that the poem was not a single work, but that a long section on the fall of man was an interpolation. In 1875 Sievers, struck by certain lexical, stylistic and metrical peculiarities, postulated that lines 235–850(1) were a translation from Old Saxon. In 1894 Sievers' theory was confirmed by the discovery in the Vatican Library of an Old Saxon fragment corresponding very closely to lines 790–816ᵃ of *Genesis*. We now follow Sievers in distinguishing between *Genesis A* and the interpolated translation from Old Saxon, *Genesis B* or *The Later Genesis*. The present edition prints the first third of *Genesis B*, or lines 246–441ᵃ in the numbering of 'the whole poem'. At 441ᵃ the narrative breaks off in the middle of a sentence, at the bottom of p. 22 in the manuscript, after which some leaves have been lost.

The linguistic peculiarities of this poem are certainly striking. They fall principally into two categories: peculiarities of diction and of metre. In both cases we find divergence from the normal lexical and metrical practice of Old English, and, more important, divergence from Old English takes the form of approximation to Old Saxon. The extraordinary number of hypermetrical lines (in circumstances where the conditions usually producing long lines in Old English are not present) must be explained as a result of Old Saxon influence. Old Saxon verse, though constructed, like Old English, according to the common Germanic metrical conventions, is characterised by much greater length of line. Timmer (*The Later Genesis* pp. 27–39) presents all the lexical peculiarities conveniently, quoting many examples of Old Saxon words, words compounded on Old Saxon principles and words used in senses strange to Old English.

The 'Saxon' character of the language of *Genesis B* has been noticed for two purposes: to demonstrate that the poem was translated from Old Saxon, and to demonstrate that the translator himself was an Old Saxon. Timmer (in company with other scholars) believes that both suppositions are true—although he does not go to the lengths of some, who have suggested that the author was none other than John the Old Saxon brought over by Alfred. It is difficult to see the necessity for using the linguistic evidence for both arguments: the discovery of the Saxon fragment puts translation beyond doubt, and the 'Saxonism' can surely be most simply explained as a result of translation from one Germanic dialect into another.

Another matter concerning the poem which has been debated since the early nineteenth century is its possible relation to Milton's *Paradise Lost*. It has been argued, on the grounds of similarity in the conception of Satan, certain parallelisms of phrasing (*PL* I, 180 ff.: *Genesis B* 332 ff.; I, 242 ff.: 356 ff.; I, 221 ff.: 446 ff.; I, 619 ff.: 338 ff.) and certain external evidence (e.g. Milton's acquaintance with Junius, the poem's first editor) that Milton borrowed from *Genesis B*. Yet it must be admitted that the internal evidence is slight and the external circumstantial; though Milton knew of Old English literature, and Bede's story of Cædmon, and had met Junius, his grasp of Old English appears not to have been great enough for him to master this relatively difficult text, and he could hardly have absorbed much of the detail of the poem after he went blind.

246 Hæfde se alwalda   engelcynna
    þurh handmægen,   halig Drihten,
    tene getrimede,   þæm he getruwode wel
    þæt hie his giongorscipe   fyligan wolden,
5   wyrcean his willan,   forþon he him gewit forgeaf
    and mid his handum gesceop,   halig Drihten.
    Gesett hæfde he hie swa gesæliglice;   ænne hæfde he swa
                           swiðne geworhtne,
    swa mihtigne on his modgeþohte;   he let hine swa micles wealdan,
    hehstne to him on heofona rice;   hæfde he hine swa hwitne
                                geworhtne,
10   swa wynlic wæs his wæstm on heofonum   þæt him com from
                                weroda Drihtne,
    gelic wæs he þam leohtum steorrum.   Lof sceolde he Dryhtnes
                                wyrcean,
    dyran sceolde he his dreamas on heofonum,   and sceolde his
                              Drihtne þancian
    þæs leanes þe he him on þam leohte gescerede — þonne lete he his
                              hine lange wealdan.
    Ac he awende hit him to wyrsan þinge,   ongan him winn up
                              ahebban
260 wið þone hehstan heofnes waldend,   þe siteð on þam halgan stole.

1. *alwalda*: *e* inserted above preceding the first *a*.
3. *tene*: first *e* dotted for erasure and *y* above; *getrimede*: *i* altered to *y*.
5. *him*: *i* dotted for erasure and *eo* above. 10. *wæstm*: MS *wæwtm*.
13. *lete*: first *e* altered from *æ*.
14. *awende, ahebban*: initial *a* inserted above in both cases.
15. *waldend*: *e* above, before *a*.

Deore wæs he Drihtne ure;   ne mihte him bedyrned weorðan
þæt his engyl ongan   ofermod wesan;
ahof hine wið his hearran,   sohte hetespræce,
gylpword ongean,   nolde Gode þeowian,
cwæð þæt his lic wære   leoht and scene,   20
hwit and hiowbeorht.   Ne meahte he æt his hige findan
þæt he Gode wolde   geongerdome,
þeodne þeowian.   Þuhte him sylfum
þæt he mægyn and cræft   maran hæfde
þonne se halga God   habban mihte   270
folcgestælna.   Feala worda gespæc
se engel ofermodes.   Þohte þurh his anes cræft
hu he him strenglicran   stol geworhte,
heahran on heofonum;   cwæð þæt hine his hige speonne
þæt he west and norð   wyrcean ongunne,   30
trymede getimbro;   cwæð him tweo þuhte
þæt he Gode wolde   geongra weorðan.
   'Hwæt sceal ic winnan?' cwæð he.   'Nis me wihtæ þearf
hearran to habbanne.   Ic mæg mid handum swa fela
wundra gewyrcean.   Ic hæbbe geweald micel   280
to gyrwanne   godlecran stol,
hearran on heofne.   Hwy sceal ic æfter his hyldo ðeowian,
bugan him swilces geongordomes?   Ic mæg wesan god swa he.
Bigstandað me strange geneatas,   þa ne willað me æt þam striðe
                                                    geswican,
hæleþas heardmode.   Hie habbað me to hearran gecorene,   40
rofe rincas;   mid swilcum mæg man ræd geþencean,
fon mid swilcum folcgesteallan.   Frynd synd hie mine georne,
holde on hyra hygesceaftum.   Ic mæg hyra hearra wesan,
rædan on þis rice.   Swa me þæt riht ne þinceð
þæt ic oleccan   awiht þurfe   290
Gode æfter gode ænegum.   Ne wille ic leng his geongra wurþan.'
   Þa hit se allwalda   eall gehyrde,
þæt his engyl ongan   ofermede micel
ahebban wið his hearran,   and spræc heahlic word
dollice wið Drihten sinne,   sceolde he þa dæd ongyldan,   50

16. *ure:* e dotted for erasure, with *v̄* above; *weorðan:* eo dotted for erasure, with
y above.
18. *hearran:* MS *herran*, with *a* above.   22. *he* added above the line.
29. *heahran:* MS originally *heanoran*, with first *n* altered to *h*, *o* erased, and *h*
and *r* joined by a thin horizontal stroke below; *cwæð:* followed by a space wide
enough for two or three letters; *speonne:* first *n* dotted for erasure.
32. *weorðan: an* inserted above.

worc þæs gewinnes gedælan, and sceolde his wite habban,
ealra morðra mæst. Swa deð monna gehwilc
þe wið his waldend winnan ongynneð
mid mane wið þone mæran Drihten. Þa wearð se mihtiga gebolgen,
300 hehsta heofones waldend, wearp hine of þan hean stole.
Hete hæfde he æt his hearran gewunnen, hyldo hæfde his
                                          ferlorene,
gram wearð him se goda on his mode. Forþon he sceolde grund
                                         gesecean,
heardes hellewites, þæs þe he wann wið heofnes waldend.
Acwæð hine þa fram his hyldo and hine on helle wearp,
60 on þa deopan dala, þær he to deofle wearð,
se feond mid his geferum eallum. Feollon þa ufon of heofnum
þurh longe swa þreo niht and dagas,
þa englas of heofnum on helle, and heo ealle forsceop
Drihten to deoflum. Forþon heo his dæd and word
310 noldon weorðian, forþon he heo on wyrse leoht
under eorðan neoðan, ællmihtig God,
sette sigelease on þa sweartan helle.
Þær hæbbað heo on æfyn ungemet lange,
ealra feonda gehwilc, fyr edneowe;
70 þonne cymð on uhtan easterne wind,
forst fyrnum cald; symble fyr oððe gar,
sum heard geswinc habban sceoldon.
Worhte man hit him to wite, hyra woruld wæs gehwyrfed,
forman siðe fylde helle
320 mid þam andsacum. Heoldon englas forð
heofonrices hehðe, þe ær Godes hyldo gelæston.
Lagon þa oðre fynd on þam fyre, þe ær swa feala hæfdon
gewinnes wið heora waldend. Wite þoliað,
hatne heaðowelm helle tomiddes,
80 brand and brade ligas, swilce eac þa biteran recas,
þrosm and þystro, forþon hie þegnscipe
Godes forgymdon. Hie hyra gal beswac,
engles oferhygd, noldon alwaldan
word weorþian; hæfdon wite micel;
330 wæron þa befeallene fyre to botme
on þa hatan hell þurh hygeleaste

---

57. *se:* a letter erased before this word.
61. *feollon: n* badly formed, probably a correction from *þ*.
72. *geswinc:* MS *gewrinc;* Sweet, Timmer, *geþwing.*
74. *siðe: e* added in another hand.   81. *þystro: o* corrected from *e*.
83. *alwaldan: e* above after *w*.   85. *wæron: n* added above.

and þurh ofermetto;   sohton oþer land,
þæt wæs leohtes leas   and wæs liges full,
fyres fær micel. Fynd ongeaton
þæt hie hæfdon gewrixled   wita unrim   90
þurh heora miclan mod   and þurh miht Godes,
and þurh ofermetto   ealra swiðost.
   Þa spræc se ofermoda cyning   þe ær wæs engla scynost,
hwitost on heofne   and his hearran leof,
Drihtne dyre   oð hie to dole wurdon,   *340*
þæt him for galscipe   God sylfa wearð
mihtig on mode yrre. Wearp hine on þæt morðer innan,
niðer on þæt niobedd,   and sceop him naman siððan:
cwæð se hehsta   hatan sceolde
Satan siððan; het hine þære sweartan helle   100
grundes gyman,   nalles wið God winnan.
Satan maðelode,   sorgiende spræc,
se ðe helle forð   healdan sceolde,
gieman þæs grundes. Wæs ær Godes engel,
hwit on heofne,   oð hine his hyge forspeon   *350*
and his ofermetto   ealra swiðost,
þæt he ne wolde   wereda Drihtnes
word wurðian. Weoll him on innan
hyge ymb his heortan;   hat wæs him utan
wraðlic wite. He þa worde cwæð: 110
   'Is þæs ænga styde   ungelic swiðe
þam oðrum   þe we ær cuðon,
hean on heofonrice,   þe me min hearra onlag,
þeah we hine for þam alwaldan   agan ne moston,
romigan ures rices. Næfð he þeah riht gedon   *360*
þæt he us hæfð befælled   fyre to botme,
helle þære hatan,   heonfonrice benumen;
hafað hit gemearcod   mid moncynne
to gesettanne. Þæt me is sorga mæst,
þæt Adam sceal,   þe wæs of eorðan geworht,   120
minne stronglican   stol behealdan,

90. *unrim:* originally *inrim.*   91. *heora:* MS *herra,* with the first *r* changed to *o.*
94. *hwitost:* MS *hwitost; heofne:* MS originally *heofne,* altered to *heofnon.*
99. *cwæð:* an abbreviated *þæt* inserted after this word.
101. *winnan:* MS *widnan.*   104. *gieman: ie* dotted for erasure, and *y* above.
105. *heofne:* second *e* changed to *o* and *n* added above, as in 94.
111. *þæs:* first element of *æ* erased; *ænga: i* inserted above, between *n* and *g*;
styde: y cancelled and *e* written above.
113. *on:* supplied in margin by original scribe.
114. *alwaldan: e* inserted above between *w* and *a.*
116. *befælled: y* written through *æ.*

wesan him on wynne,   and we þis wite þolien,
hearm on þisse helle.   Wala, ahte ic minra handa geweald
and moste ane tid   ute weorðan,

370   wesan ane winterstunde,   þonne ic mid þys werode . . .
Ac licgað me ymbe   irenbenda,
rideð racentan sal.   Ic eom rices leas;
habbað me swa hearde   helle clommas
fæste befangen.   Her is fyr micel,

130   ufan and neoðone.   Ic a ne geseah
laðran landscipe.   Lig ne aswamað,
hat ofer helle.   Me habbað hringa gespong,
sliðhearda sal   siðes amyrred,
afyrred me min feðe;   fet synt gebundene,

380   handa gehæfte.   Synt þissa heldora
wegas forworhte,   swa ic mid wihte ne mæg
of þissum lioðobendum.   Licgað me ymbe
heardes irenes   hate geslægene
grindlas greate.   Mid þy me God hafað

140   gehæfted be þam healse,   swa ic wat he minne hige cuðe;
and þæt wiste eac   weroda Drihten,
þæt sceolde unc Adame   yfele gewurðan
ymb þæt heofonrice,   þær ic ahte minra handa geweald.
Ac ðoliað we nu þrea on helle,   þæt syndon þystro and hæto

390   grimme, grundlease.   Hafað us God sylfa
forswapen on þas sweartan mistas;   swa he us ne mæg ænige
synne gestælan,
þæt we him on þam lande lað gefremedon,   he hæfð us þeah
þæs leohtes bescyrede,
beworpen on ealra wita mæste.   Ne magon we þæs wrace
gefremman,
geleanian him mid laðes wihte   þæt he us hafað þæs leohtes
bescyrede.

150   He hæfð nu gemearcod anne middangeard,   þær he hæfð mon
geworhtne
æfter his onlicnesse.   Mid þam he wile eft gesettan
heofona rice mid hluttrum saulum.   We þæs sculon hycgan georne,
þæt we on Adame,   gif we æfre mægen,
and on his eafrum swa some,   andan gebetan,

400   onwendan him þær willan sines,   gif we hit mægen wihte aþencan.

126. *irenbenda: s* suffixed above.
137. *ymbe: e* partly erased, and *utan* added above.
147. *leohtes: leo* erased; *o* partly visible.

94

Ne gelyfe ic me nu þæs leohtes furðor   þæs þe he him þenceð
                         lange niotan,
þæs eades mid his engla cræfte.   Ne magon we þæt on aldre
                         gewinnan,
þæt we mihtiges Godes mod onwæcen.   Uton oþwendan hit nu
                       monna bearnum,
þæt heonfonrice, nu we hit habban ne moton,   gedon þæt hie his
                       hyldo forlæten,
þæt hie þæt onwendon þæt he mid his worde bebead.   Þonne
            weorð he him wrað on mode,   160
ahwet hie from his hyldo.   Þonne sculon hie þas helle secan
and þas grimman grundas.   Þonne moton we hie us to giongrum
                       habban,
fira bearn on þissum fæstum clomme.   Onginnað nu ymb þa
                       fyrde þencean.

Gif ic ænegum þegne   þeodenmadmas
geara forgeafe,   þenden we on þan godan rice   410
gesælige sæton   and hæfdon ure setla geweald,
þonne he me na on leofran tid   leanum ne meahte
mine gife gyldan,   gif his gien wolde
minra þegna hwilc   geþafa wurðan,
þæt he up heonon   ute mihte   170
cuman þurh þas clustro,   and hæfde cræft mid him
þæt he mid feðerhoman   fleogan meahte,
windan on wolcne,   þær geworht stondað
Adam and Eue   on eorðrice
mid welan bewunden,   and we synd aworpene hider   420
on þas deopan dalo.   Nu hie Drihtne synt
wurðran micle,   and moton him þone welan agan
þe we on heofonrice   habban sceoldon,
rice mid rihte;   is se ræd gescyred
monna cynne.   Þæt me is on minum mode swa sar,   180
on minum hyge hreoweð,   þæt hie heofonrice
agan to aldre.   Gif hit eower ænig mæge
gewendan mid wihte   þæt hie word Godes
lare forlæten,   sona hie him þe laðran beoð.
Gif hie brecað his gebodscipe,   þonne he him abolgen wurðeþ;   430
siððan bið him se wela onwended   and wyrð him wite gegarwod,
sum heard hearmscearu.   Hycgað his ealle,

156. *him: i* changed to *e*, dotted for erasure, *eo* above; *niotan: i* altered to *e*.
164. *þegne:* 1st *e* altered from *æ*.
172. *feðerhoman:* first *e* altered from *æ* and *ð* from *d*.
180. *minum mode:* MS *mode minum* with marks for transposition.
186. *gegarwod:* an *e* added above between *g* and *a*.

hu ge hi beswicen.   Siððan ic me sefte mæg
restan on þyssum racentum,   gif him þæt rice losað.
190   Se þe þæt gelæsteð,   him bið lean gearo
æfter to aldre,   þæs we her inne magon
on þyssum fyre forð   fremena gewinnan.
Sittan læte ic hine wið me sylfne,   swa hwa swa þæt secgan cymeð
on þas hatan helle,   þæt hie heofoncyninges
440   unwurðlice   wordum and dædum
lare . . .'

III. SHORT POEMS

15. THE DREAM OF THE ROOD

The Dream of the Rood presents an interesting textual situation. The text printed here is taken from the tenth-century Vercelli Book of Old English poetry. But fragments of the poem occur in inscriptions elsewhere. Some fragments corresponding to parts of lines 39–45, 48–9, 56–9 and 62–4 are carved in runes, in the Northumbrian dialect, on the magnificent Ruthwell Cross, a stone monument in Dumfriesshire. A few words which appear to parallel parts of lines 44 and 48 are inscribed on the Brussels Cross, a presumed relic of the True Cross. The relations between the Ruthwell and Vercelli texts (the Brussels is too short to be taken into account) are uncertain. The Ruthwell Cross has been dated *ca.* 670–750, and Dickins and Ross, adding to the archaeological and historical evidence the linguistic information afforded by the inscription, favour a dating in the latter part of this period, the first half of the eighth century. They suggest 'that an original poem, selections of which appear on the Ruthwell Cross, was later expanded and added to. From this expanded version the Vercelli text is descended . . .' One cannot be sure; but it is, as they say, a 'plausible working hypothesis'.

The Vercelli text itself appears to be composite. The poem is metrically defective at 76ᵇ, and seems to break off at 77. 78–156 are an inferior continuation in a very different style. The first part is dramatic and written with an economy and figurative brilliance almost uncharacteristic of Old English; the ending is theologically and poetically conventional in its sentiments and expression: a didactic exhortation by the cross, and finally a meditation by the author.

The first half of *The Dream of the Rood* stands out from the rest of Old English poetry in several ways. It is odd stylistically: colourful in its imagery, but not stylised as is the description of the Phoenix; it has a high proportion of long lines, but the tempo does not drag; it is syntactically curious, composed almost entirely of short, inverted clauses with very little variation or expansion. Formally, it is unique. As a dream-vision it is unparalleled in Old English: the dream-vision is a device governing the form of the poem, and it is unlike the visions of later medieval literature or the prognosticating dreams of antiquity. The device of *prosopopoeia*—the speech of a personified object—has been suggested as a formal influence; in this connection note the fashion for carving epigrammatic speeches on sculptures and ornaments (cf. the Alfred Jewel *Ælfred mec heht gewyrcean* and the Brussels Cross inscription) and the form of some of the Old English

97

Riddles, where the subject of the riddle, like the cross, introduces itself in its own words. Another type of riddle employs the formula *geseah ic*, which is found regularly in this poem (4, 14, 21, 33, 36, 51). Although these formal influences may be suggested, no single source can be proposed, nor is there any analogous poem: *The Dream of the Rood* is probably unique.

Earlier scholars (e.g. A. S. Cook) have debated whether the poem is the work of Cædmon or Cynewulf; there is no real way of proving authorship, and no real advantage to be gained by a hypothesis of Cædmon's or Cynewulf's authorship, so the question is ignored here.

    Hwæt, ic swefna cyst   secgan wylle,
hwæt me gemætte   to midre nihte,
syðþan reordberend   reste wunedon.
Þuhte me þæt ic gesawe   syllicre treow
5   on lyft lædan   leohte bewunden,
beama beorhtost.   Eall þæt beacen wæs
begoten mid golde; gimmas stodon
fægere æt foldan sceatum,   swylce þær fife wæron
uppe on þam eaxlgespanne.   Beheoldon þær engeldryhte ealle
10   fægere þurh forðgesceaft;   ne wæs ðær huru fracodes gealga.
Ac hine þær beheoldon   halige gastas,
men ofer moldan,   ond eall þeos mære gesceaft.
Syllic wæs se sigebeam,   ond ic synnum fah,
forwunded mid wommum.   Geseah ic wuldres treow
15   wædum geweorðod   wynnum scinan,
gegyred mid golde;   gimmas hæfdon
bewrigen weorðlice   Wealdendes treow.
Hwæðre ic þurh þæt gold   ongytan meahte
earmra ærgewin,   þæt hit ærest ongan
20   swætan on þa swiðran healfe.   Eall ic wæs mid sorgum gedrefed.
Forht ic wæs for þære fægran gesyhðe.   Geseah ic þæt fuse beacen
wendan wædum ond bleom;   hwilum hit wæs mid wætan
                               bestemed,
beswyled mid swates gange,   hwilum mid since gegyrwed.
Hwæðre ic þær licgende   lange hwile
25   beheold hreowcearig   Hælendes treow,
oððæt ic gehyrde   þæt hit hleoðrode;
ongan þa word sprecan   wudu selesta:

2. *hwæt:* MS *hæt.*
9. *eaxlgespanne:* MS *eaxle ge spanne; engeldryhte:* MS *engel dryhtnes.*
15. *geweorðod:* MS *geweorðode.*
17. *bewrigen:* MS *bewrigene; Wealdendes:* MS *wealdes.*
20. *sorgum:* MS *surgum.*

'Þæt wæs geara iu   — ic þæt gyta geman —
þæt ic wæs aheawen   holtes on ende,
astyred of stefne minum.   Genaman me ðær strange feondas.   30
Geworhton him þær to wæfersyne,   heton me heora wergas
                                    hebban.
Bæron me ðær beornas on eaxlum,   oððæt hie me on beorg asetton,
gefæstnodon me þær feondas genoge.   Geseah ic þa Frean
                                        mancynnes
efstan elne mycle   þæt he me wolde on gestigan.
Þær ic þa ne dorste   ofer Dryhtnes word   35
bugan oððe berstan,   þa ic bifian geseah
eorðan sceatas.   Ealle ic mihte
feondas gefyllan;   hwæðre ic fæste stod.
    Ongyrede hine þa geong hæleð   — þæt wæs God ælmihtig—
strang ond stiðmod.   Gestah he on gealgan heanne,   40
modig on manigra gesyhðe,   þa he wolde mancyn lysan.
Bifode ic þa me se beorn ymbclypte;   ne dorste ic hwæðre bugan
                                        to eorðan,
feallan to foldan sceatum,   ac ic sceolde fæste standan.
Rod wæs ic aræred;   ahof ic ricne cyning,
heofona hlaford;   hyldan me ne dorste.   45
Þurhdrifan hi me mid deorcan næglum;   on me syndon þa dolg
                                        gesiene,
opene inwidhlemmas.   Ne dorste ic hira nænigum sceððan.
Bysmeredon hie unc butu ætgædere.   Eall ic wæs mid blode
                                        bestemed,
begoten of þæs guman sidan,   siððan he hæfde his gast onsended.
Feala ic on þam beorge   gebiden hæbbe   50
wraðra wyrda.   Geseah ic weruda God
þearle þenian.   Þystro hæfdon
bewrigen mid wolcnum   Wealdendes hræw,
scirne sciman;   sceadu forðeode,
wann under wolcnum.   Weop eal gesceaft,   55
cwiðdon cyninges fyll;   Crist wæs on rode.
Hwæðere þær fuse   feorran cwoman
to þam æðelinge.   Ic þæt eall beheold.
Sare ic wæs mid sorgum gedrefed,   hnag ic hwæðre þam secgum to
                                        handa,
eaðmod, elne mycle.   Genamon hie þær ælmihtigne God,   60
ahofon hine of ðam hefian wite.   Forleton me þa hilderincas
standan steame bedrifenne;   eall ic wæs mid strælum forwundod.

59. *sorgum:* not in MS, but in that part of the Ruthwell Cross inscription which
parallels this passage.

Aledon hie ðær limwerigne; gestodon him æt his lices heafdum;
beheoldon hie ðær heofenes Dryhten, ond he hine ðær hwile reste,
65 meðe æfter ðam miclan gewinne. Ongunnon him þa moldern
                                                   wyrcan
beornas on banan gesyhðe, curfon hie ðæt of beorhtan stane;
gesetton hie ðæron sigora Wealdend. Ongunnon him þa sorhleoð
                                                   galan,
earme on þa æfentide. Þa hie woldon eft siðian,
meðe fram þam mæran þeodne; reste he ðær mæte weorode.
70 Hwæðere we ðær greotende gode hwile
stodon on staðole, syððan stefn up gewat
hilderinca. Hræw colode,
fæger feorgbold. Þa us man fyllan ongan
ealle to eorðan; þæt wæs egeslic wyrd!
75 Bedealf us man on deopan seaþe. Hwæðre me þær Dryhtnes
                                                   þegnas,
freondas gefrunon;
gyredon me golde ond seolfre.
    Nu ðu miht gehyran, hæleð min se leofa,
þæt ic bealuwara weorc gebiden hæbbe,
80 sarra sorga. Is nu sæl cumen
þæt me weorðiað wide ond side
menn ofer moldan ond eall þeos mære gesceaft,
gebiddaþ him to þyssum beacne. On me bearn Godes
þrowode hwile; forþan ic þrymfæst nu
85 hlifige under heofenum, ond ic hælan mæg
æghwylcne anra, þara þe him bið egesa to me.
Iu ic wæs geworden wita heardost,
leodum laðost, ærþan ic him lifes weg
rihtne gerymde, reordberendum.
90 Hwæt, me þa geweorðode wuldres ealdor
ofer holtwudu, heofonrices weard,
swylce swa he his modor eac, Marian sylfe,
ælmihtig God, for ealle menn
geweorðode ofer eall wifa cynn.
95   Nu ic þe hate, hæleð min se leofa,
þæt ðu þas gesyhðe secge mannum;
onwreoh wordum þæt hit is wuldres beam,
se ðe ælmihtig God on þrowode
for mancynnes manegum synnum

---

65. *moldern:* MS *moldærn* with first part of *æ* dotted for erasure.
70. *greotende:* MS *reotende.*   71. *stefn:* not in MS.
91. *holtwudu:* MS *holm wudu.*

ond Adomes   ealdgewyrhtum.   100
Deað he þær byrigde;   hwæðere eft Dryhten aras
mid his miclan mihte   mannum to helpe.
He ða on heofenas astag.   Hider eft fundaþ
on þysne middangeard   mancynn secan
on domdæge   Dryhten sylfa,   105
ælmihtig God   ond his englas mid,
þæt he þonne wile deman,   se ah domes geweald,
anra gehwylcum,   swa he him ærur her
on þyssum lænum   life geearnaþ.
Ne mæg þær ænig   unforht wesan   110
for þam worde   þe se Wealdend cwyð;
frineð he for þære mænige   hwær se man sie,
se ðe for Dryhtnes naman   deaðes wolde
biteres onbyrigan,   swa he ær on ðam beame dyde.
Ac hie þonne forhtiað,   ond fea þencaþ   115
hwæt hie to Criste   cweðan onginnen.
Ne þearf ðær þonne ænig   anforht wesan
þe him ær in breostum bereð   beacna selest.
Ac ðurh ða rode sceal   rice gesecan
of eorðwege   æghwylc sawl,   120
seo þe mid Wealdende   wunian þenceð.'
    Gebæd ic me þa to þan beame   bliðe mode,
elne mycle,   þær ic ana wæs
mæte werede;   wæs modsefa
afysed on forðwege;   feala ealra gebad   125
langunghwila.   Is me nu lifes hyht
þæt ic þone sigebeam   secan mote,
ana oftor   þonne ealle men
well weorþian;   me is willa to ðam
mycel on mode,   ond min mundbyrd is   130
geriht to þære rode.   Nah ic ricra feala
freonda on foldan,   ac hie forð heonon
gewiton of worulde dreamum,   sohton him wuldres cyning;
lifiaþ nu on heofenum   mid heahfædere,
wuniaþ on wuldre;   ond ic wene me   135
daga gehwylce   hwænne me Dryhtnes rod,
þe ic her on eorðan   ær sceawode
on þysson lænan   life gefetige,
ond me þonne gebringe   þær is blis mycel,

---

113. *wolde:* MS *woḷde* preceded by an erasure, probably of *þro.*
117. *anforht:* MS *unforht.*   127. *ic* inserted above the line.
132. *foldan:* two letters erased after this word.

140   dream on heofonum, þær is Dryhtnes folc
        geseted to symle, þær is singal blis;
        ond he þonne asette þær ic syþþan mot
        wunian on wuldre, well mid þam halgum
        dreames brucan. Si me Dryhten freond,
145   se ðe her on eorþan ær þrowode
        on þam gealgtreowe for guman synnum.
        He us onlysde, ond us lif forgeaf,
        heofonlicne ham. Hiht wæs geniwad
        mid bledum ond mid blisse, þam þe þær bryne þolodan.
150   Se sunu wæs sigorfæst on þam siðfate,
        mihtig ond spedig. Þa he mid manigeo com,
        gasta weorode, on Godes rice,
        anwealda ælmihtig, englum to blisse,
        ond eallum ðam halgum þam þe on heofonum ær
155   wunedon on wuldre, þa heora Wealdend cwom,
        ælmihtig God, þær his eðel wæs.

152. *on: o* erased before this word.

16. THE WANDERER

The Wanderer, a favourite anthology piece found in the Exeter Book of Old English poetry, belongs to a class of short poems which have been characterised as 'elegies'. It is grouped with *The Seafarer, The Ruin, Deor, The Wife's Lament* and *The Husband's Message* (all in the Exeter Book) and *Beowulf* lines 2247–66 and 2444–59. The term 'elegy' is used in this context to mean, not a lament on the death of a particular individual (like *Adonais* or *Lycidas*), but a poem with an overwhelming sense of sorrow or regret, often depending on a first-person narrative of personal hardship. These poems have a distinctive and somewhat repetitive poetic diction evocative of sadness, and certain other components characteristic of the genre: expressions of physical hardship, usually complaints of hard weather, again stylised in their diction; sententious statements, either Christian or not, embedded in conventionalised forms of gnomic expression. There is a concern with the theme of mutability, a popular didactic motif in medieval literature, and one productive of moving poetry.

    It will thus be seen that the content of the elegies, and certainly of *The Wanderer* and *The Seafarer*, is distinguished by its variety. It is typical of this genre to juxtapose miscellaneous forms and themes within one poem. This fact, and the apparent contradiction of the powerful poetic impression offered by the best of the poems, has led to the growth of a considerable critical literature surrounding them. *The Wanderer* and *The Seafarer* are poems which cry out for interpretation and explanation. The extensive criticism cannot be summarised here; but a brief account of the poem's content may be given.

The opening and closing passages (1–5 and 111–15) set the body of the poem in a sententious framework, and these, and their relation to the rest of the content, have been much discussed. The opening affirms the mercy of God despite the hardships of the life of a solitary: these are noted in terms conventional to the elegies—the physical sufferings of exile and sea-faring. The closing lines, in which *fæstnung* is a key word, assert that security is to be found in heaven. Much of the intervening material consists of exemplification of the hardship and insecurity—mutability—of earthly life. An *eardstapa* explains his personal sorrows and misfortunes as a con-sequence of the death of his lord and the loss of the security of the *comitatus* (8–29[a]); in 29[b]–57 he generalises from his experiences, discussing in highly figurative and subjective language the deprivations of anyone who has been in this situation. The generalisation is taken still further in 62[b], where the poet moves from the death of nobles to a wider treatment of tran-sience, with many references (linking this section to the earlier part) to the death of nobles and warriors and the passing of their institutions. A lament on mutability, employing the conventional *ubi sunt* formula, comes near the end. All is transitory, the poet claims, and he has instanced mutability through the death of nobles and warriors and the sufferings of a lordless *eardstapa*.

Gnomic matter is interspersed with elegiac: in lines 11[b]–18 and 111–114[a] this is not specifically Christian, but at least serves to lead us to view these described hardships as moral as well as personal problems. Christian comments occur at the beginning, in line 85, and in the last line and a half, and allow us to read the poem as a Christian statement of worldly mutability. Yet we are nowhere exhorted to lead the Christian life, forsake the world and therefore earn security and bliss in heaven; and such an exhortation would agree ill with the mood of regret for the passing of earthly things communicated by the speakers in the poem.

Greater precision in the identification of the theme and of the character of the speakers depends on the interpretation of many points of detail. Is the necessary Christian detachment from the world, nowhere explicitly advocated, supplied by an allegorical reading of the *eardstapa*'s predica-ment? What is the precise significance of *anhaga, gebideð, gæstlic, fæstnung*? These have been the preoccupations of the critics. Many such points of detail are discussed in the notes.

Oft him anhaga   are gebideð,
Metudes miltse,   þeah þe he modcearig
geond lagulade   longe sceolde
hreran mid hondum   hrimcealde sæ,
wadan wræclastas: wyrd bið ful aræd.   5

5. *aræd:* MS *arẹd.*

Swa cwæð eardstapa,   earfeþa gemyndig,
wraþra wælsleahta,   winemæga hryre:
'Oft ic sceolde ana,   uhtna gehwylce,
mine ceare cwiþan.   Nis nu cwicra nan
10   þe ic him modsefan   minne durre
sweotule asecgan.   Ic to soþe wat
þæt biþ in eorle   indryhten þeaw
þæt he his ferðlocan   fæste binde,
healde his hordcofan,   hycge swa he wille.
15   Ne mæg werig mod   wyrde wiðstondan,
ne se hreo hyge   helpe gefremman.
Forðon domgeorne   dreorigne oft
in hyra breostcofan   bindað fæste;
swa ic modsefan   minne sceolde,
20   oft earmcearig,   eðle bidæled,
freomægum feor,   feterum sælan,
siþþan geara iu   goldwine minne
hrusan heolster biwrah,   ond ic hean þonan
wod wintercearig   ofer waþema gebind,
25   sohte sele dreorig   sinces bryttan,
hwær ic feor oþþe neah   findan meahte
þone þe in meoduhealle   min mine wisse,
oþþe mec freondleasne   frefran wolde,
weman mid wynnum.   Wat se þe cunnað
30   hu sliþen bið   sorg to geferan
þam þe him lyt hafað   leofra geholena.
Warað hine wræclast,   nales wunden gold;
ferðloca freorig,   nalæs foldan blæd.
Gemon he selesecgas   ond sincþege,
35   hu hine on geoguðe   his goldwine
wenede to wiste: wyn eal gedreas.
Forðon wat se þe sceal   his winedryhtnes
leofes larcwidum   longe forþolian,
ðonne sorg ond slæp   somod ætgædre
40   earmne anhogan   oft gebindað.
Þinceð him on mode   þæt he his mondryhten
clyppe ond cysse,   ond on cneo lecge
honda ond heafod,   swa he hwilum ær
in geardagum   giefstolas breac.
45   Ðonne onwæcneð eft   wineleas guma;

14. *healde*: MS *healdne*.   22. *minne*: MS *mine*.
23. *heolster*: MS *heolstre*.   24. *waþema*: MS *waþena*.
27. *min*: not in MS.   28. *freondleasne*: MS *freond lease*.

gesihð him biforan   fealwe wegas,
baþian brimfuglas,   brædan feþra,
hreosan hrim ond snaw   hagle gemenged.
Þonne beoð þy hefigran   heortan benne,
sare æfter swæsne. Sorg bið geniwad   50
þonne maga gemynd   mod geondhweorfeð;
greteð gliwstafum,   georne geondsceawað
secga geseldan: swimmað eft on weg.
Fleotendra ferð   no þær fela bringeð
cuðra cwidegiedda. Cearo bið geniwad   55
þam þe sendan sceal   swiþe geneahhe
ofer waþema gebind   werigne sefan.
Forþon ic geþencan ne mæg   geond þas woruld
for hwan modsefa   min ne gesweorce
þonne ic eorla lif   eal geondþence,   60
hu hi færlice   flet ofgeafon,
modge maguþegnas: swa þes middangeard
ealra dogra gehwam   dreoseð ond fealleþ.'
    Forþon ne mæg wearþan wis   wer ær he age
wintra dæl in woruldrice. Wita sceal geþyldig,   65
ne sceal no to hatheort   ne to hrædwyrde,
ne to wac wiga   ne to wanhydig,
ne to forht ne to fægen,   ne to feohgifre;
ne næfre gielpes to georn,   ær he geare cunne:
beorn sceal gebidan,   þonne he beot spriceð,   70
oþþæt collenferð   cunne gearwe
hwider hreþra gehygd   hweorfan wille.
Ongietan sceal gleaw hæle   hu gæstlic bið
þonne ealre þisse worulde wela   weste stondeð,
swa nu missenlice   geond þisne middangeard   75
winde biwaune   weallas stondaþ,
hrime bihrorene,   hryðge þa ederas.
Woriað þa winsalo,   waldend licgað
dreame bidrorene,   duguþ eal gecrong
wlonc bi wealle. Sume wig fornom,   80
ferede in forðwege;   sumne fugel oþbær
ofer heanne holm;   sumne se hara wulf
deaðe gedælde;   sumne dreorighleor
in eorðscræfe   eorl gehydde.
Yþde swa þisne eardgeard   ælda scyppend   85
oþþæt burgwara   breahtma lease
eald enta geweorc   idlu stodon.

53. *eft:* MS *oft.*   59. *modsefa:* MS *mod sefan.*   74. *ealre:* MS *ealle.*

Se þonne þisne wealsteal   wise geþohte
ond þis deorce lif   deope geondþenceð,

90   frod in ferðe,   feor oft gemon
wælsleahta worn   ond þas word acwið:
  'Hwær cwom mearg? Hwær cwom mago?   Hwær cwom
                                        maþþumgyfa?
Hwær cwom symbla gesetu?   Hwær sindon seledreamas?
Eala beorht bune!   Eala byrnwiga!

95   Eala þeodnes þrym!   Hu seo þrag gewat,
genap under nihthelm,   swa heo no wære!
Stondeð nu on laste   leofre duguþe
weal wundrum heah,   wyrmlicum fah.
Eorlas fornoman   asca þryþe,

100   wæpen wælgifru,   wyrd seo mære.
Ond þas stanhleoþu   stormas cnyssað,
hrið hreosende   hrusan bindeð,
wintres woma;   þonne won cymeð,
nipeð nihtscua,   norþan onsendeð

105   hreo hæglfare   hæleþum on andan.
Eall is earfoðlic   eorþan rice;
onwendeð wyrda gesceaft   weoruld under heofenum.
Her bið feoh læne,   her bið freond læne,
her bið mon læne,   her bið mæg læne;

110   eal þis eorþan gesteal   idel weorþeð.'
  Swa cwæð snottor on mode,   gesæt him sundor æt rune.
Til biþ se þe his treowe gehealdeþ,   ne sceal næfre his torn to
                                        rycene
beorn of his breostum acyþan,   nemþe he ær þa bote cunne,
eorl mid elne gefremman.   Wel bið þam þe him are seceð,

115   frofre to fæder on heofonum,   þær us eal seo fæstnung stondeð.

89. *deorce*: MS *deornce*.   100. *mære* has been altered from *mæro* in the MS.
102. *hrusan*: MS *hruse*.

17. THE SEAFARER

The Wanderer and *The Seafarer* have much in common. They are about the
same length; each divides neatly about half-way through, the halves being
distinguished by their content. In both poems the first half has as its subject a first-person narrative of grief and suffering: the narrator is cut off
from society and suffers loneliness and physical deprivation and discom-
fort. The second half, in each case, is largely a generalised treatment of the
theme of mutability. Both poems contain gnomic material. There is close
similarity in the expression of the themes of loneliness and transience,

especially in the typical 'elegiac' vocabulary, and in the use of the bitterest moods of external nature to mirror the protagonists' despair and weariness of spirit. These common features of form and content have led editors to anthologise the poems as a pair, and critics to discuss them together.

The poems have been discussed as versions of the same theme. But *The Seafarer* does need a degree of separate treatment. The difference of content between the two halves (dividing at 64^a) is more marked than it is in *The Wanderer*; it is more difficult to relate the specific narrative of the opening section to the more general moralising of the second half. This second half itself is not overwhelmingly problematical. At the break the seafaring theme comes abruptly to a close; there are no more references to seafaring after this point, and the poet shifts to a consideration of death and mutability. The speaker dismisses 'this dead, transitory life on earth'. From this point the description of mutability is quite conventional: there is the statement that the glories of the earth have passed away, that senility and death attack every man; that man's best memorial is fame after death won by courageous and Christian deeds during life. Interspersed with the explicitly Christian sentiment are details which recall the Anglo-Saxon secular gnomic tradition: the discussion of fame after death and the hypermetrical sententious lines at the end. The poem in the manuscript actually goes on to 124 lines; 109–24 are not printed here, because after 108 *The Seafarer* tails off into gnomic trivia, and the text itself becomes very corrupt.

The difficulties of the poem involve our understanding of its first section, and of the relationship between the two halves. It may appear that lines 1–64^a contain contradictory statements about seafaring: a complaint about the hardships of life at sea, and yet some insistence on the motives for going to sea. One attempt to overcome this contradiction was the 'dialogue' theory: that the first half of the poem contains a dialogue between a young man who is eager to go to sea and an old warrior who argues against him by recounting his own personal experiences of hardship at sea. No such complicated view is now taken of the narrative content of the early part of the poem. As Mrs. Gordon says (pp. 2–3 of the Introduction to her edition of *The Seafarer*), 'It is now generally accepted that the seafaring theme represents the reflections of a man who knows from experience the dangers and hardships of seafaring, and yet feels a longing to make a voyage across the ocean.' But why is there this ambivalent attitude? Has this story of a man with motives pulling two ways any more importance than as just a sketch of a personality? These questions have usually been answered by (quite properly) interpreting the seafaring section in the light of the second half of the poem: thus the first half is understood to be either an allegory or a narrative with Christian significance. Anderson and Smithers have interpreted the part of the poem overtly concerned with seafaring as an allegory. Smithers, for example, argues that the seafarer's wanderings over the sea symbolise the *peregrinatio* of man on earth, man as an exile from heaven making his way back to heaven. Professor Whitelock regards the seafarer as the type of a real *peregrinus*, a man who renounces this transitory life by voluntarily becoming an exile, a wanderer over the seas, cut off from society.

Another explanation which comes to mind, and one which removes the need for an allegorical interpretation or one attributing definite Christian motivation for the seafaring, falls more in line with our view of *The Wanderer*. In that poem the *eardstapa* sees his own experiences of suffering as a regrettable aspect of mutability, not as a way of renouncing the pleasures of the world. Likewise, the poet of *The Seafarer* offers the experiences of a mariner as an instance of the hardships of life on earth, life which appears to be attractive but which is not pleasurable but fickle and transitory. So the relation between specific narrative and general statement is roughly as in *The Wanderer;* but in *The Seafarer* there is more condemnation of the attractive, yet impermanent, life.

Mæg ic be me sylfum   soðgied wrecan,
siþas secgan,   hu ic geswincdagum
earfoðhwile   oft þrowade,
bitre breostceare   gebiden hæbbe,
5   gecunnad in ceole   cearselda fela,
atol yþa gewealc,   þær mec oft bigeat
nearo nihtwaco   æt nacan stefnan,
þonne he be clifum cnossað.   Calde geþrungen
wæron mine fet,   forste gebunden,
10   caldum clommum,   þær þa ceare seofedun
hat ymb heortan;   hungor innan slat
merewerges mod.   Þæt se mon ne wat
þe him on foldan   fægrost limpeð,
hu ic earmcearig   iscealdne sæ
15   winter wunade   wræccan lastum,
winemægum bidroren,
bihongen hrimgicelum;   hægl scurum fleag.
    Þær ic ne gehyrde   butan hlimman sæ,
iscaldne wæg.   Hwilum ylfete song
20   dyde ic me to gomene,   ganetes hleoþor
ond huilpan sweg   fore hleahtor wera,
mæw singende   fore medodrince.
Stormas þær stanclifu beotan,   þær him stearn oncwæð
isigfeþera;   ful oft þæt earn bigeal,
25   urigfeþra;   nænig hleomæga
feasceaftig ferð   frefran meahte.
    Forþon him gelyfeð lyt,   se þe ah lifes wyn

26. *frefran:* MS *feran.*

gebiden in burgum,   bealosiþa hwon,
wlonc ond wingal,   hu ic werig oft
in brimlade   bidan sceolde.   30
Nap nihtscua,   norþan sniwde,
hrim hrusan bond,   hægl feol on eorþan,
corna caldast.   Forþon cnyssað nu
heortan geþohtas,   þæt ic hean streamas,
sealtyþa gelac   sylf cunnige;   35
monað modes lust   mæla gehwylce
ferð to feran,   þæt ic feor heonan
elþeodigra   eard gesece.
Forþon nis þæs modwlonc   mon ofer eorþan,
ne his gifena þæs god,   ne in geoguþe to þæs hwæt,   40
ne in his dædum to þæs deor,   ne him his dryhten to þæs hold,
þæt he a his sæfore   sorge næbbe,
to hwon hine Dryhten   gedon wille.
Ne biþ him to hearpan hyge   ne to hringþege,
ne to wife wyn   ne to worulde hyht,   45
ne ymbe owiht elles   nefne ymb yða gewealc;
ac a hafað longunge   se þe on lagu fundað.
Bearwas blostmum nimað,   byrig fægriað,
wongas wlitigað,   woruld onetteð;
ealle þa gemoniað   modes fusne   50
sefan to siþe,   þam þe swa þenceð
on flodwegas   feor gewitan.
Swylce geac monað   geomran reorde,
singeð sumeres weard,   sorge beodeð
bitter in breosthord.   Þæt se beorn se wat,   55
esteadig secg,   hwæt þa sume dreogað
þe þa wræclastas   widost lecgað.
   Forþon nu min hyge hweorfeð   ofer hreþerlocan,
min modsefa   mid mereflode,
ofer hwæles eþel   hweorfeð wide,   60
eorþan sceatas,   cymeð eft to me
gifre ond grædig;   gielleð anfloga,
hweteð on hwælweg   hreþer unwearnum,
ofer holma gelagu.
                        Forþon me hatran sind
Dryhtnes dreamas   þonne þis deade lif,   65
læne on londe.   Ic gelyfe no
þæt him eorðwelan   ece stondað.

52. gewitan: MS gewitað.   56. esteadig: MS eft eadig.
63. hwælweg: MS wælweg.   67. stondað: MS stondeð.

Simle þreora sum þinga gehwylce
ær his tid aga to tweon weorþeð:
70 adl oþþe yldo oþþe ecghete
fægum fromweardum feorh oðþringeð.
Forþon þæt bið eorla gehwam æftercweþendra
lof lifgendra lastworda betst,
þæt he gewyrce ær he on weg scyle,
75 fremum on foldan wið feonda niþ,
deorum dædum deofle togeanes,
þæt hine ælda bearn æfter hergen,
ond his lof siþþan lifge mid englum
awa to ealdre, ecan lifes blæd,
80 dream mid dugeþum.
                           Dagas sind gewitene,
ealle onmedlan eorþan rices.
Nearon nu cyningas ne caseras
ne goldgiefan swylce iu wæron,
þonne hi mæst mid him mærþa gefremedon
85 ond on dryhtlicestum dome lifdon.
Gedroren is þeos duguð eal, dreamas sind gewitene;
wuniað þa wacran ond þas woruld healdaþ,
brucað þurh bisgo. Blæd is gehnæged,
eorþan indryhto ealdað ond searað,
90 swa nu monna gehwylc geond middangeard.
Yldo him on fareð, onsyn blacað,
gomelfeax gnornað, wat his iuwine,
æþelinga bearn eorþan forgiefene.
Ne mæg him þonne se flæschoma, þonne him þæt feorg losað,
95 ne swete forswelgan ne sar gefelan,
ne hond onhreran ne mid hyge þencan.
Þeah þe græf wille golde stregan
broþor his geborenum, byrgan be deadum
maþmum mislicum, þæt hine mid wille,
100 ne mæg þære sawle þe biþ synna ful
gold to geoce for Godes egsan,
þonne he hit ær hydeð þenden he her leofað.
    Micel biþ se Meotudes egsa, forþon hi seo molde oncyrreð;
se gestaþelade stiþe grundas,
105 eorþan sceatas ond uprodor.
Dol biþ se þe him his Dryhten ne ondrædeþ; cymeð him se deað
                                                      unþinged.

---

69. tid aga: MS tide ge. 71. feorh: MS fᵉorh. 72. bið: not in MS.
75. fremum: MS fremman. 79. blæd: MS blæð. 82. nearon: MS næron.

110

Eadig bið se þe eaþmod leofaþ; cymeð him seo ar of heofonum.
Meotod him þæt mod gestaþelað, forþon he in his meahte
gelyfeð.

18. DEOR

THIS LITTLE POEM is unique in the satisfaction given by its form. The text
in the manuscript is divided into six sections, with new paragraphs signalised
by large capitals in the margin at the beginnings of our lines 1, 8, 14,
18, 21, 28; the ends of these sections are marked by a sign used almost
invariably in the Exeter Book to point the ends of paragraphs. But this
short paragraphing is rare in the MS, and this emphasises the power of the
form of the poem in overcoming the scribe's usual practice of writing out a
whole text without a break. The form of the first five sections is determined
by the distribution of the 'refrain' *Þæs ofereode; þisses swa mæg* and by the
fact that one section is devoted to one legendary or historical figure. *Þæs*
refers to the (temporary) sorrow suffered by, or at the hands of, the subject
of the preceding paragraph. *Þisses* refers forward to the fictitious hardship
of 'Deor'. By implication, the general point is made that, just as the huge
sorrows of the legendary great passed away in time, so a man's individual
hardship will pass.

This general point is taken up at the beginning of the sixth stanza, where
it is stated that a man who thinks his troubles are overwhelming may take
comfort in the thought that God apportions good and bad fortune to men.
We are reminded of the similar statement at the beginning of *The Wanderer*:
life is a mixture of prosperity and suffering (cf. note to *Wanderer* l. 1). In
terms of the balance of specific and general in the argument of the poem,
the *scop* has a function very like that of the *eardstapa* and the other first-
person speakers in the elegies. He is a fictitious figure (credible here in
his role as a disappointed poet) who makes personal the emotions dealt
with in the poem. In this poem, unlike the others, his own personal sufferings do not dominate the work as the sole *exemplum* used to back up the
generalisations. The impact of his own experiences is only slightly greater
(because of its key position as the climax of the argument) than those of the
subjects of stanzas 1–5. I have divided off ll. 35–42 as a separate stanza, on
the analogy of the first five. As the last line makes clear, it is the story of
Deor and Heorrenda to which the repeated *þisses* refers specifically. But
we must not forget that Deor, like other figures of his type, is subordinate
to the general point. This is a consolation poem, not a personal narrative.

One should not, however, emphasise one part of the content of the poem
to the exclusion of other features of interest. Krapp and Dobbie (*The
Exeter Book*, p. liii) remind us of the prominence of the heroic matter, and
of an analogy in a poem outside the group of elegies (cf. the allusions to
history and legend in *Beowulf*): 'Though lyric and elegiac in form and mood,
Deor belongs properly with WIDSITH, as a poem in autobiographical form,
dealing with Old Germanic heroic material. And there seems to be no

doubt that here, as in Widsith, the autobiographical element is purely fictitious, serving only as a pretext for the enumeration of the heroic stories.' One would not want to press this argument exclusively, either. *Deor* was written, in its present form, in the Christian period. It contains general Christian sentiment, and material from other poetic traditions is made to fit well with this: the allusions to heroic story; the elegiac tone; the fictitious personal narrator. Like the elegies, it is composite in its content, and like them certainly not a mere patchwork of Christian and traditional.

Welund him be wurman wræces cunnade,
anhydig eorl earfoþa dreag;
hæfde him to gesiþþe sorg ond longaþ,
wintercealde wræce; wean oft onfond,
5 siþþan hine Niðhad on nede legde,
swoncre seonobende on syllan monn.
　　Þæs ofereode, þisses swa mæg.

Beadohilde ne wæs hyre broþra deaþ
on sefan swa sar swa hyre sylfre þing,
10 þæt heo gearolice ongieten hæfde
þæt heo eacen wæs; æfre ne meahte
þriste geþencan, hu ymb þæt sceolde.
　　Þæs ofereode, þisses swa mæg.

We þæt Mæðhilde monge gefrugnon
15 wurdon grundlease Geates frige,
þæt hi seo sorglufu slæp ealle binom.
　　Þæs ofereode, þisses swa mæg.

Ðeodric ahte þritig wintra
Mæringa burg; þæt wæs monegum cuþ.
20 　Þæs ofereode, þisses swa mæg.

We geascodan Eormanrices
wylfenne geþoht; ahte wide folc
Gotena rices. Þæt wæs grim cyning.
Sæt secg monig sorgum gebunden,
25 wean on wenan, wyscte geneahhe
þæt þæs cynerices ofercumen wære.
　　Þæs ofereode, þisses swa mæg.

Siteð sorgcearig, sælum bidæled,
on sefan sweorceð, sylfum þinceð
30 þæt sy endeleas earfoða dæl.

14. *Mæðhilde:* MS *mæð hilde.*　　　　　30. *earfoða:* MS *earfoda.*

Mæg þonne geþencan   þæt geond þas woruld
witig Dryhten   wendeþ geneahhe,
eorle monegum   are gesceawað,
wislicne blæd,   sumum weana dæl.

Þæt ic bi me sylfum   secgan wille,   35
þæt ic hwile wæs   Heodeninga scop,
dryhtne dyre.   Me wæs Deor noma.
Ahte ic fela wintra   folgað tilne,
holdne hlaford,   oþþæt Heorrenda nu,
leoðcræftig monn   londryht geþah,   40
þæt me eorla hleo   ær gesealde.
    Þæs ofereode,   þisses swa mæg.

IV. POETIC PARAPHRASE

19. THE PHOENIX

A POEM, from the Exeter Book, of 677 lines, which divides naturally into two parts. Lines 1–380 are a loose paraphrase and expansion of a Latin poem of 170 lines, *De Ave Phoenice*. The Latin is usually ascribed to Lactantius, who was born in Africa in the second half of the third century A.D., became a Christian (although the Christian content of this particular poem is in doubt), was tutor to Constantine's son in Gaul, and died about 340. This first part of *The Phoenix* consists of an idealised portrait of the Phoenix' paradise-like land, of its burning and resurrection, and a colourful description of the bird itself. This account differs from that of Lactantius in many ways (see the article by Emerson cited in the Bibliography); such departures as the removal of non-Christian allusions may be explained as an adaptation of the narrative–mythological material to the needs of the second half of the work. Lines 381–677 are an interpretation of the story of the Phoenix as a Christian allegory of man's preparation for heaven and of Christ and his resurrection: an integral part of the poem (it is foreshadowed in the narrative section), but distinguished from the first half by source and style. This interpretation is derived from no one particular source, although a passage from l. 443 is believed to be based on Ambrose's *Hexameron* Bk. V, Ch. 79–80.

The poem has been attributed to Cynewulf, largely on the grounds of resemblances of phraseology to his signed works (those which, unlike *The Phoenix*, incorporate his name in runes at the end). It must be said that the stylistic arguments are not compellingly convincing. Cook believed that the poem was by Cynewulf, but added:

> If it is not by Cynewulf, we can hardly say more than that the writer must have been a monk or ecclesiastic, apparently under the influence of Cynewulfian poetry, and likely to have lived either within the period of Cynewulf's poetic activities . . . or soon after.

Krapp and Dobbie comment 'a very reasonable conclusion from the facts at hand'. But Fulton as early as 1896 had argued firmly against this position, and today scholars are unwilling to accept Cynewulf as the author.

What the modern reader is likely to find most impressive is the quality of the descriptive poetry, which is evocative yet precise, highly sensuous, and in its content very different from the more normal Old English poetic landscape (contrast the gloom and haziness of the physical contexts provided in the elegies and *Beowulf*). The description of the Phoenix' paradise at the beginning of the poem is famous. As in the elegies, features of the physical environment are linked with features of human character and human fortune: not only is there no wintry weather, but there is no malice, sin or suffering. It is important to realise that this, despite its excellence as descriptive poetry, portrays no mere physical landscape, but a paradise— a landscape fitting for blissful living. Note also that much of the description is by negative statement: the Phoenix' land is seen not as a positively identified paradise but as the antithesis of the transitory and sorrowful world with which much Old English poetry is concerned.

Hæbbe ic gefrugnen   þætte is feor heonan
eastdælum on   æþelast londa
firum gefræge. Nis se foldan sceat
ofer middangeard   mongum gefere
folcagendra,   ac he afyrred is   5
þurh Meotudes meaht   manfremmendum.
Wlitig is se wong eall,   wynnum geblissad,
mid þam fægrestum   foldan stencum.
Ænlic is þæt iglond,   æþele se Wyrhta,
modig, meahtum spedig,   se þa moldan gesette.   10
Ðær bið oft open   eadgum togeanes
onhliden hleoþra wyn,   heofonrices duru.
Þæt is wynsum wong,   wealdas grene,
rume under roderum. Ne mæg þær ren ne snaw,
ne forstes fnæst,   ne fyres blæst,   15
ne hægles hryre,   ne hrimes dryre,
ne sunnan hætu,   ne sincaldu,
ne wearm weder,   ne winterscur
wihte gewyrdan,   ac se wong seomað,
eadig ond onsund. Is þæt æþele lond   20
blostum geblowen. Beorgas þær ne muntas

15. *fnæst*: MS *fnæft*, with *n* over an erasure.

Lactantius, *De Ave Phoenice*

Est locus in primo felix oriente remotus,
  Que patet aeterni maxima porta poli,
Nec tamen aestivos hiemisve propinquus ad ortus,
  Sed qua sol verno ab axe diem.
Illic planities tractus diffundit apertos,
  Nec tumulus crescit nec cava vallis hiat,
Sed nostros montes, quorum juga celsa putantur,
  Per bis sex ulnas eminet ille locus.
Hic Solis nemus est et consitus arbore multa
  Lucus, perpetuae frondis honore virens.   10

steape ne stondað,   ne stanclifu
heah hlifiað,   swa her mid us,
ne dene ne dalu   ne dunscrafu,
25 hlæwas ne hlincas,   ne þær hleonað oo
unsmeþes wiht,   ac se æþela feld
wridað under wolcnum,   wynnum geblowen.
  Is þæt torhte lond   twelfum herra,
folde fæðmrimes,   swa us gefreogum gleawe
30 witgan þurh wisdom   on gewritum cyþað,
þonne ænig þara beorga   þe her beorhte mid us
hea hlifiað   under heofontunglum.
Smylte is se sigewong;   sunbearo lixeð,
wuduholt wynlic.   Wæstmas ne dreosað,
35 beorhte blede,   ac þa beamas a
grene stondað,   swa him God bibead.
Wintres ond sumeres   wudu bið gelice
bledum gehongen;   næfre brosniað
leaf under lyfte,   ne him lig sceþeð
40 æfre to ealdre,   ærþon edwenden
worulde geweorðe.   Swa iu wætres þrym
ealne middangeard   mereflod þeahte,
eorþan ymbhwyrft,   þa se æþela wong
æghwæs onsund   wið yðfare
45 gehealden stod   hreora wæga,
eadig, unwemme,   þurh est Godes;
bideð swa geblowen   oð bæles cyme,
Dryhtnes domes,   þonne deaðræced,
hæleþa heolstorcofan,   onhliden weorþað.
50 Nis þær on þam londe   laðgeniðla,
ne wop ne wracu,   weatacen nan,
yldu ne yrmðu,   ne se enga deað,
ne lifes lyre,   ne laþes cyme,
ne synn ne sacu,   ne sarwracu,
55 ne wædle gewin,   ne welan onsyn,

Cum Phaethonteis flagrasset ab ignibus axis,
  Ille locus flammis inviolatus erat,
Et cum diluvium mersisset fluctibus orbem,
  Deucalioneas exsuperavit aquas.
15 *Non huc exsangues morbi, non aegra senectus,*
  Nec mors crudelis nec metus asper adest,
Nec scelus infandum nec opum vesana cupido
  Aut ira aut ardens caedis amore furor;
Luctus acerbus abest et egestas obsita pannis
20 *Et curae insomnes et violenta fames.*

ne sorg ne slæp,   ne swar leger,
ne wintergeweorp,   ne wedra gebregd
hreoh under heofonum,   ne se hearda forst
caldum cylegicelum   cnyseð ænigne.
Þær ne hægl ne hrim   hreosað to foldan,   60
ne windig wolcen,   ne þær wæter fealleþ,
lyfte gebysgad,   ac þær lagustreamas,
wundrum wrætlice,   wyllan onspringað,
fægrum flodwylmum   foldan leccaþ,
wæter wynsumu   of þæs wuda midle;   65
þa monþa gehwam   of þære moldan tyrf
brimcald brecað,   bearo ealne geondfarað
þragum þrymlice.   Is þæt Þeodnes gebod
þætte twelf siþum   þæt tirfæste
lond geondlace   lagufloda wynn.   70
Sindon þa bearwas   bledum gehongne,
wlitigum wæstmum;   þær no waniað o,
halge under heofonum,   holtes frætwe.
Ne feallað þær on foldan   fealwe blostman,
wudubeama wlite,   ac þær wrætlice   75
on þam treowum symle   telgan gehladene
ofett edniwe,   in ealle tid,
on þam græswonge   grene stondaþ,
gehroden hyhtlice   Haliges meahtum,
beorhtast bearwa.   No gebrocen weorþeð   80
holt on hiwe,   þær se halga stenc
wunaþ geond wynlond;   þæt onwended ne bið
æfre to ealdre,   ærþon endige
frod fyrngeweorc   se hit on frymþe gescop.
  Ðone wudu weardaþ   wundrum fæger   85
fugel feþrum strong,   se is Fenix haten.

64. *flodwylmum:* MS *fold wyl mum.*
71. *gehongne:* MS *gehongęne* (i.e. dotted under *e* for erasure).
72. *waniað:* MS *wuniað.*

Non ibi tempestas nec vis furit horrida venti
  Nec gelido terram rore pruina tegit,
Nulla super campos tandit sua vellera nubes,
  Nec cadit ex alto turbidus umor aquae.
Sed fons in medio est, quem vivum nomine dicunt,   25
  Perspicuus, lenis, dulcibus uber aquis,
Qui semel erumpens per singula tempora mensum
  Duodecies undis inrigat omne nemus.
Hic genus arboreum procero stipite surgens
  Non lapsura solo mitia poma gerit.   30

Þær se anhaga   eard bihealdeþ,
deormod drohtað;   næfre him deaþ sceþeð
on þam willwonge   þenden woruld stondeþ.

(Description of the Phoenix' song at sunrise; preparations for the burn

90   Siteð siþes fus.   Þonne swegles gim
on sumeres tid,   sunne hatost,
ofer sceadu scineð,   ond gesceapu dreogeð,
210   woruld geondwliteð,   þonne weorðeð his
hus onhæted   þurh hador swegl.
95   Wyrta wearmiað,   willsele stymeð
swetum swæccum,   þonne on swole byrneð
þurh fyres feng   fugel mid neste.
Bæl bið onæled.   Þonne brond þeceð
heoredreorges hus,   hreoh onetteð,
100   fealo lig feormað,   ond Fenix byrneð,
fyrngearum frod.   Þonne fyr þigeð
220   lænne lichoman;   lif bið on siðe,
fæges feorhhord,   þonne flæsc ond ban
adleg æleð.
                    Hwæþre him eft cymeð
105   æfter fyrstmearce   feorh edniwe,
siþþan þa yslan   eft onginnað
æfter ligþræce   lucan togædre,
geclungne to cleowenne.   Þonne clæne bið
beorhtast nesta,   bæle forgrunden,
110   heaþorofes hof;   hra bið acolad,
banfæt gebrocen,   ond se bryne sweþrað.
230   Þonne of þam ade   æples gelicnes
on þære ascan bið   eft gemeted;
of þam weaxeð wyrm,   wundrum fæger,
115   swylce he of ægerum   ut alæde,

Hoc nemus, hos lucos avis incolit unica Phoenix;
    Unica, sed vivit morte refecta sua.

Protinus instructo corpus mutabile nido
90   *Vitalique toro membra vieta locat.*
35   *Ore dehinc sucos membris circumque supraque*
        Inicit exsequiis inmoritura suis.
Tunc inter varios animam commendat odores,
        Depositi tanti nec timet illa fidem.
Interea corpus genitali morte peremptum
40   *Aestuat et flammam parturit ipse calor,*
Aetherioque procul de lumine concipit ignem:
Flagrat et ambustum solvitur in cineres.

scir of scylle. Þonne on sceade weaxeð,
þæt he ærest bið swylce earnes brid,
fæger fugeltimber; ðonne furþor gin
wridað on wynnum, þæt he bið wæstmum gelic
ealdum earne, ond æfter þon   120
feþrum gefrætwad, swylce he æt frymðe wæs,
beorht geblowen. Þonne bræd weorþeð   240
eal edniwe eft acenned,
synnum asundrad   — sumes onlice
swa mon to ondleofne eorðan wæstmas   125
on hærfeste ham gelædeð,
wiste wynsume, ær wintres cyme,
on rypes timan, þy læs hi renes scur
awyrde under wolcnum; þær hi wraðe metað,
fodorþege gefean, þonne forst ond snaw   130
mid ofermægne eorþan þeccað
wintergewædum. Of þam wæstmum sceal   250
eorla eadwela eft alædan
þurh cornes gecynd, þe ær clæne bið
sæd onsawen. Þonne sunnan glæm   135
on lenctenne, lifes tacen,
weceð woruldgestreon, þæt þa wæstmas beoð
þurh agne gecynd eft acende,
foldan frætwe. Swa se fugel weorþeð,
gomel æfter gearum, geong edniwe,   140
flæsce bifongen. No he foddor þigeð,
mete on moldan, nemne meledeawes   260
dæl gebyrge, se dreoseð oft
æt middre nihte; bi þon se modga his
feorh afedeð, oþþæt fyrngesetu,   145
agenne eard, eft geseceð.

122. *weorþeð:* MS has second *e* altered from *a.*   125. *wæstmas:* MS *wæsmas.*
130. *gefean:* MS *ge feon.*   133. *eadwela:* MS *ead welan.*

Quos velut in massam cineres natura coactos
   Conflat, et effectum seminis instar habet.   100
Hinc animal primum sine membris fertur oriri,   45
   Sed fertur vermi lacteus esse color.
Crescit, et emenso sopitur tempore certo
   Seque ovi teretis colligit in speciem.
Ac velut agrestes, cum filo ad saxa tenentur,
   Mutari tineae papilione solent,   50
Inde reformatur qualis fuit ante figura,
   Et Phoenix ruptis pullulat exuviis.
Non illi cibus est nostro concessus in orbe
   Nec cuiquam inplumem pascere cura subest.   110

I   119

Þonne bið aweaxen wyrtum in gemonge
fugel feþrum deal; feorh bið niwe,
geong, geofona ful. Þonne he of greote his
150 lic leoþucræftig, þæt ær lig fornom,
somnað, swoles lafe, searwum gegædrað
270 ban gebrosnad æfter bælþræce,
ond þonne gebringeð ban ond yslan,
ades lafe, eft ætsomne,
155 ond þonne þæt wælreaf wyrtum biteldeð,
fægre gefrætwed.

(The Phoenix returns from the scene of the burning to its native lan

291 Is se fugel fæger forweard hiwe,
bleobrygdum fag ymb þa breost foran.
Is him þæt heafod hindan grene,
160 wrætlice wrixled, wurman geblonden.
Þonne is se finta fægre gedæled,
sum brun, sum basu, sum blacum splottum
searolice beseted. Sindon þa fiþru
hwit hindanweard ond se hals grene
165 nioþoweard ond ufeweard, ond þæt nebb lixeð
300 swa glæs oþþe gim, geaflas scyne
innan ond utan. Is seo eaggebyrd
stearc, ond hiwe stane gelicast,
gladum gimme, þonne in goldfate
170 smiþa orþoncum biseted weorþeð.
Is ymb þone sweoran, swylce sunnan hring,
beaga beorhtast brogden feðrum.
Wrætlic is seo womb neoþan, wundrum fæger,

160. *wrixled:* MS *wrixleð.*   172. *brogden:* MS *bregden.*

---

55 *Ambrosios libat caelesti nectare rores,*
  Stellifero tenues qui cecidere polo.
Hos legit, his aliture mediis in odoribus ales,
  Donec maturam proferat effigiem.

60 *Principio color est, quali est sub sidere Cancri*
  Mitia quod corium punica grana tegit,
Qualis inest foliis quae fert agreste papaver,
  Cum pandit vestes Flora rubente solo.
Hoc humeri pectusque decens velamine fulget,
130   *Hoc caput, hoc cervix summaque terga nitent.*
 65 *Caudaque porrigitur fulvo distincta metallo,*
  In cuius maculis purpura mixta rubet.
Alarum pennas insignit desuper iris,
  Pingere ceu nubem desuper acta solet.
Albicat mixto viridante zmaragdo

scir ond scyne.   Is se scyld ufan
frætwum gefeged   ofer þæs fugles bæc.   175
Sindon þa scancan   scyllum biweaxen,   310
fealwe fotas.   Se fugel is on hiwe
æghwæs ænlic,   onlicost pean,
wynnum geweaxen,   þæs gewritu secgað.
Nis he hinderweard   ne hygegælsa,   180
swar ne swongor,   swa sume fuglas
þa þe late þurh lyft   lacað fiþrum,
ac he is snel ond swift   ond swiþe leoht,
wlitig ond wynsum,   wuldre gemearcad.
Ece is se Æþeling   se þe him þæt ead gefeð.   185

Et puro cornu gemmea cuspis hiat.   70
Ingentes oculi, credas geminos hyacinthos,
   Quorum de medio lucida flamma micat.
Aptata est rutilo capiti radiata corona,
   Phoebei referens verticis alta decus.   140
Crura tegunt squamae fulvo distincta metallo,   75
   Ast ungues roseo tinguit honore color.
Effigies inter pavonis mixta figuram
   Cernitur et pictam Phasidis inter avem.
Magnitiem terris Arabum quae gignitur ales
   Vix aequare potest, seu fera seu sit avis.   80
Non tamen est tarda ut volucres quae corpore magno
   Incessus pigros per grave pondus habent,
Sed levis ac velox, regali plena decore:
   Talis in aspectu se tenet usque hominum.   150

20. ALFRED'S TRANSLATION OF A METRE OF BOETHIUS

BOETHIUS WAS BORN of a noble Roman family about A.D. 480, and rose to a
position of great power under Theodoric. On the strength of a now uncertain accusation of conspiracy, however, he was cast into prison at Pavia,
where he was tortured and killed (524). His most famous work is the *De
Consolatione Philosophiae*, supposedly written while he was in prison.
Although there is almost nothing in the *Consolation* which is specifically
Christian, it was accepted in the Middle Ages as one of the great works in
the canon of religious and philosophical literature. A very great number of
medieval manuscripts exists, and vernacular translations abound. Chaucer
translated it, and was only one of the many medieval poets who were profoundly influenced by it.

   It was a natural choice for King Alfred to translate, clearly being worthy
of inclusion among those books which he regarded as 'most necessary for
all men to know'. The West Saxon version is the earliest in any vernacular
language, and has been attributed to him from a very early date. It now
exists in two forms. An early-twelfth-century manuscript, Bodley 180
('B'), contains a prose translation of both the Latin prose and metres of

Boethius. Cotton Otho A. vi ('C'), a mid-tenth-century manuscript, contains a prose translation of Boethius' prose, and a verse translation of the metres. This MS was extensively damaged in the Cotton fire of 1731. But while it was still complete Fransiscus Junius had made a copy of the verse translation of the metres, inserting them in the appropriate places of his copy of the prose from Bodley 180: his complete transcript survives as MS Junius 12 ('J'), and can be used to reconstruct the Cotton text of the metres.

As with all Alfred's translations, it is not possible to determine the exact nature of his personal contribution. Our most positive evidence is contained in the verse and prose Proems to the West Saxon translation; the latter says that 'King Alfred was the translator of this book, and turned it from Latin into English. . . . And . . . when he had learned this book, and turned it from Latin into English proses, he made it again into verse. . . .' After many ingenious arguments for and against Alfred's authorship, we are left with only this attribution and a few scraps of linguistic evidence to prove the case either way; but the statement of the Proem is positive enough, and near enough Alfred's time, not to be doubted. It is now generally accepted that Alfred was responsible for both the prose and verse translations.

As far as can be judged by internal evidence, the relationship between Boethius Latin metres, the Old English prose and the verse is consistent with the statement of the Proem. The verse translations of the *Metra* are not fresh translations from the Latin, but consist of the prose translations versified in a quite mechanical way: the Latin has not been referred to. In consequence, these verse translations of the metres are inferior Old English poetry and also lose much of the content and expression of the Latin.

Here we print the Latin verse, Old English prose and Old English verse of Boethius' Book II, Metre iii.

(*a*) PROSE

Ða ongan se Wisdom singan and giddode þus:

Þonne seo sunne on hadrum heofone beorhtost scineð, þonne aþeostriað ealle steorran, forþam þe heora beorhtnes ne beoð nan beorhtnes for hire. Þonne smylte blaweð suþanwestan wind, þonne
5   weaxeð swiðe hraðe feldes blosman; ac þonne se stearca wind cymð norðaneastan, þonne toweorpð he swiðe hraþe þære rosan wlite; swa oft þone to smylton sæ þæs norðanwindes yst onstyreð. Eala þæt nanwuht nis fæste stondendes weorces awuniende on worulde.

---

2. *beorhtost:* MS *beohtost.*   3. *steorran:* MS *þeorran; beorhtnes:* MS *beohtnes.*
6. *þære:* MS *þær.*

(b) VERSE

Ða se Wisdom eft   wordhord onleac,
sang soðcwidas,   and þus selfa cwæð:
Ðonne sio sunne   sweotolost scineð,
hadrost of hefone,   hræðe bioð aðistrod
ealle ofir eorðan   oðre steorran,   5
forðæm hiora birhtu   ne bið auht
to gesettane   wið þære sunnan leoht.
Ðonne smolte blæwð   suðan and westan
wind under wolcnum,   þonne weaxeð hraðe
feldes blostman,   fægen þæt hi moton.   10
Ac se stearca storm,   þonne he strong cymð
norðan and eastan,   he genimeð hraðe
þære rosan wlite,   and eac þa ruman sæ
norðerne yst   nede gebædeð,
þæt hio strange geondstyred   on staðu beateð.   15
Eala, þæt on eorðan   auht fæstlices
weorces on worulde   ne wunað æfre!

14. *gebædeð*: C *ge . . . ded*; J *gebæded*.

Boethius, *De Consolatione Philosophiae* II, iii.

Cum polo Phoebus roseis quadrigis
    Lucem spargere coeperit,
Pallet albentes hebetata vultus
    Flammis stella prementibus.
Cum nemus flatu Zephyri tepentis   5
    Vernis inrubuit rosis,
Spiret insanum nebulosus Auster,
    Iam spinis abeat decus.
Saepe tranquillo radiat sereno
    Immotis mare fluctibus,   10
Saepe ferventes Aquilo procellas
    Verso concitat aequore.
Rara si constat sua forma mundo,
    Si tantas variat vices,
Crede fortunis hominum caducis,   15
    Bonis crede fugacibus!
Constat aeterna positumque lege est,
    Ut constet genitum nihil.

BIBLIOGRAPHY

I. GENERAL

1. FURTHER BIBLIOGRAPHY

F. W. BATESON (ed.) *The Cambridge Bibliography of English Literature*, I (600–1660), Cambridge, 1941.

G. WATSON (ed.) *The Cambridge Bibliography of English Literature*, V (Supplement), Cambridge, 1957.

W. L. RENWICK and H. ORTON, *The Beginnings of English Literature to Skelton, 1509*, 2nd ed., London, 1952.

N. R. KER, *Catalogue of Manuscripts containing Anglo-Saxon*, Oxford, 1957.

2. LANGUAGE

J. BOSWORTH and T. N. TOLLER, *An Anglo-Saxon Dictionary*, Oxford, 1882–98, *Supplement*, Oxford, 1908–20.

A. C. BAUGH, *A History of the English Language*, 2nd ed., London, 1959.

E. E. WARDALE, *An Old English Grammar*, London, 1922. (Describes earlier West Saxon.)

R. QUIRK and C. L. WRENN, *An Old English Grammar*, 2nd ed., London, 1957. (Describes 'classical' Old English—late West Saxon.)

A. CAMPBELL, *An Old English Grammar*, Oxford, 1959. (Advanced and comprehensive.)

3. OLD ENGLISH LITERATURE

(*Note:* There is no one detailed, comprehensive and authoritative history of Old English literature, and so the individual reading-lists in Section II below must be used fully.)

G. K. ANDERSON, *The Literature of the Anglo-Saxons*, London, 1949. (Not infallible.)

A. C. BAUGH, K. MALONE and C. BROOKS, *A Literary History of England*, London, 1948. (The best short history of the period.)

W. P. KER, *The Dark Ages*, London, 1904. (Paperback, New York, 1958.)

W. P. KER, *Epic and Romance*, London, 1908. (Paperback, New York, 1957.)

K. SISAM, *Studies in the History of Old English Literature*, Oxford, 1953. (A collection of rather specialised essays.)

A. W. WARD and A. R. WALLER, *The Cambridge History of English Literature*, I, Cambridge, 1907.

E. E. WARDALE, *Chapters on Old English Literature*, London, 1935.

4. HISTORICAL AND SOCIAL BACKGROUND

P. HUNTER BLAIR, *An Introduction to Anglo-Saxon England*, Cambridge, 1956.

H. M. CHADWICK, *The Heroic Age*, Cambridge, 1926.

R. G. COLLINGWOOD and J. N. L. MYRES, *Roman Britain and the English Settlements*, 2nd ed., London, 1937.

D. C. DOUGLAS, *William the Conqueror*, London, 1964.

R. H. HODGKIN, *A History of the Anglo-Saxons*, 3rd ed., London, 1952.

SIR FRANK STENTON, *Anglo-Saxon England*, 2nd ed., London, 1947.

DOROTHY WHITELOCK, *The Beginnings of English Society*, Harmondsworth, 1952.

II. INDIVIDUAL TEXTS

(*Note:* The bracketed reference after the title of each text is to the *Cambridge Bibliography*.)

1–3. THE ANGLO-SAXON CHRONICLE (*CBEL* I. 88–9)

Facsimiles: R. FLOWER and A. H. SMITH, *The Parker Chronicle and Laws*, EETS. 208, London, 1941.

DOROTHY WHITELOCK, *The Peterborough Chronicle* (*Early English MSS in Facsimile* iv), Copenhagen, 1954.

Editions: J. EARLE and C. PLUMMER, *Two of the Saxon Chronicles Parallel*, Oxford, 1892; reprint with additional material by Dorothy Whitelock, Oxford, 1952. (Full introduction and notes; indispensable.)

A. H. SMITH, *The Parker Chronicle, 832–900*, London, 1935.

CECILY CLARK, *The Peterborough Chronicle*, Oxford, 1958.

Translations: G. N. Garmonsway, *The Anglo-Saxon Chronicle*, London, 1953. (Excellent; corresponds page-for-page with the Old English text of Earle-Plummer.)

DOROTHY WHITELOCK, D. C. DOUGLAS and SUSIE I. TUCKER, *The Anglo-Saxon Chronicle*, London, 1961.

Discussion: (The most important discussion is found in the introductions and notes to the works cited above.)

CECILY CLARK, 'Studies in the Vocabulary of the Peterborough Chronicle', *English and Germanic Studies*, v (1953), 67–89.

B. DICKINS and R. M. WILSON, *Early Middle English Texts* (London, 1952), 3–4, 153–4.

R. H. HODGKIN, *A History of the Anglo-Saxons*, 3rd ed. (London, 1952), II, 583–5, 624–9, Ch. XIX *passim*, 745–7.

F. P. MAGOUN, Jnr., 'Cynewulf, Cyneheard and Osric', *Anglia*, lvii (1933), 361–76.

F. P. MAGOUN, Jnr., 'King Alfred's Naval and Beach Battle with the Danes', *MLR* xxxvii (1942), 409–14.

SIR FRANK STENTON, 'The South-Western Element in the Old English Chronicle', *Essays in Medieval History Presented to T. F. Tout*, Manchester, 1925.

SIR FRANK STENTON, *Anglo-Saxon England*, 2nd ed. (London, 1947), 263–6, 679–84.

C. E. WRIGHT, *The Cultivation of Saga in Anglo-Saxon England*, Edinburgh, 1939.

4. ALFRED'S PREFACE TO THE PASTORAL CARE (*CBEL* I. 86)

Facsimile: N. R. KER, *The Pastoral Care* (*Early English MSS in Facsimile* vi), Copenhagen, 1956.
Edition: H. SWEET, *King Alfred's West-Saxon Version of Gregory's Pastoral Care*, EETS. 45, 50, London, 1871, 1872.
Translation: SWEET, as above.
Discussion: R. H. HODGKIN, *A History of the Anglo-Saxons*, 3rd ed. (London, 1952), 608 ff.
    F. KLAEBER, 'Zu König Alfreds Vorrede zu seiner Übersetzung der Cura Pastoralis', *Anglia*, xlvii (1923), 53–65.
    S. POTTER, 'The Old English "Pastoral Care"', *TPS*, 1947, 114–25.
    K. SISAM, 'The Publication of Alfred's *Pastoral Care*', Ch. IX of *Studies in the History of Old English Literature*, Oxford, 1953.

5. BEDE'S ACCOUNT OF THE POET CÆDMON (*CBEL* I. 86–7)

Editions: T. MILLER, *The Old English Version of Bede's Ecclesiastical History of the English People*, E.E.T.S. 95, 96, 110, 111, London 1890–1, 1898. (Based chiefly on MS Tanner X.)
    J. SCHIPPER, *König Alfreds Übersetzung von Bedas Kirchengeschichte*, Leipzig, 1897–9. (Parallel-text edition.)
    A. H. SMITH, *Three Northumbrian Poems*, London, 1933. (Cædmon's Hymn.)
Translation: MILLER, as above.
Discussion: P. F. VAN DRAAT, 'The Authorship of the Old English Bede', *Anglia*, xxxix (1916), 319–47.
    SIR I. GOLLANCZ, *The Cædmon MS*, Oxford, 1927.
    J. M. HART, 'Rhetoric in the Translation of Bede', in *An English Miscellany*, Oxford, 1901.
    F. P. MAGOUN, Jnr., 'Bede's Story of Cædman: the Case History of an Anglo-Saxon Oral Singer', *Speculum*, xxx (1955), 49–63.
    S. POTTER, *On the Relations of the Old English Bede to Werferth's Gregory and to Alfred's Translations*, Prague, 1931.
    C. L. WRENN, 'The Poetry of Cædmon', *PBA*, xxxii (1946), 277–95.

6. THE VOYAGES OF OHTHERE AND WULFSTAN (*CBEL* I. 87–8)

Facsimile: A. CAMPBELL, *The Tollemache Orosius* (*Early English MSS in Facsimile* iii), Copenhagen, 1953.
Edition: H. SWEET, *King Alfred's Orosius*, Pt. I, EETS. 79, London, 1883.
Discussion: A. L. BINNS, 'Ohtheriana VI: Ohthere's Northern Voyage', *English and Germanic Studies*, vii (1961), 43–52.
    SIR W. CRAIGIE, '"Iraland" in King Alfred's "Orosius"', *MLR*, xii (1917), 200–1.
    SIR W. CRAIGIE, 'The Nationality of King Alfred's Wulfstan', *JEGP*, xxiv (1925), 396–7.
    R. EKBLOM, 'Alfred the Great as Geographer', in *A Philological Miscellany Presented to E. Ekwall*, Uppsala, 1942.
    K. MALONE, 'King Alfred's North. A Study in Medieval Geography', *Speculum*, v (1930), 139–67.

K. MALONE, 'On King Alfred's Geographical Treatise', *Speculum*, viii (1933), 67–78.

S. POTTER, 'The Old English Orosius', *TPS*, 1939, 44–53.

A. S. C. ROSS, The *'Terfinnas'* and *'Beormas'* of Ohthere, Kendal, 1940.

A. S. C. ROSS, 'Ohthere's "Cwenas and Lakes"', *The Geographical Journal*, cxx (1954), 337–46.

W. C. STOKOE, Jnr., 'On Ohthere's *Steorbord'*, *Speculum*, xxxii (1957), 299–306.

7. APPOLLONIUS OF TYRE (*CBEL* I. 94–5)

Editions: P. GOOLDEN, *The Old English Apollonius of Tyre*, Oxford, 1958. (With reconstructed Latin text.)

J. RAITH, *Die alt- und mittelenglischen Apollonius-Bruchstücke, mit dem Text der Historia Apollonii nach der englischen Handschriftengruppe*, München, 1956.

Edition with translation: B. THORPE, *The Anglo-Saxon Version of the Story of Apollonius of Tyre*, London, 1834.

Discussion: GOOLDEN, as above.

C. O. CHAPMAN, 'Beowulf and Apollonius of Tyre', *MLN*, xlvi (1931), 439–43.

P. H. GOEPP, 'The Narrative Material of Apollonius of Tyre', *ELH*, v (1938).

8. THE END OF THE WORLD (*CBEL* I. 93)

Facsimile: R. WILLARD, *The Blickling Homilies* (*Early English MSS in Facsimile* x), Copenhagen, 1960.

Edition with translation: R. MORRIS, *The Blickling Homilies of the Tenth Century*, EETS. 58, 63, 73, London, 1874–80.

9. WULFSTAN'S ADDRESS TO THE ENGLISH (*CBEL* I. 92)

Editions: D. WHITELOCK, *Sermo Lupi ad Anglos*, 3rd ed., London, 1963.

D. BETHURUM, *The Homilies of Wulfstan* (Oxford, 1957), 255–75. (Three versions.)

Translation: A. S. COOK and C. B. TINKER, *Select Translations from Old English Prose* (Boston, 1908), 194 ff.

Discussion: WHITELOCK and BETHURUM as above.

R. FOWLER, 'Some Stylistic Features of the *Sermo Lupi'*, *JEGP*, lxv (1966).

K. JOST, *Wulfstanstudien* (*Swiss Studies in English* xxiii), Bern, 1950.

A. MCINTOSH, 'Wulfstan's Prose', *PBA*, xxxv (1949), 109–42.

D. WHITELOCK, 'Archbishop Wulfstan, Homilist and Statesman', *TRHS*, 4th series, xxiv (1942), 25–45.

10. ÆLFRIC'S LINE OF KING OSWALD (*CBEL* I. 89)

Edition: W. W. SKEAT, *Ælfric's Lives of Saints*, EETS. 76, 82, 94, 114 (London, 1881–1900), No. 26.

Translation: SKEAT, as above.

Discussion: SKEAT, as above.

C. R. BARRETT, *Studies in the Word-order of Ælfric's Catholic Homilies and Lives of the Saints*, Cambridge, 1953.

P. A. M. CLEMOES, 'The Chronology of Ælfric's Works', in Clemoes (ed.), *The Anglo-Saxons, Studies . . . Presented to Bruce Dickins* (London, 1959), 212–47.

K. SISAM, 'The Order of Ælfric's Early Books', Note E in *Studies in the History of Old English Literature*, Oxford, 1953.

II. BEOWULF (*CBEL* I. 63–8)

Facsimiles: J. ZUPITZA, *Beowulf*, 2nd ed., rev. Norman Davis, EETS. 245, London, 1959. (Zupitza's facsimile and transliteration were originally published in 1882; in the 2nd ed. his transliteration is retained, but a new and clearer photofacsimile is given.)

K. MALONE, *The Thorkelin Transcripts of Beowulf* (*Early English MSS in Facsimile* i), Copenhagen, 1951.

Editions: FR. KLAEBER, *Beowulf and The Fight at Finnsburg*, 3rd ed. with two supplements, London and New York, 1951. (The great standard scholarly edition.)

C. L. WRENN, *Beowulf with the Finnesburg Fragment*, revised and enlarged edition, London, 1958. (An excellent and informative, up-to-date students' edition.)

A. J. WYATT, *Beowulf with the Finnsburg Fragment*, new edition revised by R. W. Chambers, Cambridge, 1925.

Translation: J. R. CLARK HALL, *Beowulf and the Finnesburg Fragment*, with prefatory remarks by J. R. R. Tolkien; revised edition with introduction by C. L. Wrenn, London, 1950.

Discussion (a small selection):

A. BONJOUR, *The Digressions in Beowulf* (*Medium Ævum Monographs* v), Oxford, 1950.

A. BONJOUR, *Twelve Beowulf Papers, 1940–1960*, Neuchâtel, 1962.

A. G. BRODEUR, *The Art of Beowulf*, Berkeley, 1959.

R. W. CHAMBERS, *Beowulf, an Introduction to the Study of the Poem*, 3rd ed., with supplements, Cambridge, 1959.

R. GIRVAN, *Beowulf and the Seventh Century: Language and Content*, London, 1935.

MARGARET GOLDSMITH, 'The Christian Theme of *Beowulf*', *Medium Ævum*, xxix (1960), 81–101.

W. W. LAWRENCE, *Beowulf and the Epic Tradition*, Cambridge (Mass.), 1928.

L. E. NICHOLSON, *An Anthology of Beowulf Criticism*, Notre Dame, Indiana, 1963.

J. R. R. TOLKIEN, '*Beowulf*: The Monsters and the Critics', *PBA*, xxii (1936), 245–95.

DOROTHY WHITELOCK, *The Audience of Beowulf*, Oxford, 1951.

12. THE BATTLE OF MALDON (*CBEL* I. 83–4)

Editions: M. ASHDOWN, *English and Norse Documents relating to the Reign of Ethelred the Unready*, Cambridge, 1930.

E. V K. DOBBIE, *The Anglo-Saxon Minor Poems* (New York, 1942), 7–16.

E. V. GORDON, *The Battle of Maldon*, London, 1937.

E. D. LABORDE, *Byrhtnoth and Maldon*, London, 1936.

Translations: ASHDOWN, as above.

R. K. GORDON, *Anglo-Saxon Poetry*, revised edition (London, 1954), 329–34.

Discussion: LABORDE, ASHDOWN, and E. V. GORDON as above.

E. V. GORDON, 'The Date of Æthelred's Treaty with the Vikings: Olaf Tryggvason and the Battle of Maldon', *MLR*, xxxii (1937), 24–32.

E. B. IRVING, Jnr., 'The Heroic Style in *The Battle of Maldon*', *SP*, lviii (1961), 457–67.

E. D. LABORDE, 'The Site of the Battle of Maldon', *EHR*, xl (1925), 161–73.

E. D. LABORDE, 'The Style of the Battle of Maldon', *MLR*, xix (1924), 401–77.

BERTHA S. PHILLPOTTS, 'The Battle of Maldon: some Danish Affinities', *MLR*, xxiv (1929), 172–90.

H. B. WOOLF, 'The Personal Names in *The Battle of Maldon*', *MLN*, liii (1938), 109–12.

13. ANDREAS (*CBEL* I. 77)

Facsimile: M. FOERSTER, *Il Codice Vercellese*, Roma, 1913.

Editions: K. R. BROOKS, *Andreas and The Fates of the Apostles*, Oxford, 1961.

G. P. KRAPP, *Andreas and the Fates of the Apostles*, Boston, 1906.

G. P. KRAPP, *The Vercelli Book* (New York, 1932), 3–51.

Translation: R. K. GORDON, op. cit., 181–210.

Discussion: BROOKS and KRAPP, as above.

A. S. COOK, 'The Authorship of the Old English Andreas', *MLN*, xxxiv (1919), 418–19.

S. K. DAS, *Cynewulf and the Cynewulf Canon*, Calcutta, 1942.

R. E. DIAMOND, 'The Diction of the Signed Poems of Cynewulf', *PQ*, xxxviii (1959), 228–41.

F. P. MAGOUN, Jnr., 'Oral-formulaic Character of Anglo-Saxon Narrative Poetry', *Speculum*, xxviii (1953), 446–67.

L. J. PETERS, 'The Relationship of the Old English Andreas to Beowulf', *PMLA*, lxvi (1951), 844–63.

C. SCHAAR, *Critical Studies in the Cynewulf Group* (*Lund Studies in English*, xvii, 1949).

K. SISAM, 'Cynewulf and his Poetry', Ch. I of *Studies in the History of Old English Literature*, Oxford, 1953.

14. GENESIS B (*CBEL* I. 74)

Facsimile: SIR I. GOLLANCZ, *The Cædmon Manuscript of Anglo-Saxon Biblical Poetry, Junius xi in the Bodleian Library*, Oxford, 1927.

Editions: FR. KLAEBER, *The Later Genesis and other Old English and Old Saxon Texts Relating to the Fall of Man*, Heidelberg, 1913.

G. P. KRAPP, *The Junius Manuscript* (London and New York, 1931), 9–28.

B. J. TIMMER, *The Later Genesis*, 2nd ed., Oxford, 1954.

Translation: GORDON, op. cit., 99–103.

Discussion: H. BRADLEY, 'The "Cædmonian" Genesis', *Essays and Studies*, vi (1920), 7–29.

G. H. GEROULD, 'The Transmission and Date of Genesis B', *MLN*, xxvi (1911), 129–33.

GOLLANCZ as above.

J. W. LEVER, 'Paradise Lost and the Anglo-Saxon Tradition', *RES*, xxiii (1947), 97–106.

R. E. WOOLF, 'The Devil in Old English Poetry', *RES*, n.s. iv (1953), 1–12.

15. THE DREAM OF THE ROOD (*CBEL* I. 78)

Facsimile: M. FOERSTER, *Il Codice Vercellese*, Roma, 1913.

Editions: A. S. COOK, *The Dream of the Rood*, Oxford, 1905.

B. DICKINS and A. S. C. ROSS, *The Dream of the Rood*, 4th ed., London, 1954.

G. P. KRAPP, *The Vercelli Book* (New York, 1932), 61–5.

Translations:

GORDON, op. cit., 235–8.

COOK, *ed. cit.*, 47–54, gives an interesting selection of translations of the first twelve lines of the poem.

Discussion: COOK and DICKINS and ROSS as above.

G. BALDWIN BROWN, *The Arts in Early England* (London, 1921), V, Ch. iv–xii.

H. R. PATCH, 'Liturgical Influence in the Dream of the Rood', *PMLA*, xxxiv (1919), 233–57.

M. SCHLAUCH, 'The Dream of the Rood as prosopopoeia', in *Essays and Studies in Honor of Carleton Brown*, New York, 1940.

R. WOOLF, 'Doctrinal Influences on *The Dream of the Rood*', *Medium Ævum*, xxvii (1958), 137–53.

16. THE WANDERER (*CBEL* I. 70)

Facsimile: R. W. CHAMBERS, MAX FÖRSTER and ROBIN FLOWER, *The Exeter Book*, London, 1935.

Editions: G. P. KRAPP and E. V K. DOBBIE, *The Exeter Book* (New York and London, 1936), 134–7.

N. KERSHAW, *Anglo-Saxon and Norse Poems* (Cambridge, 1922), 7–15.

Translation: GORDON, op. cit., 73–5.

Discussion:

I. L. GORDON, 'Traditional Themes in *The Wanderer* and *The Seafarer*', *RES*, n.s. v (1945), 1–13.

S. B. GREENFIELD, 'The *Wanderer*: a Reconsideration of Theme and Structure', *JEGP*, l (1951), 451–65.

B. F. HUPPE, 'The "*Wanderer*": Theme and Structure', *JEGP*, xlii (1943), 516–38.

W. W. LAWRENCE, 'The *Wanderer* and the *Seafarer*', *JEGP*, iv (1902), 460–80.

R. M. LUMIANSKY, 'The Dramatic Structure of the Old English *Wanderer*', *Neophilologus*, xxxiv (1950), 111 ff.

G. V. SMITHERS, 'The Meaning of *The Seafarer* and *The Wanderer*,' *Medium Ævum*, xxvi (1957), 137–53, and xxviii (1959), 1–22 and 99–104.

E. G. STANLEY, 'Old English Poetic Diction and the Interpretation of *The Wanderer*, *The Seafarer* and *The Penitent's Prayer*', *Anglia*, lxxiii (1955), 413–66.

17. THE SEAFARER (*CBEL* I. 70–1)

Facsimile: CHAMBERS, FÖRSTER and FLOWER, *The Exeter Book*, London, 1935.
Editions: KRAPP and DOBBIE, *The Exeter Book* (New York and London, 1936), 143–7.
I. L. GORDON, *The Seafarer*, London, 1960.
N. KERSHAW, *Anglo-Saxon and Norse Poems* (Cambridge, 1922), 20–6.
Translation: R. K. GORDON, op. cit., 76–8.
Discussion: I. L. GORDON, as above.
O. S. ANDERSON, *The Seafarer: an Interpretation*, Lund, 1937.
J. J. CAMPBELL, 'Oral Poetry in *The Seafarer*', *Speculum*, xxxv (1960), 87–96.
S. B. GREENFIELD, 'Attitudes and Values in *The Seafarer*', *SP*, li (1954), 15–20.
S. B. GREENFIELD, 'The Formulaic Expression of the Theme of Exile in Anglo-Saxon Poetry', *Speculum*, xxx (1955), 200–6.
W. A. O'NEIL, 'Another Look at Oral Poetry in *The Seafarer*', *Speculum*, xxxv (1960), 596–600.
DOROTHY WHITELOCK, 'The Interpretation of *The Seafarer*', in *Early Cultures of North-West Europe* (*H.M. Chadwick Memorial Studies*), Cambridge, 1950.
See also Bibliography for *The Wanderer* above.

18. DEOR (*CBEL* I. 68–9)

Facsimile: CHAMBERS, FÖRSTER and FLOWER, *The Exeter Book*, London, 1935.
Editions: B. DICKINS, *Runic and Heroic Poems of the Old Teutonic Peoples*, (Cambridge, 1915), 70–7.
KRAPP and DOBBIE, *The Exeter Book* (New York and London, 1936), 178–9
K. MALONE, *Deor*, London, 1933.
Translation: GORDON, op. cit., 71–2.
Discussion: MALONE, as above.
W. W. LAWRENCE, 'The Song of Deor', *MP*, ix (1911), 23–45.
K. MALONE, *Studies in Heroic Legend* (Copenhagen, 1959), 116–23, 142–57.
F. NORMAN, '"Deor"; a Criticism and an Interpretation', *MLR*, xxxii (1937), 374–81.

19. THE PHOENIX (*CBEL* I. 77–8)

Facsimile: CHAMBERS, FÖRSTER and FLOWER, *The Exeter Book*, London, 1935.
Editions: N. F. BLAKE, *The Phoenix*, Manchester, 1964.
A. S. COOK, *The Old English Elene, Phoenix, and Physiologus*, New Haven and London, 1919.
KRAPP and DOBBIE, *The Exeter Book* (New York and London, 1936), 94–113.
Translation: GORDON, op. cit., 239–51.
Discussion: BLAKE and COOK as above.
N. F. BLAKE, 'Some Problems of Interpretation and Translation in the Old English *Phoenix*', *Anglia*, lxxx (1962), 50–62.
O. F. EMERSON, 'Originality in Old English Poetry', *RES*, ii (1926), 18–31.
E. FULTON, 'On the Authorship of the Anglo-Saxon Poem Phoenix', *MLN*, xi (1896), 73–85.

20. ALFRED'S TRANSLATION OF A METRE OF BOETHIUS (*CBEL* I. 87)

Editions: G. P. KRAPP, *The Paris Psalter and the Meters of Boethius*, New York, 1932.

W. J. SEDGEFIELD, *King Alfred's Old English Version of Boethius*, Oxford, 1899.

Translation: W. J. SEDGEFIELD, *King Alfred's Version of the Consolations of Boethius*, Oxford, 1900.

Discussion: KRAPP and SEDGEFIELD, as above.

K. SISAM, 'The Authorship of the Verse Translation of Boethius's Metra', Note D in *Studies in the History of Old English Literature*, Oxford, 1953.

NOTES

1. THE FEUD OF CYNEWULF AND CYNEHEARD

1. *755*: actually 757; there is an error of two and sometimes three years in the dating for about 100 years from this point.

Cynewulf: King of Wessex at the time when Offa, King of Mercia, held great power in England. Much of what is known about Cynewulf's reign is found in this extract from the *Chronicle*.

1–2. *West-Seaxna wiotan*: this is the first recorded instance of the contribution of the *witan* to the deposition of a king.

4. *Andred*: *Andredes weald*, the Weald of Kent and Sussex, at that time a great forest stretching into Hampshire.

5. *Pryfetes flodan*: Privett, near Petersfield, Hants.

8. *xxxi wintra*: actually, 29. Cynewulf's death took place in 786 and is again recorded in the *Chronicle* under 784.

11. *Merantune*: most probably Merton, Surrey.

bur: a small apartment separate from the main building in which the King's retainers would be. Earle-Plummer (II, 45) has a long note on the 'arrangements of a Saxon residence' which will clarify the circumstances in which this conflict took place.

15–16. *wærun feohtende*: 'went on fighting'.

17. *gebærum*: literally 'gestures'; here 'cries'.

18. *ond radost*: two MSS omit this; two others omit just *ond*. Both alterations simplify this awkward construction.

20–1. Implied here is the belief that it was disgraceful to survive one's lord unless he was avenged. The survivor's ties with Cynewulf were less strong, it is suggested, because he was a Welshman and a hostage.

21. *gisle*: cf. the position of Byrhtnoð's hostage Æscferð in *Battle of Maldon*, 265–72.

25, 26. *byrig, gatu*: *byrig* refers to the whole homestead, not just the *bur*. In such place-names as *Lundenbyrig* it denotes larger settlements. The gates are those of the protecting fence, not the door of the *bur*.

26. *him to belocen hæfdon*: (Cyneheard's men) 'had closed the gates upon themselves'.

27. *hiera agenne dom*: cf. *Battle of Maldon* 38 *hyra sylfra dom*.

27 ff. The difficulty here is caused by the ambiguity of the pronouns. A skeleton translation is given: 'And he (Cyneheard) offered them (Osric, etc.) . . . if they (O) would give him (C) . . . and told them (O) that their (O) kinsmen were with him (C) who would not leave him (C). And they (O) offered their kinsmen. . . . And they (C) said that the same offer had been made to their (O) comrades . . .; then they (C) said that they (C) regarded it 'no more than your (O) . . .' And they (O) went on fighting . . .'

29–30. *nænig mæg . . . hlaford*: Note that the tie between retainer and lord is greater than that between kinsmen. With the loyalty of these retainers contrast the behaviour of Beowulf's retainers in the fight with the dragon; the sons of Odda in *Battle of Maldon*.

K   135

34. *'þon ma . . . wærun':* Direct speech is rare in the *Chronicle.* The sudden change from reported to direct is said by Earle-Plummer to be 'characteristic of antique narration, and especially frequent in the Icelandic sagas'.

37. *aldormonnes:* i.e. Osric's.

2. ALFRED'S WARS WITH THE DANES

1–2. *þe we gefyrn ymbe spræcon:* basically, the army which the *Chronicle* says was at Fulham in 879 and which left for the Continent in the next year. It was defeated by Arnulf at the Battle of the Dyle (at Louvain) in 891, and had to return to England in the next year because of lack of food.

2. *eastrice:* the kingdom of the East Franks.

Bunnan: Boulogne.

4. *Limene muþan:* see Hodgkin's map, p. 657. The course and outlet of the River Lympne (now the East Rother) have altered considerably through silting and through shrinkage of the river as a result of clearing the Weald. The river now reaches the sea at Rye, farther south.

10. *fenne:* part of Romney Marsh, between Rye and Appledore.

12. *Hæsten:* a Viking leader who had been active on the Continent since 866.

Temese: River Thames.

13. *Middletune:* Milton Royal, near Sittingbourne, Kent.

14. *Apuldre:* the old bed of the Lympne (which was used in the construction of the Military Canal) passed Appledore.

16. *geweorc:* probably the winter camp at Louvain.

Norþhymbre ond East-Engle: the Danes settled in Northumbria and East Anglia, who continue to make Alfred's campaigns against the Danish invading armies more difficult throughout this extract.

18. *þa oþre hergas:* the two invading armies. Note that *here* is the term used in the Alfredian *Chronicle* for a Danish army, *fyrd* for an English army.

20–3. Alfred's placing himself between the great army at Appledore (*wudufæsten*) and Hæsten's army at Milton (*wæterfæsten*) was an attempt to prevent the two armies uniting and cutting off eastern Kent. The *Chronicle* does not mention here that Alfred made a truce with Hæsten's army, which moved off to Benfleet on the south coast of Essex (cf. 33 *East-Seaxe* and 51–5, 61–4).

23. *hie:* the Great Army, plundering from Appledore.

26–8. *Hæfde se cyning . . . scolden:* Alfred has divided his forces into two so that half can always remain at home, keeping up the cultivation of the land, while half is in continuous military service.

28. *þa burga:* the system of forts laid out by Alfred in the years preceding the Danish invasions. Each fortification was linked to a certain district, and the district was responsible for maintaining and manning it. The forts are listed in the early-eleventh-century *Burghal Hidage*, and are discussed in Hodgkin II, 585 ff.

33. *in on East-Seaxe ongean þa scipu:* the Great Army has moved west and north in an attempt to reunite with Hæsten at Benfleet. They had apparently sent their ships to Essex earlier.

34. *Fearnhamme:* Farnham, Surrey. They were defeated by part of the *fyrd* under Alfred's son Edward, and were driven north over the Thames and up the Colne (Hertfordshire).

36. *iggað:* Thorney Island, near Iver, Bucks.

39. *scire:* a military, not territorial, division.

41. *sæton þær behindan:* 'remained behind' despite the fact that the siege was lifted because of bad co-ordination between the divisions of the *fyrd*. Their eventual move to Benfleet is referred to in 51–2.

cyning: the identity of this commander is not known.

42–6. *þa gegaderedon . . . Exancester:* an extremely successful diversion from the Danelaw, two apparently simultaneous attacks in the west preventing Alfred from keeping up the attack on the Great Army, which is allowed to proceed to Benfleet.

44, 46. *ymbutan:* 'around the coast'.

45. *Norþsæ:* Bristol Channel.

46. *Exancester:* Exeter.

47–8. *buton . . . folces:* 'except for a very small part of the people, who remained in the east'.

49. *hie:* Edward and Æthelred, alderman of Mercia, who was co-operating with Edward on this series of engagements.

51–68. The narration is here made difficult by the fact that the chronicler is at the same time telling of the defeat of the Great Army at Hæsten's camp at Benfleet, and explaining how Hæsten came to be at Benfleet, and why leniency was shown to his family.

52. *se micla here:* that is to say, the remainder of the army which had been defeated at Farnham and allowed to escape at Thorney.

58. *þa scipu:* Hæsten's ships.

59. *Hrofesceastre:* Rochester.

61. *Æðeredes = Æðelredes.*

64. *hie:* Hæsten and his men; Hæsten had broken the truce which involved his family's baptism.

66. *cumpæder:* Earle's note is helpful: 'The Latin "compater", which probably at this date was still understood in its etymological sense, of the relation subsisting between two men who were godfathers to the same child, or between a godfather and the natural father.' (As here.)

71. *þa eodon hie to hiora scipum:* the army from the Danelaw on the way home engages in raids along the south coast.

72. *þa hergas:* the defeated Great Army and Hæsten's army.

73. *Sceobyrig:* Shoebury, Essex (east of Benfleet).

76. *gedydon æt:* 'arrived at'.

Sæferne: River Severn.

77. *Æþelm . . . Æþelnoþ:* aldermen of Wiltshire and Somerset.

79. *Pedredan:* River Parret, Somerset.

Sealwuda: Selwood, Somerset.

81. *Norðwealcynnes:* the Welsh, as distinct from the Westwalas, Cornish.

82. *Buttingtune:* either Buttington near Welshpool (Montgomery) or Buttington Tump near Chepstow (Monmouthshire), where the Wye joins the Severn Estuary. The latter is preferred by Wyatt, Plummer and Smith (in his notes), who takes the phrase about 'both sides of the river' to refer to the Wye. (Smith's glossary entry 'Buttington Tump (Montgomery)' confuses the issue.) Hodgkin (p. 665), Sweet-Onions (13th ed., p. 206) and Stenton (p. 264 and fn. 2) favour Buttington near Welshpool. If the Welshpool identification is correct, this is consistent with the direction taken in the Danes' two subsequent raids towards the north-west along the boundary

of the Danelaw (see Hodgkin's map, p. 664). N.B. *'up be Sæferne'*, implying motion towards the source, i.e. in the direction of Welshpool.

85. *hie:* the Danes.

88. *Cristnan:* the opposition between 'Christians' (English) and 'heathens' (Danes) is observed in this section of the *Chronicle.*

89. *cyninges þegn:* a personal servant of the king, and therefore a man of some rank.

92–6. Another remarkable journey by the Danes across country, this time to Chester. The next sentence acknowledges the Danish superiority in this sort of manœuvre.

95–6. *anre westre ceastre . . . seo is Legaceaster gehaten: Legaceaster* is derived from *Legionis castra,* 'city of the legion' (the Twentieth Legion). Its desolation probably dated from the Battle of Chester in about 616, when Ethelfrith of Northumbria defeated a British army and massacred 1,200 monks.

97–100. The deliberate destruction of the crops around Chester to starve out the Danes was a unique and desperate action. Note, however, that this succeeds only in driving the Danes out, not defeating them: their superior speed across country allows them to escape.

109. *Meresig:* Mersea Island, off the coast of Essex south of Colchester.

111. *Cisseceastre:* Chichester.

114. *Lygan:* River Lea, Herts.

128. *Cwatbrycge:* Bridgenorth, Shropshire. Earle pointed out the existence of Quat and Quatford slightly to the south; Hodgkin gives 'Quatford' for *Cwatbrycg.*

138. *foron to Sigene:* the departure of this part of the Danish host to the River Seine marks the end of this particular set of campaigns.

138–9. *Næfde se here . . . gebrocod:* this rare passionate outburst by the chronicler testifies to the strain and terror of these wars. The Danes had had the initiative throughout, as the *Chronicle* itself acknowledges.

145. *æt Dorceceastre:* Plummer suggests that the pronoun *æt* rather than *on* may be accounted for by the removal of the see of Leicester to Dorchester in consequence of the Danish raids: that Ealhheard was only residing at Dorchester, not Bishop of Dorchester.

151 ff. On the construction of this fleet, see Hodgkin, II, 583–5. He comments: 'So far as we know, it was Alfred who first showed the Scandinavian nations that they could be beaten in the art of shipbuilding, in which for some centuries they had had the lead.'

157. *Wiht:* the Isle of Wight.

159–60. *þone muðan:* Wyatt, *Anglo-Saxon Reader,* p. 206, suggests Poole Harbour as the scene of this battle; Southampton Water has also been suggested. On this encounter, see the article by Magoun cited in the Bibliography.

160. *foron hie:* i.e. the Danes. (Notice the ambiguity of pronouns here, as in extract 1.)

161. *ufeweardum:* the upper, i.e. north, end of the harbour.

on drygum: beached, because the crews had gone ashore raiding.

172. *Friesa:* Frisians, famous as sailors, were used by Alfred to sail his new warships (although these particular names look English); one is reminded that he had also to import Continental scholars to supply another deficiency in England.

3. A PORTRAIT OF WILLIAM THE CONQUEROR

1–9. Note the conventional didactic sentiments and cf. the ending, 91–3. William's death is used as an *exemplum* of one of the most frequently expressed arguments in medieval didactic literature: even great men die, because of the mutability of the world; no man should consider himself immune from death, and everyone should therefore prepare himself for it.

2. *Seo:* note inconsistency of gender; cf. *Se* l. 1.

3. *nextan dæg æfter Natiuitas Sancte Marie:* September 9.

4. *Capum:* Caen.

12. *we* requires *willað* or (subj.) *willen;* the singular form is consistent with the use of *we* for *ic.*

12–13. This profession of direct knowledge (true or not) is rare in the *Chronicle.*

15. *ænig his foregenga:* 'any predecessor of his' not 'any of his predecessors'.

15–17. *He was . . . his willan:* note the rhetorical balance in this sentence, common enough in the later homilies, and becoming increasingly common in the *Chronicle* in the eleventh century. The style reflects the author's intention to give a balanced account.

18. *mære mynster:* Battle Abbey.

20. *mære mynster on Cantwarbyrig:* the rebuilding of the ruined Canterbury Cathedral by Lanfranc, on the model of St-Étienne de Caen, mentioned in l. 4.

22. *Sanctes Benedictus regule:* the Benedictine Rule had in fact provided the basis for the revival of monasticism in the tenth and eleventh centuries.

23–4. *ælc man . . . wolde:* Miss Tucker translates 'each man who wished followed out whatever concerned his order'; Professor Garmonsway 'every man who wished to, whatever considerations there might be with regard to his rank, could follow the profession of a monk'.

25. *bær his cynehelm:* William's institution of 'crown-wearing' was a lavish ceremonial associated with a full assembly of his Court on major Church festivals.

27. *Gleaweceastre:* Gloucester. It was at one of these 'crown-wearings', at Gloucester at Christmas, 1085, that the Domesday survey was planned.

29. *cnihtas:* 'knights' rather than the earlier OE 'boys'. The knight was originally a household retainer engaged for protection; after the Conquest knights were a class of aristocratic landowners or retainers with some specialised military obligations.

34. *ne sparode his agene broðor, Odo het:* Odo's arrest is noted under the annal for 1082. The chronicler has less sympathy for him in the annal for 1088, when he reports his revolt. Ordericus Vitalis (*English Historical Documents*, II, 288–9) reports at length William's death-bed attitude to Odo, and his unwillingness to release him while he was freeing his other prisoners.

35. *Baius:* Bayeux.

36. *eorldom:* the earldom of Kent.

40–1. *an man . . . ungederad:* Plummer rightly comments that this 'is traditional and proverbial', Cf. Peterborough Chronicle, 1135, 12–13 (of Henry I), and other parallels quoted by Miss Clark, p. 71.

44. *þa limu:* castration was not an unusual penalty. William's decree to this effect is found in F. Liebermann, *Gesetze der Angelsachsen*, I, 504.

47. *his gewrit:* Domesday Book; cf. the annal for 1085.

48. *Brytland:* Wales. William did not 'conquer' Wales; but after the establishment of powerful earldoms on the border there was gradual penetration into that area during his reign.

casteles: the construction of castles, an invaluable policy for the Normans, was often viewed by the chroniclers as an act of oppression. Cf. 56–7 and the annals for 1051 and 1137.

51. *Mans:* Maine, conquered by William in 1063.

67. *deorfriδ:* possibly the New Forest.

84. *his sehta:* 'peace with him', 'his favour'.

88. 'And consider himself [to be] above all men.'

92. *forleon:* 'avoid', 'eschew'; a mistake for *forlætan* or *forfleon?*

4. ALFRED'S PREFACE TO THE PASTORAL CARE

1 ff. *Ic* is to be supplied in the second clause. Sweet notes that the change of person seems to have been frequent in prefaces and dedications, and instances Ælfric's preface to his translation of the Heptateuch: Ælfric munuc gret Æðelweard ealdormann eadmodlice. Ðu bæde me leof ðæt ic sceolde ðe awendan of Ledene ða boc Genesis.

Wærferð: Bishop of Worcester from 873, a helper of Alfred and translator for him of Gregory's *Dialogues*.

14. *Humbre:* River Humber.

18–19. *Gode . . . lareowa:* presumably a reference to the imported clerics.

25. *lufodon:* the other MSS have *hæfdon*, and this form is usually preferred, *lufodon* being explained as a slip following *lufodon* in the previous lines. I have preserved the MS reading, as in fact it makes good sense.

28. *forhergod . . . ond forbærned:* a reference to the Danish invasions and plundering. The most notorious sacking of churches took place at Lindisfarne and Jarrow in 793–4.

30. *swiðe . . . wiston:* 'had very little use for the books'.

45. *Ebriscgeðiode:* Hebrew.

46. *Creacas:* Greeks.

47. *Lædenware:* Romans.

58. *Lædengeðiode:* Latin (language).

65. *Plegmunde:* Plegmund was, like Wærferð, a Mercian; Alfred made him Archbishop of Canterbury in 890.

66. *Assere:* Alfred's biographer, a Welshman from St. David's who joined Alfred about 885 and was created Bishop of Sherborne.

Grimbolde: an old scholar whom Alfred had obtained from Fulco, Archbishop of Rheims; he had lived for many years at the monastery of St. Bertin, near St. Omer. He was placed in charge of the New Minster at Winchester after Alfred's death.

67. *Iohanne:* John the Old Saxon had been brought over to be set in charge of a rather unsuccessful community of monks, largely from Gaul, which Alfred established at Athelney.

68. *hie:* i.e. the book.

71. *æstel:* This word occurs only here and in Ælfric's *Glossary*, where it glosses *indicatorium*. The precise function of this object is not known, but the translation 'book-mark' is usually suggested. The famous 'Alfred Jewel' may provide corroboration. This is a small oval gold and enamel jewel bearing the inscription (in OE) 'Alfred had me made.' It has a socket at the base

which could have held a quill to be used as a pointer for following the lines in the manuscript. The jewel was discovered at Newton Park, four miles north-west of Athelney. But other derivations and explanations have been offered.

mancessan: the mancus was a coin worth thirty pence, so the *æstel* was of considerable value.

5. BEDE'S ACCOUNT OF THE POET CÆDMON

1. *abbudissan:* Hild, Abbess of Whitby 658–80.

10. *Ongelþeode:* England.

14–15. *ac efne þa an þa þe:* 'but just those alone which . . . '

15. *þa æfestan tungan:* Sweet emends *þa* to *þære* because *gedafenode* would usually demand a dative. Bede's Latin has the accusative *religiosam . . . linguam,* and the accusative *þa* is doubtless due to this. The translator often follows the Latin 'slavishly' as Sweet puts it.

18. *gelyfedre yldo:* Cædmon's exact age is not known.

19. *intinga:* the Latin is *laetitiae causa decretum;* the translator has misinterpreted *causa* as nominative.

25–6. *him . . . æt:* 'by him'.

31. *Sing me frumsceaft:* 'Sing to me about the Creation.'

35–43. Cædmon's *Hymn.* Seventeen copies of this poem survive, of which four are in the Northumbrian dialect and thirteen (including this one, of course) West Saxon: this very considerable number accords well with Bede's account of Cædmon's popularity and the veneration he enjoyed. The technique of the poem is notable, with its fully developed lexical variation and repetition. (Note especially the profusion of alternative terms for God.) It is composed almost entirely of formulae—conventional phrases shared by many poets which occur time and again in different poems—each roughly one half-line in length.

39. *eorðan bearnum:* there is another group of MSS which has *ælda barnum* 'sons of men'.

45–6. *þæm wordum . . . togeþeodde:* again, the influence of the Latin is seen here in the word-order and inflexions: *eis mox plura in eundem modum verba Deo digni carminis adjunxit.*

50. *him andweardum:* 'in their presence'.

69 ff. This list of Cædmon's works has been the basis for the suggestion that the closely corresponding contents of MS Junius XI are the work of Cædmon.

84. *fægere ende:* most of the remainder of the story of Cædmon, omitted here, is concerned with his death.

6. THE VOYAGES OF OHTHERE AND WULFSTAN

[It is assumed that readers will use a map—for example Malone's, *Speculum* v, 1930, 166–7—while following these voyages.]

2–3. *He cwæð . . . Westsæ:* in l. 73 his home is located in the district of Halgoland (modern Helgeland); it is usually said to be in the region of Malangen Fjord: more precise guesses (e.g. Austein, Senja) are difficult to corroborate.

3. *Westsæ:* i.e. the North Sea, from the viewpoint of Norway.

5. *Finnas:* Lapps.

9. *norþryhte:* few of Alfred's terms of direction make sense if taken literally. In this case, for example, Ohthere could not have sailed 'due north along the coast' because the coast of Norway extends Northeast. Several attempts have been made to explain Alfred's error, the most famous being Kemp Malone's proposal of a 45° shift in Alfred's terms of direction. In fact, the error is not consistent enough to support such a proposal, and it is best to assume that the terms are just being used imprecisely.

10. *steorbord . . . bæcbord:* starboard was the right side of the boat, from which the steering oar projected; *bæcbord* the left (port) side, behind the back of the steersman.

13 ff. *gesiglan:* note the distinction between this, 'reach by sailing' and *siglan* 'sail', 'be in the process of sailing'.

13. *Þa beag . . .:* this point is the North Cape, or somewhat to the east of it.

16. *ðær:* probably at Cape Sazonova, on the east of the Kola Peninsula. Ohthere is about to sail along the east coast of the White Sea.

19. *an micel ea:* the River Varzuga.

25. *Beormas* = ON Bjarmar. The existence of 'Bjarmaland' is well attested in ON writings, although they often locate it around the River Dvina (on the east of the White Sea, meeting it at Archangel). Ross ('The *Terfinnas* and *Beormas* of Ohthere') supposes that there were two groups of *Beormas* (= Karelians, according to him), one around the Dvina, and a western branch near the *Terfinnas* on Kandalaks Bay, identified only by Ohthere.

27. *Terfinna land:* Ross on place-name evidence identifies the *Terfinnas* as a group of Lapps particularly associated with the Kola Peninsula.

31–2. *Þa Finnas . . . an geþeode:* both Finno-Ugrian languages. See Ross, op. cit., pp. 48–51.

33. *horschwælum:* i.e. 'horse-whales'. The modern 'walrus' is the same word with the components reversed.

40. *þe . . . beoð:* 'in which their riches consist'.

41. *wildrum:* a contraction of *wild* + *deor.*

42. *hranas:* ON *hreinir* (which gives the root of Modern English 'reindeer'). The regular vowel-alternation has been supplied in this loan-word (cf. OE *stan,* ON *steinn*).

53–4. *ægþer . . . sioles:* 'each must be sixty ells long, one made of whaleskin, the other of seal (skin)'.

56. *his:* 'of it'. 'Every part of it which can either be grazed or ploughed . . . .'

58. *moras:* 'mountains' (as often in OE), not 'moors'.

59. *eastweard:* 'in the south'. Malone argues that this refers to the land in relation to the Skagerak, in Ohthere's view part of the *Austmarr* (East Sea, i.e. Baltic).

67. *Sweoland:* Sweden.

68. *Cwena land:* Ross (*Ohthere's 'Cwenas and Lakes'*, p. 338) says of the *Cwenas:* 'They were . . . Northern Finns and were certainly widespread over North Norway and North Sweden in Ohthere's time.' Ross reconstructs a journey from Lake Torne to Malangen Fjord which may well have been followed by the *Cwenas* on raids to the region of Ohthere's home.

72. *swyðe lytle scypa and swyðe leohte:* kayaks?

75. *Sciringes heal:* a port on Oslo Fjord.

78. *Iraland:* Ireland or Iceland? Iceland fits the description better; but Malone argues for Ireland (the assumed 45° shift would 'expose' Ireland),

Craigie for Iceland. Alfred calls Ireland *Scotland* or *Ibernia* elsewhere in the *Orosius*, and Iceland *Thila*.

79. *ða igland:* Hebrides, Man, etc.

þissum lande: England.

81. *Norðweg:* Norway.

81–2. *swyðe mycel sæ:* the Skagerak.

83. *Gotland:* Jutland.

Sillende: Holstein.

85–6. *æt Hæþum:* Hedeby, now Slesvig. Sweet's note (*Reader*, 13th ed., p. 200) identifies *æt* as a primitive place-name element.

86. *Winedum:* Wends, occupying the area fronting the south of the Baltic.

88. *Denamearc:* by this Ohthere presumably means the North Danish kingdom in the southern part of what is now Sweden.

94. *Wulfstan:* an Englishman, according to Sir William Craigie.

Truso: a town on the Frisches Haff (*Estmere*, 105).

97. *Langaland, Læland, Falster, Sconeg:* Danish islands—Langeland, Laaland and Falster—and Skaane, a territory of the Northern Danes on the south-eastern tip of the Scandinavian peninsula.

98. *Burgenda land:* the island of Bornholm.

100. *Blecingaeg:* Blekinge, Sweden.

101. *Eowland, Gotland:* Öland and Gotland, large islands considerably to the north of Wulfstan's course.

102. *Wislemuðan:* the delta of the Vistula; for a map, see Malone, *Speculum*, v (1931), facing p. 162.

104. *Estum:* Esthonians.

106. *Ilfing:* River Elbing.

108–9. *And þonne . . . hire naman:* 'And at that point the Vistula deprives the Elbing of its name'; i.e. the Elbing loses its identity by merging with the greater river.

119. *swa micle lencg swa hi maran speda habbað:* 'As much longer as they have greater wealth' or 'longer, in proportion to the amount of their wealth'.

126 ff. *Alecgað . . . :* Sweet (*Reader*, p. 201) reproduces from Bosworth a charming diagram explaining the principle of these races.

142. *þæt þær sceal ælces geðeodes man beon forbærned:* 'that, in that country, men, whatever their tribe, be cremated'.

7. APOLLONIUS OF TYRE

1. *se cyning:* Arcestrates, King of Cyrene, chief city of Cyrenaica in Libya.

2. *dohtor:* Arcestrate.

7–8. *on ðam plegan:* Apollonius' entertainment of Arcestrates in the gymnasium is recorded in the preceding scene.

13. *sege me . . . arece me:* note the rhetorical variation in word-order in these two clauses.

20–2. *Leofe . . . sar:* Goolden quotes a Vergilian echo, *Aeneid*, ii, 3: *Infandum, regina, iubes renovare dolorem.*

37. *gefeol:* translates *incidit*; she 'fell' into the skill of harping, without formal instruction.

44. *Apollines:* Apollo.

50. *plegode:* the erasure in the MS (brought about by clerical anti-drama zeal?) and the imprecise paraphrase conceal the exact nature of Apollonius'

performance. The Latin indicates that he was miming: . . . *deponens liram induit statum comicum et inauditas actiones expressit. Deinde induit se tragicum.*

54–5. *gefeol . . . on . . . lufe:* the first instance of the English idiom 'fall in love'.

59. *Lareow:* Arcestrate anticipates Apollonius' future function.

64. *bure:* usually in OE 'private room', 'bedroom'. Here it translates *triclinium* ('dining-room'), not *cubiculum* as elsewhere. Obviously the public room is meant here.

65. *ðe hig gesawon:* 'who saw it'.

66. *þe:* a rare late OE form of the definite article.

76. *cuman:* 'may come'.

87. *cuman:* N.B. that this is a noun.

88. *pearle:* most often used to intensify unpleasant adjectives.

94 ff. Note the tone of gently implied humour in this scene.

96. *ceastre stræte:* both are loan-words from Latin.

107. *morgengife:* a gift made by the husband to the wife on the morning after the wedding.

111. *swa:* 'if'.

115. *hwi gæst ðu ana:* the girl is surprised that Apollonius enters her bedroom alone.

  næs git yfel wif: Goolden explains *næs* as derived from *ne + ealles* (as 8/30), not *ne + wæs*, and paraphrases 'mistress, not yet a bad woman' (i.e., still innocent).

131. *þurh weax:* i.e. 'in writing'.

137. *Se oðer:* 'One of the others'.

8. THE END OF THE WORLD

1–2. *geseon . . . oncnawan . . . ongeotan:* note the tautologous parallelism (here and throughout the sermon), a constant feature of the late homilies.

7–8. *worldricra . . . wære:* 'the death of prosperous men whose life was dear to men . . .'; an awkward construction which illustrates the incompleteness of the relative pronoun system of this time.

20. *myngige and manige manna gehwylcne:* alliteration arranged very much like that of OE verse.

22. *Syn:* 'let us be'. The exhortations which follow are conventional to OE homilies and legal codes.

24. *gepwærnesse . . . habban:* cf. 9/176–7.

30. *næs na þa anum þe:* 'not just those who . . .'

35–8. *ne beo . . . to:* for the formula, cf. 16/66–9.

48–9. *growan and blowan:* note the rhyme.

55. *þis is se rihta geleafa:* it is, of course, a series of echoes of the Creed, the learning of which was much advocated by Anglo-Saxon homilists and ecclesiastical legislators.

66 ff. *Geseo . . . .:* here the theme of *contemptus mundi* is introduced.

74. *Nis þæt nan wundor:* cf. 9/114.

  hwæt biþ . . . .: rhetorical questions inviting disdain and disgust at the impermanence of the body and of the world are standard in the expression of this theme.

76 ff. *Hwær beoþ . . . .:* the *ubi sunt* formula, found also in 16/92–3.

9. WULFSTAN'S ADDRESS TO THE ENGLISH

1–2. *hit nealæcð þam ende:* Wulfstan was much concerned about the end of the world and the advent of Antichrist. His early homilies are eschatological, and in the present one he suggests that contemporary devastation and anarchy (largely a result of the prolonged onslaughts of the Danes) are signs of the reign of Antichrist. Although no English source mentions A.D. 1000 as the date of the end of the world, many writings suggest that popular feeling was high in this period, and continued to be so in the eleventh century.

10. *unlaga:* 'violations' or 'abuses of law', not 'bad laws'.

15–16. *godiende weorðan:* a rare construction, presumably meaning 'begin to get better'.

19. *Godes gerihta:* most of the legislation drawn up by Wulfstan insists on the payment of church dues, presumably withheld on account of the oppressions of the Danes.

20 ff. *On hæþenum þeodum . . . .:* frequently Wulfstan displays a keen consciousness of the distinction between paganism and Christianity; see further, note to 119–20 *hæþene unsida.*

24–5. *we habbað . . . berypte:* not a reference to the Danes' plundering of churches, but to enforced use of church treasures to pay off the invaders.

34–5. *on unriht:* 'wrongly (in the eyes of the Church)'—perhaps by being forced to marry within the first year of widowhood, such marriage being frowned on by the Church.

36–7. *ut . . . gesealde:* a reference to the slave-trade, condemned especially where Christians were sent to non-Christian countries.

37. *swyþe unforworhte:* 'even though quite innocent'. Wulfstan acknowledges, without condoning it, the (illicit) practice of sending criminals into slavery.

39. *freoriht fornumene:* curtailment of the rights of freemen was yet another result of the social upheavals caused by the Danish invasions.

þrælriht genyrwde: one of the principal rights of slaves, which might wel be interfered with, was the right to keep their earnings gained on certain days stipulated by law.

46 ff. *here and hunger . . . :* the first example in this homily of the word-lists so frequent in Wulfstan.

48. *stric:* a word peculiar to Wulfstan, meaning either 'plague' (suggested by the context and by a gloss *sekenes* in one MS), or 'sedition' (*gestric* glosses *seditionem* in *Leechdoms*).

49. *ungylda:* a reference to the heavy taxation necessary to pay the Danegeld. The *Chronicle* makes special mention of the large amounts paid to the Danes in 991, 994, 1002, 1007 (when £30,000 was paid) and 1014.

50. *unwedera:* note especially the reference to famine in *Chronicle* 1005 ('the great famine throughout England, such that no man ever remembered one so cruel') and to flood in 1014.

55. *regollice:* i.e. according to the Rule of his monastic order or the obligations of his priesthood.

worhtan: supply *we.*

62. *hlafordswican manege:* as Professor Whitelock says, 'the frequency of references to treachery is one of the most striking features of this period'. She lists a number of examples of conspiracy and treachery.

66. *Eadweard:* Edward the Martyr, Edgar's eldest son and Ethelred's half-

brother, who was murdered at Corfe on March 18, 978 or 979, probably at the instigation of Ethelred, 'under circumstances of abominable treachery' (Stenton, *Anglo-Saxon England*, p. 368). Only Wulfstan says that his body was subsequently burned; other authorities record that it was buried at Wareham and later transferred to Shaftesbury.

67. *Æpelred:* Ethelred was expelled after Christmas 1013. If we believe that this reference was part of the original (it is omitted in three MSS) it is thus important for setting the earliest date at which the homily could have been written.

69–70. *and ealles to mænege . . . gelogode:* this could be just a reference to unsuitable admissions to monasteries or, more specifically, to the occupation of monastic houses by secular clerks, an infringement of monastic discipline severely condemned by contemporary reformers.

75. *sceotað togædere:* 'club together' as Professor Whitelock suggests.

78, 80. *wið weorðe:* 'for a price'.

92–3. *and gif . . . þegengylde:* Professor Whitelock comments: 'Apparently the grievance here is the exaction by the Danes of the same price even when the slain man was a deserting slave.' The wergeld of a thane was £25, the price of a slave £1.

94–5. *fela ungelimpa gelimpð:* near-puns are found occasionally in Wulfstan's works.

119–20. *hæþene unsida:* Wulfstan's writings, like others in the period, are full of condemnations of paganism, often credibly particularised. It is uncertain whether the strain of the Danish invasions caused a reversion to paganism in this period, so long after the Conversion. Most probably the moralists refer to unorganised superstition of a sort which is widely evidenced in OE literature.

121. *hadbrycas:* not 'violation of holy orders' but 'attacks on persons in holy orders'.

122. *siblegeru:* marriage within the prohibited degrees, not 'incest' as defined today.

125. *freolsbrycas and fæstenbrycas:* both secular and ecclesiastical regulations are insistent on the keeping of Church festivals.

126. *apostatan:* a word peculiar to Wulfstan.

141. *bec:* the penitentials, an important body of English and Continental works in the late OE period.

147. *wælcyrian:* the Valkyries of Norse mythology were supernatural women who collected the slain from the battlefield. The normal use of the derived word in OE is as a gloss to the names of roughly comparable mythological figures (e.g. Furies, Bellona). Wulfstan presumably means a kind of witch. But no real distinction between *wiccan and wælcyrian* may be intended; the second word may have been selected because of the demands of the rhythm and alliteration.

158. *Gildas:* sixth-century author of the *Liber Querulus de Excidio Britanniae*, a book which contains one of the earliest accounts of the Germanic invasion of Britain; but its value as historical record is vitiated by the violence of his argument that the invasion was God's judgement on the sins of the Britons. Before Wulfstan, Alcuin had used a similar argument of the first series of Danish raids (late eighth century).

167 ff. *Ac wutan:* strings of constructions with *(w)utan* form frequent endings to Wulfstan's homilies.

10. ÆLFRIC'S LIFE OF KING OSWALD

1. *Augustinus:* Augustine's mission to Kent took place in 597.

2. *Oswold:* son of Æthelfrith of Bernicia.

Norðhymbra lande: the separate kingdoms of Deira and Bernicia were united by the Deiran Edwin on his defeat of Æthelfrith in 616.

3. *Se ferde . . . to Scotlande:* Oswald had lived in exile under Deiran rule, and had received Christianity from the monks of Iona.

5. *Eadwine:* a powerful king, but defeated and killed by Cadwallon, the Christian king of Gwynedd, at Hatfield Chase in 632.

7. *æftergengan:* after Edwin's death Northumbria split up again into Deira and Bernicia, ruled by Edwin's cousin Osric and Eanfrith, Oswald's brother, respectively. Both were killed by Cadwallon.

10 ff. Oswald defeated and killed Cadwallon in 633 at Rowley Burn, south of Hexham, and succeeded to the throne of the whole of Northumbria.

24. *Bede:* Bede's account, on which Ælfric's version is based, occurs in *Ecclesiastical History,* III, 1–13.

Sum man: identified by Bede as one Bothelm, a monk of Hexham.

35. *Scotland:* i.e. Iona.

39. *Aidan:* he and his followers settled on Lindisfarne.

75-8. *Oswoldes . . . wurðode:* Bede, perhaps exaggerating through his admiration of Oswald as a Christian king, is the authority for this statement.

79. *Eferwic:* York.

86 ff. The conversion of Cyngyls of Wessex is dated 635 by the *Chronicle.*

89. *papan:* Pope Honorius I.

94-5. *Oswold . . . wæs cumen to Cynegylse:* his visit to Cynegyls at this time concerned his impending marriage to a daughter of the West Saxon king.

97. *Dorcanceaster:* Dorchester-on-Thames, Oxon.

100. *Hædde:* Bishop of Winchester from 676.

102. *Ealdanmynstre:* so called to distinguish it from Edward's New Minster.

105. *ofslagen:* on August 5, 641.

110. *Maserfelda:* not certainly identified; Oswestry is one suggestion.

118. *Oswig:* Oswiu actually ruled Bernicia only, Deira falling to Oswine, son of Osric. In 654 Oswiu defeated and killed Penda and established himself as a powerful king.

125. *Bebbanbyrig:* Bamburgh.

126. *broðor dohtor:* Osthryth.

127. *Bardanige:* Bardney in Lindsey.

143. *Cuðberht:* the date of his birth is not known. He entered Melrose as a novice in 651 and died on March 20, 687.

144. *Aidanes sawle:* Aidan died in 651.

11. BEOWULF

5. *hie* is the object of *bregdan.*

10. *Godes yrre bær:* God's curse on Grendel as a member of Cain's tribe is mentioned in *Beowulf,* 104–8.

11. *manscaða* has the root *mān,* 'evil, wickedness'; not to be confused with *man(n),* 'man'.

14. *goldsele:* Heorot was both a place where gold was distributed and a hall decorated with gold.

24. *on fagne flor:* the floor of the hall was of many colours; possibly a recollection of Roman tessellated paving used as a floor when Anglo-Saxon halls were built over the ruins of Romano-British villas. The place-name Fawler comes from *fag flor;* at Fawler, Berks, Roman pavings were discovered.

35. *beheold:* 'waited to see'.

48. *wið earm gesæt:* Klaeber gives 'sat up supporting himself on his arm'; Wrenn 'sat right up violently (*gesæt* with perfective force) so as to drive back Grendel's arm (lit. *wið earm* = "against the arm")'. *He* is, of course, Beowulf.

50. *middangeardes:* adverbial genitive, 'in the world', as *sceata* 51.

53. *meahte:* verb of motion omitted.

58. *æfenspræce:* his boasting speech (*gylpworda sum*) of the evening before, *Beowulf* 677–87 (and 632–8). Cf. the *beot* of *Maldon.*

68. *ealuscerwen:* a much-discussed word which seems to have the same function as the related (derived?) *meoduscerwen* of *Andreas* 1526. In both cases a time of terror (a flood after feasting in *Andreas*) follows a period of joy, and the contrast is sharpened by an ironic metaphor recalling the pleasures of merry-making. The etymology of *ealuscerwen* is difficult to establish: *ealu-* most probably means 'ale' (and this is how the poet of *Andreas* evidently understood it), but it has been connected with ON *ǫl*, 'good luck.' If *ealu* = 'ale', then we must postulate a verb **scerwan* meaning the opposite of *bescerwan*, i.e. 'grant', 'allot'. If *ealu* = 'good luck' we must take **scerwan* as similar in meaning to *bescerwan*, i.e. 'deprive'. For fuller discussion, see the glossary to Wrenn's *Beowulf;* G. V. Smithers, *English and Germanic Studies,* iv (1951–2), 67 ff.

78. *hit:* the hall; but neither *sele* nor *heal(l)* is neuter.

80–1. *nympe . . . swapule:* an allusion to the burning of Heorot as a result of the feud between the Danes and the Heathobards. Cf. *Beowulf*, 81–5, 2024–69; *Widsith*, 45–9. Hroðgar attempted to settle this feud by marrying his daughter Freawaru to Ingeld, son of Froda, king of the Heathobards, who had been killed by the Danes; but the feud was revived.

82. *Norð-Denum:* cf. *East-Denum*, 128, *West-Denum*, 319; the variation seems to be attributable to nothing but the demands of the alliteration.

88–9. Quite closely paralleled in *Beowulf*, 196–7; the power of Beowulf's grip is constantly emphasised.

94. *eorl:* singular implying plural: '(each) noble'; note the compensating change of number in 96.

ealde lafe: excellent weapons are conventionally called 'old', acknowledging the fact that they were treasured heirlooms and handed down as such. Wrenn suggests that a reason for this reverence of ancient weapons was a decline in craftsmanship from the fourth to sixth centuries.

97. *þæt* is the object of *wiston* and the clause beginning *þone synscaðan* (100 ff.) is in apposition to *þæt.*

109. *myrðe:* see Glossary. This is only one possible interpretation. If *myrðe* is taken as a noun, the inflexion is uncertain—gen.pl. dependent on *fela* is a reasonable suggestion. But it could be a noun meaning 'mirth', *modes myrðe* (dat.) meaning 'light-heartedly', referring to Grendel's earlier state of mind when plundering. Wrenn suggests that it is an adjective, 'wicked'.

135. *under geapne hrof:* Beowulf places the arm under the vaulted roof over the entrance to the hall, where it could be seen by all, as a token of his victory.

136. *Ic:* Hroðgar is the speaker.

140, 142. *oðer . . . oðer:* 'one . . . the other'.

143. *wræclastas træd:* cf. 16/5.

148 ff. The account of the region occupied by Grendel and his mother is the most elaborate and evocative description in the poem. It has several parallels, but exact indebtedness and relations are difficult to work out. Echoes of *Æneid* VI have been proposed, but we cannot be sure of the *Beowulf*-poet's direct dependence. The ON *Grettissaga*, Ch. 66, may have some relation to this part of the narrative. Finally, certain elements are reminiscent of early medieval conceptions of the Christian Hell. A Latin *Vision of St. Paul* bears a clear though general resemblance (itself taking some details from Virgil). *Blickling Homily XVII*, perhaps remembering *Beowulf*, supplies the features of the northern wintry landscape wanting in its source, the *Vision of St. Paul.*

154. *hrinde bearwas:* cf. *Blickling Homily XVII hrimige bearwas . . ., on ðæm isgean bearwum.*

158. *þæt þone grund wite:* 'who knows the depth of it'.

170. *secg:* Wrenn notes that Grendel's mother is given (grammatically) masculine sex in several places, and suggests that '*qua* mother she is thought of as f., but *qua* demon as of either sex' (cf. 183, 185).

173. *wundnum:* several editors read *wundini* and identify this as an archaic instrumental form of *wunden*. Such an inflexion could be dated not later than the middle of the eighth century, and thus, if accepted as a 'fossilised' relic of an earlier stage of the poem, would be important for dating the work.

177–80. Cf. 17/68–80.

196–7. *magoþegna . . . þone selestan:* Æschere, Hroðgar's dearest retainer, carried off by Grendel's mother in revenge for the death of her son.

201. The line appears verbatim as l. 58 of *Exodus*, a poem whose earliest stage of composition may have come before *Beowulf.* Other possible parallels to 200–2 are the Vulgate Exodus xiii, 18, 20, and *Æneid*, XI, 522 ff.

220. *sorhfulne:* their journey is 'grievous' in that they cause trouble to passing ships.

221. *hruron:* 'sank'—rushed to the bottom to escape.

231. *wægbora:* the word appears here only, and is of uncertain meaning. *Wæg-* 'wave' is clear; *-bora* has been connected with *beran*, 'bear', and *borian*, 'pierce.' Meanings suggested include 'wave-roamer, -traveller, -traverser, -piercer, -disturber', 'offspring of the waves'.

233. *þæm wordum:* Beowulf's speech to Hroðgar, omitted here.

236. *hwil dæges:* 'a good part of the day'.

238. *se ðe:* Grendel's mother.

249. *no he þæs modig wæs:* 'however brave he was' (literally 'not at all was he brave to that extent').

264. *beadoleoma:* a genuine totally periphrastic kenning of the ON type.

275ᵇ–7. For another example of the tendency of OE epic to break off to insert moral comment, see 14/52–4.

284–5. As *feþecempa* and *werigmod* evidently refer to Beowulf, *oferwearp* must have an intransitive sense, 'fall over', 'stumble'.

291. *Hæfde:* 'would have'.

298. *on:* 'among'.

299. *eotenisc*, 303. *giganta geweorc:* cf. *enta ærgeweorc, Beowulf*, 1679, *ealdsweord etonisc, Beowulf*, 2616, *eald enta geweorc*, 16/87 and note. Wrenn comments, 'Things belonging to a more skilled age or an older civilisation no longer comprehended, were so thought of in OE poetry, as in other ancient literature.'

312–13. *efne . . . candel:* one of the very few similes of OE poetry. Another occurs 349 ff.

326. *to ðæs þe:* 'when'.

330. *he* is Grendel; the implied subject of *becearf*, Beowulf.

339–40. *þa . . . hæfde:* 'Then it seemed to many that the she-wolf of the lake had killed him.'

341. *non dæges:* the ninth hour of the day, or 3 p.m. From the ecclesiastical *nona hora*, the Church office of None; this is the first recorded secular usage of the term.

343. *goldwine gumena:* Hroðgar.
  gistas: Beowulf's party.

345. *wiston:* see Glossary *wiscan*.

350. *forstes bend:* cf. *Wanderer* 24 and note.

358. *ættren:* Wrenn suggests 'so venomous', making the adj. parallel to *to þæs hat* of the previous line.

363. *þas lænan gesceaft:* a conventional reference to mutability, automatic by its alliteration but hardly appropriate in this context, for neither a tone of regret nor an invocation of transience is apt to Grendel's passing.

365. *ða aglæcean:* Beowulf and the dragon.

369 ff. With the cowardice of these followers of Beowulf, cf. the disloyalty of the sons of Odda in *Maldon* 185 ff.

376. *Scylfinga:* a name for the Swedish royal family. See further, next note.

384 ff. Eanmund was the nephew of the Swedish king Onela, who had seized the throne after the death of his brother Oht(h)ere (Eanmund's father). Weohstan killed Eanmund and was rewarded by Onela with the gift of Eanmund's weapons. At this time the Geats had been sheltering Eanmund. The Geats' motive in harbouring the grandson of their old enemy Ongenþeow, the good relations between Weohstan and his son and Beowulf, and the relationship between Wiglaf and Beowulf implied by the linking name *Wægmundingas* remain doubtful.

386. *wræccan wineleasum:* refers to Eanmund's exile among the Geats; cf. *Resignation* 45 *wineleas wræcca.*

387. *his:* Eanmund's.
  magum: refers to Onela.

392. *his broðor bearn:* Eanmund.

406–33. With the sentiments of this speech by Wiglaf compare the many invocations of the spirit of the *comitatus* in *Maldon*, especially 212 ff.

411. *on:* Klaeber gives 'from among'.

422. *hyt:* as this word takes main stress it is much more likely to be a noun 'heat' than a pronoun; (although, if it is taken as a pronoun, the translation 'as long as it lasts' is quite acceptable).

426–9. Cf. *Maldon*, 220–3, 246–53.

441. *fullæstu:* the inflexion is an early Anglian form; cf. *hafo*, 2150, *hafu*, 2523.

446. *bord wið rond: rond* often means just 'shield', but here it has a more particular sense. The half-line probably means '(with waves of flame he

completely burned) the shield (*bord*) as far as its boss (*rond*)'. 'Metal rim/ border' has also been proposed: '. . . the shield right down to its rim'.

448. *his mæges scyld:* Beowulf has had a metal shield made (*eallirenne . . . wigbord wrætlic*, 2338–9).

460. *wundrum heard:* note that the MS reads *wundum;* all editors except von Schaubert and, following her, Wrenn, emend as I have done. The very plausible justification for retaining *wundum* rests on *Beowulf,* 1459–60:

> ecg wæs iren,   atertanum fah,
> *ahyrded heaþoswate*

'hardened by the blood of battle'. This is presumably a pseudo-chemical rationalisation of the belief that a sword gained excellence through its prowess in earlier combats.

470–2. Translate: 'He did not care for (i.e. aim at) the head, but the brave man's hand was burnt when, helping his kinsman, he struck the evil foe somewhat lower down.'

479. *ferh ellen wræc:* 'strength drove out life'.

481. *secg:* the poet has Wiglaf and other young warriors in mind, presumably.

491. *stanbogan:* note that the dragon's lair is a stone structure, not just a hole in the ground.

527. *hringnet beran:* a characteristic circumlocution for 'went'; but it suggests a state of armed readiness on entering the dragon's den.

533. *uhtflogan:* the dragon is described in 2271 as *uhtsceaða*; on the possible connotations of the first element of these compounds see note to *Wanderer* 8[b] *uhtna gehwylce.*

537[b]–9. *Sinc . . . wylle:* Klaeber calls this an 'apparently uncalled-for ethical reflection on the pernicious influence of gold'. But the poem makes it clear (2210[b]–2286) that the gold in the dragon's hoard was the beginning of the trouble which ended in Beowulf's death. The sentiment is not merely anti-materialistic; there is a condemnation of the practice of burying grave-goods: NB *hæðen gold,* 2276, and cf. 2216 and *Seafarer,* 97–102.

540. *segn eallgylden:* a *segen gylden,* symbol of royalty, is associated with the ship burial of Scyld described at the beginning of *Beowulf.* Wrenn believes that the presence of the golden standard in the dragon's hoard suggests that the barrow was originally a king's burial-chamber. He refers to the so-called 'standard' found in the Sutton Hoo ship-burial.

564. *wæteres:* this is an instrumental genitive—'splashed him with water'.

565[b]. Various suggestions have been made for supplying the missing half-line, which was probably a speech-introducing formula.

575–81. Beowulf's instructions for his funeral barrow are paralleled widely. The closest is the oft-cited description of the funeral pyre of Achilles and Patroklos in the *Odyssey,* XXIV, 80 ff.: 'Then around (Achilles' bones) did we . . . pile a great and glorious tomb, on a jutting headland above the broad Hellespont, that it might be seen afar from off the sea by men, both by those who now are, and by those who shall be hereafter.'

602. *homera lafe:* 'products of hammers', i.e., swords.

627. *wehte:* 'tried to wake him'.

630. *Wealdendes wiht:* translate 'anything ordained by the Lord'.

659–61. *londrihtes . . . hweorfan:* 'each man of your family must wander deprived of his right to land . . .'

12. THE BATTLE OF MALDON

2. *hors forlætan:* horses were used in Anglo-Saxon times for transport rather than battle.

3. *feor afysan:* 'drive (the horses) away'.

6. *eorl:* In the earlier poetry the word implies nobility but no special rank or office. Byrhtnoth is called *ealdormann* in the *Chronicle,* and it appears that here *eorl* = *ealdormann,* a high-ranking regional administrative officer responsible to the king. *Eorl* in this sense has evidently been influenced by its cognate ON *jarl.*

8. *þæs holtes:* the wood near Hazeleigh, behind the English army. This is presumably the wood to which the sons of Odda escape.

15. *beot:* a customary vow or oath of service and allegiance made before battle. Cf. 198–201, 289–93.

17–24. The poet distinguishes between Byrhtnoth's personal followers (*heorðgeneatas*) and the local army supporting him (*fyrd*); he instructs the *fyrd* in their duties, and then takes up his position with his *comitatus.*

24. An ambiguous line for which Miss Ashdown gives three interpretations: (1) 'Where he knew his bodyguard, a most loyal band, to be.' (2) 'Where he knew his bodyguard, most loyal of all, (i.e. more loyal than the *folc*) to be.' (3) 'In that part of his bodyguard which he knew to be most loyal.' She comments: 'The last interpretation would suggest that Byrhtnoth foresaw the treachery of such unfaithful retainers as the sons of Odda.' But Laborde argues that if Byrthnoth had known that some of his men were cowardly he would have been more cautious in his subsequent actions.

32. *gafole:* it seems that the Vikings' first object in seeking this confrontation was to exact tribute. See quotation from the *Chronicle* in the introduction to this extract.

38. *syllan . . . on hyra sylfra dom:* cf. extract 1/27; ON *selja sjalfdœmi.*

42. For similar epic formulae at the beginning of speeches, cf. ll. 230, 244, 255, 309–10.

44. *yrre and anræd:* the half-line occurs in *Beowulf,* 1575[a] (11/316).

47. *ættrynne ord:* cf. 146. It is not likely that the spear-point was actually poisoned. Klaeber, discussing *atertanum fah, Beowulf,* 1459[b] (of a sword) comments: '*ater* is perhaps used figuratively with regard to the acid employed in the process of (false) damascening. Another possibility is that serpentine ornamentation . . . was supposed to have a miraculous poisoning effect . . ., the figures of serpents suggesting their well-known attribute.'

ealde swurd: old weapons were viewed as the best and most trustworthy. Cf. *Beowulf,* 795, 1458, 1488, 2563, etc.; cf. note to 11/94.

55. *hæþene:* a standard epithet for the Vikings, much used in the *Chronicle.* See note to 2/88.

60. *ord and ecg:* spear-point and sword-edge. Cf. *Exeter Gnomic Verses* 202: *ecg [sceal] on sweorde ond ord spere.*

66. *lucon lagustreamas:* Laborde's suggestion is that this refers to the conjunction of the tidal streams at the west of Northey Island after the tide has flowed round both sides of the island.

69. *æschere:* the Viking army, so called because their ships were made of ash-wood.

74. *bricge:* the causeway.

75. *Wulfstan* was a local landowner; see Gordon's edition, pp. 48, 85–6.

77. *francan:* etymologically, 'a Frankish spear'—a barbed thrusting spear with a long socket to prevent one's opponent cutting the head off. In 140 it appears to be used as a thrusting spear, but here it is thrown.

80. *Maccus:* a Celtic name; but we can guess nothing about this man.

83. *wæpna wealdan:* a dead kenning, = 'fight'; cf. 168, 272; *Beowulf,* 1509, 2038.

87. *upgang:* Miss Ashdown says that 'the literal meaning of *up-* need not be pressed'. But Laborde (*EHR,* xl (1925), pp. 167–8), using the word as evidence against *bricg* = 'bridge', concludes that it 'would rather suit some other means of crossing which ended in an ascent of the river bank'.

89. *ofermode:* this word, which occurs elsewhere (particularly in *Genesis B*) as noun or adjective meaning 'pride/proud', must imply a slighter degree of censure here: 'overconfidence' is usually suggested.

91. *ceallian:* regarded as a loan from ON *kalla,* this is the only instance of the verb in OE.

102. *wihagan* = *scyldburh* (242) and *bordweall* (277); cf. *bordhaga, Elene,* 652, *scildweall, Beowulf,* 3118. Gordon describes it as a formation of two rows of overlapping shields held by two ranks of men, the second holding their shields over their heads and those of the rank in front.

109ᵃ. *gegrundene:* Gordon suggests *grimme gegrundene* as an emendation of this defective half-line, and quotes several parallels.

113. *Wulfmær:* not to be confused with *Wul(f)mær (se geonga)* of 155, 183.

115. *swuster sunu:* according to Tacitus (*Germania* 20) the relationship between uncle and sister's son was a close one. It involved the uncle in the obligation of guardianship if the child's father died.

117. *Eadweard:* an unidentified retainer of Byrhtnoth's; it is uncertain whether this is *Eadweard se langa* of 273.

134. *superne gar:* not 'spear from the south' (which is inconsistent with Laborde's interpretation of the site of the battle) but 'spear of southern make' ('foreign'?).

137. *sprengde: he* (Byrhtnoth) is the subject: he dashed the spear away with his shield.

143. *operne:* another Viking (*he,* l. 144), not another spear.

149. *drenga sum: dreng* is a loan-word from ON, and here implies a Viking warrior.

152 ff. Miss Ashdown notes the motif of the young retainer by the side of the old dying chief (as at the end of *Beowulf*) and suggests that the obligation of vengeance by the man who removes the murder weapon prompts Wulfmær's actions.

160–1. Laborde explains this plundering by referring to the 'special honour paid to those who spoiled the leader of the enemy' and comments, 'It was not a case of mere cupidity.'

180. *hi:* refers to *sawul.*

181. *heowon:* the twelfth-century *Liber Eliensis* says that Byrhtnoth was decapitated in the battle.

185 ff. A pointed passage varying between irony and explicit condemnation. Note especially that the sons of Odda flee immediately after their lord's death, whereas his death is a call to even more intense fighting by the loyal retainers; that their flight is presented as above all else ungrateful. N.B. the ironical juxtaposition of 188 and 189, and cf. 2ᵇ–3ᵃ.

186. *Odda* may be a name of Scandinavian origin; but the three sons named subsequently have English names.

194. *þæt fæsten* = *þone wudu* 193.

198. Offa appears to play a leading part in the battle after Byrhtnoth's death. With his observation of 198–201, cf. notes to ll. 15 and 24.

207–8. Cf. *Waldere*, 8–11.

209. *Ælfric* is believed to have been an *ealdormann* of Mercia who was banished in 985 or 986; this would explain the presence of his expatriate son Ælfwine among Byrhtnoth's followers.

212–14. Cf. *Beowulf*, 2633–8 (11/404–11).

225. *fæhðe gemunde:* Miss Ashdown comments, 'i.e. he kept in mind the duty of vengeance'.

242^b. *Abreoðe his angin:* two interpretations are possible. Ashdown has 'may what he has set on foot come to nothing' (referring to the results of his action, 241–2ᵃ, 243): Gordon 'may his conduct have an evil end', i.e. 'curse him for behaving thus'.

249. *Sturmere:* Sturmer, Essex.

256. *unorne:* 'simple', 'not of noble rank'; a representative figure of the *fyrd*, as the other speakers are of Byrhtnoth's personal retinue. In view of this interpretation, perhaps *beorna gehwylc* (257) has the force 'everyone' (not only the *heorðgeneatas*).

261. *hiredmen:* cf. ON *hirðmaðr*. The simple *hired* occurs earlier, but the compound appears for the first time here.

265. *gysel:* a hostage of noble rank was expected to fight on his 'host's' side in repayment for good treatment. Cf. the position of the hostage in extract 1. We cannot know why Byrhtnoth had a Northumbrian hostage; however, the *Liber Eliensis* describes him as *Northanimbrorum dux:* he may possibly have had responsibility in Northumbria on his king's account.

277. *bordweall:* editors have been undecided whether this refers to the English formation or that of the invaders.

283. *cellod:* a word of uncertain meaning.

284. *lærig:* occurs here and in *Exodus*, 239. The most probable meaning is 'rim', as Gordon suggests; see his note (p. 59). But neither Ashdown nor Laborde is so positive.

286–7. *Offa* and *Gaddes mæg* are usually taken to be the same person.

300. *Wigelmes bearn:* Gordon suggests that this refers to Offa, and draws attention to a possible parallel with ll. 181–4, where Ælfnoth and Wulfmær die in avenging their dying lord.

309. *Byrhtwold:* Gordon notes a possible identification with one Byrhtwold who is named in the will of Æthelflæd, Byrhtnoth's sister-in-law.

310. *eald geneat: eald* probably refers primarily to his long service, not to his age; he is a member of the *duguþ*, the core of senior retainers.

315. *mæg* has the force of future tense.

13. ANDREAS

1 ff. A variation of the conventional opening formula found in many OE narrative poems; cf. the openings of *Beowulf*, *Exodus*, *Daniel*, *Phoenix* Krapp's edition has long note on the formula.

3. *þeodnes þegnas:* a commonplace phrase used frequently of the followers of a secular master. The adaptation of a heroic phrase to religious use is

common in this poem, which is, incidentally, insistent on the *comitatus* relationship within the various groups that enter into the narrative.

5. *gedældon:* 'parted, dispersed'.

6. *hlyt:* according to other versions of the story, the disciples cast lots to determine where each of them was to preach.

15. *igland:* used as in *Phoenix* 9: 'a (remote) land reached by water'.

25ᵇ. This half line is found in *Beowulf* 178ᵇ, of the Danes' reversion to paganism.

34. *dryas:* a word of Celtic origin, often used in OE with an evil (heathen) connotation.

38. *heorogrædige:* refers to *hie*, 37; both Krapp and Brooks point out that the word seems more appropriate to the Mermedonians than to their victims.

42. *Mermedonia:* the city is not named in the Greek original, but occurs in the other accounts (Latin and OE) variously as *Mermedonia, Mirmidonia, Marmadonia.* On the difficult question of its identification, see Krapp, pp. lxv–lxvii, Brooks, pp. xxvii–xxx. The city is possibly to be identified with Strabo's *Myrmecium* in Scythia, which, according to Brooks, 'was a generic name for the land of the tribes contiguous to the Black Sea; especially to the Greeks it signified everything wild and barbarous'.

43. *deofles þegnas:* cf. 3 and note.

50. *heafdes segl* (= *sigel*): 'suns of the head', i.e. 'eyes'; cf. *heafodgimmas,* 31.

59–62. The elaboration of a formula introducing direct speech (*wordum cwæð*) is very typical of OE epic. Note also *sigedryhten, gumena brego, weoruda wilgeofan* formed on the pattern of secular heroic diction.

72. *sweordum aswebban:* this circumlocution for 'kill' occurs in *Beowulf,* 567, 679.

78. *billhete:* cf. *ecghete, Beowulf,* 84, 1738; here 'the hateful deeds of swords'.

88–90. Krapp and Brooks both accuse the poet of failing to mention that Matthew's sight is restored; but these lines might be said to be a symbolic representation of this fact.

109. *synne ðurh searocræft:* Brooks translates the MS reading 'by evil artifices'; Krapp emends to *synnige.*

115. *nihtgerimes:* the Anglo-Saxons followed the usual Germanic practice of reckoning fairly long periods of time by counting nights, not days.

118. *holmwearde:* often emended to *helmwearde;* but Brooks argues against this, and translates the MS reading 'Him who was their protector on the sea'.

119–21. Cf. *Beowulf,* 38–9:

> ne hyrde ic cymlicor   ceol gegyrwan
> hildewæpnum   ond heaðowædum.

128 ff. The storm is not mentioned in the Greek original, and is much more elaborately described here than in any of the Latin or OE versions. Note the vigour of the lines deriving from the staccato verbal phrases; cf. 151–3.

129. *Hornfisc:* probably not 'swordfish' but 'whale' (cf. *Beowulf,* 540, *hronfixas*).

134. *wædo gewætte:* nom. pl. 'drenched sails', parallel to *strengas.*

136ᵇ–9. Cf. *Beowulf,* 691–2.

149. *firigendstream:* literally 'mountain stream'; used of Grendel's mere in *Beowulf* 1359 and 2128. Brooks suggests 'stream that is a mountain (of immensity)', i.e. 'the mighty ocean'.

164 ff. In this retort, Andrew's disciples voice the feeling which is one of the most productive Germanic motifs in OE poetry: the necessity of absolute loyalty of the *comitatus* to its chief. Cf. *Beowulf* 2864–91; *Maldon* 220–53. Note also the conventional, and perhaps inappropriate, military phraseology at the end.

185. *torngeniðlan:* i.e. the Mermedonians. The object *hine* (Andrew) must be understood, as in the next sentence, although Krapp emends *deormode* and *stærcedferþþe* to acc. sg. (*-ne*) to make them refer to Andrew.

190. *enta ærgeweorc:* a common phrase, found with slight variation in, for example, *Beowulf,* 1562, 1679, 2717 and 2774; *Wanderer,* 87; *Ruin,* 2. Its most usual reference is to buildings surviving from an earlier civilisation. Cf. 11/299, 16/87 and notes.

191. *stræte stanfage:* cf. *Beowulf,* 320 *stræt wæs stanfah,* 725 *on fagne flor.* Commentators on *Beowulf,* noting the Latin origin of *stræt,* take *stanfah* as a reference to Roman tessellated pavements.

210 ff. The cold weather, not obviously appropriate to Mermedonia, is a conventional OE poetic attendant of descriptions of personal sorrow. Cf. especially *The Wanderer* and *The Seafarer, passim.* Krapp, emphasising the personification *hare hildstapan,* 213, has a long note on 'the mythic feeling pervading this passage'.

217. *blæce:* Krapp glosses this 'black,' but Brooks points out that this hardly fits and derives *blæce* from *blac,* 'shining', which occurs elsewhere in the poem.

231. *blodlifrum:* probably 'in clots (of blood)', parallel to *yðum* and *hatan heolfre*; but see the notes of Krapp and Brooks for alternative explanations.

232[b]. Krapp translates, 'His body did not cease from, or have relief from, suffering.'

14. GENESIS B

2. *handmægen:* occurs only once elsewhere in OE, but several times in OS.

3. *tene:* ten orders of angels.

4. *giongorscipe:* based on OS *jungarskepi.*

6[b]. *halig Drihten:* so 2[b]. This poem is extremely repetitive, in both ideas and phrasing.

9. *hehstne to him:* 'next below him'.

13. *leohte:* used (as in OS) in the rare sense of 'world, life'.
    lete: 'would have let'.

17. *ofermod:* for a less damning meaning, see *Maldon* 89.

26. *folcgestælna:* cf. l. 42. God and Satan respectively are seen in this Germanic military expression as leaders of bands of retainers.

30. *west and norð:* North-west—a location commonly ascribed to Satan.

37. *æfter . . . ðeowian:* 'try to obtain by service'. OS *thionôn aftar.*

38. *swilces geongordomes:* adverbial genitive.

39. *striðe:* OS *strîd.*

39–42. Note the heroic vocabulary.

52–4. The interruption of the narrative for moral comment is common to both secular and religious epics; cf. 11/275–7.

62. *þurh longe swa:* usually emended to *þurh swa longe swa*; but left as

it stands it makes sense, although the construction is unparalleled. Timmer quotes this as an example of 'faulty OE used by the translator'.

67. *sigelease:* the term in heroic diction for 'defeated'.

71. *gar:* probably used figuratively: 'piercing cold'.

73–4. *Worhte man . . . fylde . . .:* to be translated as passive constructions.

77. *fynd:* more usually means 'enemy'.

81. *þegnscipe:* in OE usually 'bravery'; OS *theganskepi* = 'service', the meaning here.

93. *cyning:* the applicability of this term to Satan is hardly clear.

115. *romigan:* Timmer cites OS *rômon* and other cognate forms, with the meaning 'aim at', 'try to obtain'.

117. *heofonrice benumen:* genitive is more usual with this verb.

120–2. An awkward set of clauses, of which the skeleton is: *Adam sceal . . . stol behealdan . . . (sceal) wesan . . .*

125. *winterstunde:* a winter hour is a short hour because of the division of the period of daylight (shorter in winter) into equal 'hours'.

131. *landscipe:* an OS compound.

139. *grindlas greate:* the subject of *Licgað* 137.

142. *þæt . . . gewurðan:* 'that it would fare ill between us two, Adam and me . . .'

146. *swa:* 'although'.

156. *Ne gelyfe ic me . . .:* 'I do not expect for myself . . .'

157. *cræfte:* Timmer notes (p. 33): 'The sense of "hosts" is not known in OE, but OS *kraft* is very common in this meaning.'

164 ff. Note Satan's appeal to his retainers in the typical manner of the Germanic prince; cf. 190 ff.

172. *feðerhoman:* 'wings', literally 'feather covering.' The cognate *fjarðr-hamr* in ON is used of artificial wings used by Weland and Loki.

187. *hearmscearu:* OS *harmskara*.

15. THE DREAM OF THE ROOD

2–3. Cf. *Daniel* 122–3:

> hwæt hine gemætte
> þenden reordberend   reste wunode.

8. *foldan sceatum:* possibly 'surface of the earth' (cf. l. 43), i.e. the foot of the Cross. But an alternative explanation is that of Patch (p. 246) 'the corners of the earth, to which the cross reaches as it spreads over the sky'. In *Daniel* 501–2 the Cross (in Nebuchadnezzar's vision) towered to heaven and *ofer-fæðmde foldan sceatas/ealne middangeard;* the tree Yggdrasill in Norse mythology reached from hell to heaven and spread its branches over the earth.

10. *fægere þurh forðgesceaft:* ambiguous. Dickins and Ross give 'beautiful in virtue of an ancient decree'; or 'beautiful through their creation', i.e. 'created beautiful'.

15. *wædum:* Cook suggests that the poet has in mind streamers attached to the processional Cross.

18–19. The dreamer's perception of a Cross of triumph changes to one of a Cross of suffering.

21. *fuse:* usually means 'eager', and Cook gives 'mobile' by extension of meaning; Dickins and Ross 'bright'.

21–3. The changing decorations are explained by Patch (pp. 249–51) by reference to changes customary in the Church: 'the plain red cross was carried during Lent, but on Palm Sunday a more ornamental cross appeared. . . . And on Easter Day . . . the "crux de christallo" was used. . . .'

33. *Frean:* the Norse pagan derivation of this word (cf. *Freyr, Freyja*), sometimes pointed out by the commentators, seems to have been forgotten by Christian poets; it is used in Cædmon's *Hymn*, for example, and the cognate *frauja* is standard in the Gothic biblical translations.

39. *Ongyrede . . . hæleð:* the impression of the half-line is of a warrior stripping preparatory to arming himself for battle.

42. *ymbclypte:* Cook comments 'to represent Christ as embracing the cross is a poetic mode of emphasising his voluntary sacrifice'.

52. *þenian:* do not confuse with *þe(g)nian* 'to serve'.

55. *Weop eal gesceaft:* commentators have pointed out the similarity with the Norse lament for Baldr, for whom all things wept except the goddess Þǫkk.

57. *fuse:* probably a reference to Joseph and Nicodemus.

62. *strælum:* the nails? Usually the word means 'arrow'; cf. possibly the missiles thrown at Baldr.

67. *sorhleoð galan:* Dickins and Ross compare *Beowulf*, 2460, and suggest that this is 'probably an archaic feature of the Old English burial rite and therefore evidence of antiquity'.

70. *we (us*, 73, 75): the three crosses.
greotende: weeping and flowing with blood.

73. *feorgbold:* unique; cf. the quite common *feorhhus*.

76. A half-line at least is missing. For the finding of the True Cross, cf. *Elene*, 827 ff., and A. S. Cook, *The Old English Elene, Phoenix, and Physiologus* (New Haven, 1919), pp. xiv–xxiv.

98. *se ðe . . . on:* 'on which'.

101. *Deað . . . byrigde* = Vulgate *gustare mortem*.

109. *lænum life:* the utter conventionality of this second part of the poem is typified in this gratuitous reference to the transience of life.

115. *fea:* adv. 'little'; probably not 'a little' (Dickins and Ross).

130. *mundbyrd:* '(hope of) protection'.

131 ff. With this lament on dead friends cf. *The Wanderer*, 37 ff., 78 ff.; *The Seafarer*, 80 ff.

149. *bryne þolodan:* Cook explains: 'The reference is to the spirits in prison who were released by the Harrowing of Hell. This theme is continued to the end of the poem.'

16. THE WANDERER

1. *anhaga:* the etymology is in doubt; the word has been connected with *hogian* 'to think' and with the noun *haga* 'enclosure', giving the meanings 'one who meditates by himself' (cf. 111) or 'one who is restricted to one place', 'recluse'. Other occurrences of *anhaga* and *anhoga* (referring, e.g. to Beowulf, the Phoenix, a wolf; glossing *solitarius* and explained by *anwuniende*) suggest a less precise meaning, 'a solitary person or thing'. The closest parallel is the *Exeter Book* poem *Resignation* l. 45, where the word is applied to one who is, like the *eardstapa, leodwynna leas, wineleas wræcca*.

gebideð: probably 'experiences' rather than 'waits for, seeks', although the word is not unambiguous. Cf. a very similar context, *Beowulf*, 1060–2:

> Fela sceal gebidan
> leofes ond laþes se þe longe her
> on ðyssum windagum worolde bruceð.

5. *wadan wræclastas:* a conventional expression or 'formula'; cf. *Seafarer*, 57; *Beowulf*, 1352.

wyrd bið ful aræd: on *wyrd* see B. J. Timmer, 'Wyrd in Anglo-Saxon prose and poetry', *Neophilologus*, xxvi (1941), 24–33, 213–28. He views *wyrd* as a deterministic concept rather than a pagan god, and paraphrases 'man's lot is determined', taking *aræd* as the past participle of *arædan* 'determine'; so l. 15 speaks of man's inability to change his lot.

8. *uhtna gehwylce:* the morning seems to have been the time traditionally associated with hardship and the bewailing of hardship. Cf. *Resignation*, 96, *mod morgenseoc; Wife's Lament*, 7, *uhtceare;* 11/533, *uhtflogan.*

10. *þe him:* 'to whom' (but not in 31).

11–14. For the same sentiment, that an unhappy man does not complain about his sorrows, see *Precepts*, 54, 57–8:

> Seldan snottor guma sorgleas blissað . . .
> Wærwyrde sceal wisfæst hæle
> breostum hycgan, nales breahtme hlud.

Cf. *Homiletic Fragment II (Exeter Book, p. 224)*, 2–3.

21. *feterum sælan* continues the metaphor of *ferðlocan, hordcofan, breostcofan.* Individual kennings are more common than sustained figures of this type.

23. *heolster:* MS *heolstre* emended to make it subject of *biwrah.*

24. *wintercearig:* 'winter-sad'—an epithet which sums up the association of winter and sorrow; see note to 101–5 below.

waþema gebind: 'the binding of the waves', i.e. 'the frozen waves'; for the same metaphor see 11/350, *forstes bend; Exeter Gnomic Verses*, 75, *forstes fetre.*

25. *dreorig* modifies *ic* 23, not *sele.*

27. *min mine:* the personal pronoun *min* is added, *mine* being taken as a noun; cf. *Beowulf*, 169, *ne his myne wisse*, although this too is not absolutely clear.

32. *wunden gold:* 'twisted gold'—gold wire or braid, interlace decoration or, more simply, 'rings'.

41–2. For embraces between men in OE, cf. *Beowulf*, 1870.

50–5. *Sorg . . . cwidegiedda:* The difficulty of these lines is considerable. The passage can be punctuated in several ways, and this edition largely follows Krapp and Dobbie. The semicolon after *geondhweorfeð* is meant to indicate a change of subject: 'he' should be supplied as a subject for *geondscawað, Secga geseldan* is the object of *geondscawað*, and we must supply 'they', referring back to *geseldan*, as subject of *swimmað. Ferð* is understood as 'company' or 'troop,' following Smithers, *English and Germanic Studies*, iv (1951–22), 84–5.

55–7. Cf. *Seafarer*, 58–62.

58–9. 'For I can think of no reason in this world why my heart should not grow gloomy when . . .'

61. *flet ofgeafon:* a circumlocution for 'died'. This general statement links up with the list of specific causes of death, 80–4.

62. *middangeard:* cf. ON *miðgarðr:* a term derived from pagan, not Christian, cosmology.

64–5ᵃ. Cf. Cotton *Gnomic Verses,* 11ᵇ–12 (*Anglo-Saxon Minor Poems,* p. 56).

72. *hreþra:* plural for singular, as *breostum,* 113.

73. *gæstlic:* usually means 'spiritual', 'divine' as opposed to 'bodily', 'earthly', but this meaning hardly fits here. The suggestions 'unearthly', 'mysterious' (by extension of meaning) are inappropriate and strained. We need a meaning lexically consistent with that of the following clause, and 'terrible', derived from *agæstan* 'to frighten', is chosen.

75. This line occurs practically verbatim in the next poem in the Exeter Book, *The Gifts of Men* (l. 28).

76 ff. The meditation on mutability inspired by the contemplation of a ruined building invites comparison with the OE poem *The Ruin.*

77. *hryðge:* presumably from an adj. *hryðig,* of uncertain meaning. Explanations include 'storm-beaten', 'ruined', 'snow-covered'. Cf. *hrið* 102.

80–4. The catalogue of ways of death, and the repeated *sum* formula, have parallels. Cf. *The Gifts of Men,* 30–96, based on clauses beginning with *sum; The Fortunes of Men,* in which paragraphs describing the various misfortunes of men begin with *sum.*

80–1. *sume . . . forðwege: forniman,* with *wig* or *deað* as subject, is a common circumlocution for 'die'.

81–2. *sumne . . . holm:* an unusual association of birds with death if it is meant that the bird *caused* death. The predatory action of birds after battle is usual (cf. 12/106–7), and, in view of 80ᵇ–81ᵃ, this may be intended here.

82–3. *sumne . . . gedælde:* cf. *The Fortunes of Men,* 12–13; Exeter *Gnomic Verses,* 146–7:

> Wineleas, wonsælig mon   genimað him wulfas to geferan,
> felafæcne deor.   Ful oft hine se gefera sliteð . . .

83–4. *sumne . . . gehydde: dreorighleor* modifies *eorl.* This is a reference to burial: cf. 22–3.

85. This has been taken as a reference to Doomsday, but it is difficult to see why, in this case, *Yþde* should be past tense.

87. *eald enta geweorc:* the dragon's lair in *Beowulf* (a stone structure) is described as *enta geweorc* (2717) and *eald enta geweorc* (2774); in the Cotton *Gnomic Verses, ceastra* are described an *enta geweorc* (2). It is believed that there was some tendency among the Anglo-Saxons (who built in wood, apart from the later churches) to regard the ruins of Roman stone buildings as the work of supernatural beings; see further, note to 11/299.

92 ff. Cf. 8/76–81; this is established formula in OE, the equivalent of the Latin *ubi sunt . . .* formula used in treatments of mutability. See J. E. Cross, '"Ubi sunt" passages in Old English—sources and relationships'. Vetenskaps-Societeten i Lund, *Årsbok,* 1956, pp. 25–44.

98. *wyrmlicum fah:* 'decorated with serpent shapes': serpent interlace, applied to jewellery, weapons, armour, manuscripts, stonework; cf. *Beowulf* 1698 *wyrmfah* (of a sword).

101–5. For the association of winter landscapes with the mood of sorrow, cf. 5, 24, 76–7; *Seafarer,* 8–10, 14–17, etc.

108–9. *Her . . . læne:* Mrs Gordon quotes an apt parallel from the ON poem *Hávamál:*

> Deyr fé, deyja frændr,
> deyr sjalfr it sama . . .

(Cattle die, kinsfolk die, one dies oneself just the same.)

111. *æt rune:* this is often inappropriately interpreted 'in council'. The literal meaning of *run* is 'secret', 'mystery' (runes were a form of secret writing); the translation 'in meditation' (i.e. *private* thought) is preferred.

112–15. Hypermetrical lines with antithetical syntax and sententious content are found often enough elsewhere to establish this as a set form associated with moralising. See *Seafarer,* 106–8; Exeter *Gnomic Verses,* 35–7; and the non-hypermetrical *Beowulf,* 183–9.

17. THE SEAFARER

1–2ᵃ. Cf. *The Wife's Lament,* 1–2ᵃ:

> Ic þis giedd wrece   bi me ful geomorre,
> minre sylfre sið

a use of first-person narrative characteristic of the elegiac genre, apparently giving rise to a set opening formula.

5. *cearselda:* not recorded elsewhere.

8. *cnossað:* related to *cnyssan* (cf. 33), but intransitive. Mrs. Gordon translates 'dashes'; perhaps 'is dashed' conveys better the type of movement intended.

8ᵇ–17: cf. 23ᵃ, 31–3ᵃ and *Wanderer* passim for the conventional association of sorrow and winter landscape.

12. *merewerges:* adj. used as noun.

13. *þe him . . . limpeð:* literally 'whom it befalls most pleasantly on land'.

16. *winemægum bidroren:* cf. the situation of the Wanderer after *winemæga hryre* (7).

23. *him,* 24. *þæt:* the antecedents of these pronouns are not clear, and it is best to leave them out of translation; cf. *him* 27.

oncwæð: the tern responds to the noise of the waves like an echo from the cliffs.

27. *forþon:* usually 'therefore' or 'because'; but here it seems to mean just 'indeed' or 'truly'.

ah: probably used here as an auxiliary.

34. *hean streamas: heah* is such contexts has an ambiguity like that of Latin *altus* : either 'deep' or 'high' (i.e. waves whipped up by the storm).

36. *mæla gehwylce:* 'all the time'.

39–43. A form of expression found in homilies with the phrasing 'there is no man so . . . nor so . . . that he will not have to face death'.

41. *dryhten,* 43. *Dryhten:* secular and spiritual lord respectively.

47. *longunge:* not longing for the sea, but depression, weariness of spirit (cf. *sorge* 42), which is so strong as to overcome all thoughts of pleasure (44–5).

48. *fægriað* probably has *Bearwas* as its subject and *byrig* its object.

50. *fusne:* adj. as noun; *sefan* is parallel to it.

55. *breosthord:* the same metaphor as in *Wanderer* 13–18.

58 ff. For the movement of the mind or spirit over the sea, cf. *Wanderer*, 55–7.

62. *anfloga*: usually taken to refer to the cuckoo.

64ᵇ. Note that a new paragraph is started here. If no sentence-break were made, and *forþon* translated 'because', the sense of the whole passage would be altered. It could be taken to imply 'because the joys of the Lord are more inspiring than this transitory life on earth, I turn my back on the world by a sea-journey'.

67. *him*: used reflexively with *stondað*.

68–80. There is a close mingling of Christian and heroic sentiments in these lines. There are the ideas that death is, by virtue of mutability and through one of a range of causes, inevitable; that the best reward for a hero is praise after his death; that he should earn this praise, and a place in heaven, by virtuous and brave deeds.

74. *gewyrce* is intransitive; *fremum* 75 and *deorum dædum* 76 are given almost adverbial function by their dative inflexions.

80–90. As in *The Wanderer*, we have a conventional poetic treatment of the theme of mutability (introduced in 64–7) in terms of the death of the leaders of society. Missing is the rhetorical question, the *ubi sunt* formula.

82–3. Cf. *Wanderer*, 92–5; Wulfstan (ed. Napier), 263: *Hwær syndon þa rican caseras and þa cyningas þe jo wæron . . . hwær is heora ofermedla?*

84. *mid him*: 'amongst themselves'.

87. *wacran*: Mrs. Gordon points out that this means '(morally) inferior', not 'less powerful'.

91–6. The idea of the degeneration of the body with senility and death is a standard component of medieval sermons on mutability and *contemptus mundi*; we do not find it in *The Wanderer*.

97–102. A difficult, but not incomprehensible, passage. We find, as elsewhere in the poem, a doubtful logic through the conflation of two ideas: that treasure placed in a man's grave by his kin will not help him at the Last Judgement if he is *synna ful*; nor will gold hoarded in his own lifetime.

99ᵇ. *þæt hine mid wille*: 'that he wishes (to go) with him'.

100. *mæg*: *beon* must be supplied to complete the verb (of which the subject is *gold*).

103. *hi*: i.e. *seo molde* (reflexive pronoun).

106–8. On these hypermetrical lines, see note to 16/112–15.

106. Cf. Exeter *Gnomic Verses* 35.

18. DEOR

1. *Welund*: a figure celebrated in ON mythology as a skilful smith: see especially the ON *Vǫlundarkviða*. Captured by King Niðhad (ON Níðuðr), he was hamstrung and forced to work for the King. In revenge he killed the sons of Niðhad (l. 8), raped his daughter Beadohild (Bǫðvildr) and flew off.

be wurman: a crux which has been 'resolved' with many explanations. See Kemp Malone, *Deor*, p. 6: F. Klæber, *Anglia Beiblatt*, xxxii (1921), 38–40, *JEGP*, xxiii (1924), 121–4; Krapp and Dobbie, *Exeter Book*, 318–19.

3. Cf. 16/30.

4. *wintercealde*: cf. 16/24 and note.

6. *seonobende*: presumably a reference to the hamstringing of Welund: he is 'bound' figuratively (immobilised) by the cutting of his sinews.

7. The verbs are impersonal; the pronouns in the genitive almost adverbial. A literal translation would be: 'It (sorrow) passed away in that case; so may it in this.' Cf. the similar construction l. 26.

10ᵃ–11ᵃ. *þæt . . . wæs:* the whole clause, which includes another clause 11ᵃ, is in apposition to *þing.*

12ᵇ. This excessively elliptical half-line has been interpreted as impersonal: 'how that came about' or 'how that would turn out'. L. Whitbread, *MLN,* lv (1940), 205–6, suggests 'how (she) would go about it', i.e. deal with her situation.

14. *Mæðhilde:* the MS has *mæð hilde,* and this is usually taken as a woman's name. *Geat* is assumed to be a man's name. We cannot identify these characters. For an attempt, see Malone's edition, pp. 8–9; for a justly sceptical criticism of Malone's views, and a speculative interpretation, see F. Norman, *MLR,* xxxii (1940), 374–81.

14. *monge,* 15. *frige:* words of unknown meaning.

18. *Ðeodric:* Theodoric the Ostrogoth, whose particular affliction was his exile at *Mæringa burgu.* (But Malone identifies Ðeodric with Theodoric the Frank.)

21. *Eormanric:* King of the Goths, died *ca.* A.D. 375. The poet of *Widsith* speaks of him as a great and good king; but *Beowulf* (1197–1201) hints at his tyranny by a laconic reference to the death of Hama at his hands. The king seems not to have been generally remembered for his oppression of his subjects, however.

25. *wean on wenan:* 'in the expectation (*wenan,* dat. pl.) of woe (*wean,* gen. sg.)'.

28–30. These lines have been understood as an 'if' clause dependent on *mæg* 31. It is more natural to take them as a subjectless sentence of a type perfectly common in the poetry, and 31–4 similarly.

Notice how the vocabulary here is like that of the elegies; cf. notes to ll. 3, 4. On the mixture of good and evil meted out by God (31–4) cf. opening lines of *Wanderer* and note.

35. *þæt . . . wille:* a common opening formula in this type of poetry; cf. the first lines of *The Seafarer* and *The Wife's Lament.* The situation described in the last stanza is fictitious, and there is no point in trying to identify the names. The fictitious personal situation concerns the loss of the lord, and is described with precision, as in *The Wanderer.*

19. THE PHOENIX

1. *Hæbbe ic gefrugnen:* a conventional opening formula; cf. note to *Andreas,* 1.

2. *eastdalum on:* i.e. *on eastdalum;* paradise, in Christian tradition, was located in the East.

7. *Wlitig is se wong eal:* the inverted construction, with the complement at the beginning of the half-line, is found also in 9, 33, 185.

9. *iglond:* Cook has a note on this pointing out that the word often means 'land that is reached by water'. He suggests that it had connotations of remoteness, exoticness, which would be appropriate here.

10. *modig, meahtum spedig:* cf. *Guthlac,* 695: *modig Mundbora, meahtum spedig.*

14^b–18. Note that the land of the Phoenix is above all free from wintry weather, and cf. the association of winter and misery in *The Wanderer* and *The Seafarer*.

15–16. The half-lines are linked together by rhyme—a rare device; cf. 54–5.

23, 31. *her:* 'in this world' (as opposed to the Phoenix' paradise, not 'in England').

25. *hlæwas:* the word has become more general in meaning as compared with its original sense 'tumulus' (as in *Beowulf*, 2802, 3157).

29^b–30. The poet here stresses (as in 1. 179 and outside the present extracts 176) that his observations are based on (authoritative) sources. Cf. *Judith*, 7, 246; *Beowulf*, 1–2, 74, 2484, 2752, etc.; *Maldon*, 117, for this convention.

33. *sigewong:* normally 'battlefield', as in *Judith*, 294.

sunbearo: it is made evident in Lactantius that the grove is sacred to Phoebus; an instance of the Anglo-Saxon poet's suppression of pagan references.

40–1. The motive for stressing this virtue of permanence until the end of the world is perhaps to be found in the medieval preoccupation with mutability; but cf. the Latin, where the land of the Phoenix is said to remain untouched on the devastation of the world by the flames of Phaeton's chariot. However, in the light of 47–9, 82–4, it may be that this is an anticipatory reference to the fire of Doomsday—an intrusion of the allegorical interpretation into the literal narrative.

56. *ne sorg ne slæp, ne swar leger:* the Latin to which 56^a corresponds is *curae insomnes*. The line would appear to be almost a stock formula, not a translation of the Latin. Parallels cited by Cook are: *Wanderer*, 39^a *sorg ond slæp; Christ*, 1661^a *slæp ne swar leger; Solomon and Saturn* 313; *sorg bið swarost byrðen, slæp bið deaðe gelicost*; pseudo-Wulfstan XIX (Napier, *Wulfstan*, p. 139, lines 27–9) *sorh ne sar . . . ne hefelic slæp*. These parallels demonstrate that 56^a does not contain a slip which needs to be emended, and that *slæp* was a word with unpleasant connotations.

59. *ænigne:* 'anyone'.

61. *windig wolcen:* a verb needs to be supplied: 'nor (is) there . . .'

66. *þa* refers to *wæter* (plural).

80. *weorþeð*, 83. *bið*, 88. *scepeð:* these verbs must be translated in the future tense.

87. *anhaga:* translates Latin *unica*.

90. *siteð*, 92. *dreogeð*, 93. *geondwliteð:* i.e. the Phoenix.

97. *fyres feng:* cf. *Beowulf*, 1764^a.

99. *heoredreorges:* a word from the heroic vocabulary.

102. *lif bið on siðe:* cf. 90. The idea of death as a journey is behind many OE expressions. Cf. *Wanderer*, 81^a *ferede in forðwege; Chronicle* (frequently) *forðferan* 'die'.

110. *heaþorofes:* a heroic term.

118. *fugeltimber: timber* has the general sense 'material out of which something is made'—not specifically wood.

124. *synnum asundrad:* probably a reference (with the subsequent allegorical interpretation in mind) to the purging of men's sins by the fire of Doomsday.

124–5. *sumes onlice swa:* 'in somewhat the same way as'. Similes are infrequent in OE; the one which follows is unusually long and fully developed.

155. *wælreaf:* a word which, like *sigewong* (33) seems out of place. Cf. *Beowulf* 1205.

157 ff. This description of the Phoenix differs considerably from that of Lactantius. Cook (pp. 117–18) quotes several other descriptions which illustrate well the differences of opinion on this picture. Blake notes that: 'The commonly recurring features are the brilliant colours, the diadem, its resemblance to the eagle or the peacock and, particularly in the Christian authors, its radiance.'

159. *Is him þæt heafod:* 'His head is . . .'

170. *smiþa orðoncum:* cf. *Beowulf* 406, *smiþe orþancum.*

177. *fotas:* the normal form is, of course, *fet. Fotas* occurs in Cynewulfian poems, and its presence in *Phoenix* has been taken as a sign of Cynewulf's authorship; but it is not restricted to Cynewulf's poems only.

178. *pean:* Lactantius mentions both the peacock and the pheasant.

182. *lacað fiþrum:* 'flies'; for a similar periphrasis, cf. *Beowulf,* 514 *mundum brugdon* 'swam'.

20. ALFRED'S TRANSLATION OF A METRE OF BOETHIUS

ALFRED HAS TURNED his prose translation of Metre II, iii into verse in a most mechanical way. Metrical 'padding' is prominent: for example, the unsatisfactory expansion of the single words *suþanwestan* and *norðaneastan* into the intractably unalliterating *suðan and westan* (20b/8) and *norðon and eastan* (20b/12), the latter being quite unacceptable in an 'a' half line; the introduction of adverbial phrases and of adjectives whose chief function is to fill out the half-lines (e.g. *under wolcnum* 20b/9, *stearca* 20b/11). Some lines (for example, 20b/6–7) are only ostensibly metrical—prose split up and given a little alliteration.

The opening lines are closest in form and feeling to poetry in the traditional vein. They are conventional in their device of elaborating a speech-introducing formula, which here is based on the kenning *wordhord onleac* (cf. *Beowulf* 259), with the verb varied in the phrases of 20b/2ª and 2ᵇ. Elsewhere, variation leads to tautology which has only metrical function: *swetolost/hadrost* (20b/3–4); *stearca/strong* (20b/11).

GLOSSARY

IN THIS GLOSSARY the aim has been comprehensiveness; but this has had to be managed within the bounds of economy and in the interests of simplicity. All spellings of all words have been listed with, where necessary, cross-references, except where a particular spelling falls within ten places of the main entry of the word of which it is a variant. So a spelling with -ie- will be listed, and the reader directed to the main -y- spelling, or vice versa. What spelling of a word is chosen for its chief entry is determined by frequency of occurrence, not dialect normalisation; this means that the orthography of the primary entries is inconsistent, but that the glossary is easier to use given the variety of spelling conventions found in these excerpts.

Words beginning with **æ** are listed separately after words beginning with **a**; medial **-æ-** follows **-a-**, not **-ad-**; **þ** and **ð** occur (without distinction) after **t**; the affix *ge* is ignored in the sequence, **geferan** coming after **feran**, **ealdgestreon** between **ealdormonn** and **ealdsweord**. A bracketed *ge-* means that the prefix is only sometimes present in the various forms of the word.

Usually, three examples of each word are cited. The convention of numerical reference is to extract and line number; thus 1/1 means 'extract 1, line 1'. Where the nominative singular of nouns, or the masculine nominative singular of pronouns and adjectives, or the infinitive of verbs, is found in the book, it is listed first in the glossary; after this (and in other cases) references are given in numerical sequence. Words found in more than one spelling are given two references each. Full details of the forms of strong verbs and of pronouns are provided (with cross-references) in the belief that discovering how to look these up causes the beginner much difficulty, and that what he learns of these essential paradigms from his grammar may well be reinforced by the use of this glossary.

A good range of meanings is given for each word, bearing in mind actual (or at least apparent) meanings in the texts. Where distinctly separate semantic areas appear to emerge, these are listed, with groups of references. Specialised or idiosyncratic meanings are noted individually.

The following abbreviations are used:

acc. accusative	*gen.* genitive
adj. adjective	*imp.* imperative
adv. adverb	*impers.* impersonal
comp. comparative	*indef.* indefinite
conj. conjunction	*inf.* infinitive
dat. dative	*infl.* inflected
def. art. definite article	*instr.* instrumental
dem. demonstrative	*inter.* interrogative
excl. exclamation	*intr.* intransitive
f. feminine	*irr.* irregular verb

lit. literally
m. masculine
n. neuter
neg. negative
nom. nominative
num. numeral
p. participle
pl. plural
poss. possessive
prep. preposition
pres. present
pret. preterite

pron. pronoun
refl. reflexive
sg. singular
subj. subjunctive
supl. superlative
tr. transitive
vb. verb
w.*1* (*2*, etc.) weak verb of the first (second, etc.) class
1 (*2*, etc.) strong verb of the first (second, etc.) class.

ā *adv.* ever, always 6/25, 9/7, 10/32; aa 9/2; āwa 17/79; ō 19/72; oo 19/25; ā leng 7/107 any longer.
abbod *m.* abbot 3/28–9, 33.
abbotrice *n.* office of abbot, abbey 3/33.
abbudysse *f.* abbess 5/1, 48, 60.
ābēag *see* ābūgan.
ābēodan *2* declare; ābēod *imp. sg.* 12/49; ābēad *3 sg. pret.* 12/27, 13/96; āboden *pret. p.* 7/132.
ābisgian *w.2* occupy 2/72.
āblendan *w.1* blind 13/78.
ābolgen *adj.* (*pret. p.*) enraged 14/185.
ābrecan *5* break, destroy; ābræc *3 sg. pret.* 2/68; ābrǣcon *3 pl. pret.* 2/9, 56; ābrocen *pret. p.* 13/195.
ābredwian *w.2* kill 11/392.
ābrēotan *2* kill, destroy; ābrēoton *3 pl. pret.* 13/51; ābroten *pret. p.* 11/340, 480.
ābrēoðan *2* fail 12/242n; ābroþen *pret. p.* degenerate 9/126.
ābūgan *2* start, fall awayi ābēag *3 sg. pret.* 11/74.
ac *conj.* but 1/20, 2/64, 168; ah 8/39.
ācennan *w.1* beget, bring forth 8/50, 11/147, 19/123.
acol *adj.* afraid 13/221.
ācōlian *w.2* cool 19/110.
acolmōd *adj.* terror-stricken 13/136.
ācweccan *w.1* brandish; ācwehte *3 sg. pret.* 12/255, 310.
ācwelan *4* die; acwolen *pret. p.* 2/86.
ācwellan *w.1* kill; ācwealde *3 sg. pret.* 9/66.

ācwencan *w.1* extinguish 9/18.
ācweðan *5* speak; ācwið *3 sg. pres.* 16/91; ācwæð fram *3 sg. pret.* 14/59 dismissed.
ācȳþan *w.1* make known 16/113.
ād *m.* funeral pyre 6/123, 19/112, 154.
ādl *f.* disease 7/137, 8/9, 17/70.
ādlēg *m.* flame of the pyre 19/104.
ādlig *adj.* sick 10/27.
ādrǣdan *irr.* fear; ādrēd *3 sg. pret.* 7/73.
ādrǣfan *w.1* drive 1/4, 8.
ādrēogan *2* practise, commit 13/128; ādrēoganne *infl. inf.* 13/73; ādrēogað *3 pl. pres.* 9/76.
ādwǣscan *w.1* extinguish, put an end to 10/9.
āfaran *6* go; āfaren *pret. p.* 2/54.
āfeallan *7* decline, die; āfeallen *pret. p.* 4/60, 12/202.
āfēdan *w.1* sustain 19/145.
āfirsian *w.2* remove 7/29.
āflyman *w.1* cause to flee 12/243.
āfyllan *w.1* fill 3/21.
āfyllan *w.1* (=āfellan) kill 10/15, 9/91, 92.
āfyrht *adj.* (*pret. p.*) frightened 10/134.
āfyrran *w.1* deprive of, remove from 14/134, 19/5.
āfȳsan *w.1* drive away, impel 12/3, 15/125.
āgalan *6* sing; āgōl *3 sg. pret.* 11/262.
āgan *irr.* possess, have 12/87, 14/114, 177; āgenne *infl. inf.* 8/70; āh *1 sg. pres.* 12/175, *3 sg. pres.* 15/107, 17/27; āge *3 sg. pres.*

subj. 16/64; **āhte** *1 sg. pret.* 18/38, *1 sg. pret. subj.* 14/123, 143, *3 sg. pret.* 9/92, 12/189, 18/18; **nāh** *neg. 1 sg. pres.* 15/131.

āgān *irr.* go; **āgā** *3 sg. pres. subj.* 17/69; **of āgāne** *pret. p.* 2/162 gone away.

āgeald *see* **āgyldan.**

āgen *adj.* (*pret. p. of* **āgan**) own 1/27, 3/34, 4/32.

āgenne 8/70 *see* **āgan.**

āgetan *w.1* destroy 13/32.

āgifan 5 restore, give back; **āge(a)f** *3 sg. pret.* 2/60, 64, 5/58; **āgēfan** *3 pl. pret.* 13/160; **āgyfen** *pret. p.* 12/116.

āginnan *3* begin; **āginnan** *1 pl. pres. subj.* 9/150.

āgitan 5 understand, know; **āgēaton** *1 pl. pret.* 3/12.

āglǣca, ǣglǣca *m.* demon 11/31, 38, 115; enemy 11/365.

āgōl *see* **āgalan.**

āgyldan *3* pay, give 8/82; **āgeald** *3sg. pret.* 11/463.

āh *see* **ac, āgan.**

āhēawan 7 cut down; **āhēawen** *pret. p.* 15/29.

āhebban 6 raise up 3/87, 14/14, 49; **āhōf** *1 sg. pret.* 15/44, *3 sg. pret.* 12/130, 244; **āhōfon** *1 pl. pret.* 12/213, *3 pl. pret.* 15/61; **āhafen** *pret. p.* 12/106.

āhebbian *w.2* ebb, recede 2/168.

āhlēapan 7 leap up; **āhlēop** *3 sg. pret.* 11/188.

āhlihhan 6 laugh; **āhlōg** *3 sg. pret.* 11/29.

āhōn 7 hang 2/178.

āhrǣrde *see* **ārǣran.**

āhreddan *w.1* rescue 2/35, 10/14, 16.

āht *n.* anything; 3/40 of any account; 9/18 *see* **tō āhte.**

āhte *see* **āgan.**

āhwār *adv.* anywhere 9/169.

āhwētan *w.1* expel 14/161.

ālǣdan *w.1* take away, lead out 2/130, 19/133; 19/115 emerged.

ālǣg *see* **ālicgean.**

ālǣtan 7 give up, leave 11/523; **ālǣte** *2 sg. subj.* 11/438.

aldor, ealdor *n.* life 11/121, 162, 372; 11/225 vital organs; **on, tō (e)aldre** (for) ever 14/157, 182, 191, 17/79.

aldor 13/55 *see* **ealdor.**

aldordagas, ealderdagas *m. pl.* life 11/17, 56.

aldorgedāl *n.* death 11/104.

aldorlēas *adj.* dead 11/328.

aldorman(n), -mon, (e)aldormann, -monn *m.* alderman, chief officer of a shire 1/3, 5, 24, 2/77.

ālecgan *w.1* lay (down), lay low, defeat; **ālecgað** *3 pl. pres.* 6/126, 141; **ālegde** *3 sg. pret.* 11/133; **ālēdon** *3 pl. pret.* 10/19, 15/63; **ālēd** *pret. p.* 6/127.

gealgean see **ealgian.**

ālicgean 5 fail 11/659; **ālǣg** *3sg. pret.* 11/269, 13/3.

ālimpan *3* befall; **ālumpen** *pret. p.* 11/32.

alle *see* **eal(l).**

al(l)walda *m.* Almighty 14/1, 47, 83.

ālȳfan *w.1* permit, allow 12/90, 7/24.

ālȳsan *w.1* release 13/100, 112.

amber *f.* measure 6/51.

ambyre *adj.* favourable 6/77.

āmyrran *w.1* wound, hinder 12/165, 14/133.

ān *num.* one 1/37, 2/3, 163; *indef. art.* a(n) 1/4, 8, 21; *adj.* only, alone 4/25 (**ǣnne**), 7/33, 35.

and, ond *conj.* 5/2, 3, 6; 1/1, 2, 3.

anda *m.* anger, hostility 11/7, 14/154, 16/105.

andefn *f.* amount 6/125.

andettan *w.1* confess 8/49.

andgit *n.* sense; 4/65 **andgit of andgite** according to the sense.

andgitfullicost *supl. adv.* most intelligibly 4/69.

andlēan *n.* reward, requital 11/282.

andlongne *see* **ondlang.**

andsaca *m.* enemy 11/85, 14/75.

andsund *see* **onsund.**

andswarian, andswerian *w.2* answer 5/27, 7/100.

andswaru, ondswaru *f.* answer 11/633, 5/32, 12/44; 11/234, 13/160.

andweard *adj.* present, in person 7/143, 5/50, 7/48.

andwlita *m.* face 7/145, 5.

andwyrdan, andwirdan *w.1 with dat.* answer 4/41, 7/137.

ānfloga *m.* solitary bird 17/62 n.

anforht *adj.* afraid 15/117.

ānforlǣtan 7 forsake, leave alone; **ānforlǣtaþ** *1 pl. pres.* 8/14.

ānga *adj.* only 11/288.

angin *n.* action 12/242 n.

ānhaga, -hoga *m.* solitary 16/1 n., 19/87 n., 16/40.

ānhȳdig *adj.* resolute 11/440, 18/2.

geānlǣcan *w.1* unite; **-lǣhte** *3 sg. pret.* 10/77.

ānlēpe *adj.* single 4/17.

anmedla *m.* pride, pomp, 8/77.

ānne *see* **ān.**

ānpæð *m.* single track 11/201.

ānrǣd *adj.* resolute 11/270, 316, 12/44.

ānrǣdnes *f.* resolution 7/124.

ānstreces *adv.* direct 2/94.

ansȳn *see* **onsȳn.**

ānwealda *m.* Lord 15/153.

apostata *m.* apostate 9/126.

ār *m.* messenger, disciple 11/556, 12/26, 13/159.

ār *f.* (1) honour, benefit, mercy 11/379, 13/76, 16/1, 114; (2) revenue 6/47.

ār *f.* oar 2/153.

arǣdan *w.1* (1) read 4/58, 61–2; (2) determine 16/5 n.

ārǣran *w.1* build, raise 3/4, 10/12, 22; **ārērde** *3 sg. pret.* 3/18; **āhrǣrde** *3 sg. pret.* 10/61.

ārgeblond *n.* mingling of waves, tumultuous sea 13/142.

arcebiscop, ærce- *m.* archbishop 3/28, 4/66.

āreccean *w.1* (1) tell 7/13; **arehte** *3 sg. pret.* 7/18; (2) translate 4/16, 69.

ārēdian *w.2* decide on 7/105.

ārēodian *w.2* blush 7/145.

ārfæstnes *f.* virtue 5/3.

ariht *adv.* properly 9/108.

ārīsan *1* (a) rise; **ārīseþ** *3 sg. pres.* 8/6; **ārīs** *imp. sg.* 11/181; **ārās** *3 sg. pret.* 5/21, 44, 13/191; **ārison** *3 pl. pret.* 7/66.

ārwurð *adj.* venerable 10/39.

ārwurðian *w.2* honour 10/105.

ārwurðlīce *adv.* reverently 10/44, 124, 137.

ārwurðnys *f.* reverence 10/121, 135.

āsændan *w.1* send 7/108.

asca 16/99 *see* **æsc.**

asce *f.* ashes 19/113.

āsceacan 6 shake; **āscēoc** *3 sg. pret.* 12/230.

geāscode, geāscodon *see* **geāxian.**

āscūfan 2 push, launch 2/175.

āscȳran *w.1* make clear 8/44.

āsecgan *w.1* say, tell 16/11; **āsǣde** *3 sg. pret.* 12/198.

āsettan *w.1* (1) set, place 6/146, 15/32, 142; (2) transport (oneself) 2/3.

āsingan *3* sing; **āsong** *3 sg. pret.* 5/58.

āsittan *5* run aground; **āsǣton** *3 pl. pret.* 2/165, 166; **āseten** *pret. p.* 2/166, 167.

āsmēagan *w.2* investigate 9/153.

āsmiþian *w.2* forge 10/124.

āsolcennes *f.* laziness 9/163.

āspendan *w.1* expend 6/137.

āstandan 6 stand up; **āstandaþ** *3 pl. pres.* 8/43; **āstōd** *3 sg. pret.* 11/58, 297.

āstīgan *1* arise; **āstīgeð** *3 sg. pres.* 11/164; **āstāg** *3 sg. pret.* 11/81, 15/103.

āstirian, astyrian *w.2* move 7/46, 15/30.

āstreccan *w.1* extend; **astreht** *pret. p.* 10/131.

āsundrian *w.2* separate 13/198, 19/124.

āswāmian *w.2* cease 14/131.

āswebban *w.1* kill 13/72.

atelīc *adj.* dreadful 11/83.

ātēon 2 draw, take; **ātēah** *3 sg. pret.* 11/65; **ātuge** *3 sg. pret. subj.* 5/80.

atol, atul *adj.* horrible, dire 11/31, 115, 443, 13/53.

attor *n.* poison 11/488, 13/53.

attorsceaða *m.* venomous foe 11/612.

āð *m.* oath, pledge 2/17, 63, 9/176.

āðbrice *m.* perjury 9/123.

āþencan *w.1* think, plan 14/155; āðōhte *3 sg. pret.* 11/416.

āþēostrian, āþīstrian *w.2* be eclipsed 20a/3, 20b/4.

āþer *see* ǣgþer.

āðum *m.* son-in-law 7/104.

āwa *see* ā.

āweaxan 7 grow; āweaxen *pret. p.* 19/147.

āweccan *w.1* rouse, incite; āwehte *3 sg. pret.* 5/81; āwehton *3 pl. pret.* 7/85.

āweg *see* onweg.

āwendan *w.1* turn, translate 4/69, 10/45, 14/14.

āweorpan 3 cast out; āwearp *3 sg. pret.* 10/40; āworpene *pret. p.* 14/175.

āwiht *n.* anything 8/44; āuht 20b/9, 16; ōwiht 17/46; *cf.* āht.

āwiht *adv.* at all 14/45.

āwrītan *1* write 3/12; āwrītað *imp. pl.* 7/107; āwrāt *3 sg. pret.* 7/125, 131, 9/158; āwritene *pret. p.* 4/32.

āwuni(g)an *w.2* remain 8/12, 20a/8.

āwyrdan *w.1* destroy 19/129.

āxsian *w.2* ask 7/9, 14.

geāxian *w.2* learn (of) 1/10, 8/4, 9.

ǣ *f.* law (of God) 4/45.

ǣdre, ēdre *adv.* at once 13/110, 160.

ǣfæst *adj.* pious 5/81, 10, 15.

ǣfæstnes, ǣfestnes *f.* piety 5/15, 3.

ǣfen, ǣfyn *m.* evening 13/200, 14/68.

ǣfensprǣc *f.* evening-speech 11/58.

ǣfentīd *f.* evening 15/68.

ǣfre *adv.* ever 4/42, 9/130, 10/78.

æftan *adv.* from behind 9/59.

æfter *prep. with dat.* (1) after 2/12, 102, 3/3; (2) through, along 2/23, 11/194, 216; (3) because of, on account of 11/523.

æfter *adv.* after(wards) 5/42, 11/180, 504.

æfter ðan ðe *conj.* after 10/1.

æftercweðende *adj. pl.* people speaking after a man's death 17/72.

æftergenga *m.* successor 10/7.

ǣg *n.* egg 19/115.

ǣghwā *pron.* everyone, everything; ǣghwǣm *m. dat. sg.* 11/175; ǣghwǣs *n. gen. sg.* 11/397.

ǣghwǣr *adv.* everywhere 9/22, 52, 129.

ǣghwǣs *adv.* entirely 19/44, 178.

ǣghwǣðer, ǣgþer *pron.* each, either 11/617; 2/22, 6/53, 147, 9/65.

ǣghwilc, ǣghwylc *pron.* each (one) 6/50, 12/234, 8/56, 9/31.

ǣglǣca *see* āglǣca.

ǣgþer *conj.* (1) ǣgþer ge . . . ge both . . . and 2/74–5, 104, 154; (2) ǣgðer . . . and both . . . and 12/224; (3) āþer oððe . . . oððe either . . . or 6/56.

ǣgylde *adj.* unpaid for (by wergild) 9/91.

æht *f.* council 13/169.

ǣht, ēaht *f.* property, possessions 6/40, 3/83.

ǣlan *w.1* burn 19/104.

ǣlc *pron. and adj.* each, any 3/23, 2/25, 35.

ǣlda *see* ylde.

ǣlmæsriht *n.* charitable duty 9/40.

ǣlmesgeorn *adj.* charitable 10/60, 8/23.

æl(l)mihtig *adj. and noun* almighty, the Almighty 5/43, 13/76, 124, 4/18–19.

ǣlmysse *f.* alms 10/66, 67.

ǣlwiht *f.* alien creature, monster 11/241.

geǣmetigan *w.2 with gen.* free, disengage 4/21.

ænde *see* ende.

ænga *see* enge.

ænglas *see* engel.

ǣnig, ǣneg *pron. and adj.* any 3/15, 85, 6/8, 14/46; ǣnige þinga 11/90 by any means.

ǣnlic *adj.* unique 19/9, 10/79, 19/178.

ǣnne *see* ān.

æppel *m.* apple 19/112.

ǣr (1) *prep. with dat.* before 4/60, 8/17, 9/3; (2) *adv.* before, previously 1/25, 32, 2/7; ǣrer, ǣror, ǣrur *adv. comp.* earlier 3/4, 11/108, 427, 3/6, 15/108; ǣrest, ǣrost *adv. supl.* 2/30, 4/45, 5/39, 12/124; (3) *conj.* before 1/12, 2/30, 62.

ǣr ðām ðe, ǣr ðan ðe *conj.* before, 4/27–8, 10/12.

ǣrænde *n.* message 12/28.

ǣrcebiscepe *see* **arcebiscop.**

ǣrendwreca *m.* messenger 4/6.

ǣrend*gewrit* *n.* letter 4/15.

ǣrest *adj. supl.* first 5/71, 6/133; *see also* **ǣr** (2)

ǣrfæder *m.* (old) father 11/395.

ǣrist *m.* resurrection 8/53.

ærnan *w.1* ride 6/131, 141, 12/191.

***ge*ærnan,** *w.1* ride to 6/135.

ǣror, ǣrost, ǣrur *see* **ǣr** (2).

ǣrþan, ǣrþon *conj.* before, until 15/88; 11/30, 19/40, 83.

ǣrwacol *adj.* awake early 7/85.

ǣrwela *m.* ancient wealth 11/520.

ǣr*geweorc* *n.* ancient work 13/190.

ǣr*gewin* *n.* former suffering 15/19.

ǣs *n.* carrion 12/107.

æsc *m.* (ash-tree) (1) ship made of ash wood 2/151, 152; (2) spear made of ash wood 12/43, 310; **asca** *gen. pl.* 16/99.

æscberend *m.* spear-bearer 13/47.

æschere *m.* Viking army 12/69 n.

æscholt *n.* ash-wood spear 12/230.

æstel *m.* bookmark? 4/71 n., 72.

æswic *m.* fraud, deception 9/121.

æt *prep. with dat.* (1) at 1/5, 2/5, 27; (2) from 4/65, 66, 67; 11/168 *see* ***ge*lang æt.**

ætberan 4 carry 11/302; **ætbær** *3 sg. pret.* 11/387.

æteowan *w.1* appear 8/3.

ætforan *prep. with dat.* before 12/16.

ætgædere *adv.* together 2/74, 9/157, 11/28.

ætgifan 5 give 11/651.

æthlēapan 7 escape; **æthlēape** *3 sg. pres. subj.* 9/89.

æthrīnan *1 with gen. or dat.* touch; **æthrān** *3 sg. pret.* 11/21.

ætsomne *adv.* together 11/620, 19/154.

ætsteppan 6 step forth; **ætstōp** *3 sg. pret.* 11/44.

ættren, ættryn, ættern *adj.* poisonous 11/358; 12/47 n.; 12/146.

ætwītan *1 with dat.* reproach 12/220.

æþelboren *adj.* of noble birth 7/97.

æðelborennes *f.* nobility 7/12, 15.

æðele *adj.* noble, fine 10/1, 6/34, 7/103; **æþelast** *supl.* 19/2.

æþeling *m.* noble, prince 1/19, 9, 14.

æþelo *n. pl.* descent 12/216.

ǣðm *m.* breath, breathing 11/366.

ǣwbryce *m.* adultery 9/122.

(*ge*)bād *see* **gebīdan.**

baldlīce *adv.* boldly 12/311; **-licost** *supl.* 12/78.

bām *see* **bēgen.**

bān *n.* bone, tooth 6/34, 48, 143.

bana, bona *m.* slayer 11/386, 12/299, 1/30; 11/597, 13/17.

bāncofa *m.* body 13/231.

band *see* **bindan.**

bānfāg *adj.* adorned with bone (antlers?) 11/79.

bānfæt *n.* body 19/111.

bānhring *m.* bone ring, vertebra 11/308.

bānhūs *n.* body 13/195.

bānloca *m.* joint, body 11/41, 117.

bār *m.* boar 3/72.

***ge*barn** *see* **(*ge*)byrnan.**

basu *adj.* purple, crimson 19/162.

bāt *see* **bītan.**

baþian *w.2* bathe 16/47.

bæc *n.* back 19/175; **ofer bæc** 12/276 backwards.

bæcbord *n.* port side 6/10, 25, 81.

bæd, bædon *see* **biddan.**

***ge*bǣdan** *w.1* oppress 11/599, 20b/14.

bǣl *n.* burning, funeral pyre 19/98, 11/576, 591.

bǣlþracu *f.* violence of fire 19/152.

bǣr *see* **beran.**

***ge*bǣran** *w.1* bear oneself, behave 11/597.

***ge*bǣre** *n.* gesture, cry 1/17 n.

bærnan *w.1* burn 9/111.

bærst *see* **berstan**

(*ge*)bǣtan *w.1* bridle, saddle 11/190.

be, bī, big *prep. with dat.* by, along, about 2/36, 128, 4/64, 2/24; 123, 5/75; 12/182.

be þām þæt *conj.* because 10/107.

bēacen *n.* sign 15/6, 11/550, 15/21.

***ge*bēad** *see* **(*ge*)bēodan.**

beadolēoma *m.* battle-light, i.e. sword 11/264.

beadu *f.* battle 11/8, 280, 12/185.
beadulāc *n.* battle-sport, battle 11/302.
beadurǣs *m.* onslaught 12/111.
beadurōf *adj.* valiant in battle 13/96.
beaduscearp *adj.* battle-sharp 11/477.
beaduscrūd *n.* war-garment 11/433.
beaduserce *f.* coat of mail 11/528.
beaduwang *m.* battlefield 13/172.
bēag, bēah *m.* ring 11/408, 585, 12/31.
bēag, gebēah *see* (*ge*)**būgan.**
bēahgifa *m.* ring-giver, benefactor 12/290.
bēahhord *n.* treasure-hoard 11/599.
beald *adj.* bold 8/36.
bealo *n.* evil, misery 8/36, 11/599.
bealohȳdig *adj.* hostile 11/22.
bealoniŏ *m.* wickedness; *dat. sg.* 11/487 *adv.* wickedly, fiercely.
bealosīþ *m.* journey or experience of hardship 17/28.
bealuware *m. pl.* wicked men 15/79.
bēam *m.* (1) tree 19/35; (2) Cross 15/97, 6, 114.
(*ge*)**bearh** *see* (*ge*)**beorgan.**
bearhtm *m.* noise 11/222.
bearm *m.* bosom 11/548.
bearn *n.* child, son 2/57, 9/53, 80.
bearnmyrŏra *m. or* **-myrŏre** *f.* infanticide 9/146.
bearo *m.* wood 11/154, 17/48, 19/67.
bēatan 7 beat; **bēateŏ** *3 sg. pres.* 20b/15; **bēotan** *3 pl. pret.* 17/23.
beæftan *prep. with dat.* behind 1/22, 24.
bebēodan 2. command; **bebīode** *1 sg. pres.* 4/20, 71; **bebēad** *3 sg. pret.* 8/23, 14/160, **bibēad** 19/36; **bebudon** *3 pl. pret.* 5/55; **beboden** *pret. p.* 5/58, 7/78, 8/29; 5/24 'entrusted.'
bebycgan *w.* 1 sell; **bebohte** 1 *sg. pret.* 11/572.
bebyrgan *w.1* bury 3/3, 10/100.
bēc *see* **bōc.**
beceorfan 3 *with acc. of pers. and gen. of thing* cut off, deprive of by cutting; **becearf** *3 sg. pret.* 11/331.
beceorian *w.2* complain 3/78.

becuman 4(1) come; **becōm** *3 sg. pret.* 7/3, 10/1, 42; **becōmon** *2 pl. pret.* 12/58; (2) befall; **becwōm** *3 sg. pret.* 11/656; **becōmon** *3 pl. pret.* 4/23.
gebed *n.* prayer 10/17, 80, 83.
bedǣlan, bidǣlan *w.1 with dat.* deprive (of) 11/20; 9/26, 16/20.
bedd *n.* bed 7/84, 10/25.
bedelfan 3 bury; **bedealf** *3 sg. pret.* 15/75.
bedīglan *w.1* conceal 8/45.
bedrīfan *1* sprinkle; **bedrifenne** *pret. p.* 15/62.
bedyrnan *w.1* conceal 14/16.
beebbian *w.2* strand 2/170.
befæstan *w.1* (1) secure, entrust 2/93, 132, 7/87; (2) apply 4/22.
befeallan 7 fall; **befeallene** *pret. p.* 14/85, **befeallan** 3/65.
befēolan *w.1 with dat.* apply (oneself) to 4/56.
befōn 7 seize, envelop; **befongen** *pret. p.* 11/368, **bifongen** 19/141, **befangen** 14/129.
beforan, biforan (1) *prep. with dat.* in front of, before 7/64, 84, 8/60; 16/46; (2) *adv.* in front 11/203.
befyllan *w.1* cast down; **befælled** *pret. p.* 14/116.
begān *irr.* (1) surround; **beēode** *3 sg. pret.* 1/12; (2) practise 8/14; **beēode** *3 sg. pret.* 8/81.
bēgen *num.* both 2/72, 73, 10/111; **būtū** *n.acc.* 15/48; **bām** *n.dat.* 11/433.
begēotan 2 cover, pour over; **begoten** *pret. p.* 15/7, 49.
beginnan 3 begin; **begunnon** *pret. p.* 10/79.
begiondan *prep. with dat.* beyond 4/16.
begitan, begietan 5 (1) get 4/16; **begē(a)ton** *3 pl. pret.* 2/138, 4/34; (2) reach **begēte** *3 sg. pret. subj.* 13/137; (3) befall **begēt** *3 sg. pret.* 11/645; (4) occupy **bigēat** *3 sg. pret.* 17/6.
begong *m.* circuit, region 11/238.
behātan 7 promise; **behēt** *1 sg. pret.* 7/63; *3 sg. pret.* 10/89; **behētan** 1 *pl. pret.* 9/174.

behealdan 7 (1) look, see **behēold**
1 sg. pret. 15/25, 58; *3 sg. pret.*
11/35; **behēoldon** *3 pl. pret.*
10/133, 15/9; (2) watch over,
occupy 14/121; **bihealdeþ** *3 sg.
pres.* 19/87; **behēold** *3 sg. pret.*
11/239.

behindan *adv.* behind 2/41.

behionan *prep. w. dat* on this side
of 4/14.

behōfian *w.2 with gen.* require,
need, 11/420.

behrēosan 2 *with dat.* (1) deprive
behrorene *pret. p.* 11/535; (2)
cover **bihrorene** *pret. p.* 16/77.

(*ge*)belgan *3* enrage; **gebolgen**
pret. p. 11/22, 280, 14/54.

belimpan *3* belong, befit; **belimpeð**
3 sg. pres. 6/104; **belumpe** *3 sg.
pret. subj.* 3/24; **belumpon** *3 pl.
pret.* 5/3, 15.

belūcan 2 close; **belocen** *pret. p*
1/26.

bēn *f.* prayer 10/36.

benc *f.* bench 12/213.

bend *f.* bond, fetter 3/32, 11/350.

beniman *4 with gen. or dat.* deprive of; **benimð** *3 sg. pres.* 6/108;
benam *3 sg. pret.* 1/1, 3/59,
binōm 18/16; **benumen(e)** *pret.
p.* 2/104, 14/117 n.

benn *f.* wound 11/497, 16/49.

(*ge*)bēodan 2 (1) offer; **bēodeð** *3
sg. pres.* 17/54; **gebēad** *3 sg. pret.*
1/19, 27; **budon** *3 pl. pret.* 1/31;
geboden *pret. p.* 1/32; (2) command; **bēodaþ** *3 pl. pres.* 9/129.

bēon, bīon *irr.* be 2/156, 6/63, 122,
6/60; **bēo** *1 sg. pres.* 13/72; **bið**
3 sg. pres. 4/71, 6/35, 111; **bið on**
4/71 is worth, 6/48 consists of;
bīoð *1 pl. pres.* 13/167; **bēoð** *3 pl.
pres.* 6/37, 43, 49; **bēo** *2 sg. pres.
subj.* 7/138; **bēo** *3 sg. pres. subj.*
8/35; **bēon** *2 pl. pres. subj.* 7/69;
bēo *imp. sg.* 13/98, **bīo** 11/520.

beorg, biorh *m.* hill, mound, barrow 11/528, 615, 15/32, 50, 11/580.

*ge*beorg *n.* protection 12/31, 131,
245.

(*ge*)beorgan *3 with dat.* protect,
save 9/142, 156, 178; **beorge** *3 sg.*

pres. subj. 9/43; (*ge*)**bearh** 9/52,
11/289; **burgon** *3 pl. pret.* 12/194,
burgan 11/372.

beorht *adj.* bright, splendid, clear
13/84, 96, 202; **beorhtost** *supl.*
11/550, 13/103, 15/6, **beorhtast**
19/80, 109, 172.

beorhte *adv.* brightly, splendidly
11/258, 19/31; **beorhtost** *supl.*
20a/2.

beorhtnes *f.* brightness 20a/3, 4.

beorn *m.* warrior 16/70, 12/17, 62.

(*ge*)bēorscipe *m.* banquet 7/66,
5/19, 23, 7/55.

bēot *n.* vow 12/15, 213, 16/70; **on
bēot** *adv.* 12/27 threateningly.

bēotan *see* bēatan.

bēotian *w.2* vow 12/290.

bera *m.* bear 6/51.

beran *4* bear, carry 6/123, 11/527,
12/12; **bereð** *3 sg. pres.* 15/118,
byrð 6/138; **berað** *3 pl. pres.*
6/70; **beren** *1 pl. pres. subj.*
11/426; **beron** *3 pl. pres. subj.*
12/67; **berað** *imp. pl.* 7/62; **bær**
3 sg. pret. 3/25, 7/126, 10/64;
bǣron *3 pl. pret.* 12/99, 13/176,
15/32, **bǣran** 11/623.

berēafian *w.2 with dat.* deprive, rob
7/76, 11/519, 598.

beren *adj.* bearskin 6/52.

berīdan *1* surround; **berād** *3 sg.
pret.* 1/11.

berōwan 7 row round 2/177.

berstan *3* break, strain 15/36;
bærst *3 sg. pret.* 12/284; **burston**
3 pl. pret. 11/59, 117.

berȳpan *w.1* despoil 9/25, 33.

bescyrian *w.1 with gen.* deprive of
14/147, 149.

besēon *5* look; **beseah** *3 sg. pret.*
7/70, 99, 118.

besettan, bisettan *w.1* surround,
cover 13/210, 19/163, 170.

besittan *5* besiege, sit round;
besittaþ 13/169 *in* æht besittaþ
debate in council; **besæt** *3 sg. pret.*
2/36; **besǣton** *3 pl. pret.* 2/83, 97;
beseten *pret. p.* 2/70, 110.

besmiþian *w.2* fasten 11/74.

besorgian *w.2* grieve about 7/6,
124.

bestandan 6 surround; **bestōdon** 3 pl. pret. 12/68.

bestēman w.1 drench 13/194, 15/22, 48.

bestrȳpan w.1 with gen. strip 9/34.

beswillan w.1 drench 15/23.

beswīcan 1 deceive; **beswīce** 3 sg. pres. subj. 9/63; **beswīcen** 2 pl. pres. subj. 14/188; **beswāc** 3 sg. pret. 14/82; **beswicene** pret. p. 9/36, 12/238.

besyrwan w.1 ensnare, trick 11/12, 9/36.

bet adv. comp. better 9/12; **betst** supl. 7/7.

(ge)bētan w.1 make amends for, atone for 6/143, 8/39, 9/45.

gebētan w.1 remedy, improve 11/129.

betǣcan w.1 deliver, commit; **betǣht(e)** pret. p. 9/24, 10/114.

betlīc adj. splendid 11/79.

betre adj. comp. better 4/51, 8/62, 12/31; **betst** supl. 5/58, 6/37, 17/73.

betwēonan prep. with dat. between, among 6/115, 8/24, 9/177.

bet(w)uh, bet(w)ux, betwyx prep. with dat. between, among 2/20, 3/39, 6/79, 86, 10/5, 58.

betȳnan w.1 finish 5/84.

beþencan w.1 call to mind, consider 9/152, 170.

bewǣndan w.1 (refl.) turn 7/20.

beweaxan 7 grow over, cover; **beweaxen** pret. p. 10/27, **biweaxen** 19/176.

beweorpan 3 throw; **beworpen** pret. p. 14/148.

bewindan 3 encompass, surround; **bewunden** pret. p. 13/19, 58, 14/175.

bewitan w.1 preside over, take care of; **bewiste** 3 sg. pret. 10/66.

bewitian w.2 watch, carry out 11/219.

bewrēon 1 cover; **biwrāh** 3 sg. pret. 16/23; **bewrigen** pret. p. 15/17, 53.

bī see **be**.

bibēad see **bebēodan**.

bicgan w.1 buy 9/76.

gebicgan w.1 obtain; **gebohte** 3 sg. pret. 9/79.

(ge)bīdan 1 with gen. (1) await 6/16, 11/177, 235; **bīdeþ** 3 sg. pres. 8/40; **bād** 3 sg. pret. 6/14, 11/8; (2) receive, experience, suffer 9/12; **gebīdeð** 3 sg. pres. 16/1 n.; **(ge)bād** 1 sg. pret. 11/509, 12/174, 15/125, 3 sg. pret. 11/114, 359; **gebiden** pret. p. 9/11, 15/50, 79; (3) intr. wait 16/70; **gebīdan** 3 pl. pres. subj. 13/158; **gebād** 3 sg. pret. 7/83.

bidǣled see **bedǣlan**.

(ge)biddan 5 ask, pray 10/14, 82 (refl.), 13/84; **bidde** 1 sg. pres. 7/22, 86, 1 pl. pres. 7/103; **gebiddaþ** 3 pl. pres. 15/83; **gebǣd** 1 sg. pret. 15/122; **(ge)bǣd** 3 sg. pret. 10/36, 74, 113; **bǣdon** 1 pl. pret. 7/100, 3 pl. pret. 7/67, 10/134, 12/87.

bidrēosan 2 with dat. deprive (of); **bidroren(e)** pret. p. 16/79, 17/16.

bifian w.2 tremble 15/36, 42.

bifongen see **befōn**.

biforan see **beforan**.

big see **be**.

gebīgan w.1 convert, turn 10/34, 50, 52.

bigēat see **begitan**.

bigiellan 3 scream around; **bigeal** 3 sg. pret. 17/24.

bigstandan 6 surround; **bigstandað** 3 pl. pres. 14/39.

bigwist f. food, sustenance 10/141.

bihealdeþ see **behealdan**.

bihongen adj. (pret. p.) hung 17/17.

bihrorene see **behrēosan**.

bil(l) n. sword 11/308, 298, 394.

billhete m. violence of the sword 13/78.

gebind n. binding 16/24 n., 57.

(ge)bindan 3 bind, seal; **bindeð** 3 sg. pres. 16/102; **(ge)bindað** 3 pl. pres. 16/18, 40; **binde** 3 sg. pres. subj. 16/13; **band** 3 sg. pret. 13/210; **bond** 17/32; **gebundon** 3 pl. pret. 13/48, 177; **gebunden** pret. p. 11/272, 17/9, 18/24.

binnan, binnon (1) *prep. with dat. or acc.* within, into 2/131, 10/7, 102, 7/94; (2) *adv.* within 2/56.

binōm *see* **beniman.**

bīo, bīon, bīoŏ *see* **bēon.**

biorh *see* **beorg.**

bīorsele *m.* beer-hall 11/408.

birhtu *f.* brightness 20b/6.

bisceop, biscop, biscep *m.* bishop 10/39, 2/143, 145, 3/35, 4/1, 75.

biscoprīce *n.* bishopric 3/33.

bisc(e)opstōl *m.* see (bishop's seat) 3/35, 4/70, 10/97.

biseted *see* **besettan.**

bisgo, bisgu *f.* (1) occupation 4/62–3; (2) trouble 17/88.

bisy *see* **bysig.**

bītan *1* cut, bite 11/264; **bāt** *3 sg. pret.* 11/41.

biteldan *w.1* cover 19/155.

bit(t)er *adj.* bitter, sharp, fierce 11/222, 465, 477.

bitere *adv.* cruelly 13/33.

biþ *see* **bēon.**

biwāwan *7* blow upon; **biwāune** *pret. p.* 16/76.

biweaxen *see* **beweaxan.**

biwrāh *see* **bewrēon.**

biwrītan *1* copy; **biwrīte** *3 sg. pres. subj.* 4/76.

blāc *adj.* shining 11/258, 13/217, 19/162.

blācian *w.2* grow pale 17/91.

geblandan *7* mix; **geblēndan** *3 pl. pret.* 13/33; **geblonden** *pret. p.* 19/160.

blāwan *7* blow; **blāweŏ** *3 sg. pres.* 20a/4, **blǣwŏ** 20b/8.

blǣd, blēd *m.* life, glory 16/33, 13/17, 103, 15/149.

blǣdgifa *m.* life-giver 13/84.

blǣst *m.* blaze 19/15.

blēate *adv.* wretchedly, pitiably 11/597.

blēd *f.* fruit 19/35, 38, 71.

blēdum 16/33 *see* **blǣd.**

blendian *w.2* blind 3/70.

bleo *m.* colour 15/22.

bleobrygd *m. or n.* variety of colours 19/158.

bletsian *w.2* bless 10/73.

blinnan *3 with gen.* cease from; **blon** *3 sg. pret.* 13/220.

blis(s), blys(s) *f.* bliss 15/139, 5/19, 10/71, 15/141.

blissian *w.2* rejoice, bless 7/27, 88, 120.

blīþe *adj.* glad, blissful 10/48, 144, 15/122; **blīþra** *comp.* 12/146.

blīðe *adv.* happily 7/59.

blīðheort *adj.* joyful in heart 13/217.

blōd *n.* blood 11/357, 41, 213.

blōdegian *w.2* make bloody 11/465.

blōdgyte *m.* bloodshed 9/47.

blōdig *adj.* bloody 12/154.

blōdlifer *f.* blood-clot? 13/231 n.

blon *see* **blinnan.**

geblonden *see* **geblandan.**

blondenfeax *adj.* grey-haired 11/335.

blōs(t)ma *m.* flower 17/48, 19/21, 74.

blōwan *7* bloom, flower 8/49; **geblōwen** *pret. p.* 19/21, 27, 47.

blysse *see* **blis(s).**

bōc *f.* book 4/29, 30, 63; **bēc** *dat. sg.* 4/72, *nom. pl.* 9/141 n., 151, *acc. pl.* 4/39, 47, 51.

bōccræft *m.* reading (school education) 7/138.

bōcere *m.* scribe 5/4.

gebod *n.* command 19/68.

boda *m.* messenger 12/49, 9/129.

geboden *see* (**ge**)**bēodan.**

bodian *w.2* preach 10/90, 51, 57.

gebodscipe *m.* command 14/185.

bodung *f.* preaching 10/48.

boga *m.* bow 12/110.

gebohte *see* **gebicgan.**

boldwela *m.* happy home 13/103.

gebolgen *see* (**ge**)**belgan.**

bolgenmōd *adj.* enraged 11/8, 13/176.

bona *see* **bana.**

bond *see* (**ge**)**bindan.**

bord *n.* shield 11/446, 12/15, 42.

bordweall *m.* shield-wall 12/277.

geboren *adj.* (*pret. p.* of **beran**) born 7/103; 17/98 born brother.

bōsum *m.* bosom 3/41.

bōt *f.* remedy 9/17, 8, 12.

botm *m.* bottom 11/247, 14/85, 116.

brād *adj.* broad, wide 2/7, 6/61, 63;
 brādre *comp.* 6/62, 82, **brǣdre**
 6/61; **brādost** *supl.* 6/60.
brādswurd *n.* broadsword 12/15.
brand *see* **brond.**
gebrǣc *n.* clash 12/295.
brǣd *f.* flesh 19/122.
brǣdan *w.1* spread 16/47.
brēac *see* **brūcan.**
breahtm, brehtm *m.* revelry 16/86,
 noise 13/226.
brecan *4* break, transgress, destroy;
 brecað *3 pl. pres.* 14/185; 19/67
 burst forth; **brǣc** *3 sg. pret.* 11/252,
 308, 12/277; 11/557 tormented;
 brǣcan *1 pl. pret.* 9/45, 172;
 (*ge*)**brocen** 12/1, 19/80, 111.
bregd *m.* fraud, deceit 8/37.
gebregd *n.* vicissitude 19/57.
(*ge*)**bregdan** *3* (1) move quickly,
 draw, throw 11/6; (*ge*)**brǣgd** *3 sg.*
 pret. 11/93, 280, 305, 476, **brǣd**
 12/154, 162; (2) knit, weave;
 brō(g)den *pret. p.* 11/289, 528,
 19/172.
brego *m.* lord 13/61.
brengan *w.1* bring 2/124, 127;
 (*ge*)**brōhte** *3 sg. pret.* 2/60, 10/127;
 (*ge*)**brōhton** *3 pl. pret.* 2/57, 59,
 6/34, 2/132; (*ge*)**brōht** 9/24,
 10/146. *Cf.* (*ge*)**bringan.**
brenting *m.* ship 11/580.
brēost *n.* and *f.* (*often pl.*) breast
 11/487, 12/144, 13/51.
brēostcearu *f.* sorrow of heart 17/4.
brēostcofa *m.* heart 16/18.
brēosthord *n.* breast, heart 11/565,
 17/55.
brēostgehygd *f.* intimate thought
 11/591.
brēostnet *n.* corslet 11/289.
brēowan *2* brew; **gebrowen** *pret.*
 p. 6/115.
bricg *f.* (bridge), causeway 12/74, 78.
bricgweard *m.* guardian of the
 causeway 12/85.
brid *m.* chick 19/117.
brim *n.* sea, water 11/335, 576.
brimcald *adj.* cold as the sea 19/67.
brimfugol *m.* seabird 16/47.
brimlād *f.* ocean-path 17/30.
brimlīþend *m. pl.* seafarers 12/27.

brimman *m.* seaman, viking 12/49,
 295.
brimrād *f.* water-path 13/217.
brimwylf *f.* she-wolf of the lake
 11/247, 340.
brimwylm *m.* surging of the water
 11/235.
(*ge*)**bringan** *3* lead, take; (*ge*)-
 bringeð *3 sg. pres.* 9/137, 16/54,
 19/153; **gebringe** *3 sg. pres. subj.*
 15/139; **bryng** *imp. sg.* 7/112.
 Cf. **brengan.**
(*ge*)**brocen** *see* **brecan.**
brocian *w.2* afflict 2/139, 140,
 10/25.
brōden, brogden *see* (*ge*)**bregdan.**
brōdenmǣl *n.* damascened sword
 11/357.
(*ge*)**brōhte,** (*ge*)**brōhton** *see* **bren-**
 gan.
brond, brand *m.* fire 19/98, 14/80.
brosnian *w.2* wither 19/38, 152.
brosnung *f.* decay 10/72, 123.
brōþor, brōþur *m.* (1) brother
 9/54, 81, 1/10; (2) monk 5/1.
(*ge*)**brōþru** *m. pl.* brothers 12/191,
 305.
gebrowen *see* **brēowan.**
brūcan *2 with gen.* enjoy, use 11/585,
 13/17, 106; **brūconne** *infl. inf.*
 13/23; **brūcað** *3 pl. pres.* 17/88;
 brēac *3 sg. pret.* 16/44.
brūn *adj.* brown 19/162.
brūnec(c)g *adj.* bright-edged
 11/287, 12/163.
brūnfāg *adj.* shining 11/388.
bryce *m.* offence 9/16.
brycgian *w.2* span 13/216.
bryne *m.* fire 9/46, 17, 179.
bryng *see* (*ge*)**bringan.**
brytta *m.* giver 16/25.
būan *irr.* (*some strong and some weak*
 forms) live, dwell in, cultivate;
 būon *inf.* 11/615; **būgeað** *3 pl.*
 pres. 2/43; **būde** *3 sg. pret.* 6/2, 9,
 73; **gebūn** *pret. p.* 6/21, 22; **gebūd**
 pret. p. 6/26.
budon *see* (*ge*)**bēodan.**
būfan *prep. with dat.* above 2/117,
 6/120.
(*ge*)**būgan** *2* (1) bend, bow 9/171,
 14/38, 15/36; **bēag** *3 sg. pret.* 6/13

177

17; (2) sink, fall; **gebēah** *3 sg.*
pret. 11/281; (3) flee 12/276;
bugon *3 pl. pret.* 11/371, 12/185.
*ge*bunden, -on *see* **bindan.**
būne *f.* cup 16/94, 11/548.
būr *m.* private room, chamber
1/11 n., 7/64 n.
burg, burh *f.* fortified settlement,
town 2/26, 28, 70, 6/111, 10/97;
byrig *gen. sg.* 2/121, *dat. sg.* 1/25,
2/79, 6/112.
burgan, burgon *see* (*ge*)**beorgan.**
burgware *f. pl.* citizens 2/111,
50, 118.
burston *see* **berstan.**
būrþēn *m.* chamberlain 12/121.
būte *conj.* but 2/155.
būton, būtan (1) *prep. with dat.*
except, without 1/2, 2/35, 47, 1/21,
37, 2/28; outside 7/139; (2) *conj.*
except (that), unless 6/4, 14,
11/301; (3) *adv.* outside 2/98.
būtū *see* **bēgen.**
bydel *m.* officer, messenger 9/164.
byldan *w.1* encourage 12/169, 209,
234.
bȳne *adj.* (*cf.* **buan**) cultivatable,
arable 6/58, 59.
gebyrd *f.* rank 6/50, 7/103.
byrde *adj.* high-born; **byrdesta**
supl. 6/50.
byre *m.* son 11/394.
byre *m.* opportunity 12/121.
byrgan *w.1* bury 17/98.
*ge*byrian *w.2 with dat.* befit, pertain
to 8/56, 9/130.
byrig *see* **burg.**
(*ge*)**byr(i)gan** *w.1* taste, eat 15/101,
19/143.
(*ge*)**byrnan** *3* burn (*intr.*); **byrneð**
3 sg. pres. 19/96, 100; *ge*barn *3 sg.*
pret. 11/470.
byrne *f.* corslet, coat of mail 11/433,
388, 446.
byrnsweord *n.* flaming sword 8/41.
byrnwiga *m.* armed warrior 16/94.
byrst *m.* injury 9/42, 11.
byrð *see* **beran.**
(*ge*)**bysgian** *w.2* trouble 13/154,
19/62.
bysig, bisy *adj.* busy 12/110, 7/106.
bysmerian *w.2* revile 15/48.

bysmor *m.* insult 9/11, 42, 109.
bysnian *w.2* set an example 10/53.

cāf *adj.* valiant 12/76.
cāflīce *adv.* valiantly 12/153.
cald *n.* cold 17/8.
cald, ceald *adj.* cold 14/71, 12/91,
17/10, 13/215; **caldast** *supl.* 17/33.
*ge*camp *m.* battle 12/153.
camprǣden(n) *f.* warfare 13/4.
candel *f.* candle 11/313.
canōn *m.* canon 5/73.
canst *see* **cunnan.**
carcern *n.* prison 13/57, 90, 205.
carlman *n.* man 3/43.
cāsere *m.* emperor 17/82.
castel *m.* castle 3/48, 56.
cēafl *m.* jaw 9/165.
cealdum *see* **cald.**
ceallian *w.2* shout 12/91 n.
cēap *m.* (1) property, cattle 2/98,
104, 140; (2) purchase 9/75, 79.
cearian *w.2* care, be anxious 11/277
cearo *f.* grief 16/55, 9, 17/10.
cearseld *n.* abode of care 17/5.
*ge*cēas *see* (*ge*)**cēosan.**
ceaster *f.* fort, city 2/95, 7/96, 139.
ceasterbūend *m.* town-dweller,
castle-dweller 11/67.
ceasterhof *n.* city dwelling 13/192.
ceaster*gewara* *m.* citizen 7/103.
cellod *adj.* ? 12/283 n.
cempa *m.* warrior 11/292, 326,
12/119.
cēne *adj.* brave 12/215, 11/67,
12/283; **cēnre** *comp.* 12/312.
cēnlīce *adv.* boldly 10/10.
cēnðu *f.* bravery 11/469.
cēol *m.* ship 13/120, 139, 17/5.
ceorfan *3* carve; **curfon** *3 pl. pret.*
15/66.
ceorl *m.* man, husband, man of low
rank 12/256, 9/35, 11/332.
(*ge*)**cēosan** *2* choose 7/128; *ge*cēose
1 sg. pres. 7/120, *2 sg. pres. subj.*
7/104, 122, *3 sg. pres. subj.* 7/108;
*ge*cēas *3 sg. pret.* 11/411, 12/113;
cure *3 sg. pret. subj.* 11/591;
curon *3 pl. pret. subj.* 13/163;
*ge*coren *pret. p.* 5/51, 14/40.
gecīgan *w.1* call 7/29, 10/7.
cinges *see* **cyning.**

178

ciricean see cyrce.
cirlisc adj. rustic 2/10.
cirm see cyrm.
cirr m. time, occasion 2/156, 6/7.
cirran w.1 turn 6/20.
clæne adj. pure 5/66, 19/108.
clæne adv. completely 4/13, 9/25, 33.
clænsian w.2 purify 9/176.
cleofan 2 split; clufon 3 pl. pret. 12/283.
cleowen(n) n. ball 19/108.
clif n. rock 17/8.
clingan 3 shrink; clang 3 sg. pret. 13/215; geclungne pret. p. 19/108.
cliopodon see clypian.
clomm m. grasp, bond 11/243, 14/128, 163.
cludig adj. rocky 6/57.
clumian w.2 mumble 9/165.
clustor n. barrier 14/171.
clypian w.2 call, cry out 9/165, 10/13, 71, 115; cliopodon 3 pl. pret. 7/49.
clyppan w.1 embrace 5/60, 16/42.
cnapa m. boy 10/143.
gecnāwan 7 understand: gecnāwen inf. 4/53; gecnāwe 3 sg. pres. subj. 9/42, 86; gecnāwað imp. pl. 9/1.
cneo n. knee 16/42.
gecneordnesse f. accomplishment 7/85–6.
cniht m. (1) boy, young man 12/9, 2/64, 7/109; (2) knight 3/29 n.
cnossian w.2 knock 17/8 n.
cnyssan w.1 buffet, agitate 16/101, 17/33, 19/59.
cnyttan w.1 bind 9/103.
colian w.2 cool, grow cold 8/12, 13/211, 15/72.
collenferð adj. bold of spirit 11/558, 16/71.
cōm, cōman, cōme, cōmon see cuman.
con, const see cunnan.
gecoren see (ge)cēosan.
corn n. corn, grain 2/100, 104, 121.
cradolchild n. infant 9/38.
cræft m. skill, strength 7/46, 54, 11/469, 13/49, 14/24, 27, 157 n.

(ge)crincgan 3 fall (in battle), die 12/292; gecrong 3 sg. pret. 11/309, 16/79, gecranc 12/250, 324; cruncon 3 pl. pret. 12/302.
cristen adj. Christian 2/88, 4/25, 49.
cristendōm m. Christianity 9/89.
cuædon see (ge)cweðan.
cuma m. guest 7/87.
cuman 4 come 6/26, 14/171; cymest 2 sg. pres. 11/173; cym(e)ð 3 sg. pres. 6/80, 106, 132; cumað 3 pl. pres. 6/107, 8/80; cyme 2 sg. pres. subj. 13/159; cume 3 sg. pres. subj. 8/69; cuman 3 pl. pres. subj. 7/76; cōme 2 sg. pret. 7/139; c(w)ōm 3 sg. pret. 2/12, 29, 50, 11/442; cōmon 1 pl. pret. 7/102, 3 pl. pret. 2/4, 30, 49; c(w)ōman 3 pl. pret. 6/91, 15/57; cōme 3 sg. pret. subj. 2/62, 6/89; cumen pret. p. 2/51, 5/52, 10/95.
cumbol n. banner 13/4.
cumpæder m. godfather 2/66 n.
cunnan irr. (1) know; canst 2 sg. pres. 7/90 13/68; const 11/168; can 3 sg. pres. 7/132; cunnon 3 pl. pres. 11/146; cunne 3 sg. pres. subj. 16/69, 71; cūðe 1 sg. pret. 5/29, 3 sg. pret. 10/49, 109, 14/140; cūðon 1 pl. pret. 4/44, 14/112; (2) be able to; con 1 sg. pres. 5/28; cunnon 1 pl. pres. 4/35; cunne 3 sg. pres. subj. 9/42, 86, 94; cunnen 3 pl. pres. subj. 4/57; cūþon 1 pl. pret. 9/108, 3 pl. pret. 4/61; cūðen 3 pl. pret. subj. 4/14.
cunnian w.2 try, explore, experience, suffer 11/217, 241, 12/215.
cure, curon see (ge)cēosan.
curfon see ceorfan.
cūð adj. known, familiar, famous 13/139, 11/4, 16/55.
cwalu f. murder 9/48.
cwealmcuma m. murderous visitor 11/91.
cwearten n. prison 3/33–4, 38.
gecwēman w.1 please 7/7.
cwēn, cwēne f. queen, woman 7/69, 65, 67; 9/75, 101.
(ge)cweðan 5 speak, say 15/116; cweðenne infl. inf. 9/40, 149;

179

cwyŏ *3 sg. pres.* 15/111; **cwe-ŏende** *pres. p.* 7/111, cwæŏende 10/72; **cwæŏ** *1 sg. pret.* 4/41; **(ge)cwǣde** *2 sg. pret.* 7/77, 11/437; **(ge)cwæŏ** *3 sg. pret.* 5/28, 29, 31, 7/1, 10/123; **cwǣdan** *1 pl. pret.* 9/123; **cuǣdon** *3 pl. pret.* 1/29, 32, 33; **cwǣden** *3 pl. pret. subj.* 4/32.

cwic *adj.* alive 11/91, 558, 16/9.

cwidegiedd *n.* greeting 16/55.

cwild *m. or f.* death 2/140.

cwīþan *w.1* lament 16/9, 15/56.

cwōm, cwōman *see* **cuman.**

cwyde *m.* message 7/149.

cyle *m.* cold, cooling 6/144, 146.

cylegicel *m.* icicle 13/215, 19/59.

cyme *m.* coming 19/53, 5/75, 10/44.

cyme, cymest, cymŏ *see* **cuman.**

cymlīce *adv.* splendidly; -licor *supl.* 13/120.

gecynd *f.* nature 19/134, 138.

gecynde *adj.* natural 3/51, 11/469.

cynedōm *m.* rule 10/103.

cynehelm *m.* crown 3/25, 7/41.

cynelic *adj.* royal 7/80, 113, 10/64.

cynerīce, kynerīce *n.* kingdom 10/75, 4/63.

cyning(c), kyning, cing, cyng(c) (*and other variants*) *m.* king 1/13, 23, 25, 1/12, 4/1, 2/38, 46, 78.

cynn *n.* race, people 11/11, 34, 109.

cyr(i)ce, cirice *f.* church 4/28, 8/52, 10/31.

cyrichata *m.* persecutor of the Church 9/126.

cyrm, cirm *m.* uproar 13/41, 12/107, 13/192.

gecyrrednys *f.* conversion 10/95–6.

cyssan *w.1* kiss 7/2, 16/42.

cyst *f.* choice, the best of 11/101, 300, 15/1.

cystig *adj.* virtuous 10/61.

(ge)cȳŏan *w.1* make known, show, tell 4/2, 1/28, 3/89.

(ge)dafenian *w.2 with dat. or acc.* befit 5/16, 7/10.

dala *see* **dæl.**

daroŏ, dareŏ *m.* javelin 11/621, 12/149, 255.

dǣd *f.* deed 1/2, 5/81, 8/7.

dǣdfruma *m.* lord 13/75.

dæg *m.* day 7/83, 2/25, 122; **dæges** *gen. sg.* by day 2/94.

dæghwamlīce *adv.* daily 9/9, 111.

dæghwīl *f.* day 11/499.

dægrīm *n.* number of days 11/122.

dægweorc *n.* day's work 12/148.

dæl *n.* valley 14/60, 176, 19/24.

dǣl *m.* part, share 2/80, 48, 86.

(ge)dǣlan *w.1* (1) divide up, share (in, out) 14/51, 10/42, 12/33; **gedǣled** *pret. p.* 19/161 variegated; (2) part (from) 8/73, 11/30, 13/5.

dēad *adj.* dead 6/117, 129, 140.

gedēaf *see* **gedūfan.**

dēah *see* **dugan.**

deal *adj.* proud 19/148.

dear *see* **durran.**

dēaŏ *m.* death 3/1, 8/5, 8.

dēaŏrǣced *n.* grave 19/48.

dēman *w.1* decree, judge 13/75, 5/19, 15/107.

dēmend *m.* judge 13/87.

denn *n.* lair 11/532.

denu *f.* glen 19/24.

dēofol *m.* demon, (the) devil 9/5, 11/55, 13/43.

dēop *n.* sea 2/166.

dēop *adj.* deep 13/199, 14/60, 176.

dēope *adv.* deeply, profoundly 13/153, 16/89.

dēor *n.* animal 6/42, 48.

dēor, dēore, dȳre *adj.* precious, brave 17/41, 14/16, 6/43.

deorc *adj.* dark 15/46, 16/89.

dēore *adv.* dearly, at great cost 9/79.

dēorfriŏ *n.* park, protection for game 3/67.

dēormōd *adj.* fierce, brave 19/88, 13/187.

dēorwurŏe *adj.* costly 7/61.

derian *w.1 with dat.* injure 12/70, 9/49, 58.

dest, deŏ, dide, didon *see* **(ge)dōn.**

gedihtan *w.1* compose, write 10/138.

dimm *adj.* dim 13/225.

ding *see* **dung.**

disc *m.* dish, plate 10/65, 68, 69.

dōgor *n.* day 11/122, 186, 16/63.

dōgorgerīm *n.* number of days 11/501.

dohte *see* dugan.

dohtor *f.* daughter 7/2, 6, 20.

dol *adj.* foolish 17/106, 14/95.

dolg *n.* wound 15/46.

dolgslege *m.* gash 13/199.

dollic *adj.* audacious 11/419.

dollīce *adv.* foolishly 14/50.

dōm *m.* (1) judgement 11/631, 5/76, 8/53; (2) choice 1/27, 12/38; (3) glory 11/269, 179, 439.

dōmdæg *m.* day of judgement 15/105.

dōmgeorn *adj.* eager for glory 16/17.

dōmlēas *adj.* inglorious 11/663.

dōmlīce *adv.* gloriously; -licost *supl.* 13/222.

(*ge*)dōn *irr.* (1) do, make 3/31, 4/10, 5/11; gedō *1 sg. pres.* 7/26; dēst *2 sg. pres.* 7/34; dēð *3 sg. pres.* 9/136, 11/632; (*ge*)dōð *3 pl. pres.* 6/147, 9/74; dō *2 sg. pres. subj.* 4/20, *3 sg. pres. subj.* 3/90, 9/60; gedōn *1 pl. pres. subj.* 4/53; dyde *3 sg. pret.* 5/22, 10/70, dide 7/78; gedydon *3 pl. pret.* 2/157, dydan 3/32, 13/27, didon 7/109; gedōn *pret. p.* 3/10, 43, 7/64; (2) place; dōn *inf.* 4/59 promote; dō . . . from *3 sg. subj.* 4/72 remove; dyde . . . of *3 sg. pret.* 11/582 take off; (3) arrive; gedydon *3 pl. pret.* 2/76, 95, 118.

dorste, dorston *see* durran.

drāf *f.* band 9/106.

dragan 6 drag; drōgon *3 pl. pret.* 13/187.

dranc *see* drincan.

drǣfan *w.1* drive 9/67.

gedrǣg *n.* company 13/43, 11/55.

drēam *m.* joy 15/140, 11/20, 14/12.

(*ge*)dreccan *w.1* afflict; gedrehte *3 sg. pret.* 13/39; drehton *3 pl. pret.* 2/149, gedrehtan 9/49.

drēfan *w.1* stir up, trouble 11/208, 13/128, 153.

dreng *m.* warrior 12/149 n.

drēogan 2 act, commit, experience 13/199; drēogeð *3 sg. pres.* 19/92; drēogað *3 pl. pres.* 9/74, 17/56;

drēag *3 sg. pret.* 18/2; drugon *3 pl. pret.* 11/97, 130; gedrogen *pret. p.* 11/499.

drēorig, drīorig *adj.* (1) bloody 11/208, 562; (2) sad 16/25, 17.

drēorighlēor *adj.* with sad face 16/83.

(*ge*)drēosan 2 fall, decline 11/439; drēoseð *3 sg. pres.* 16/63, 19/143; drēosað *3 pl. pres.* 19/34; gedrēas *3 sg. pret.* 16/36; gedroren *pret. p.* 17/86.

drepan 5 strike; drep *1 sg. pret.* 11/653.

drepe *m.* blow 11/330.

drīfan *1* drive; drīfað *3 pl. pres.* 9/106, 11/581; drife *3 sg. pres. subj.* 9/65.

drihten *see* dryhten.

drihtguma *m.* retainer 11/179.

drincan 3 drink; drincað *3 pl. pres.* 6/113, 114; dranc *3 sg. pret.* 11/41.

gedrogen *see* drēogan.

drōgon *see* dragan.

drohtað, drohtoð *m.* abode 19/88, way of life, lot 11/55, 13/128.

drohtnung *f.* way of life 10/40.

drugon *see* drēogan.

drȳ *m.* magician 13/34.

drȳge *adj.* dry 2/161.

dryhten, drihten *m.* lord, God 5/38, 42, 11/526, 562.

dryhtlic *adj.* magnificent; -licestum *supl.* 17/85.

dryhtmāðum *m.* noble treasure 11/616.

dryhtsele *m.* splendid hall 11/66.

drync *m.* drink 13/22, 34, 53.

gedrync *n.* drinking 6/122, 124.

dryre *m.* fall 19/16.

drysmian *w.2* become gloomy 11/166.

gedūfan 2 plunge in; gedēaf *3 sg. pret.* 11/473.

dugan *irr.* avail, prosper; dēah *3 sg. pres.* 12/48; dohte *3 sg. pret.* 9/46, 95.

duguð, dugeð, dugoð *f.* (1) veterans, elders 13/153, 9/161, 11/431; (2) gift, benefit 12/197.

dumb *adj.* dumb 13/67.

dung *f.* prison(-cell); **ding** *dat. sg.* 13/225.

dūnscræf *n.* mountain cave, ravine 13/187, 19/24.

durran *irr.* dare; **durre** *1 sg. pres.* 16/10; **dyrre** *2 sg. pres.* 11/170; **dear** *3 sg. pres.* 9/20, 22, 26; **dorste** *1 sg. pret.* 15/35, 45, 47, *3 sg. pret.* 3/31, 42, 11/508; **dorston** *3 pl. pret.* 6/20, 26, 11/621.

duru *f.* door 11/20, 1/13, 19/12.

dwǣs *adj.* foolish 9/141.

dwelian *w.2* lead astray 9/6.

dwolcræft *m.* sorcery 13/34.

gedwolgod *m.* false god 9/21, 23, 26.

gedwyld *n.* error 10/129.

dydan, dyde, (ge)dydon see **(ge)-dōn.**

dȳgel *adj.* secret 11/148.

dynnan *w.1* resound 11/66.

dȳran *w.1* esteem 14/12.

dȳre see **dēor.**

dyrne *adj.* secret, mysterious 11/148.

dyrstig *adj.* bold 11/611.

dysig *adj.* foolish 9/128.

ēa, ē *f.* river 2/7, 8, 84, 123; **ēas** *gen. sg.* 2/125, 6/22.

ēac (1) *adv.* also, moreover 2/25, 26, 52; (2) *prep. with dat.* besides 2/147.

ēaca *m.* reinforcement 2/74.

ēacen *adj.* (1) large 11/362; (2) pregnant 18/11.

ēad *n.* prosperity, bliss 14/157, 19/185.

ēadgifa *m.* giver of happiness 13/74.

ēadig *adj.* blessed 19/20, 10/9, 13/54.

ēadmōd, ēaðmōd *adj.* humble 10/60, 15/60, 17/107.

ēadwela *m.* blessedness 19/133.

eafera *m.* offspring, son 11/288, 14/154.

eafoð *n.* strength 13/30.

ēage *n.* eye 7/19, 11/25, 13/30.

ēaggebyrd *f.* nature of the eye 19/167.

ēagorstrēam *m.* sea 13/138.

ēahta 3/83 see **ǣht.**

eahta *num.* eight 6/36, 10/106.

eahtian *w.2* watch over, rule 11/198.

ēalā *excl.* alas 3/5, 7/35, 123.

ēaland *n.* land beyond the sea 13/28; *cf.* **igland** (2).

ealað see **ealo.**

eald *adj.* old 11/536, 9/33, 11/94; 19/120 fully grown; **ieldran** *comp.* 4/33 ancestors.

ealderdagum see **aldordagas.**

ealdhlaford *m.* old lord 11/551.

ealdian *w.2* grow old 17/89.

ealdor, aldor *m.* chief, lord 12/202, 11, 53, 13/55, 70.

ealdor, ealdre see **aldor.**

ealdormonn, -mann, see **aldor-mann.**

ealdgestrēon *n.* ancient treasure 11/172.

ealdsweord *n.* ancient sword 11/299, 389.

ealdgewyrht *n.* desert 11/430, 15/100.

ealgian *w.2* defend, protect 11/95, 428, 441; **gealgean** *inf.* 12/52.

eall, all (1) *adj.* all 2/56, 58, 81; 1/15, 20; (2) *adv.* completely 7/145, 11/43; *cf.* **ealles.**

ealles *adv.* (*gen. sg. of* **eall**) altogether, entirely 2/139, 141, 9/10.

eallgylden *adj.* all golden 11/540.

eallwealdend *m.* God 10/18.

ealneg *adv.* always 4/75.

ealo *n.* ale 6/115; **ealað** *gen. sg.* 6/146.

ealubenc *f.* ale-bench 11/640.

ealuscerwen *f.* dispensing of ale? 11/68 n.

ēam *m.* uncle 10/5.

eard *m.* land, homeland 11/168, 9/37, 50.

eardgeard *m.* dwelling-place 16/85.

eardian *w.2* dwell 6/59, 91.

eardstapa *m.* wanderer 16/6.

earfoþ, earfeþ *n.* hardship 18/2, 30, 16/6.

earfoðhwīl *f.* time of hardship 17/3.

earfoðlic *adj.* full of hardship 16/106.

earfoðlīce *adv.* with difficulty, sorrowfully 11/595.

earfoþnes *f.* trouble, hardship 8/16.

earh *adj.* cowardly 12/238.

earhlic *adj.* cowardly 9/93.

earm *m.* arm 10/25, 116, 123.
earm *adj.* wretched, poor 3/57, 78, 8/23.
earmbēag *m.* bracelet 11/536.
earmcearig *adj.* miserable 16/20, 17/14.
earmlic *adj.* miserable 11/107.
earmlīce *adv.* wretchedly 9/153.
earmsceapen *adj.* wretched 11/142.
earn *m.* eagle 12/107, 17/24, 19/117.
(*ge*)earnian *w.2* earn, deserve 8/46, 9/13, 179; **ernian** 9/12.
earnung *f.* (de)merit 9/13, 14.
geearnung *f.* merit, favour 10/28, 78, 12/196.
eart *see* **wesan.**
ēast *adv.* east 2/50, 6/15.
ēastan *adv.* from the east 6/106, 107, 20b/12; **be ēastan** 2/79, **wiŏ ēastan** 6/58 to the east of.
ēastdǣl *m.* eastern part 19/2.
ēastende *m.* eastern end 2/5.
ēasterdæg *m.* Easter Day 10/64.
ēasterne *adj.* east(ern) 14/70.
ēasteŏ *n.* river-bank 12/63.
ēastewe(a)rd (1) *adj.* eastern 2/5, 48, 108; (2) *adv.* to the east 6/59, 60.
ēasthealf *f.* east side 2/87.
ēastlang *adv.* to the east 2/6.
ēastrēam *m.* river 13/216.
ēastrīce *n.* the eastern kingdom 2/2 n., 16.
ēastryhte *adv.* due east 16/13.
ēaŏe *adv.* easily 4/53, 7/142, 9/152; **eaŏ** *comp.* 13/127.
ēaŏmōd *see* **ēadmōd.**
ēaŏmōdlīce *adv.* humbly 5/82.
eaxl *f.* shoulder 11/115, 134, 278.
eaxl*ge*spann *n.* point of intersection of two members of the Cross 15/9.
ebba *m.* ebb 12/65.
ēce *adj.* eternal 5/38, 42, 8/75.
ēcelīce *adv.* eternally 8/66.
ecg *f.* (sword-)edge, sword 11/104, 290, 299.
ecghete *m.* violence of the sword 17/70.
ēcnys *f.* eternity 10/32, 149.
ēder *f.* vein 11/41.
edlēan *n.* requital 13/183.

ednīwe, ednēowe *adj.* renewed 19/77, 105, 123, 14/69.
ednīwian *w.2* renew 7/22.
edor *m.* dwelling 16/77.
ēdre *see* **ǣdre.**
edwenden *f.* change, end 19/40.
edwītlīf *n.* life of disgrace 11/664.
edwītsprǣc *f.* scornful speech 13/81.
efenehŏ *f.* neighbourhood 2/100.
efes *f.* edge, side 2/24.
efnan *w.1* perform 11/395.
efne, emne *adv.* even, just 5/14, 13/114.
efne swā *conj.*, *adv.* just as 11/312, 13/189.
efnēce *adj.* co-eternal 8/51.
efstan *w.1* hasten 8/18, 11/234, 12/206.
eft *adv.* afterwards, again, back 2/2, 60, 66.
eftsīŏ *m.* return 11/556.
ege *m.* fear 5/76, 9/135.
eg(e)sa *m.* terror 11/83, 509, 13/221.
egeslic *adj.* terrible 11/598, 9/4, 74.
ēhtan *w.1 with gen.* pursue 11/253.
elcung *f.* delay 7/101.
eldum *see* **ylde.**
ellen *n.* courage 11/479, 234, 270.
ellenheard *adj.* valorous 13/209.
ellenmǣrþu *f.* heroic deed 11/127.
ellenrōf *adj.* valiant 13/169.
ellensīoc *adj.* deprived of strength 11/560.
ellenweorc *n.* courageous deed 11/416.
ellenwōdnes *f.* zeal 5/83–4.
elles *adv.* else, otherwise 8/74, 75, 17/46.
ellorgāst, ellorgǣst *m.* alien spirit 11/106, 140, 358, 362.
el(l)þēodig *adj.* foreign 13/16, 26, 63.
eln *f.* ell 6/36, 38, 53.
elra *adj. comp.* another 11/51.
embe *see* **ymb(e).**
emne *see* **efne.**
emnlange *prep. with dat.* along 6/58.
ende *m.* end 8/2, 2/66, 5/84; **ænde** 9/31.
endebyrdnes *f.* order, succession 5/20, 34.

endeláf *f.* last survivor 11/586.
endeléas *adj.* endless 18/30.
(ge)endian *w.2* end, die 5/85, 7/66, 19/83.
geendung *f.* end 7/55, 10/113.
enge, ænge *adj.* narrow 11/201, 19/52, 14/111.
engel, *m.* angel 14/27, 12/178, 13/74, **engyl** 14/17; **ænglas** *nom. pl.* 10/144.
engelcynn *n.* race of angels 14/1.
engeldryht *f.* host of angels 15/9.
ent *m.* giant 11/490, 547, 13/190 n., 16/87 n.
ēode, ēodon *see* **gān.**
eodorcende *adj.* (*pres. p.*) ruminating 5/66.
eofersprēot *m.* boar-spear 11/228.
eoh *m.* steed 12/189.
eom *see* **wesan.**
ēoredgeatwe *f. pl.* military equipment 11/639.
eorl *m.* (1) man, warrior 11/60, 68, 90; (2) earl 12/51, 3/29, 12/6 n.
eorldōm *m.* earldom 3/36, 51.
eorlscipe *m.* nobility, heroism 11/395.
eornost *f.* earnest 9/108.
eornoste *adv.* earnestly 12/281.
eorre *see* **yrre.**
eorŏdraca *m.* earth-dragon 11/485, 598.
eorŏe *f.* earth (world) 5/39, 11/51, 101.
eorŏreced *n. or m.* earth-house 11/492.
eorŏrīce *n.* earth 14/174.
eorþscræf *n.* grave 8/39, 16/84.
eorŏweg *m.* earth 15/120.
eorŏwela *m.* earthly wealth 17/67.
eoten *m.* giant 11/60.
eotenisc, etonisc *adj.* made by giants, gigantic 11/299, 389.
ēow, ēower, ēowre, ēowerne, ēowrum *see* **þū.**
erian *w.1* plough 6/56, 46.
ernian *see* **(ge)earnian.**
ēst *f.* grace, will 19/46.
ēstēadig *adj.* prosperous, well-living 17/56.
ettan *w.1* graze 6/56.
ēŏbegēte *adj.* easy to obtain 11/634.

ēŏel *m.* country 13/21, 4/7, 12/52.
ēŏellēas *adj.* homeless 13/74.
ēŏelwyn *f.* enjoyment of a home 11/658.

fācen *n.* wickedness 13/20.
fadian *w.2* arrange, regulate 9/175, 54.
fāg, fāh *adj.* hostile 11/110, 444; **fāne** *m. acc. sg.* 11/428 foe.
fāg, fāh *adj.* decorated, shining, stained 15/13, 11/15, 24 n., 335, 356.
fand *see* **findan.**
fandian *w.2* test, find out 6/7.
(ge)faran 6 (1) *intr.* act, proceed, go 2/31, 159, 3/41; **fareŏ** *3 sg. pres.* 17/91; **faraþ** *3 pl. pres.* 6/11; **fare** *3 sg. pres. subj.* 7/76; **fōr** *3 sg. pret.* 2/1, 20, 102; **fōron** *3 pl. pret.* 2/19, 23, 44; **gefōre** *3 sg. pret. subj.* 6/94; **gefaren** *pret. p.* 2/71, 9/153; (2) *tr.* suffer **gefōre** *2 sg. pret.* 7/139.
fatu *see* **fæt.**
fæc *n.* period of time, interval 5/5.
fæder *m.* father 3/74, 7/2, 3.
fæge *adj.* doomed to die 12/119, 11/268, 309.
fægen *adj.* glad 10/95, 16/68, 20b/10.
fæger *adj.* fair 19/85, 5/84, 7/50; **fægrost, -est** *supl.* 13/103, 19/8.
fægere, fægre *adv.* beautifully, suitably, well 12/22, 19/156, 161; **fægrost** *supl.* 17/13.
fægnian *w.2 with gen.* rejoice in 10/44.
fægrian *w.2* make beautiful 17/48.
fæhŏ(o) *f.* feud, battle 11/171, 278, 12/225 n.
fælsian *w.2* cleanse, purge 11/124, 361.
fæmne *f.* girl 7/130.
fær *n.* journey 2/39.
fær *m.* (sudden) danger 14/89.
færgripe *m.* sudden grip or attack 11/257, 37.
færinga *adv.* suddenly 7/1 11/205.
færlīce *adv.* suddenly 16/61.
færsceaŏa *m.* raider 12/142.
fæst *adj.* firm, strong 11/155, 21, 491.
fæste *adv.* firmly 5/44, 11/59, 72.

fæsten *n.* fortification, secure place 2/83, 12/194.

fæstenbryce *m.* violation of a fast 9/125.

fæstlic *adj.* firm 20b/16.

fæstlīce *adv.* firmly, resolutely 12/82, 254.

(ge)fæstnian *w.2* fasten, confirm 12/35, 10/120, 13/49.

fæstnung *f.* security 16/115.

fæt *n.* vessel 11/534.

fǣt *n.* (gold) plate 11/15.

fǣted *adj.* (*pret. p.*) ornamented, plated 11/474.

fǣtels *m. or n.* vessel 6/146.

fæþm *m.* bosom, embrace 11/80, 184.

fæðmian *w.2* embrace, enfold 11/425.

fæðmrim *n.* cubit 19/29.

fēa *adj. pl.* (a) few 2/10, 4/14, 4/17.

fēa *adv.* little 15/115 n.

gefēa *m.* joy 11/513, 19/130.

(ge)feaht *see* **(ge)feohtan.**

feala, fealo *see* **fela.**

(ge)feallan 7 fall, prostrate oneself, fall dead 10/13, 12/54, 105; **fealleþ** *3 sg. pres.* 16/63; **feallað** *3 pl. pres.* 19/74; **feallende** *pres. p.* 10/113; **(ge)fēol(l)** *3 sg. pret.* 7/37, 54, 10/24, 11/71, 12/119; **fēollon** *3 pl. pret.* 7/19, 10/16, 111.

gefeallan 7 fall on to; **gefēoll** *3 sg. pret.* 11/607.

fealo *adj.* pale, yellow 19/100, 16/46, 19/74.

fealohilte *adj.* golden-hilted 12/166.

fēasceaft *adj.* destitute, friendless 13/126.

fēasceaftig *adj.* needy 17/26.

fēawa, fēawe, fēawum *see* **fēa** (*adj.*).

(ge)feccan, gefecgan *w.1* fetch 7/28, 30, 88, 12/160; **fette** *3 sg. pret.* 10/26.

gefēgan *w.1* join together 19/175.

gefeh *see* **gefēon.**

fela, feala, fealo (1) *with gen.* many, much 2/83, 151, 10/148, 13/198, 11/530; (2) *adv.* much 11/176.

gefēlan *w.1* feel 17/95.

felasinnig *adj.* very sinful 11/170.

feld *m.* open country, field, plain, battlefield 19/26, 2/23, 12/241.

fel(l) *n.* skin, hide 6/48, 51, 13/23.

feng *m.* grip, attack 19/97.

(ge)fēng(on) *see* **(ge)fōn.**

fengel *m.* prince 11/191.

fenhlið *n.* fen-slope 11/119.

fenhop *n.* fen-retreat 11/63.

fengelād *n.* fen-path 11/150.

fenn *m. or n.* fen 2/10.

feoh *n.* property, money 16/108, 1/19, 27.

feohgīfre *adj.* avaricious 16/68.

feohlēas *adj.* without money 2/137.

gefeoht *n.* war, battle 1/7, 2/42, 8/6.

(ge)feohtan 3 fight 12/16, 261; **feohtende** *pres. p.* 1/16, 20, 35; **(ge)feaht** 1/7, 2/34, 10/10; **gefuhton** *3 pl. pret.* 2/88, 171.

gefeohtan 3 win in battle 12/129.

feohte *f.* battle 12/103.

(ge)fēol(l), fēollon *see* **(ge)feallan.**

fēolan 3 penetrate; **fylð** *3 sg. pres.* 6/81; **fulgon** *3 pl. pret.* 1/35.

fēolheard *adj.* hardened by the file *or* hard as a file 12/108.

gefēon 5 rejoice; **gefeh** *3 sg. pret.* 11/126, 310.

fēond, fīond (*pl. often* **fȳnd**) *m.* enemy, fiend 11/24, 9/78, 10/19, 11/444.

feor (1) *adv.* far 6/11, 12, 11/107; **firrest** *supl.* 6/11; (2) *adj. with dat.* far from 16/21.

feorgbold *n.* body 15/73 n.

feorh, feorg *m.* life 19/105, 1/19, 37, 17/94; **ferh** *acc. sg.* 11/479; **tō wīdan feore** 13/106 'for the rest of your life'.

feorhbenn *f.* mortal wound 11/513.

feorhhord *n.* soul 19/103.

feorhhūs *n.* body 12/297.

feorhlegu *f.* life 11/573.

feorhgeniðla *m.* deadly enemy 11/281.

feorhsēoc *adj.* mortally wounded 11/119.

feormendlēas *adj.* without a polisher 11/534.

feormian *w.2* consume 11/43, 19/100.

feorran *adv.* from afar 11/124, 161, 581.

feorrancumen *adj.* (*pret. p.*) foreign 13/24.

feos *see* **feoh.**

fēower *num.* four 2/120, 6/16, 7/60.

fēowertig *num.* forty 2/44, 6/38.

gefēra *m.* companion 12/280, 1/32, 34.

fēran *w.1* go 11/181, 10/3, 51.

gefēran *w.1* reach 11/617.

gefēre *adj.* accessible 19/4.

ferh *see* **feorh.**

fer(h)ð *m., n.* mind, heart 11/53, 16/90, 17/26.

ferhðgeniðla *m.* deadly foe 11/654.

(ge)ferian *w.1* (1) *tr.* transport, carry 2/32, 42, 10/101; (2) *intr.* go 12/179, 13/156.

ferlorene *see* **forlēosan.**

fers *n.* verse 5/33.

fersc *adj.* fresh 6/70.

ferð *m. or n.* company 16/54.

ferðloca, fyrhðloca *m.* heart 16/33, 13, 13/58.

fēsan *w.1* drive away 9/99.

fēt *see* **fōt.**

fetelhilt *n.* hilt with a chain 11/304.

feter *f.* fetter 16/21.

gefetian *w.2* fetch 2/130, 15/138.

fette *see* **(ge)feccan.**

fēþa *m.* foot-troop 11/215, 12/88.

fēðe *n.* movement 14/134.

fēþecempa *m.* foot-soldier, warrior 11/285, 626.

feðer *f.* feather, wing 6/48, 52, 16/47.

feðerhoma *m.* wings 14/172 n.

fierd, fird, fyrd *f.* army, levy 2/30, 20, 27, 96, 107, 129, 12/221; 14/163 battle.

fierdian *w.2* be on military service 2/39.

fierdlēas *adj.* unguarded 2/24.

fīf *num.* five 6/19, 51, 2/164.

fīftēne *see* **fȳftȳne.**

fīftig, fīfteg *num.* fifty 11/506, 6/38, 4/71.

findan 3 find, meet 7/77, 140, 11/169; **findeð** *3 sg. pres.* 6/143; **fand** *3 sg. pret.* 11/18, 562; **fundon** *3 pl. pret.* 12/85; **funde** *3 sg. pret.*

subj. 7/117, 11/206; **funden** *pret. p.* 4/45.

finger *m.* finger 11/59, 63, 246.

finta *m.* tail 19/161.

fīonda *see* **fēond.**

fiorm *f.* use 4/30.

fīras *m. pl.* men, mankind 5/43, 11/514, 13/24.

fird *see* **fierd.**

firigendstrēam *see* **fyrgenstrēam.**

gefirn *see* **gefyrn.**

firrest *see* **feor.**

first, fyrst *m.* time 4/57, 8/68, 10/99.

fiscað *m.* fishing 6/113, 5.

fiscere *m.* fisherman 6/24, 28.

fiþer *n.* wing 19/163, 182.

flān *m.* arrow 12/71, 269.

flānboga *m.* bow 11/224.

flǣsc *n.* flesh 8/75, 10/122, 19/103.

flǣschoma *m.* body 8/44, 11/309, 13/24.

flēam *m.* flight 2/90, 11/662, 12/81.

flēogan 2 (1) fly 12/7, 109, 150; **flēag** *3 sg. pret.* 17/17; (2) flee 12/275.

flēon 2 flee 11/54, 63, 119; **flugon** *3 pl. pret.* 2/35, 12/194.

flēotend *m.* (*pres. p.*) seafarer 16/54.

flet *n.* (floor of a) hall 11/281, 309, 16/61 n.

geflīeman, geflȳman *w.1* put to flight 2/34, 55, 111, 11/161.

flocc *m.* troop 2/25.

flocrād *f.* gang, troop 2/24.

flōd *m.* flood, tide 2/175, 11/152, 157.

flōde *f.* channel 1/5.

flōdweg *m.* ocean-path 17/52.

flōdwylm *m.* spring 19/64.

flōr *m.* floor 11/24.

flot *n.* sea 12/41.

flota *m.* (1) sailor (Viking) 12/72, 227; (2) ship 13/156.

flotman *m.* sailor (Viking) 9/98.

flōwan 7 flow; **flōwende** *pres. p.* 12/65.

flugon *see* **flēon.**

flyht *m.* flight 12/71.

geflȳmed *see* **geflīeman.**

fnǣst *m.* breath, blast 19/15.

fōddor *n.* food 19/141.

fōdorþegu *f.* sustenance 19/130.

folc *n.* people, troop 12/45, 2/48, 118.

folcāgend *m.* ruler of a people 19/5.

folccyning *m.* king of a nation 11/506, 646.

folclagu *f.* public law 9/32.

folcriht *n.* public right 11/381.

folc*ge*stealla *m.* companion in war 14/26, 42.

folcstede *m.* country 13/20.

folctoga *m.* chieftain 13/8.

foldbold *n.* building 11/72.

foldbūend *m.* man, earth-dweller 11/146.

folde *f.* ground, earth 5/43, 11/152, 184.

folgaŏ *m.* office 18/38.

folgian *w.2 with dat.* follow, serve 1/30, 3/24, 81.

folm(e) *f.* hand 11/21, 44, 12/21, 108.

(*ge*)fōn 7 seize, take 14/42; **fōŏ** *3 pl. pres.* 6/43; **fēng** *1 sg. pret.* 4/18; (*ge*)**fēng** *3 sg. pret.* 10/118, 11/39, 242, 278, 283; (*ge*)**fēngon** *3 pl. pret.* 2/32, 162; **fēngon tōgædere** 10/111 joined battle.

for *prep. with dat.* (1) because of 1/2, 4/23, 43; (2) before 11/554; (3) in the face of 17/101.

fōr *see* (*ge*)**faran.**

for hwī *int. adv.* why 7/84.

foran *adv.* from the front, at the front, 2/34, 99, 160, 19/158.

forbærnan *w.1* (*tr.*) burn up, cremate 2/58, 100, 6/122.

forbēodan 2 forbid; **forbēad** *3 sg. pret.* 3/71.

forberstan 3 break apart; **forbærst** *3 sg. pret.* 11/453.

forbūgan 2 flee away from; **forbēah** *3 sg. pret.* 12/325.

forbyrnan 3 (*intr.*) burn up; **forbarn** *3 sg. pret.* 11/357, **forborn** 11/445.

ford *m.* ford 2/36, 12/81, 88.

fordōn *irr.* destroy 9/161; **fordenera** *pret. p. gen. pl.* 13/43 damned.

fore *prep. with acc.* instead of 17/21, 22.

*ge*fōre *see* (*ge*)**faran.**

foregenga *m.* predecessor 3/15.

foregīsel *m.* preliminary hostage 2/17.

foresecgan *w.1* mention before; **foresǣdon** *1 pl. pret.* 10/122; **foresǣdan** *pret. p.* 10/26 aforesaid.

forespeca *m.* sponsor 9/175.

foresprecen *adj.* (*pret. p.*) aforesaid, above-mentioned 2/116.

forfaran 6 obstruct; **forfōron** *3 pl. pret.* 2/159.

forgeorne *adv.* very well 8/66.

forgifan 5 give; **forgeaf** *3 sg. pret.* 7/72, 11/260, 379; **forgeafe** *1 sg. pret. subj.* 14/165; **forgifen, forgyfen, forgiefene** *pret. p.* 7/70, 5/53, 17/93; **forgif** *imp. sg.* 13/76.

forgifenes *f.* forgiveness 3/90.

forgrindan 3 destroy; **forgrunden** *pret. p.* 11/450, 13/172, 19/109.

forgyldan 3 repay, requite 11/318; **forgilde** *3 sg. pres. subj.* 13/146; **forgyldon** *2 pl. pres. subj.* 12/32; **forgeald** *3 sg. pret.* 11/282, 325; **forgolden** *pret. p.* 11/616.

forgȳman *w.1* neglect 14/82.

forgytan 5 forget; **forgytane** *infl. inf.* 3/39.

forhabban *irr.* restrain oneself 11/382.

forhæfednys *f.* temperance 10/54.

forhealdan 7 withhold 9/20; **forhealdaŏ** *1 pl. pres.* 9/21.

forheard *adj.* extremely hard 12/156.

forhēawan 7 hew down; **forhēawen** *pret. p.* 12/115, 223, 288.

forhergian *w.2* ravage 4/28.

forhicgan *w.1/2* despise; **forhogode** 12/254.

forhohnes *f.* contempt 5/8.

forht *adj.* afraid, fearful 11/53, 13/98, 15/21.

forhtian *w.2* be afraid 12/21, 15/115.

forhwæga *adv.* about 6/126, 130.

forlǣtan 7 (1) leave, desert, abstain from, neglect 9/172, 11/91, 12/2, **forlǣton** 8/65; **forlǣteŏ** *3 sg. pres.* 8/69; **forlǣten** *3 pl. pres. subj.* 8/65; **forlǣten** *3 pl. pres. subj.* 14/159, 184; **forlēt** *1 sg. pret.* 7/16; *3 sg. pret.* 5/23, 7/49, 11/560; **forlēton** *3 pl. pret.* 2/127,

4/43, 15/61; **forlēte** *3 sg. pret.*
subj. 5/61; **forlēton** *3 pl. pret.*
subj. 13/162; **forlǣten** *pret. p.*
4/36; **forlǣt** *imp. sg.* 7/25; (2) let
(go); **forlēt** *3 sg. pret.* 12/149, 321;
(3) spare; **forlēt** *3 sg. pres.* 3/1.
forlǣtnes *f.* remission 8/53.
forlegen *adj.* (*pret. p.*) adulterous
9/147.
forlēogan *2* perjure oneself ; **for-
logen(e)** *pret. p.* 9/84, 124.
forlēon 3/92 n.
forlēosan *2* lose, ruin; **forlēas** *1 sg.
pret.* 7/15; *3 sg. pret.* 3/44; **forlure**
2 sg. pret. subj. 7/91; **forloren,
ferlorene** *pret. p.* 9/124, 14/56.
forliden *adj.* shipwrecked 7/7, 129,
135.
forlidennes *f.* shipwreck 7/140.
forliger *n.* fornication 9/122.
forma *adj.* first 11/15, 39, 268.
formoni *adj.* very many 12/239.
forniman *4* carry off, destroy; **fornime** *3 sg. pres. subj.* 7/137;
fornōm *3 sg. pret.* 16/80, 19/150,
fornam 11/227, 545; **fornāmon**
3 pl. pret. 11/601, **fornōman**
16/99; **fornumene** *pret. p.* 9/39.
fornȳdan *w.1* force 9/34.
foroft *adv.* very often 9/50, 52,
115.
fōron *see* (*ge*)**faran**.
forrǣdan *w.1* betray 9/65, 66.
forrīdan *1* intercept 2/99; **forrād**
3 sg. pret. 2/33.
forrotian *w.2* decay 10/72.
forsacan *6* refuse, deny; **forsōcon**
3 pl. pret. 10/136.
forscieppan *6* transform; **forscēop**
3 sg. pret. 14/63.
forsēon *5* despise; **forsawene**
pret. p. 9/41.
forsīðian *w.2* perish 11/291.
forspanan *6* lead astray; **forspēon**
3 sg. pret. 14/105.
forspendan *w.1* squander 6/139.
forspillan *w.1* kill 9/68.
forst *m.* frost 13/212, 11/350, 14/71.
forstandan *6* (1) withstand, prevent; **forstōd** *3 sg. pret.* 11/290;
(2) understand; **forstōd** *1 sg. pret.*
4/68.

forswāpan *7* sweep off; **forswēop**
3 sg. pret. 11/587; **forswapen**
pret. p. 14/146.
forswelgan *3* swallow, eat 17/95.
forswerian *6* (1) lay curse on; **forsworen** *pret. p.* 11/103; (2) for-
swear; **forsworene** *pret. p.* 9/84.
forswīðe *adv.* very greatly, excessively 2/139.
forsyngod *adj.* (*pret. p.*) corrupt(ed)
9/117, 151.
forð *adv.* (1) forward 2/49, 6/20,
7/50; (2) thenceforth, henceforth
14/75, 103, 192; **tō forð** 9/137 too
much, 12/150 too far.
forð heonon *adv.* henceforth 15/132.
forðām, forþan, forþǣm, forðon
(**þe**) *conj.* (1) because 2/41, 103,
5/2, 29; (2) therefore 4/19, 35,
5/14, 18.
forðbringan *w.1* produce; **forð-
brōhte** *3 sg. pret.* 5/7.
forðearle *adv.* grievously 10/25.
forðfēran *w.1* die 2/142.
forðgān *irr.* go forth; **forðēode**
3 sg. pret. 15/54.
forðgeorn *adj.* eager to advance
12/281.
geforþian *w.2* accomplish 12/289.
forþolian *w.2 with dat.* forgo 16/38.
forðgesceaft *n.* creation? decree?
15/10 n.
forðweg *m.* way forth, departure
11/398, 15/125, 16/81.
forðȳ *adv.* therefore 2/175, 4/50, 74.
forðȳ þe *conj.* because 2/103-4.
forwandigend *adj.* (*pres. p.*) respect-
ful 7/11.
forweard *adv.* in front, forward
19/157.
forwegan *5* kill; **forwegen** *pret. p.*
12/228.
forweorpan *3* throw away; **forwurpe** *3 sg. pret. subj.* 11/645.
forweorðan *3* perish; **forweorðan**
1 pl. pres. subj. 9/157; **forwearð**
3 sg. pret. 2/180; **forwurdan** *3 pl.
pret.* 9/69, 167.
forwiernan, -wyrnan *w.1* deny
2/122, 7/80.
forwrītan *1* cut apart; **forwrāt** *3 sg.
pret.* 11/478.

forwundian *w.2* wound severely 2/180, 15/14, 62.

forwyrcan *w.1* obstruct, dam, destroy 2/123-4; **forwyrcan** *3 pl. pres. subj.* 9/139; **forworhtan** *3 pl. pret.* 9/166-7; **forworhte** *pret. p.* 14/136.

forwyrde *f.* destruction 8/19.

foryrman *w.1* make destitute 9/35.

fōt *m.* foot *(dat. sg. and nom. acc. pl.* fēt) 10/58, 11/44, 12/119; **fōtas** *nom. pl.* 19/177.

fōtmǣl *n.* foot (measure) 3/7, 12/275.

fōð *see (ge)*fōn.

fracod, fracoð *adj.* worthless, vile 11/316, 15/10, 13/168.

fram, from (1) *prep. with dat.* from, away from, by 2/9, 6/87, 7/24, 1/29, 2/169; (2) *adv.* away 11/53, 12/317, 1/31.

franca *m.* spear 12/77 n., 140.

frǣcnessum *see* frēcnes.

gefrǣge *n.* information; *usually dat. sg. in* mine gefrǣge as I heard 11/75, 458, 610.

gefrǣge *adj.* famous 19/3.

gefrǣgn *see* gefrignan.

frǣt *see* fretan.

frǣtwe *f. pl.* ornaments, treasure, precious weapons 19/139, 11/393, 557, 19/73 fruit.

frǣtwian *w.2* decorate 8/79, 19/121, 156.

frēa *m.* lord, God 5/43, 11/435, 15/33 n.

frēadrihten *m.* lord 11/95.

freca *m.* warrior 11/304.

frēcne *adj.* terrible, dangerous 11/150, 169, 462; **frēcnost** *supl.* 13/186.

frēcnes, frǣcnes *f.* danger, disaster 8/3, 16.

frēfran *w.1* comfort 13/126, 16/28, 17/26.

fremde *adj.* strange 6/141, 9/37, 53.

(*ge*)fremman *w.1* perform, do 10/90, 8/82, 11/110.

fremsumnes *f.* benefit 5/78.

fremu *f.* benefit 14/192, 17/75 n.

frēo, frio *adj.* free 3/76, 4/55.

frēod *f.* peace, love 12/39, 13/149.

frēodryhten *m.* noble lord 11/400.

gefreogum *see* gefrige.

frēolsbryce *m.* non-observance of a festival 9/125.

frēomǣg *m.* free kinsman 16/21.

frēond *m.* friend 16/108, 6/118, 7/64; **frȳnd** *dat. sg.* 7/29, *acc. pl.* 12/229.

frēondlēas *adj.* friendless 16/28.

frēondlīce *adv.* in a friendly way 4/2.

frēorig *adj.* freezing, cold 16/33, 13/214.

frēoriht *n.* rights of freemen 9/39.

freoðolēas *adj.* savage 13/29.

fretan *5* devour, eat; **frǣt** *3 sg. pret.* 11/322; **freten** *pret. p.* 2/86.

frettan *w.1* graze 2/100.

gefricgan *5* learn; **gefricgean** *3 pl. pres. subj.* 11/662.

frige? 18/15 n.

gefrige *n.* information; **gefreogum** *dat. pl.* 19/29.

gefrignan *3* learn (of); **gefrǣgn** *1 sg. pret.* 11/467, 525, 546; **gefrugnon** *1 pl. pret.* 18/14, **gefrūnan** 13/1; **gefrūnon** *3 pl. pret.* 15/76; **gefrugnen** *pret. p.* 19/1.

frīnan *3* ask; **frīneð** *3 sg. pres.* 15/112.

frīora *see* frēo.

frið *n.* peace 3/39, 12/39, 41.

frōd *adj.* wise, old 11/157, 11/398, 573.

frōfor *m.* solace, comfort 7/80, 13/95, 16/115.

from *adj.* active, bold 13/8.

from *prep., adv. see* fram.

fromweard *adj.* about to die 17/71.

fruma *m.* beginning 5/70.

frumgār *m.* chieftain 11/629.

frumsceaft *f.* creation 5/31.

gefrūnon, gefrūnan *see* gefrignan.

frymdi *adj.* desirous, requesting 12/179.

frymþ *m., f.* beginning 19/84, 121.

frȳnd *see* frēond.

fugel *m.* bird 16/81, 6/48, 19/86.

fugelere *m.* fowler 6/24, 28.

fugeltimber *n.* young bird 19/118.

(*ge*)fuhton *see* (*ge*)feohtan.

fūl *adj.* foul 9/146, 165.

fulgon *see* **fēolan.**

fūlian *w.2* decay 6/145.

full *adj.* full 3/41, 8/37, 14/88; **be fullan** 4/39, completely, perfectly.

ful(l) *adv.* very 9/16, 93, 131.

fullæstan *w.1 with dat.* help 11/441 n.

fullian *w.2* baptise 10/4.

fullīce *adv.* completely 9/91, 92.

fulluht *m. or n.* baptism 9/174, 10/52, 95.

fulnēah *adv.* almost 2/152.

fultum *m.* help, support 2/50, 4/54, 11/435.

fultumian *w.2* assist 5/13.

fulwihthād *m.* baptismal vow 8/33.

fulwyrcan *w.1* complete; **fulworhte** *3 sg. pret.* 10/78.

funde(n), fundon *see* **findan.**

fundian *w.2* make one's way, hasten 15/103, 17/47.

furlang *n.* furlong 2/168.

furðor, furður *adv. comp.* further 4/59, 58, 11/60; 14/156 any more.

furþum *adv.* just, even 2/126, 4/15, 17.

fūs *adj.* eager 12/281, 15/21 n., 57.

fūslic *adj.* ready 11/215, 391.

fȳftȳne, fīftēne *num.* fifteen 6/51, 11/323, 6/105.

fylgean, fyligan *w.2 with dat.* (*cf.* **folgian**) follow 9/173, 14/4, 8/45.

fyl(l) *m.* fall, death 10/9, 115, 11/285.

fyllan *w.1 (with gen.)* fill (with) 4/29, 14/74; 10/121 fulfil.

fyllan *w.1* fell, kill 11/428, 479, 15/38.

(ge)fylstan *w.1 with dat.* help 12/265, 10/11, 109.

fylþ *f.* filth, sin 9/76, 77.

fylð *see* **fēolan.**

fȳnd *see* **fēond.**

fȳr *n.* fire 11/474, 9/17, 11/157.

fȳrbend *f.* band forged with fire 11/21.

fyrd *see* **fierd.**

fyrdhom *m.* coat of mail 11/245.

fyrdhrægl *n.* corslet 11/268.

fyrdhwæt *adj.* valiant 13/8.

fyrdlēoð *n.* warsong 11/215.

fȳrdraca *m.* fire-dragon 11/462.

fyrdrinc *m.* warrior 12/140.

fyrdsearo *n.* armour 11/391.

fyrdgestealla *m.* comrade in battle 11/646.

fyren *f.* crime 11/49, 110; **fyrnum** *dat. pl.* (*adv.*) excessively 14/71.

fyrenlust *m.* lust 8/80.

fyrgenbēam *m.* mountain-tree 11/205.

fyrgenholt *n.* mountain-wood 11/184.

fyrgenstrēam, firigendstrēam *m.* mountain-stream (waterfall?) 11/150, 13/149 n.

fyrhto *f.* terror 5/76.

fyrhðlocan *see* **ferðloca.**

fyrhðlufe *f.* heartfelt love 13/83.

fyrlen *adj.* distant 10/91.

fȳrlēoht *n.* fiery light 11/257.

fyrmest *adj. supl.* foremost, first 3/36, 12/323.

gefyrn, gefirn *adv.* formerly 2/1, 7/101.

fyrndagas *m. pl.* days of old 13/1.

fyrngēar *n. pl.* past years 19/101.

fyrnmann *m.* man of old 11/534.

fyrngesetu *n. pl.* ancient home 19/145.

fyrnum *see* **fyren.**

fyrngeweorc *n.* ancient work 19/84.

fyrst *adj.* chief 6/44.

fyrste *see* **first.**

fyrstmearc *f.* proper time 19/105.

(ge)fyrōran *w.1* impel 11/557.

fyrwet *n.* curiosity 11/557.

fȳrwylm *m.* surge of fire 11/444.

fȳsan *w.1* shoot 12/269.

gafol, gofol *n.* tribute 6/48, 47, 12/32, 61.

gegadrian *w.2* assemble 2/20, 42, 76; **gegædrað** *3 sg. pres.* 19/151.

gāl *n.* pride 14/82.

galan *6* sing 11/85, 223, 15/67.

gālscipe *m.* pride 14/96.

gān *irr.* go 7/96, 13/124; **gǣst** *2 sg. pres.* 7/115; **gā** *3 sg. pres. subj.* 11/185; **gān** *1 pl. pres. subj.* 7/72, *3 pl. pres. subj.* 3/93; **ēode** *1 sg. pret.* 5/29, *3 sg. pret.* 1/13, 5/22, 57; **ēodon** *3 pl. pret.* 1/27, 31; **gegān tōgædre** *pret. p.* 11/403

come together (in battle); **gāð**
imp. pl. 12/93.

gegān *irr.* (1) obtain 3/18, 11/276;
(2) come to pass; **geēode** *3 sg.
pret.* 10/73; (3) go **geēode** *3 sg.*
11/449.

gang *m.* path, track 8/26, 11/182,
195; 15/23 flowing.

gangan, gongan 7 go 12/3, 40, 62;
11/10, 421; **gangon** *2 pl. pres.
subj.* 12/56; **gongende** *pres. p.*
5/23; **gīong** *3 sg. pret.* 11/488,
gēong 11/529; **gegongen** *pret. p.*
11/121; **gēong** *imp. sg.* 11/516.

gegangan 7 (1) gain 12/59; (2) hap-
pan; **gegongen** *pret. p.* 11/594.

ganet *m.* gannet 17/20.

gār *m.* spear 12/13, 46, 67; 14/71 n.

gārberend *m. pl.* spear-warriors
12/262.

gārrǣs *m.* battle 12/32.

gārsecg *m.* ocean 13/151, 130.

gārwiga *m.* warrior 11/447, 584.

gārwigend *m.* warrior 11/414.

gegarwod *see* **gearwian**.

gāst *m.* (1) spirit 15/11, 152; 11/148
demons; (2) soul 8/73, 12/176,
15/49; (3) *in* **Halga Gāst** 8/51
Holy Ghost.

gatu *see* **geat**.

gædeling *m.* kinsman 19/390.

gegædrað *see* **gegadrian**.

gǣlsa *m.* luxury 9/166.

gærs *n.* grass 13/38.

gǣst *see* **gān**.

gǣstlic *adj.* 16/73 n.

gē *pron. see* **þū**.

ge *conj.* and, or 6/118.

ge ... ge *conj.* both ... and 2/26,
56–7, 79–80.

gēac *m.* cuckoo 17/53.

geador *adv.* together 11/134.

geaf *see* **gifan**.

geaflas *m. pl.* jaws 19/166.

gēafon *see* **gifan**.

gealga *m.* (gallows), cross 15/10,
40.

gealgan *see* **ealgian**.

gealgmōd *adj.* cruel 13/32.

gealgtrēow *n.* cross 15/146.

gēap *adj.* curved, vaulted 11/135.

gēapscipe *n.* cunning 3/45.

gēar *n.* (*some cases* **gēr(e)**) year 2/1,
15, 102.

gēara *adv.* (*gen. pl. of* **gēar**) long ago
11/437, 14/165, 15/28.

gēardagas *m. pl.* days of yore 11/145,
16/44.

gearelīce, gearolīce *adv.* readily,
clearly 8/1, 18/10.

gearo *adj.* ready 1/18, 12/72,
100.

gearwe, geare, gearo *adv.* readily,
well 11/498, 16/71, 11/429, 10/15,
11/521; **gearwost** *supl.* 11/14.

gearwian *w.2* prepare 9/180, 14/186.

geat *n.* gate 7/139; **gatu** *acc. pl.*
1/26, 35.

geatolic *adj.* splendid, adorned
11/192, 303.

gefeð *see* **gifan**.

gegnum *adv.* forwards, straight
11/195.

gēn, gīen, gīn *adv.* yet 11/450, 475,
14/168, 19/118; **ne ... þā gēn**
11/33 by no means.

gēna *adv.* still 11/573.

gengan *w.1* go 11/192, 203.

gēnunga *adv.* completely 11/644.

gēoc *f.* help 11/447, 17/101.

gēocor *adj.* sad 11/64.

geofon *m. or n.* sea 13/152; **gyfenes**
gen. sg. 11/185.

geofona *see* **gifu**.

geoguðe *see* **gioguð**.

geoguðfeorh *m., n.* youth 11/437.

geohðo, giohðo *f.* sorrow 13/66,
11/566.

geolo *adj.* yellow 11/383.

geōmor *adj.* sad 11/405, 13/61,
17/53.

geōmormōd *adj.* sad at heart
13/165.

geond, giond, gynd *prep. with acc.*
through, throughout, along 6/70,
8/5, 4/3, 4, 9/10, 39.

geondfaran 6 pass through; **-farað**
3 pl. pres. 19/67.

geondhweorfan 3 pass through;
-hweorfeð *3 sg. pres.* 16/51.

geondlācan 7 flow through; **-lāce**
3 sg. pres. subj. 19/70.

geondscēawian *w.2* consider 16/52.

geondstyrian *w.1* agitate 20b/15.

geondþencan *w.1* consider 16/60, 89.

geondwlīteð *see* **giondwlītan.**

geong, iung- *adj.* young 12/210, 11/399, 447, 7/2, 4, 7; **gingæste** *supl.* 11/590 last.

gēong *vb. see* **gangan.**

geongordōm *m.* service 14/22, 38 n.

geongra, giongra *m.* disciple, servant 14/32, 8/16, 14/162.

georn, giorn *adj.* eager, zealous 8/36, 11/556, 4/9.

georne *adv.* eagerly, readily, certainly 8/61, 9/5, 8; **geornor** *comp.* 11/120; **geornost** *supl.* 8/59, 9/156.

geornful(l) *adj.* desirous (of), eager 12/274, 8/18.

geornfulnes, -nys *f.* eagerness, zeal 5/80–1, 10/62–3.

geornlīce *adv.* eagerly, zealously 5/79, 12/265.

gēotan *2* pour, surge; **gēotende** *pres. p.* 13/152.

gēr(e) *see* **gēar.**

gesthūs *n.* lodging 7/72.

giddian *w.2* sing 20a/1.

giefstōl *m.* throne 16/44.

gielpes *see* **gilp.**

giellan *3* scream; **gielleð** *3 sg. pres.* 17/62.

gīeman *see* **gȳman.**

gīen *see* **gēn.**

gīet *see* **gȳt.**

gif, gyf *conj.* if 1/27, 2/22, 3/10, 11/173.

gifan *5* give 7/56; **gife** *1 sg. pres.* 7/59; **gefeð** *3 sg. pres.* 19/185; **gife** *2 sg. pres. subj.* 7/23, *3 sg. pres. subj.* 13/147; **geaf** *3 sg. pret.* 11/396, 408, 413; **gēafon** *3 pl. pret.* 10/96; **gif** *imp. sg.* 7/58.

gīfernes *f.* greed 9/118.

gifeðe, gyfeþe *adj.* granted 11/455, 503, 118.

gīfre *adj.* eager 17/62.

gifu, gyfu *f.* gift 5/53, 7/65, 5/2, 13; **geofona** *gen. pl.* 19/149.

gīgant *m.* giant 11/303.

gilp, gielp *n.* boast 11/128, 16/69.

gim(m) *m.* jewel 13/223, 3/8, 15/7.

gīn *see* **gēn.**

gingæste *see* **geong.**

gioguð, geoguð, iugoð *f.* youth, young men 4/54, 16/35, 17/40, 10/3.

giohðe *see* **geohðo.**

giond *see* **geond.**

giondwlītan *1* look over, survey 11/544; **geondwlīteð** *3 sg. pres.* 19/93.

gīong *vb. see* **gangan.**

giongorscipe *m.* service 14/4.

giongrum *see* **geongra.**

giorne *see* **georn.**

girnan *w.1* desire 7/89, 97.

girran *3* rattle; **gurron** *3 pl. pret.* 13/133.

girstandæg *adv.* yesterday 7/86.

gīsle, gīslas *see* **gȳsel.**

gist, gyst *m.* stranger 11/263, 232, 343, 12/86.

gīt *see* **gȳt.**

gītsung *f.* avarice 3/65, 9/118, 162.

giū *see* **iū.**

glæd *see* **glīdan.**

glæd *adj.* bright 19/169.

glǣm *m.* ray 19/135.

glæs *n.* glass 8/44, 19/166.

glēaw *adj.* wise 16/73, 19/29.

glen(c)gan *w.1* adorn 5/6, 58.

glēd *f.* fire, flame 11/425, 450.

glēdegesa *m.* terrible fire 11/423.

glenge *m.* ornament 8/78.

glīdan *1* glide 13/203; **glād** *3 sg. pret.* 13/130.

glitinian *w.2* glitter, shine 11/531.

glīwstafas *m. pl.* joy; **-stafum** *dat. pl.* 16/52 joyfully.

gnorn *m. or n.* sorrow 11/431.

gnornian *w.2* grieve 12/315, 17/92.

god *m.* god, God 7/44, 9/12, 14/38.

gōd *n.* (1) goodness 8/11, 55; (2) benefit 12/176, 13/165, 14/46; (3) *in pl.* goods, property 5/63.

gōd *adj.* good, noble 12/315, 3/91, 6/35; **sēl(re)** *comp.* 11/460, 175, 8/62; **sȳllan** 18/6; **sēlest** *supl.* 11/180, 2/141, 11/197.

godbearn *n.* godchild 9/68.

godcund *adj.* divine 4/3, 9, 5/1–2.

godcundlīce *adv.* divinely 5/12.

gōddǣd *f.* good deed 9/132, 133.

godfyrht *adj.* godfearing 9/133.

gōdian *w.2* (*intr.*) improve 9/15.

gegōdian *w.2* enrich, endow 3/5, 19, 7/75.

gōdlec *adj.* excellent; gōdlecran *comp.* 14/36.

gōdnes, -nys *f.* goodness 3/92, 10/143.

godsibb *m.* sponsor (at baptism) 9/68.

godspell *n.* gospel 8/60, 13/12.

godsunu *m.* godson 1/37, 2/61.

gofol *see* gafol.

gold *n.* gold 11/538, 3/41, 60.

goldǣht *f.* gold-treasure 11/521.

goldfāh *adj.* decorated with gold 11/584.

goldfæt *n.* gold-setting (for a jewel) 19/169.

goldgyfa, -giefa *m.* lord 11/425, 17/83.

goldhord *n.* treasury 7/57.

goldsele *m.* gold-hall 11/14 n.

goldwine *m.* gold-friend, benefactor 11/343, 16/22, 35.

gomel, gomol *adj.* old 11/188, 336, 383, 455.

gomelfeax *adj.* grey-haired 17/92.

gomen *n.* merriment 17/20.

gongan, *ge*gongen, gongende *see* gangan, *ge*gangan.

gram *adj.* hostile, fierce 14/57, 11/64, 76.

grāp *f.* grasp 11/64, 135, 283.

grāp *vb. see* grīpan.

grāpian *w.2* grasp 11/307.

grǣdig *adj.* greedy, full of desire 11/240, 263, 17/62.

grǣdinæs *f.* gluttony 3/66.

grǣf *n.* grave 17/97.

grǣg *adj.* grey 13/130.

grǣgmǣl *adj.* marked with grey 11/455.

gegrǣmian, *ge*gremian *w.2* enrage 9/159–60, 12/138, 296.

grǣswong *m.* grassy plain 19/78.

grēat *adj.* massive 14/139.

grēne *adj.* green 19/164, 13, 36.

grēot *n.* dust 12/315, 19/149.

grēotan *2* weep; grēotende *pres. p.* 15/70 n.

grētan *w.1* (1) greet 4/1, 5/26, 7/67; (2) approach, touch 11/102, 508.

gegrētan *w.1* attack 9/134.

grim, grimm *adj.* fierce, grim 11/240, 9/127, 11/283.

grimlic *adj.* terrible, cruel 9/4.

grindan *3* grind; grundon *3 pl. pret.* 13/132; *ge*grundene *pret. p.* 12/109.

grindel *m.* bar 14/139.

grīpan *1* grasp; grāp *3 sg. pret.* 11/242.

grið *n.* sanctuary, peace 9/71, 12/35.

griðian *w.2* protect 9/29.

griðlēas *adj.* violated 9/32.

grōwan *7* grow 8/48.

grund *m.* (1) ground, bottom, depths 13/152, 11/158, 185; (2) earth 17/104.

grundlēas *adj.* bottomless, endless 14/145, 18/15.

grundwong *m.* bottom, floor 11/237, 543.

grundwyrgen *f.* hag of the deep 11/259.

gryrelēoð *n.* terrible song 11/85, 12/285.

gryrelic *adj.* terrible 11/232.

guma *m.* man 11/175, 14, 158.

gumcynn *n.* mankind 11/538.

gumfēþa *m.* troop on foot 11/192.

gurron *see* girran.

gūð *f.* war, battle 11/276, 399, 651.

gūðbill *n.* war-sword 11/102.

gūðcyning *m.* war-king 11/450.

gūðhorn *n.* war-horn 11/223.

gūðhrēð *m. or n.* glory in battle 11/118.

gūðlēoð *n.* war-song 11/263.

gūðplega *m.* battle (*lit.* battle-play) 12/61.

gūðrǣs *m.* attack 11/318.

gūðrinc *m.* warrior 12/138, 11/242, 421.

gūð*ge*tāwa *f. pl.* war-equipment 11/409.

gūð*ge*wǣde *n.* armour 11/390, 396, 503.

gūðwērig *adj.* weary with fighting, dead 11/327.

gūðwine *m.* sword (*lit.* war-friend) 11/508.

gyf *see* gif.

gyfenes *see* geofon.

gyfeþe *see* gifeðe.

gyfe *see* gifu.

gyldan *3* pay, repay 6/50, 11/409, 14/168; **gylt** *3 sg pres.* 6/50; **gyldað** *1 pl. pres.* 9/109, 110, *3 pl. pres.* 6/47; **gylde** *3 sg. pres. subj.* 9/92.

gylden *adj.* golden 11/582.

gylpan *3 with dat.* boast (of) 11/647.

gylpword *n.* boasting word 12/274, 14/19.

gȳman, gīeman *w.1* care, take care of, pay heed to 14/101, 104, 5/79.

gynd *see* geond.

gynn *adj.* spacious, wide 11/292.

*ge*gyrela *m.* garment 8/79.

gyrwan *w.1* build, decorate 14/36, 15/16, 23.

gȳsel, gīsel *m.* hostage 12/265, 1/21, 2/63.

gystas *see* gist.

gȳt, gīt, gīet *adv.* yet, still 3/52, 9/83, 152, 7/38, 11/168, 4/34; **gȳta** 15/28.

habban *irr.* (*2 uses: tr.* 'have' *and as auxiliary; for economy of space they are not separated here*) 3/82, 4/12, 7/105; **habbanne, hæbbenne** *infl. inf.* 14/34, 8/70; **hæbbe** *1 sg. pres.* 7/131, 15/50, 79; **habbe** 7/26; **hafast** *2 sg. pres.* 7/22, 12/231; **hæfð** *3 sg. pres.* 9/180, 12/237, 14/116, **hafað** 6/132, 11/351, 14/118; **habbað** *1 pl. pres.* 3/91, 4/19, 54, *3 pl. pres.* 6/33, 72, 99; **habban** *1 pl. pres. subj.* 8/24; **hæbben** *3 pl. pres. subj.* 4/55, **habban** 8/25; **hæfde** *1 sg. pret.* 4/68, *3 sg. pret.* 1/2, 8, 2/21; **hæfdon** *3 pl. pret.* 1/16, 26, 2/16; **hafa** *imp. sg.* 11/186; *negative forms:* **næfð** *3 sg. pres.* 7/37, 14/115, **nafað** 8/67; **nabbe** *2 pl. pres.* 7/105; **næbbe** *3 sg. pres. subj.* 17/42; **næfde** *3 sg. pret.* 2/138, 3/7, 42.

hād *m.* order, rank 3/23, 4/4, 9.

hādbryce *m.* attack on a priest 9/121.

*ge*hādod *adj.* (*pret. p.*) in holy orders 9/55.

hādor *adj.* bright 13/89, 19/94, 20a/2.

hādre *adv.* brightly 11/312; **hādrost** *supl.* 20b/4.

hafela, heafola *m.* head 11/163, 212, 452, 470.

hafenian *w.2* raise 11/314, 12/42, 309.

hafoc *m.* hawk 12/8.

hagle *see* hægl.

hāl *adj.* sound, unhurt 7/138, 10/122, 11/244.

hālettan *w.1* salute 5/26.

hālgian *w.2* consecrate 8/52.

hālig, hāleg *adj.* holy, *weak as noun* saint 5/40, 54, 64, 13/104.

hālignes *f.* sanctuary 9/32.

hals, heals *m.* neck 19/164, 12/141, 11/307, 464, 582.

hām *m.* home, base 2/28, 55, 78.

hāmweard *adv.* home 2/109.

hāmweardes *adv.* on the way home 2/40.

hand, hond *f.* hand 10/73, 7/42, 11/382, 457.

handbred *n.* (palm of) hand 10/85.

handmægen *n.* might 14/2 n.

hand*ge*stealla *m.* comrade 11/369.

hār *adj.* grey, grey-haired 12/169, 11/206, 517.

hara *m.* hare 3/75.

hāt *n.* heat 11/378, 14/138.

hāt *adj.* hot 11/464, 214, 357; **hātran** *comp.* 17/64 more inspiring; **hātost** *supl.* 19/91.

hātan *7* (1) call 14/99; **hǣt** *3 sg. pres.* 6/75, 85, 110; **hātað** *1 pl. pres.* 2/6, *3 pl. pres.* 6/42; **hātan** *3 pl. pres. subj.* 11/579; **hēt** *3 sg. pret.* 3/34; (*ge*)**hāten** *pret. p.* 1/9, 2/96, 109, 3/51; **hātte** *3 sg. pret. passive* 6/73, 7/136, 9/158; (2) command; **hāte** *1 sg. pres.* 4/2, 15/95; **hāteð** *3 sg. pres.* 4/1; **hēt** *3 sg. pret.* 2/152, 158, 179, **hēht** 13/124; **hāt** *imp. sg.* 7/28, 37, 77; **hātað** *imp. pl.* 11/575.

*ge*hātan *7* promise; *ge*hāte *1 sg. pres.* 11/183, 12/246; *ge*hēt *3 sg. pret.* 12/289; *ge*hēton *1 pl. pret.* 11/407; *ge*hāten *pret. p.* 8/55.

hātheort *adj.* passionate 16/66.

gehātlond *n.* promised land 5/72.

gehāwian *w.2* observe 2/123.

hæbbe, hæbben(ne), hæfde, hæfdon *see* habban.

hæft *m.* captive 11/87.

hæftan *w.1* make captive, emprison 14/135, 140.

hægelscur *m. or f.* hailstorm 13/212.

hægl, hagl *m.* hail 17/17, 32, 19/60, 16/48.

hæglfaru *f.* hailstorm 16/105.

hæl *f.* salvation 8/14.

(ge)hǣlan *w.1* heal 15/85, 10/23, 27.

hæle *m.* man. 16/73.

hǣlend *m.* Saviour (Christ) 8/13, 50, 10/91.

hæleð *m.* hero, warrior 13/228, 12/74, 214; hælæð 12/249.

hǣlo *f.* luck, health 11/18, 13/95.

hǣman *w.1* copulate 3/43.

hǣrfest *m.* autumn, harvest 2/120, 19/126.

hǣs *f.* command 7/65.

hǣt *see* hātan.

hǣto, hǣtu *f.* heat 14/144, 19/17.

hǣðen *adj.* heathen 10/88, 7/44, 9/20.

hǣðstapa *m.* heath-stalker, stag 11/159.

hē *personal pron.* he. *Singular forms:* m. nom. hē 1/2, 3, 4; *acc.* hine 1/12, 14, 15, hyne 11/227, 366, hiene 1/3, 4, 4/22; *gen.* his 1/1, 23, 2/51, hys 6/135, 137, 139; *dat.* him 1/3, 22, 28, hym 6/91; *f. nom.* hēo 5/49, 7/24, 25, hīo 4/13, 76, 6/103, hīe 4/75; *acc.* hī 7/32, 35, hīe 4/46, 48, 65, hig 7/16, 65, hēo 3/46; *gen.* hire 7/24, 3/44, hyre 7/2, 24, 32; *dat.* hire 5/48, 7/24, 27, hyre 7/28, 58; *n. nom.* hit 9/1, 2, 3, hyt 6/136, 7/94, 11/452; *acc.* hit 1/19, 11/78, 183; *gen.* his 6/56. *Plural forms:* nom. hī 2/8, 37, 60, hȳ 11/371, hīe 1/16, 20, 23, hig 11/337, hēo 14/64, 68; *acc.* hī 7/110, hȳ 7/96, 11/365, hīe 2/96, 127, 4/12, hig 7/67, hēo 14/63, 65; *gen.* hira 2/93, 94, 100, hyra 6/71, 121, hiera 1/18, 19, 27, hiora 2/91,

4/6, 7, heora 2/19, 37; *dat.* him 1/26, 27, 2/34, heom 7/51, 71, 99.

hēadēor *n.* noble beast 3/73.

hēafod *n.* head 10/119, 7/42, 10/116.

hēafodgimm *m.* eye (*lit.* jewel of the head) 13/31.

hēafodmann *m.* elder, leader 10/36.

heafolan *see* hafela.

hēah *adj.* high, lofty, deep 11/578, 11/12, 17/34 n.; hērra, hiera, hēarra, hēahra *comp.* 19/28, 2/154, 4/59, 14/37, 29; hēhst *supl.* 8/22, 14/9 n., 15.

hēahcyning *m.* noble king (God) 13/6.

hēahdiacon *m.* archdeacon 8/31.

hēahfæder *m.* noble father (God) 15/134.

hēahlic *see* hēalic.

hēahgestrēon *n.* noble treasure 13/121.

hēahðungen *adj.* high-born 6/119.

(ge)healdan 7 hold, keep, possess, inhabit 2/28, 66; gehealdeþ 3 sg. pres. 16/112; (ge)healde 3 sg. pres. subj. 8/56, 16/14; gehealdan 3 pl. pres. subj. 8/34; hēold 1 sg. pret. 11/505, 510, 524; (ge)hēold 3 sg. pret. 7/95, 10/103, 11/87, 393; hēoldon 3 pl. pret. 14/75; gehēolde 3 sg. pret. subj. 10/81; hēoldan 1 pl. pret. subj. 8/24, 9/56; hēoldon 3 pl. pret. subj. 12/20, (ge)hīoldon 4/7, 33; gehealden pret. p. 19/45 protected.

healf *f.* side 2/19, 83, 84.

healf *adj.* half 2/27, 28, 6/120.

hēalic, hēahlic *adj.* noble, proud 10/132, 14/49.

heall *f.* hall 7/45, 113, 12/214.

healp *see* helpan.

heals *see* hals.

healsittend *m.* hall-dweller 11/641.

healðegn *m.* retainer 11/18.

hēan *adj.* humble, abject 16/23, 3/2.

hēan(ne) *see* hēah.

hēanlic *adj.* humiliating 12/55.

hēap *m.* band, troop 11/29, 369.

heard (1) *adj.* hard, strong, brave 11/280, 226, 294; heardra *comp.*

12/312, 11/18; **heardost** *supl.*
15/87; (2) *adv.* hard 11/307.

hearde *adv.* hard, strongly 11/229,
12/33, 13/18.

heardhicgende *adj.* (*pres. p.*) stern-
minded 11/98.

heardlīce *adv.* fiercely 12/261.

heardmōd *adj.* brave 14/40.

hearm *m.* sorrow 12/223, 14/123.

hearmcwide *m.* cruel speech 13/79.

hearmloca *m.* sorrowful prison
13/95.

hearmscaþa *m.* harmful foe 11/65.

hearmscearu *f.* affliction 14/187 n.

hearpe *f.* harp 5/20, 21, 7/29.

hearpenægl *m.* plectrum 7/46.

hearpestreng *m.* harp-string 7/46.

hearpian *w.2* play the harp 7/31.

hēarra *m.* lord, master (*cf.* **hēah**)
14/43, 18, 34; **hēorra** 12/204.

heaðobyrne *f.* war-corslet 11/293.

heaþodēor *adj.* brave in battle 11/71.

heaðogrim *adj.* fierce 11/464.

heaðomǣre *adj.* renowned in battle
11/575.

heaþorōf *adj.* brave 19/110.

heaðoscearp *adj.* battle-sharp
11/602.

heaðosīoc *adj.* battle-sick, wounded
11/527.

heaþoswāt *m.* blood of battle
11/347.

heaðowylm, -welm *m.* hostile
flame 11/592, 14/79.

hēawan *7* hew, cut down, stab
11/99; **hēaweð** *3 sg. pres.* 9/59;
hēow *3 sg. pret.* 12/324; **hēowon**
3 pl. pret. 12/181.

hebban *6* raise up 15/31.

hēdan *w.1 with gen.* care about
11/470.

hefene *see* **heofon.**

hefig *adj.* grievous 7/13, 15/61;
hefigran *comp.* 16/49.

hēhstan *see* **hēah.**

hēht *see* **hātan.**

hēhðu *f.* height 14/76.

heldor *n.* gate of hell 14/135.

hell *f.* hell 9/179, 11/87, 14/59.

hellewīte *n.* torment of hell 14/58
(*for metrical reasons this compound
is unlikely in* 9/179).

hellfūs *adj.* damned 13/50.

helm *m.* (1) protection, cover
11/183; (2) helmet 11/432, 267,
388; (3) protector, lord 11/478.

helmberend *m.* warrior 11/415.

help *f.* help 11/293, 13/91, 15/102.

(**ge**)**helpan** *3 with gen. or dat.* help
10/140, 11/422, 457; **helpe** *3 sg.
pres. subj.* 9/181; **healp** *3 sg. pret.*
11/471.

helsceaða *m.* fiend of hell 12/180.

gehende *adj. with dat.* near 12/294.

hēnðo *f.* suffering 13/117.

hēo *see* **hē.**

heofon, hefen, hefon *m.* heaven
5/40, 74, 11/312, 20b/4.

heofoncyning *m.* heavenly king
13/92, 14/194.

heofone *f.* heaven 10/80, 3/93.

heofonlic *adj.* heavenly 10/131, 5/8,
53.

heofonrīce *n.* kingdom of heaven
5/35, 13/52, 56, 14/117 n.

heofontorht *adj.* shining in the sky
13/224.

heofontungol *n.* star 19/32.

hēold, hēoldon *see* (**ge**)**healdan.**

heolfor *m. or n.* blood, gore 11/214,
13/196, 232.

heolster *m.* hiding-place 11/54.

heolstor *n.* darkness 16/23.

heolstorcofa *m.* grave 19/49.

heolstorscūwa *m.* shadow of darkness 13/208.

heom *see* **hē.**

heonanforð *adv.* henceforth 9/15,
19.

heonon, heonan *adv.* hence 7/76,
11/152, 17/37, 19/1.

heord *f.* custody 5/24.

heora *see* **hē.**

hēore *adj.* pleasant 11/163.

heorodrēorig, heoredrēor(i)g *adj.*
(1) blood-stained 11/493; (2) dis-
consolate 19/99.

heorogīfre *adj.* fiercely greedy
11/239.

heorogrǣdig, heorugrǣdig *adj.*
ravenous, bloodthirsty 13/38, 79.

heorogrim(m) *adj.* fierce 11/305,
13/31.

heorohocyhte *adj.* barbed 11/229.

heorosweng *m.* sword-stroke 11/331.

heorra *see* **hearra.**

heor(o)t *m.* hart 11/160, 3/69, 71.

heorte *f.* heart 12/312, 8/48, 10/40.

heorðgenēat *m.* hearth-companion 11/321, 12/204.

heorðwerod *n.* personal retainers 12/24.

hēow, hēowon *see* **hēawan.**

hēr *adv.* (1) here 4/44, 11/569, 574; (2) now 4/34; (3) in this year 1/1, 2/1.

here *m.* (1) army, devastation 9/46, 96, 11/411; (2) a Danish army 2/1, 13, 18.

herefeld *m.* battlefield 13/10, 18.

heregeatu *f.* war-gear 12/48.

heregrīma *m.* helmet 11/378.

herehȳð *f.* booty 2/32, 35, 106.

herenes *f.* praise 5/32.

herenet *n.* corslet 11/294.

herestrǣl *m.* war-arrow 11/226.

heresyrce *f.* coat of mail 11/252.

hergaþ *m.* plundering 2/54, 67.

hergian *w.2* plunder 2/65, 105, 110.

herian *w.2* praise 5/35, 7/32, 34; **heregian** *inf.* 9/136.

*ge***hernes** *f.* hearing 5/65.

hērra *see* **hēah.**

hērtōēacan *adv.* besides 9/152.

hēt, gehēt *see* **hātan, gehātan.**

hete *m.* hatred 9/48, 96, 14/56.

hetelīce *adv.* hostilely 9/86.

hetesprǣc *f.* hostile speech 14/18.

hetol *adj.* hostile 9/127.

hēton, gehēton *see* **hātan, gehātan.**

hettend *m.* enemy 13/31.

hicgan, hycgan *w.1* think of, consider, care about 12/4, 14/152; **hogode** *3 sg. pret.* 10/81, 12/128, 133; **hogodon** *3 pl. pret.* 12/123.

hī *see* **hē.**

hīd *f.* hide of land 3/46.

hider *adv.* hither 2/101, 115, 135; **hieder** 4/11.

hīe, hiene, hiera *see* **hē.**

hīeran *see* **hēah.**

hīerde, gehierdun *see* (*ge*)**hȳran.**

hīersumian *w.2* obey 4/6.

hig *n.* hay 13/38.

hig *pron. see* **hē.**

hige, hyge *m.* mind, thought, courage 12/4, 312, 11/54, 13/36.

higeþihtig *adj.* strong-hearted 11/45.

hiht *see* **hyht.**

hild *f.* battle 11/329, 457, 496.

hildebill *n.* battle-sword 11/261, 452.

hildecyst *f.* valour 11/371.

hildedēor *adj.* brave in battle 11/133.

hildegicel *m.* battle-icicle 11/347.

hildemecg *m.* warrior 11/98.

hilderinc *m.* warrior 12/169, 11/236, 317.

hildetūx *m.* battle-tusk 11/252.

hildfruma *m.* battle-chief 11/422, 608.

hildlata *m.* coward 11/619.

hildstapa *m.* marching warrior 13/213 n.

hilt *n. or f.* hilt 11/315, 355.

him *see* **hē.**

hindan *adv.* from the rear, at the rear 2/82, 96, 19/159.

hindanweard *adv.* at the back 19/164.

hinde *f.* hind 3/69.

hinderweard *adj.* slothful 19/180.

hine *see* **hē.**

hinfūs *adj.* eager to get away 11/54.

hīo *see* **hē.**

(*ge*)**hīoldon** *see* (*ge*)**healdan.**

hiora *see* **hē.**

hioroweallende *adj.* (*pres. p.*) surging fiercely 11/554.

hīowbeorht *adj.* bright of hue 14/21.

hira *see* **hē.**

(*ge*)**hīrde** *see* (*ge*)**hȳran.**

hire *see* **hē.**

hīred *m.* court 3/13.

hīredman *m.* retainer 12/261 n.

his, hit *see* **hē.**

hīw *n.* colour, beauty 19/81, 157, 168.

hladan *6* load; **hladon** *inf.* 11/548; **gehladen** *pret. p.* 13/120, 19/76.

hlāf *m.* bread 13/21, 148.

hlāford *m.* lord 1/30, 3/7, 11.

hlāfordlēas *adj.* lordless 12/251, 13/164.

hlāfordswica *m.* traitor 9/62.

hlāfordswice *m.* treachery 9/63, 64.

hlǣfdige *f.* lady 7/115.

hlǣw *m.* mound, barrow, hill 11/546, 575, 19/25 n.

hleahtor *m.* laughter 17/21.

gehlēapan 7 mount, leap upon; **gehlēop** *3 sg. pret.* 12/189.

hlēo *m.* protector 11/90, 12/74, 13/111.

hlēomǣg *m.* protector 17/25.

hleonian *w.2* lean 11/206, 19/25.

hlēoþor *n.* song, music 17/20, 19/12.

hlēoðrian *w.2* speak 15/26.

hlīfian *w.2* tower 11/578, 15/85, 19/23.

hlihhan 6 laugh; **hlōh** *3 sg. pret.* 12/147.

hlimman, hlymman 3 resound, roar 17/18; **hlymmeð** *3 sg. pres.* 13/151.

hlinc *m.* hill 19/25.

hlīsfullīce *adv.* gloriously 10/103.

hlōð *f.* band, gang 13/42, 2/24.

hlūttor *adj.* pure 14/152.

hlynsian *w.2* resound 11/69.

gehlystan *w.1* listen 12/92.

hlyt *m.* lot, fate 13/6, 14.

hnǣgan *w.1* lay low 17/88.

hnīgan *1* bend down; **hnāg** *1 sg. pret.* 15/59.

hnītan *1* clash together; **hneotan** *3 pl. pret.* 13/4.

hōcer *n.* scorn 9/133.

hōcorwyrde *adj.* derider 9/128.

hof *n.* dwelling 19/110, 11/248.

hogode, hogodon *see* **hicgan**.

hōl *n.* malice 9/48.

gehola *m.* protector 16/31.

hold *adj.* loyal 17/41, 14/43, 18/39; **holdost** *supl.* 12/24.

holm *m.* sea, water 11/226, 333, 13/155.

holmclif *n.* cliff 11/212.

holmweard *m.* protector on the sea 13/118 n.

holmweg *m.* way over the sea 13/141.

holt *n.* wood 19/81, 11/371, 619.

holtwudu *m.* wood, tree 11/160, 15/91.

homer *m.* hammer 11/602 (*cf.* **lāf**).

gehōn 7 hang (*with dat.* with); **gehongen(e)** 19/38, 71.

hond *see* **hand**.

hondgemōt *n.* hand-meeting, battle 11/267.

hondgeweorc *n.* act of strength 11/608.

hondwundor *n.* wonderful thing made by hand 11/541.

hongian *w.2* hang 11/154.

hord *n.* hoard, treasure 11/517, 541, 546.

hordærn *n.* treasure-house 11/604.

hordcofa *m.* heart, thoughts 16/14.

hordweard *m.* guardian of a hoard 11/366.

hōring *m.* fornicator 9/147.

horn *m.* horn 11/214, 160.

hornfisc *m.* whale 13/129 n.

hornreced *n.* gabled building 11/3.

hors *n.* horse 11/190, 2/3, 86.

horschwæl *m.* walrus 6/33.

horsþegn *m.* marshal 2/147.

hrā, hrǣw *n.* corpse, body 11/329, 13/232, 15/53, 72.

hrān *m.* reindeer 6/42 n., 44, 51.

hraþe, hræþe, raþe *adv.* soon, quickly 10/42, 50, 11/228, 13/227, 7/73, 11/23; **radost** *supl.* 1/18, **hrædest** 9/40, 149.

hrǣding *f.* haste 9/153.

hrǣdwyrde *adj.* hasty of speech 16/66.

hrægl *n.* dress, clothing 6/139.

hræðre *see* **hreðer**.

hrēam *m.* outcry 12/106.

hremm *m.* raven 12/106.

hrēo(h) *adj.* rough, fierce 11/305, 19/58, 19/45.

hrēo(w) *adj.* sad 16/16.

hrēodan 2 adorn; **gehroden** *pret. p.* 19/79.

hrēosan 2 fall, rush 16/48; **hrēosað** *3 sg. pres.* 19/60; **hrēas** *3 sg. pret.* 11/604; **hruron** 3 *pl. pret.* 11/221 n.; **hrēosende** *pres. p.* 16/102.

hrēowan 2 grieve; **hrēoweð** *3 sg. pres.* 14/181.

hrēowcearig *adj.* sorrowful 15/25.

hrēowlīce *adv.* cruelly 9/36.

hrēran *w.1* stir 16/4.

hreðer, hræðer *m.* heart, breast 11/366, 13/36, 69, 11/592.

hreþerloca *m.* breast 17/58.

hrīm *m.* hoar-frost 13/212, 16/48, 77.

hrīmceald *adj.* cold as frost 16/4.

hrīmgicel *m.* icicle 17/17.

hrīnan *I* touch 11/256.

hrīnde *adj.* (*pret. p.*) covered with frost 11/154.

hring *m.* (1) ring 11/248, 582, 12/161, **ringe** *dat. sg.* 7/110; (2) ring-mail 11/244.

hringed *adj.* (*pret. p.*) made of rings 11/388.

hringloca *m.* ring-mail 12/145.

hringmǣl *n.* ring-marked sword 11/262 n., 305.

hringnet *n.* coat of mail 11/527.

hringsele *m.* ring-hall 11/613.

hringþegu *f.* receiving of rings 17/44.

hrīð *f.* storm 16/102.

gehroden *see* **hrēodan.**

hrōf *m.* roof 5/40, 11/135, 528.

hrōfsele *m.* roofed hall 11/256.

hrōðor *n.* comfort 13/111.

hruron *see* **hrēosan.**

hrūse *f.* ground 11/71, 604, 16/23.

hryre *m.* fall, death 19/16, 16/7.

hrȳðer *n.* cattle 6/45.

hryðge *adj.* ? 16/77 n.

hū *adv.* how 3/5, 10, 11.

huilpe *f.* curlew 17/21.

hund *m.* dog 9/77, 11/159.

hund *num.* hundred 2/43, 4, 112.

hundred *n. as num.* hundred 3/60.

hundtwelftig *num.* one hundred and twenty 2/6.

hunger, hungor *m.* hunger, famine 9/46, 17/11, 2/86, 8/10.

hunig *n.* honey 6/112.

hunta *m.* hunter 6/24, 27.

huntoð *m.* hunting 6/5.

hūru *adv.* indeed, however, truly 6/105, 8/65, 9/4.

hūs *n.* house, dwelling 19/94, 5/22, 23.

hwā (1) *inter. pron.* who, which, what; *m. nom. sg.* 12/95, 215, 13/140; *n. nom. sg.* **hwæt** 7/4, 9 (? *refers to m. noun*), 8/74, 75; *n. acc sg.*

hwæt 3/1, 9/115; *n. gen. sg.* **hwæs** 3/47 how much; (2) *indef. pron.* anyone, whatever; *m. nom. sg.* 3/10, 4/76, 12/71; *m. acc. sg.* **hwæne** 12/2 each one; *n. acc. sg.* **hwæt** 3/23; *n. instr. sg.* **hwan** 16/59, **hwon** 17/43.

gehwā *pron.* each; *m. nom. sg.* 9/154; *m. acc. sg.* **gehwane** 11/458, **gehwone** 11/99, 538; *m. gen. sg.* (*referring to f.*) 11/611; *m. dat. sg.* **gehwǣm** 11/156 (*referring to f.*), 211, **gehwām** 13/65, 17/72; *n. gen. sg.* **gehwæs** 5/37; *n. dat. sg.* **gehwām** 13/167, 16/63.

hwanon, hwonon *adv.* whence 7/9, 5/52.

gehwanon *adv.* from all quarters 10/67.

hwaþerre *see* **hwæðer.**

hwæl *m.* whale 6/35, 36, 48.

hwælhunta *m.* whale-hunter 6/11.

hwælhuntað *m.* whaling 6/37.

hwælmere *m.* whale-ocean 13/129.

hwælweg *m.* whale's way, sea 17/63.

hwæne *see* **hwā.**

hwænne, hwonne *conj.* (until the time) when 12/67, 13/159, 15/136, 8/40.

hwǣr, hwār (1) *conj* where 2/123, 9/80, 7/77, 139; (2) *adv.* anywhere 4/76; (3) *int. adv.* where 8/76, 77, 78.

hwæs, gehwæs, hwæt *see* **hwā, gehwā.**

hwæt *adj.* vigorous, valiant 17/40, 11/342, 415.

hwæt *excl.* lo! 8/81, 9/16, 13/1.

hwæthwegu ? something 5/27.

hwæðer *pron.* which 6/14, 18; **swa hwaþerre . . . swa** 2/24 whichever.

hwæðer *conj.* whether 6/8, 11/147, 558.

gehwæþer *pron.* each 11/113, 12/112.

hwæþere, hwæðre *adv.* however, yet 5/10, 30, 11/647.

hwelce, gehwelcum *see* **hwylc, gehwylc.**

hwēne *adv.* somewhat 6/61, 11/472; *cf.* **hwon.**

hweorfan *3* turn, go 11/661, 16/72;
hweorfest *2 sg. pres.* 13/117;
hweorfeð *3 sg. pres.* 17/58, 60;
hweorfað *1 pl. pres.* 13/164;
hwearf *3 sg. pret.* 11/314, 605.
hwettan *w.1* incite 17/63.
hwī, hwȳ *adv.* why 7/115, 14/37.
hwider *adv.* whither 13/164, 16/72.
hwīl *f.* time 11/236 n., 3/13, 6/77;
 þa hwīle þe *dat. sg.* 2/37, 121,
4/56 while; **hwīlum, hwȳlum,
hwīlon** *dat. pl.* 4/64, 65, 6/125,
12/270 sometimes; **hwīlon** *dat. pl.*
3/8 once.
hwilc, gehwilc *see* **hwylc, gehwylc.**
hwīlwendlic *adj.* transitory 10/81.
hwīt *adj.* white, bright 14/105, 9, 21.
hwon *pron. see* **hwā.**
hwōn *adv.* somewhat 6/15, 7/146,
17/28; *cf.* **hwēne.**
gehwone *see* **gehwā.**
hwōnlīce *adv.* slightly, barely 10/82.
hwonne *see* **hwænne.**
hwonon *see* **hwanon.**
hwȳ *see* **hwī.**
hwylc, hwilc, hwelc *inter. pron.*
which, what 13/170, 5/47, 3/11,
7/104, 4/3, 23.
gehwylc, gehwilc, gehwelc *indef.
pron.* each, any 12/128, 8/20, 9/18,
14/52, 1/19; *also* **hwilc** 3/43,
hwylc 9/88.
hwȳlum *see* **hwīl.**
gehwyrfan *w.1* turn (*tr.*) 5/56, 67,
14/73.
hycgan *see* **hicgan.**
hȳd *f.* hide 6/35, 49, 53.
(ge)hȳdan *w.1* hide 11/163, 539,
16/84.
gehygd *n.* thought 16/72, 13/68.
hyge *see* **hige.**
hygegǣlsa *adj.* frivolous 19/180.
hygelēast *f.* folly 14/86.
hygesceaft *f.* heart 14/43.
hyht, hiht *m.* joy, hope 15/126,
17/45, 15/148.
gehyhtan *w.1* trust 8/51.
hyhtlic *adj.* joyful; **hyhtlicost** *supl.*
13/104.
hyhtlīce *adv.* joyfully 19/79.
gehyld *n.* protection 13/117.

hyldan *w.1* bow 15/45.
hyldo *f.* kindness, favour 13/148,
14/37, 56.
hym *see* **hē.**
hȳnan *w.1* humiliate 12/180, 9/35,
111.
hyne, hyra *see* **hē.**
(ge)hȳran, (ge)hīeran *w.1* (1) hear
15/78, 5/33, 1/22, 2/46; (2) belong
to 6/87, 93, 98; (3) obey 11/527.
hyrde *m.* keeper, guardian 11/49,
417.
hyre *see* **hē.**
hyrst *f.* ornament 11/535.
gehyrstan *w.1* equip 13/45.
gehȳrsum *adj.* obedient 7/90.
hyrtan *w.1* encourage 11/366.
hyrwan *w.1* abuse 9/133, 136.
hys, hyt *see* **hē.**
hys(s)e *m.* young warrior 12/152, 2,
112.
hyt *f.* heat 11/422 n.

ic *pers. pron. Singular forms: nom.*
ic 2/70, 148, 3/1; *acc.* **mē** 7/85,
12/29, **mec** 11/423, 508, 16/28;
gen. **mīn** 7/4, 122, 127 (*also inflected as poss. pron.* 4/70, 7/15,
34); *dat.* **mē** 4/2, 41, 50; *plural
forms: nom.* **wē** 2/1, 5, 7; *acc.* **ūs**
3/93, 7/72, 75, **ūsic** 11/411, 413;
gen. **ūre** 4/32, 37, 7/75 (*also
inflected as poss. pron.* 7/8, 87,
8/13); *dat.* **ūs** 6/98, 100, 102;
dual forms: acc. **unc** 14/142,
15/48.
īcan *w.1* add, increase; **īhte** *3 sg.
pret.* 9/9.
īdel *adj.* empty, vain, idle 5/14,
8/78, 9/140.
ides *f.* woman 11/142.
ieldran *see* **eald.**
iggað *m.* island 2/36.
igland, -lond *n.* (1) island 2/108,
6/79, 90; (2) land beyond the sea
13/15 n., 19/9 n.; *cf.* **ēaland.**
ilca, ylca *adj.* same 1/32, 2/66, 5/45,
6/123.
in (1) *prep. with dat.* in, at 5/24,
11/12; (2) *adv.* in 2/33, 6/13, 17,
inn 10/65.
in gemonge *prep. see* **on gemang.**

inbryrdnes *f.* inspiration 5/6.
indryhten *adj.* noble 16/12.
indryhto *f.* nobility 17/89.
ingong, ingang *m.* entry, entrance 5/72, 11/290.
innan, innon (1) *prep. with acc. or dat.* within, among, in 2/132, 3/46, 7/45, 64; (2) *adv.* (from) within 9/34, 11/73, 492.
innanbordes *adv.* at home 4/7.
inne *adv.* within 2/10, 97, 6/117.
geinseglian *w.2* seal 7/110, 125.
intinga *m.* cause, sake 5/19 n.
into *prep. with dat.* into 10/147.
ingeþanc *m. or n.* thought, conscience 9/176, 13/35.
inwidhlemm *m.* wound of malice 15/47.
inwidsorg *f.* evil sorrow 11/130.
inwit *n.* guile, evil 8/37.
inwitgæst *m.* malicious foe 11/443.
inwitþanc *m.* hostile purpose 11/48.
inwitweorc *n.* evil deed 8/46.
inwitwrāsen *f.* cruel bondage 13/63.
īow *see* **þū**.
īren *n.* iron, sword 12/253, 11/101, 456.
īren *adj.* of iron 11/551.
īrenbend *f.* iron band 11/73, 14/126.
is *see* **wesan**.
is *n.* ice 13/216, 10/24, 11/349.
isc(e)ald *adj.* ice-cold 17/14, 19.
īsigfeþera *adj.* icy-winged 17/24.
iū, giū *adv.* formerly 4/3, 15/28, 87, 4/39.
iugoðe *see* **gioguð**.
iung *see* **geong**.
iūwine *m.* old friend 17/92.

kynerīce *see* **cynerīce**.
kyning *see* **cyning**.
kyrtel *m.* coat 6/52.

lā *excl.* lo, indeed 8/74, 75, 9/16.
lāc *n.* booty, offering 9/24, 11/325.
gelāc *n.* tumult 17/35.
lācan 7 (1) fly **lācað** 3 *pl. pres.* 19/182; **lācende** *pres. p.* 11/605; (2) fight 11/621.
gelād *n.* way 11/201.
lāf *f.* (1) remainder 2/92, 6/124, 8/76; (2) what is left by (*gen. of noun*)

homera lāf 11/602 *i.e.* sword, **swolēs lāf** 19/151 *i.e.* ashes; (3) heirloom, specifically sword 11/94, 384.
gelafian *w.2* wash, refresh 11/495.
gelagian *w.2* ordain 9/21.
lāgon *see* **licg(e)an**.
lagu *m.* water 17/47.
lagu *f.* law 3/68, 9/19, 28.
gelagu *n. pl.* expanse of water 17/64.
lagufæsten *n.* mighty sea 13/157.
laguflōd *m.* water 19/70.
lagulād *f.* watery way 16/3.
lagustrēam *m.* (tidal) stream 12/66, 19/62.
lahbryce *m.* breach of law 9/120.
lahlīce *adv.* lawfully 9/55.
gelamp *see* **gelimpan**.
land, lond *n.* land 3/21, 6, 1/27, 2/30.
landleod *f.* people of the land, subjects 3/63.
landscearu *f.* countryside 13/184.
landscipe *m.* region 14/131.
lang, long *adj.* long 2/7, 6/3, 11/364, 553; **lengra** *comp.* 2/7, 6/36.
gelang æt *prep. with dat.* dependent on 11/167–8.
lange, longe *adv.* long, far 6/145, 7/97, 4/73, 6/7, 14/62 n.; **leng** *comp.* 7/82, 107, 9/2, **lencg** 6/119; **lengest** *supl.* 1/3, 2/37.
langscip *n.* ship of war 2/152.
langunghwīl *f.* time of weariness 15/126.
lār *f.* teaching 4/43, 9, 11.
lārcwide *m.* advice 16/38.
lārēow *m.* teacher, master 7/59, 4/19, 5/68.
lārsmið *m.* counsellor; **-smeoðas** *acc. pl.* 13/175.
lāst *m.* track, path 11/193, 16/97, 17/15.
lāstword *n.* epitaph 17/73.
late *see* **læt**.
latian *w.2* delay 9/155.
lāð *n.* injury 14/147, 149.
lāð *adj.* hateful, hated 11/114, 9/41, 72; **lāðra** *comp.* 12/50, 14/131, 184; **lāðost** *supl.* 15/88.
lāðettan *w.1* loathe 9/137.
gelaðian *w.2* invite 7/8.

lāðlic *adj.* hideous 8/74, 11/325.
lāðgenīðla *m.* enemy 19/50.
(*ge*)lǣdan *w.1* lead, take 12/88, 2/178, 5/48; lett *3 sg. pres.* 3/93.
lǣfan *w.1* leave 1/25, 4/34.
lǣg(e), lǣgon *see* licg(e)an.
lǣgde *see* lecgan.
lǣn *n.* loan 4/76.
lǣne *adj.* transitory 16/108, 11/363, 618.
lǣran *w.1* teach 4/59, 58, 5/12.
gelǣred *adj.* (*pret. p.*) learned 7/40, 4/73, 7/96; gelǣrdestan *supl.* 5/49.
lǣrig *m.* shield-rim? 12/284 n.
lǣrincgmǣden *n.* pupil 7/112.
lǣs *noun* less, fewer 9/99.
lǣssa *adj. comp.* less, smaller 6/36; lǣsta *supl.* 6/128, 134.
(*ge*)lǣstan *w.1* serve, perform, carry out 9/173, 8/56, 9/20.
lǣt *adj.* slow 11/270, 13/46, 19/182.
lǣtan 7 (1) leave; lēt *3 sg. pret.* 6/9; (2) cause, allow, let; lǣte *1 sg. pres. subj.* 14/193, lēt *3 sg. pret.* 3/56, 9/160, 12/7; lēton *3 pl. pret.* 12/108; lēte *3 sg. pret. subj.* 14/13; lǣt *imp. sg.* 13/156; (3) consider; lǣt *3 sg. pret.* 9/102.
lǣwed *adj.* lay 9/55, 10/58.
lēaf *n.* leaf 19/39.
lēaf *f.* permission 7/26, 60, 128.
gelēafa *m.* faith, belief 8/55, 47, 58.
gelēaffull *adj.* faithful 8/29, 10/47, 94.
gelēaffulnes *f.* faith, belief 8/49.
lēan *n.* reward, repayment 14/190, 11/325, 13/146.
gelēanian *w.2 with dat. and acc.* reward 14/149, 11/171.
lēas *adj.* vain, empty 3/5, 14/88, 16/86; 14/127 deprived of.
lēasung *f.* falsehood 5/14, 9/124.
leccan *w.1* water 19/64.
lecgan *w.1* lay, establish; lǣgde *3 sg. pret.* 3/68, legde 18/5; gelēd *pret. p.* 10/123.
gelēfan *see* gelȳfan.
lēfdon *see* līefan.
leger *n.* (1) lying in state 6/140; (2) disease 9/56.
lehtrian *w.2* revile 9/133.

lencg *see* lange.
lencten *m.* spring 19/136.
gelend *adj.* gone 2/67.
leng *see* lange.
gelenge *adj.* belonging to 11/505.
lengest *see* lange.
lengra *see* lang.
lēod *m.* prince, man 11/128, 223, 233.
lēodbiscop *m.* sufragan bishop 3/28.
lēode *f. pl.* people 10/8, 16, 34.
lēodhata *m.* tyrant 9/127.
lēodhete *m.* persecution 13/112.
lēodsceaða *m.* ravager 13/80.
lēodscipe *m.* nation 11/524.
lēof *adj.* dear 8/71, 7/6, 20; lēofra *comp.* 1/30, 11/424, 14/167; lēofost, lēofest *supl.* 8/64, 70, 7/4, 127.
leofað, leofodan, leofian *see* libban.
lēoflic *adj.* admirable 11/376.
leofode *see* libban.
lēoht *n.* light 10/131, 11/26, 311; 14/13 n. world.
lēoht *adj.* (1) light (weight) 19/183, 6/72; (2) light (brightness) 14/20, 7/83, 14/11; (3) joyful 13/206.
lēohtfruma *m.* creator of life 13/146.
lēoma *m.* light 11/311, 258, 542.
leornere *m.* novice 5/50.
(*ge*)leornian, (*ge*)liornian *w.2* study, learn 5/65, 4–5, 4/40, 46.
leornunga *see* liornung.
lēoð *n.* song, lay 5/3, 10, 14.
lēoþcræft *m.* art of poetry 5/12.
lēoðcræftig *adj.* skilled in poetry 18/40.
lēoðocræft *m.* skill of hands 11/542.
leoðosyrce *f.* coat of mail 11/246.
lēoðsong *m.* poem 5/7, 56.
leoðubend *f.* fetter 13/100.
leoþucræftig *adj.* nimble 19/150.
lēt(e) *see* lǣtan.
lett *see* (*ge*)lǣdan.
gelettan *w.1* prevent 12/164.
lēw *f.* blemish 9/142.
gelēwed *adj.* (*pret. p.*) injured 9/143.
libban *irr.* live 3/52, 82; leofað *3 sg. pres.* 10/140, 11/157, 17/102; lifiaþ *3 pl. pres.* 15/134; lifge *3 sg.*

202

pres. subj. 8/21, 17/78; **leofode**
3 *sg. pret.* 10/53, 58; **leofodan** 3 *pl.*
pret. 3/22; **lif(i)gende** *pres. p.*
9/65, 10/35, 11/114.
lic *n.* body 6/121, 10/100, 11/32.
gelīc *adj. (with dat.)* like 14/11,
9/141; **gelīcost** *supl.* 11/26, 349,
gelīccast 9/77, **gelīcast** 19/168.
gelīce *adv.* like, alike 5/11, 19/37.
licg(e)an 5 lie, lie dead, extend
11/218, 327, 12/319; **liŏ** 3 *sg. pres.*
2/8, 6/56, 84, **ligeŏ** 6/109, 11/518,
12/222; **licgaŏ** 3 *pl. pres.* 6/57,
120, 145; **licge** 3 *sg. pres. subj.*
9/91; **læg** 3 *sg. pret.* 1/26, 3/8,
6/19; **lǣgon** 3 *pl. pret.* 1/20,
lāgon 12/112, 183, 14/77; **lǣge**
3 *sg. pret. subj.* 6/8, 12/279, 300;
licgende *pres. p.* 15/24.
līchoma, līchama *m.* body 8/73,
36, 38, 11/424.
līcian *w.2* please; *impersonal, with
dat.*, like 7/52, 75, 8/29.
gelīcnes *f.* likeness 19/112.
līcrest *f.* bier, hearse 10/130.
licsār *n.* wound 11/114.
lid *n.* ship 13/157, 162.
lidman *m.* Viking 12/99, 164.
liefan *w.1* allow; **lȳfdest** 2 *sg. pret.*
7/56; **lēfdon** *1 pl. pret.* 4/24.
geliefe *see* **gelȳfan**.
līf *n.* life 8/8, 3/22, 5/8.
līfdagas *m. pl.* life 11/93, 363.
lifge, lif(i)gende, lifiaþ *see* **libban**.
gelīfst *see* **gelȳfan**.
līfwraŏu *f.* life-protection 11/650.
līg *m.* flame 14/131, 11/26, 80.
līgegesa *m.* terror of fire 11/553.
līgþracu *f.* violence of the fire
19/107.
līgȳŏ *f.* wave of flame 11/445.
lihtan *w.1* alight, dismount 12/23.
lim *m.* limb 5/25; 3/44 sexual organs.
gelimp, gelymp *n.* fortune, cir-
cumstance(s) 7/22, 9/112, 7/13, 18.
(ge)limpan 3 (1) happen, come to
pass; **gelamp** 3 *sg. pret.* 7/94,
10/46, 63; **gelumpe** 3 *sg. pret.
subj.* 11/410; **gelumpen** *pret. p.*
11/123; (2) *with dat.* befall (some-
one) 9/87; **gelimpŏ** 3 *sg. pres.*
9/95, **limpeŏ** 17/13.

gelimplic *adj.* suitable 5/25.
limwērig *adj.* weary of limb 15/63.
lind *f.* shield (made of linden wood)
11/383, 12/99, 244.
lindgecrod *n.* troop bearing shields
13/175.
lindhæbbend *m.* warrior with shield
11/193.
lindwiga *m.* warrior 11/376.
(ge)liornian *see* **(ge) leornian**.
liornung, leornung *f.* learning,
scholarship 4/10, 56, 7/106.
lioŏobend *m.* fetter 14/137.
list *m.* skill 11/80.
littelre *see* **lytel**.
liŏ *see* **licg(e)an**.
lixan *w.1* shine 11/311, 19/33,
165.
locen *see* **lūcan**.
lōcian *w.2* look 1/14, 3/13, 9/102.
lof *m.* praise, renown 17/73, 10/98,
11/277.
gelōgian *w.2* lodge, accommodate
9/70, 10/101, 137.
gelōme *adv.* often, frequently 8/7,
9/22, 42.
gelōmlīcian *w.2* become frequent
8/11.
lond *see* **land**.
londbūend *m.* land-dweller 11/136.
londriht, -ryht *n.* privilege of land,
estate 11/659, 18/40.
long *see* **lang**.
longaþ *m.* longing 18/3.
longe *see* **lange**.
longsum *adj.* enduring 11/277.
longung *f.* depression 17/47 n.
losian *w.2* (1) *with dat.* be lost to
14/189, 17/94; (2) escape 11/183.
lūcan 2 lock, link, join 19/107;
lucon 3 *pl pret.* 12/66, 13/214;
(ge)locen *pret. p.* 11/246, 542.
lufe *f.* love 5/80, 8/57; *cf.* **lufu**.
lufen *f.* joy, comfort 11/659.
lufian *w.2* love 5/60, 3/16, 66.
luflīce *adv.* lovingly 4/1.
lufu *f.* love 8/13, 7/55, 81; *cf.* **lufe**.
gelumpe, gelumpen *see* **(ge)lim-
pan**.
lungre *adv.* quickly 11/516, 13/46,
77.
lust *m.* desire 17/36, 9/55.

gelȳfan, gelēfan w.1 believe 8/53,
54, 4/20, 7/36, 9/73.
lȳfdest see liefan.
gelȳfed adj. infirm 5/18.
lyft f. sky 11/166, 605, 15/5.
gelymp see gelimp.
lyre m. loss 19/53.
lȳsan w.1 ransom, redeem 12/37,
15/41.
lysu adj. false 13/175.
lȳt (1) noun (indeclinable) with gen.
few, little 11/609, 655, 16/31;
(2) adv. little 13/182.
lytegian w.2 use guile 12/86.
lytel, litel adj. little, small 1/10,
4/30, 3/64.
lȳtlian w.2 grow less 12/313.
lȳŏre adj. wicked 9/164.

mā noun with gen. more 2/153,
3/60, 4/44; mǣst supl. most
11/418.
macian w.2 make 3/40.
mādme see māŏ(ŏ)um.
maga m. young man 11/448.
māga see mǣg.
magan irr. be able (to); mæg 1 sg.
pres. 3/1, 4/18, 11/512; meaht 2
sg. pres. 5/30, miht 7/120, 11/169,
15/78; mæg 3 sg. pres. 4/34, 6/56,
60; magon 1 pl. pres. 4/53, 7/72,
8/1, magan 9/156; magon 3 pl.
pret. 6/144, 9/142, 152; mæge 1 sg.
pres. subj. 7/17, 11/522, 2 sg. pres.
subj. 4/21, 22, 3 sg. pres. subj. 6/83,
8/39, 48; mægen 1 pl. pres. subj.
4/53, 11/427, 14/153, 3 pl. pres.
subj. 4/56, 57; meahte 1 sg. pret.
4/69, 11/650, 16/26, mihte 7/133;
meahte 3 sg. pret. 5/11, 14, 6/12,
mehte 2/22, 96, 107, mihte 3/40,
5/55, 65; meahton 3 pl. pret. 4/31,
11/96, 141, mehton 2/42, mihton
11/456; meahten 3 pl. pret. subj.
2/156, mehten 2/175.
māgas see mǣg.
māge f. kinswoman 11/182.
mago m. son, man 16/92.
magorinc m. warrior 11/29.
magoþegn, maguþegn m. retainer
11/530, 196, 13/94, 125.
māgum see mǣg.

man, mann, mon, monn m. man
(dat. sg. and nom. acc. pl. men(n))
3/10, 36, 2/87, 141, 1/36, 5/61;
mænn nom. pl. 9/115.
man, mon pron. one 2/25, 60, 67,
3/3, 30, 70.
mān n. crime, evil 9/149, 14/54.
geman see gemunan.
mancus m. coin of value of 30
pence 4/71.
mancyn(n), moncynn n. mankind
13/69, 15/41, 5/41, 70; 3/49
inhabitants, population.
māndǣd f. wicked deed 5/80, 9/118.
mandrēam m. human joy 13/37.
mandryhten, mondryhten m. lord
11/420, 622, 377, 638.
mānfremmende adj. (pres. p.)
wicked 19/6.
mānful adj. wicked 13/42.
manian, monian w.2 exhort 12/228,
8/20, 5/61, 17/31.
manig, monig, maneg, mǣnig,
mæneg adj. many 2/141, 147,
2/89, 5/72, 8/10, 9/10, 6/84, 9/84,
9/35, 69.
manigeo see menigeo.
manigfeald see mænigfeald.
mannslaga m. murderer 9/144.
mannsylen f. selling of men 9/119.
mānscaŏa m. evil-doer 11/11 n., 36.
manslyht m. manslaughter 9/121.
mānswora m. perjurer 9/145.
māra see micel.
marc n. mark (unit of currency)
3/59.
māre see micel.
marne see morgen(n).
maþelian w.2 speak, make a speech
11/174, 404, 497.
māŏmǣht f. treasure 11/354, 606.
māŏ(ŏ)um m. treasure 4/29, 11/269,
413.
māŏŏumgyfa m. treasure-giver
16/92.
māŏŏumsigle n. precious jewel
11/530.
maŏŏumwela m. wealth of treasure
11/523.
mǣden n. girl 7/10, 16, 23.
mǣg m. kinsman 1/30, 28, 31.
mæg see magan.

mǣgburg *f.* kinsmen 11/660.

mǣge, mǣgen *see* **magan.**

mǣgen, mǣgyn *n.* strength 12/313, 7/91, 8/18, 14/24.

mǣgenāgende *adj.* (*pres. p.*) powerful 11/610.

mǣgenrǣs *m.* mighty stroke 11/260.

mǣgenstrengo *f.* great strength 11/451.

mǣgester *m.* master 3/38.

mǣgrǣs *m.* attack on kinsman 9/121.

mǣgslaga *m.* slayer of a kinsman 9/144.

mǣgð *f.* tribe, family 6/144, 9/92.

mǣl *n.* time 11/352, 406; speech 12/212.

mǣlan *w.1* speak 12/26, 43, 210.

mǣl*ge*sceaft *f.* destiny 11/510.

mǣnan *w.1* complain of 3/77.

*ge***mǣne** *adj.* (in) common, shared 9/42, 75, 76.

mǣneg *see* **manig.**

gemǣngde *see* **(*ge*)mengan.**

mǣnifealdlice *adv.* variously, in many ways 3/5.

mǣnig *see* **manig.**

mǣnige 15/112 *see* **menigeo.**

mǣnigfeald, manigfeald *adj.* manifold, various; 4/62, 9/117, 166; **mǣnigfealdre** *comp.* 9/83.

mǣnn *see* **man.**

mǣran *w.1* make famous 5/2.

mǣre *adj.* famous, notorious 3/18, 20, 10/31.

mǣrðo *f.* fame, famous deed, glory 9/180, 11/271, 413.

mǣsseprēost, -prīost *m.* (mass-) priest 4/67, 8/31, 4/67.

mǣsserbana *m.* murderer of a priest 9/144-5.

mǣst *adv.* most, mostly 6/47, 9/58, 59; *see also* **mā, micel.**

gemǣtan *w.1* (*impersonal*) dream 15/2.

mǣte *adj.* small (= no) 15/69, 124.

mǣð *f.* respect, fitness 12/195, 9/25, 71.

mǣw *m.* seagull 13/130, 17/22.

mē *see* **ic.**

meahte(n), meahton *see* **magan.**

meaht *noun see* **miht.**

gemealt *see* **gemeltan.**

mearcian *w.2* mark out, determine 14/118, 150, 19/184.

mearcland *n.* borderland 13/19.

mearcstapa *m.* wanderer in the borderland 11/139.

mear(g) *m.* horse 16/92, 12/188, 239.

mearn *see* **murnan.**

mearð *m.* marten 6/51.

mec *see* **ic.**

mēce *m.* sword 11/387, 458, 12/167.

medmicel, -mycel *adj.* small 5/5, 8/68.

medo *m.* mead 6/116, 114, 11/406; **meodo** *dat. sg.* 12/212.

medodrinc *m.* mead-drinking 17/22.

medubenc *f.* mead-bench 11/75.

mehte(n), mehton *see* **magan.**

meledēaw *m.* honeydew, nectar 19/142.

gemeltan *3* melt (*intr.*); **gemealt** *3 sg. pret.* 11/349, 356, 401.

men *see* **man(n).**

(*ge*)mengan *w.1* mix, mingle 11/334, 16/48; **gemǣngde** *3 sg. pret.* 7/31, 47.

menig(e)o *f.* multitude 4/30, 13/101; **mǣnige** *dat. sg.* 15/112, **manigeo** 15/151.

mennisc *adj.* human 10/129.

menniscnes *f.* incarnation 5/73-4.

meodo *see* **medo.**

meoduheall *f.* mead-hall 16/27.

meolc *f.* milk 6/113.

mēos *n.* moss 10/26.

meotud *see* **metod.**

meotudwang *m.* field of doom 13/11.

mere *m.* lake 11/153, 6/70, 71.

mereflōd *m.* ocean 17/59, 19/42.

merewērig *adj.* sea-worn 17/12.

merewīf *n.* woman of the lake 11/260.

mergen *see* **morgen.**

gemet *n.* (1) measure; **ofer eall gemett** 3/16 immeasurably, immoderately; (2) power, ability 11/652; **mid gemete** 11/78 by any means; (3) metre 5/46.

(*ge*)mētan *w.1* meet, find, come upon 1/25, 6/22, 11/50.

mete *m.* food 2/37, 38, 8/76.
meteliest, -least *f.* lack of food 2/85, 13/39.
meteþearfende *adj.* starving 13/27.
metod, meotud *m.* God 11/5, 5/36, 13/69, 145.
metodsceaft *f.* decree of fate, death 11/588.
mēðe *adj.* weary 15/65, 13/39, 15/69.
meþelstede *m.* meeting-place 12/199.
micel, mycel *adj.* great, large 2/74, 1/7, 3/42, 50; **micle** *inst. sg. as adv.* much, greatly 2/140, 6/119, 11/320; **mic(c)lum** *dat. pl. as adv.* much, greatly 1/15, 6/143, 10/128; **māra** *comp.* 4/44, 6/119, 9/83; **mǣst** *supl.* 2/25, 5/5, 6/38.
mid (1) *prep. with dat.* with, through, among 1/12, 28, 32; (2) *adv.* with them 2/19, 6/44.
mid þām þe *conj.* when 7/114.
mid þæm þæt *conj.* through the fact that 2/141.
mid þī (þȳ) þe *conj.* when 7/1, 140, 19, 53.
mid(d) *adj.* mid, middle of 15/2, 19/144.
middaneard *m.* earth 3/6.
middangeard, middongeard *m.* earth 16/62 n., 5/69, 41.
midde *f.* middle 11/478.
middel *m.* middle 19/65.
middelniht *f.* middle of the night 11/555, 606.
middeweard *adv.* in the middle 6/61.
miht, meaht *f.* might, power 5/36, 13/104, 17/108, 19/6.
miht(e), mihton *see* **magan.**
mihtig *adj.* mighty 11/189, 260, 14/8.
mīl *f.* mile 2/6, 7, 9.
milde *adj.* gentle 3/15, 12/175.
mildheortnesse *f.* kindheartedness 7/128.
mildheortnis *f.* mercy 3/89.
mīlgemearc *n.* measure by miles 11/153.
milts *f.* mercy, favour 8/19, 16/2.
gemiltsian *w.2* pity 7/69, 10/115.
mīn *pron. see* **ic.**

mine *m.* love 16/27 n., *in* **mīn mine wisse** loved me.
misbēodan *2 with dat.* ill-use 9/26.
misdǣd *f.* misdeed 9/117, 132, 141.
mislic, mistlic *adj.* various 4/62, 8/9, 9/62, 122.
mislician *w.2* displease 7/111.
mislimpan *w.1* go wrong 9/114.
missenlic *adj.* various 16/75; *or adv.* **missenlīce ?**
missēre *n.* half-year 11/239, 393.
mist *m.* mist 14/146.
misthliþ *n.* misty hill; **-hleoþum** *dat. pl.* 11/9 cover of darkness.
mōd *n.* mind, spirit, heart 11/29, 4/37, 5/7.
mōdcearig *adj.* sorrowful 16/2.
mōdelic *adj.* magnificent 8/67.
mōdelīce *adv.* boldly 12/200.
mōdig *adj.* brave, proud 15/41, 8/35, 10/15; **mōdi** 12/147, **mōdega** 11/112.
mōdigan *w.2* become proud 3/86.
mōdor *f.* mother 9/81, 11/279, 15/92.
mōdsefa *m.* mind, spirit 11/401, 16/10, 59.
mōdgeþoht *m.* thought 14/8.
mōdgeþonc *m.* thought 5/36.
mōdwlonc *adj.* proud-hearted 17/39.
molde *f.* earth, soil 17/103, 3/9, 8/39.
moldern *n.* tomb 15/65.
gemolsnian *w.2* decay 8/40.
mon *see* **man(n), man.**
gemon *see* **gemunan.**
mōnað *m.* month 2/15, 101, 6/76.
monað, moniað *see* **manian.**
moncynn *see* **mancynn.**
mondryhten *see* **mandryhten.**
monge ? 18/14.
monig *see* **manig.**
monigfealdian *w.2* multiply 8/3–4.
monode *see* **manian.**
mōr *m.* (1) marsh, waste land 11/9, 139, 196; (2) mountain 6/58 n., 59, 63.
morgen *m.* morning, morrow 1/22, 5/57; **marne** *dat. sg.* 5/46, **mergen** 10/17, 134.
morgengifu *f.* marriage gift 7/107 n.
morðdǣd *f.* murder or deadly sin 9/118.

morðor *n.* (1) murder, death 11/555;
(2) evil 13/19; (3) torment 14/52,
97.
morðorbealo *n.* murder 11/515.
morþorwyrhta *m.* murderer
9/145–6.
mōs *n.* food 13/27.
gemōt *n.* meeting, council 12/199;
12/301 combat.
mōtan *irr.* (1) can, be able (to), be
allowed (to); mōt *1 sg. pres.*
15/142; mōst *2 sg. pres.* 13/105,
115; mōton *1 pl. pret.* 14/159,
162; *3 pl. pres.* 14/177, mōtan
6/136; mōte *3 sg. pres. subj.* 7/89,
8/38, 48; mōste *1 sg. pret.* 7/56,
128, 11/570; *3 sg. pret.* 3/18, 11/5,
34; mōston *3 pl. pret.* 3/81,
10/135, 12/83; mōste *1 sg. pret.
subj.* 14/124; *3 sg. pret. subj.* 3/52;
mōsten *3 pl. pret. subj.* 3/76; (2)
must; mōst *2 sg. pres.* 12/30; mōt
3 sg. pres. 11/659; mōte *1 pl. pres.*
9/12.
gemunan *irr.* remember 8/59;
geman *1 sg. pres.* 11/406, 15/28;
gemon *3 sg. pres.* 16/34, 90;
gemunde *1 sg. pret.* 4/27, 38, 45,
3 sg. pret. 11/57, 379, 451; gemundon *3 pl. pret.* 12/196; gemunaþ
imp. pl. 12/212.
mund *f.* protection 9/25.
mundbora *m.* protector 11/552.
mundbyrd *f.* protection 15/130 n.
mundgripe *m.* hand-grip 11/52,
275.
munec *m.* monk 3/19, 21, 8/32.
munt *m.* mountain 19/21.
munuchād *m.* monastic orders 5/62.
munuclic *adj.* monastic 10/39–40.
munuclīce *adv.* as a monk 10/58.
murcnung *f.* grief 7/26.
murnan *w.1* care (about) 13/37.
murnan *3* (1) mourn; murne *3 sg.
pres. subj.* 11/176; murn *imp. sg.*
13/99; (2) care about 12/259;
mearn *3 sg. pret.* 11/278; mur-
non *3 pl. pret.* 12/96.
mūð *m.* mouth 5/68.
mūþa *m.* mouth, opening, estuary
2/5, 4, 9.
mycel *see* micel.

myltestre *f.* harlot 9/146.
gemynd *f.* remembrance 16/51, 4/2,
5/45.
gemyndig *adj.* mindful of 11/271,
462, 13/218.
(ge)myngian *w.2* (1) remember
5/66; (2) remind 8/20.
mynster *n.* monastery, church 3/20,
4, 18.
mynsterhata *m.* persecutor of
monasteries 9/145.
mynsterlic *adj.* monastic 10/62.
mynstermann *m.* monk 10/128,
134.
myntan *w.1* intend 11/11, 30,
61.
myrce *adj.* dark 11/196.
myrcels *m.* mark 10/117.
mȳre *f.* mare 6/113.
myrhð *f.* joy 9/180.
myrð(u) *f.* trouble 11/109 n.

nā *see* nō.
nabbe *see* habban.
naca *m.* boat 17/7.
nafað *see* habban.
nāh *see* āgan.
nālas, nālæs, nālles *see* nealles.
(ge)nam(on) *see* (ge)niman.
nama, noma *m.* name 12/267, 4/25,
72, 18/37.
nān *pron.* no 3/41, 2/168, 3/31,
nǣnne *m. acc. sg.* 4/40.
nānwuht *see* nōht.
genāp *see* genīpan.
nāst, nāt *see* (ge)witan.
nāthwylc *pron.* some 11/254.
nāwðer ne...ne *conj.* neither...
nor 2/155; nāþor...ne...ne
9/56.
næfde *see* habban.
næfne *see* nefne.
nǣfre *adv.* never 1/30, 3/42, 5/14.
næfð *see* habban.
genǣgan *w.1* assail 11/230.
nægl *m.* nail 15/46.
nǣnig *pron.* no, none 1/19, 29, 5/10.
nǣnne *see* nān.
nǣre, nǣren, nǣron, næs *see*
wesan.
næs = ne ealles *adv.* not 7/115 n.,
8/30.

næshliŏ *n.* headland-slope; **-hleo-ŏum** *dat. pl.* 11/218.

næss, næs *m.* headland 11/149, 151, 202, 230.

ne (1) *adv.* not 1/33, 2/29, 42; (2) *conj.* nor 11/15, 17, 92.

ne . . . ne *conj.* neither . . . nor 3/1–2.

nēah (*in some cases allocation to a particular word-class is difficult, but the following illustrate the range*) (1) *adj.* near 8/2, 11/501, **nēh** 12/103; **nīehst** *supl.* 2/21, **nēxtan** 3/3, **æt nēxtan, æt nȳhstan** in the end 3/34, 9/160, then, afterwards 7/96; (2) *adv.* near, nearly 6/32, 11/643, 16/26; **nēar** *comp.* 11/44; (3) *prep. with dat.* 2/111, 13/118, **nēh** 13/207.

geneahhe, genehe *adv.* sufficiently, very, frequently 11/82, 16/56, 12/269; **genehost** *supl.* 11/93.

(ge)nēalǣcan *w.1 with dat.* approach 5/21, 8/19, 9/2, **genēalēcan** 10/112–13.

nealles *adv.* not at all 11/369, 646; **nālas** 11/234, 270, 278; **nālles** 11/605, 14/101; **nālæs** 5/11.

nearo *n.* straits, difficulty 11/367, 13/173.

nearo *adj.* narrow, difficult 11/200, 17/7.

nearon *see* **wesan.**

nearonēd *f.* cruel bondage 13/102.

nearwian *w.2* press hard 11/229.

nēat *n.* cattle 5/23, 13/67.

genēat *m.* companion 2/173, 12/310, 14/39.

nēawest, nēawist *f.* (1) neighbourhood 2/121; (2) fellowship 8/73.

nebb *n.* beak 19/165.

nēd *see* **nēod.**

nēdŏearf, nȳdþearf *f.* necessity 8/58, 45, 9/18.

nēdþearf *adj.* needful 8/33.

nefne, næfne, nemne *conj.* (1) unless, if . . . not 11/293, 427; (2) except (that) 17/46, 11/144, 19/142.

nēh *see* **nēah.**

genehe *see* **geneahhe.**

nēhmǣg *m.* kinsman 8/71.

genehost *see* **geneahhe.**

nellaŏ, nelle, *see* **willan.**

nemnan *w.1* call, name 2/148, 4/63, 5/27.

nemþe *see* **nymþe.**

nēod, nēd *f.* (1) need, necessity 9/156, 3/64, 7/14; (2) compulsion, affliction 13/114, 206/14; (3) fetters 18/5.

neorxnawang *m.* paradise 13/102.

nēotan, nīotan *2 with gen.* use, enjoy 12/308, 14/156.

neoŏan *adv.* beneath, down 14/66, 19/173; **neoŏone** 14/130.

neowol *adj.* steep 11/202.

nerian *w.1* protect, save, spare 1/38, 2/90, 11/126.

nest *n.* nest 19/97, 109.

nēten, nȳten *n.* animal 5/66, 10/23.

nēxtan *see* **nēah.**

nicor *m.* water-monster 11/218.

nicorhūs *n.* sea-monster's dwelling 11/202.

nīedbeŏearfost *adj. supl.* most necessary 4/51.

nīehst *see* **nēah.**

nigon *num.* nine 2/159.

nigoŏa *num.* ninth 10/105.

niht *f.* night 2/26, 5/24, 6/95; **nihtes** *irr. gen. sg. as adv.* 2/94 by night.

nihthelm *m.* shades of night 16/96.

nihtgerīm *n.* reckoning by nights 13/115 n.

nihtscūa *m.* shadow of night 16/104, 17/31.

nihtwaco *f.* night-watch 17/7.

nihtweorc *n.* night's work 11/126.

(ge)niman *4* seize, take 12/39, 252; **(ge)nim(e)ŏ** *3 sg. pres.* 6/134, 20b/12; **nimaŏ** *3 pl. pres.* 6/141, 17/48; **niman** *3 pl. pres. subj.* 3/92; **(ge)nam** *3 sg. pret.* 3/61, 7/42, 3/2, 7/46, **(ge)nōm** 11/353, 549; **genāmon** *3 pl. pret.* 2/56, 98, 112, **genāman** 15/30; **genāme** *3 sg. pret. subj.* 12/71; **genumen** *pret. p.* 2/106, 6/134; **nim** *imp. sg.* 7/111, 115, 141; **nimaŏ** *imp. pl.* 7/71.

nīobedd *n.* bed of death 14/98.

nīosian *w.1 with gen.* seek out, attack 11/444.

nīotan *see* **nēotan.**

niopoweard *adj.* below, lower part of 19/165.

genip *n.* darkness, mist 11/151, 581.

(ge)nīpan *1* grow dark; nīpeð *3 sg. pres.* 16/104; (ge)nāp *3 sg. pret.* 16/96, 17/31.

nis *see* wesan.

niste *see* (ge)witan.

nīð *m.* hostility, force, violence 3/80, 8/36, 11/126.

niper *adv.* down 11/151, 14/98; nioðor *comp.* 11/472 lower down.

niðgæst *m.* malicious stranger 11/472.

nīðplega *m.* battle 13/173.

nīðsele *m.* battle-hall 11/254.

nīðwundor *n.* fearful wonder 11/156.

nīwe *adj.* new 11/82, 2/159, 11/367.

nīwian *w.2* restore, renew 15/148, 16/50, 55.

nō, nā *adv.* not, not at all, never 11/146, 183, 2/96, 3/39.

nō þȳ ǣr *adv.* none the sooner 11/53, 243.

genōh, genōg (1) *adj.* enough, abundant 6/116, 15/33; (2) *adv.* enough 9/102.

nōht (1) *adv.* not 4/16; (2) *as noun* nothing 5/14, 28, 29, nānwuht 4/31, 20a/8.

nōhwæðer ne . . . ne *conj.* neither . . . nor 4/24.

nōlæs *adv.* (*used as noun*) no less 2/180.

nolde, noldon *see* willan.

(ge)nōm *see* (ge)niman.

noma *see* nama.

nōn *f.* ninth hour (= 3 pm.) 11/341 n.

norþ *adv.* north 2/44, 6/3, 11; norðor *comp.* 6/60.

norþan *adv.* from the north 6/15, 16/104, 17/31; be norþan *prep.* on the north of 2/80, 6/8, 74.

norðanēastan *adv.* from the north-east 20a/6.

norðanwind *m.* north wind 20a/7.

norþerne *adj.* northern 20b/14.

norðeweard *adv.* in the north 6/62.

norþmest *adv.* furthest north 6/2.

norþryhte *adv.* due north 6/8, 9, 12.

norþweard, norðeweard *adj.* the north of, northern 6/2, 67, 68.

norþweardes *adv.* north 2/32.

nose *f.* promontory 11/576.

notian *w.2* consume 2/38.

notu *f.* use, employment 4/57.

nū *adv.* now 4/12, 74, 5/35.

nū hwīle *adv.* just 8/15.

genumen *see* (ge)niman.

nȳdan *w.1* compel, force 11/453.

nȳde *adv.* necessarily, of necessity 9/3, 17.

nȳdgyld *n.* exaction 9/93.

nȳdmāge *f.* near kinswoman 9/101.

nȳdþearf *see* nēdþearf.

nȳhst *see* nēah.

nymþe, nemþe *conj.* unless 11/80, 16/113.

nyrwan *w.1* reduce 9/39.

nys *see* wesan.

nysse, nyste *see* (ge)witan.

nȳtena *see* nēten.

nytlic *adj.* useful 8/33.

nytt *adj.* useful 11/93.

nytwyrðe *adj.* useful; -wyrðoste *supl.* 2/156.

ō *see* ā.

of (1) *prep. with dat.* from 2/2, 5/28, 11/25; (2) *adv.* away 2/162.

ofāslēan *6* cut off 10/116; ofāslagen *pret. p.* 10/126.

ofbiþ *see* ofwesan.

ōfer *m.* bank, shore 11/162, 12/28.

ofer (1) *prep. with acc., dat.*: (*a*) over, across 2/33, 101, 128, ofir 20b/5; (*b*) after 11/35; (*c*) beyond 17/58; (*d*) despite 2/18, 11/497; (*e*) contrary to 15/35; (2) *adv.* over 2/3, 6/82.

oferbrǣdan *w.1* overspread 7/149.

ofercuman *4* overcome; -cumen *pret. p.* 18/26.

oferfēran *w.1* cross 6/64, 66.

oferfrēosan *2* freeze over; -froren *pret. p.* 6/147.

oferfyll(u) *f.* gluttony 9/166.

ofergān *irr.* pass over, pass away; -ēode *3 sg. pret.* 11/199; 18/7, 13, 17 *etc.* (*impers.*).

oferhelmian *w.2* overhang 11/155.

oferhīgian *w.2* overpower 11/539.

oferhoga *m.* despiser 9/127.

oferhygd *f. or n.* pride 14/83.

oferlīce *adv.* excessively 9/159.

ofermægen *n.* great power 19/131.

ofermēde *n.* pride 14/48.

ofermētto *f.* pride 14/106, 87, 92.

ofermōd *n.* pride, overconfidence 12/89 n., 14/27.

ofermōd *adj.* proud 14/17 n., 93.

oferrǣdan *w.1* read through 7/118, 134.

ofersēcan *w.1* overtax; -sōhte *3 sg. pret.* 11/459.

oferweorpan *3* fall over; -wearp 11/284 n.

oferwinnan *3* defeat; -wann *3 sg. pret.* 10/30.

oferwrēon *2, 3* cover over; -wrogen *pret. p.* 3/8–9.

ofett *n.* fruit 19/77.

offaran *6* pursue, overtake 2/96; offōron *3 pl. pret.* 2/81.

offerian *w.1* carry off 11/324.

ofgifan *5* give up, leave; ofgēafon *3 pl. pret.* 11/341, 16/61 n., ofgēfan 11/619.

oflǣtan *7* leave, relinquish; oflēt *3 sg. pret.* 11/363.

ofost, ofst *f.* haste, speed 11/520, 556, 9/1.

ōfre *see* ōfer *m.*

ofscēotan *2* kill by stabbing; -scēat *3 sg. pret.* 12/77.

ofsittan *5* sit upon; -sæt *3 sg. pret.* 11/286.

ofslēan *6* slay; ofslōg *3 sg. pret.* 1/3; ofslōgon *3 pl. pret.* 1/36, 2/99, 112; ofslōge *3 sg. pret. subj.* 6/39; ofslægen *pret. p.* 1/16, 23, 26, ofslagen 10/5, 105.

ofstingan *3* stab; -stang *3 sg. pret.* 1/5.

ofstlīce *adv.* quickly 12/143.

oft *adv.* often 1/7, 38; swa oft swa as often as 2/18, 3/25; oftor *comp.* 2/29, 9/45, 11/320; oftost *supl.* 4/21, 9/129, 10/82.

oftēon *2* withhold; -tēah *3 sg. pret.* 11/261.

oftrǣdlīce *adv.* habitually 7/101.

ofþincan *w.1* (*impers.*) grieve 7/119.

ofwesan *irr.* be absent, disappear; ofbiŏ *3 sg. pres.* 8/75.

ōleccan *w.1 with dat.* flatter 14/45.

oll *n.* contempt 9/134.

ōmig *adj.* rusty 11/536.

on (1) *prep. with acc. dat.*, on, in, into, in 1/4, 10, 11/1, 7; (2) *adv.* within 2/10.

on innan (1) *prep. with dat.* within 13/196, 14/108; (2) within 11/488.

on gemang *prep. with dat.* among 4/62; in gemonge in the midst of 19/147.

onarn *see* onirnan.

onǣlan *w.1* kindle, excite 7/81, 19/98.

onbǣrnan *w.1* incite, inspire 5/9, 84.

onbregdan *3* swing open; -brǣd *3 sg. pret.* 11/22.

onbryrdnys *f.* ardour 10/84.

onbyrigan *w.1* taste 15/114.

oncirran, oncyrran *w.1* change 11/630, 8/28, 13/36.

oncnāwan *7* acknowledge, know 8/1, 12/9; oncnāwe *1 sg. pres.* 7/39.

oncweŏan *5* speak, respond; oncwæŏ *3 sg. pret.* 12/245, 13/155, 17/23.

oncȳŏ *f.* grief 11/211, 129.

ond *see* and.

ondlang, andlong *adj.* (extending) (1) whole (*of periods of time*) 13/209, 229; (2) standing at his side 11/468.

ondleofen *f.* food 19/125.

ondrǣdan *7* fear; ondrǣdeþ *3 sg. pres.* 17/106.

onswaru *see* andswaru.

onemn *prep. with dat.* close by 12/184.

onettan *w.1* hasten, become active 17/49, 19/99.

onfindan *3* discover, perceive; onfand *3 sg. pret.* 11/263, 403, 486, onfond 18/4; onfundon *3 pl. pret.* 1/17; onfunde *3 sg. pret. subj.* 11/49, 108, 238; onfunden *3 pl. pret. subj.* 1/12.

onfōn *7 with acc., gen. or dat.* receive; onfēng *3 sg. pret.* 5/13, 32, 48; onfēngc 7/92; onfēnge *3 sg. pret.*

subj. 5/62, 13/53; **onfangen** *pret. p.* 2/62, 5/57.

onforan *prep. with acc.* before 2/93 113.

ongeador *adv.* together 11/336.

ongēan, ongēn (1) *prep. with acc.* towards, against, opposite 2/33, 3/31, 2/152, 160; (2) *adv.* out, back, opposite 6/83, 7/3, 11/46, 12/49.

onginnan, ongynnan 3 begin; **ongynneð** 3 *sg. pres.* 14/53; **onginnað** 3 *pl. pres.* 19/106; **onginnen** 3 *pl. pres. subj.* 15/116; **ongan** *1 sg. pret.* 4/62, 11/651; **ongan** 3 *sg. pret.* 5/32, 60, 7/31, **ongon** 11/474, 484, 563; **ongunnon** 3 *pl. pret.* 5/10, 7/32, 12/86; **ongunne** 3 *sg. pret. subj.* 14/30; **onginnað** *imp. pl.* 14/163; **ongunnen** *pret. p.* 2/126.

ongitan, ongytan 5 perceive, see, understand 11/543, 237, 15/18, **ongeotan** 8/2, 19, **ongietan** 16/73, **ongiotan** 4/31; **ongytaþ** *1 pl. pres.* 8/6; **ongite** *1 sg. pres. subj.* 7/36, 11/521; **ongeat** 3 *sg. pret.* 1/13, 7/144, 149, **onget** 2/126; **ongēaton** 3 *pl. pret.* 11/222, 12/84, 14/89; **ongieten** *pret. p.* 18/10.

ongyldan 3 atone for 14/50.

ongyrwan *w.1* strip, undress 15/39.

onhǣtan *w.1* ignite 19/94.

onhlīdan *1* reveal (oneself); **onhlād** 3 *sg. pret.* 13/224; **onhliden** *pret. p.* 19/12, 49.

onhrēran *w.1* arouse, stir 17/96, 13/129, 152.

onirnan 3 give way; **onarn** 3 *sg. pret.* 11/20.

onlǣtan 7 release; **onlǣteð** 3 *sg. pres.* 11/350.

onlēon 2 give; **onlāg** 3 *sg. pret.* 14/113.

onlīc *adj.* like; **-ost** *supl.* 19/178.

onlīce *adv.* in the same manner 19/124.

onlīcnes, -næs *f.* likeness, image 14/151, 11/142.

onlūcan 2 unlock, reveal; **onlēac** 3 *sg. pret.* 20b/1.

onlūtan 2 incline 4/37.

onlȳsan *w.1* redeem 15/147.

onmēdla *m.* pomp 17/81.

onmōd *adj.* resolute 13/54.

onmunan *irr. with acc. and gen.* (1) remind of; **onmunde** 3 *sg. pret.* 11/413; (2) care about; **onmundon** 3 *pl. pret.* 1/33.

onsāwan 7 sow; **onsāwen** *pret. p.* 19/135.

onsǣge *adj.* attacking 9/45.

onscungend *m.* (*pres. p.*) one who shuns 8/72.

onscyte *m.* attack 9/60, 140.

onsendan *w.1* send 4/70, 13/110, 15/49.

onslǣpan *w.1* go to sleep 5/25.

onsponnan *irr.* unfasten; **onspēon** 3 *sg. pret.* 11/496.

onspringan 3 spring up, spring apart; **onspringað** 3 *pl. pres.* 19/63; **onsprungon** 3 *pl. pret.* 11/116.

onstāl *m.* supply 4/19.

onstellan *w.1* establish 5/38.

onstyrian *w.1* stir up 20a/7.

onsund, andsund *adj.* changeless, unscathed 19/20, 44, 10/125.

onsȳn, ansȳn *f.* appearance, form, face 11/545, 17/91, 19/55, 11/607.

ontȳnan *w.1* open 13/105.

onwald, onweald *m.* power, rule 4/5, 7.

onwǣcan *w.1* soften 14/158.

onwæcnan *w.1* awake 16/45.

onweg *adv.* away 2/165, **āweg** 2/90.

onwendan *w.1* remove, change, transgress 11/374, 8/28, 14/155.

onwindan 3 unwind; **onwindeð** 3 *sg. pres.* 11/351.

onwrēon *1* reveal; **onwrēoh** *imp. sg.* 15/97.

oo see **ā**.

open *adj.* open 15/47, 19/11.

orc *m.* cup, pitcher 11/533.

ord *m.* (1) beginning 11/564, 5/38; 13/32 (**gāra**) **ordum** point *hence* (2) spear 12/60, 47, 110; (3) van (front division of army) 12/69, 273.

ōretta *m.* warrior 11/273.

oreð *n.* breath 11/612.

orfcwealm *m.* murrain 9/48.

orfeorm *adj.* (*with dat.*) deprived (of) 13/165.

orlege *n.* battle 13/47.

orþonc *m.* art 19/170.

orwēna *adj.* (*with gen.*) despairing (of) 11/306.

oþ (1) *conj.* until 1/3, 14, 20, **oþþe** 2/49, 6/127; (2) *prep. with acc.* until, as far as 2/8, 4/57, 5/17.

oþberan 4 carry away; **oþbær** 3 sg. pret. 16/81.

oðer *adj.* (1) (the) other 2/12, 18, 25; (2) second, next 6/127, 10/17.

oþfæstan *w.1* set 4/56.

oðfeallan 7 decline 4/43; **oðfeallenu** *pret. p.* 4/13.

oðrōwan 7 row away; **oðrēowon** 3 *pl. pret.* 2/176.

oþþæt *conj.* until 1/4, 16, 35.

oððe *conj.* or 2/7, 26, 3/10; **oððe ... oððe** either ... or 2/19, 58, 58–9.

oððon *conj.* or 9/65, 174.

oðþringan 3 wrest; **oðþringeð** 3 *sg. pres.* 17/71.

oðwendan *w.1 with dat. and acc.* deprive of 14/158.

oðwindan 3 escape; **oðwand** 3 *sg. pret.* 2/163–4.

ōwer (= **ōhwǣr**) *adv.* anywhere 11/643.

ōwiht *see* **āwiht**.

pāpa *m.* pope 10/89.

pēa *m.* peacock 19/178.

plega *m.* festivity, game 6/122, 125, 7/8.

ple(a)gian *w.2* play, act 3/44, 7/50, 13/129.

port *m.* port 6/74, 85.

prass *n.* proud array 12/68.

prȳte *f.* pride 9/141.

pund *n.* pound 3/60, 7/60.

racente *f.* fetter(s) 14/127, 189.

rād *see* **rīdan**.

radost *see* **hraþe**.

ranc *adj.* brave 9/102.

randas *see* **rond**.

raþe *see* **hraþe**.

(ge)rǣcan *w.1* reach 2/22, 107; **(ge)rǣhte** 3 *sg. pret.* 11/46, 12/142.

rǣd *m.* advice, help, plan 11/167, 10/89, 14/41.

(ge)rǣdan *irr.* (*some weak and some strong forms, but all w.1 forms here*) (1) instruct 12/18; (2) decide 12/36; (3) control 11/631, 14/44; (4) read 8/60, 7/116, 117.

rǣdend *m.* God 11/296.

rǣding *f.* reading 10/54, 56.

gerǣdu *n. pl.* trappings 12/190.

rǣran *w.1* set up 9/9.

rǣs *m.* onslaught 11/399.

(ge)rǣsan *w.1* rush 1/14, 11/463, 612.

rǣsbora *m.* leader 13/144.

ræst *see* **rest**.

rǣðe *see* **rēþe**.

rēaf *n.* clothes 7/61, 12/161.

rēafere *m.* plunderer 9/148.

rēafian *w.2* rob, plunder 11/546, 9/111.

rēaflāc *m. or n.* robbery, plundering 9/49, 162.

rēc *m.* smoke 14/80.

reccan *w.1* care; **rōhte** 3 *sg. pret.* 3/80; **rōhtan** 3 *pl. pret.* 9/115, **rōhton** 12/260 (*with gen.*).

(ge)reccan, reccean *w.1* tell, explain 8/60; **(ge)rehte** 3 *sg. pret.* 10/24, 47; **rehton** 3 *pl. pret.* 5/54.

reccelēas *adj.* careless 4/42.

reced *m.* building, hall 11/69, 19, 23.

gerēfa *m.* reeve 2/171.

re(g)nian *w.2* adorn 11/76, 12/161; **rēnigenne** *infl. inf.* 8/38 'lay, set (a trap)'.

regollic *adj.* regular, monastic 5/82.

regollīce *adv.* regularly, according to the Rule 9/55.

regul *m.* (monastic) rule 3/22.

rēn *m.* rain 19/14, 128.

renweard *m.* guardian of the hall 11/69.

reord, gereord *n.* language, voice 10/48, 50, 13/60.

reordberend *m. pl.* men, people 15/3, 89.

reordian *w.2* speak 13/123.

gereordian *w.2* feast 13/144.

rēotan 2 weep; **rēotað** 3 *pl. pres.* 11/167.

rest, ræst *f.* rest, bed 5/25, 15/3, 11/46, 326.

(*ge*)restan *w.1* rest 7/72, 78, 14/189.

rēþe, rǣðe *adj.* fierce 11/326, 10/16, 11/69, 3/30.

rīce *n.* kingdom 1/1, 8, 28.

rīce *adj.* powerful, mighty 3/6, 1, 14; **rīcost** *supl.* 6/113, 12/36.

ricene, rycene *adv.* quickly 12/93, 16/112.

rīcsode *see* **rīxian**.

rīdan *I* ride 10/57, 12/291; **rīdeð** *3 sg. pres.* 6/135, 14/127; **rād** *3 sg. pret.* 2/122, 129, 10/119; **ridon** *3 pl. pret.* 1/23.

riht, ryht *n.* right 8/82, 9/19, 130, 11/296.

riht *adj.* right 8/25, 26, 47.

***ge*rihta** *n. pl.* rights, dues 9/30, 19, 22.

rihtan *w.1* direct 15/131.

rihte *adv.* rightly 9/58, 12/20.

rihtlagu *f.* just law 9/128.

***ge*rihtlǣcan** *w.1* guide 10/98.

riht*ge*lēfed *adj.* of true faith, orthodox 8/52.

rihtlīce *adv.* righteously 8/21, 9/175, 10/16.

rinc *m.* man, warrior 11/19, 27, 40.

ringe *see* **hring**.

rīp rȳp *n.* crop, harvest 2/122, 19/128.

***ge*rīpan** *I* reap; **gerypon** *3 pl. pret.* 2/121.

***ge*risene** *n.* what is fitting 9/34.

***ge*risenlic** *adj.* proper 5/2.

rīxian, rīcsian *w.2* rule, hold sway 3/45, 51, 10/149, 9/7.

rōd *f.* cross, the Cross 10/22, 12, 15/56, 119.

roder, rodor *m.* sky 11/167, 296, 313, 19/14.

rōf *adj.* brave 11/439, 463, 13/9.

rōhte, rōhton *see* **reccan**.

rōmigan *w.2 with gen.* possess, (try to) obtain 14/115 n.

rond, rand *m.* shield 13/9, 11/382, 426, 12/20; 11/446 n. shield-boss.

rōse *f.* rose 7/148, 20a/6, 20b/13.

rudu *f.* redness 7/149.

rūm *m.* opportunity 11/463.

rūm *adj.* spacious, broad 19/14, 20b/13.

rūmmōd *adj.* generous 8/22.

rūn *f.* mystery, secret 16/111 n.

rycene *see* **ricene**.

ryht *see* **riht**.

ryhtnorþanwind *m.* due north wind 6/16.

(*ge*)rȳman *w.1* extend, make way (for) 4/8, 10/75, 12/93.

rȳmet *n.* space 2/21.

rȳpan *w.1* plunder 9/111.

rȳpere *m.* robber 9/49, 148.

gerypon *see* **gerīpan**.

rypes *see* **rīp**.

***ge*rysne** *adj.* becoming, proper 11/426.

sacu *f.* strife 19/54.

sāl *m.* chain 14/127, 133.

sam . . . sam *conj.* whether . . . or 6/147.

same *see* **swā same**.

(*ge*)samnod(e) *see* **(*ge*)somnian**.

samod, somod *adv.* together, also 6/107, 10/4, 11/355; **samod (somod) ætgædere** 11/28, 16/39.

samworht *adj.* half-built 2/11.

sanct *m.* saint 10/131, 129, 135.

sand *f.* (what is sent) course of food 10/68.

sang *see* **singan, song**.

sann *see* **sinnan**.

sār *n.* pain, wound 13/201, 7/22, 11/86.

sār *adj.* grievous, painful 14/180, 15/80, 16/50.

sārbenn *f.* grievous wound 13/194.

sāre *adv.* sorely, grievously 9/36, 143, 11/519.

sārgian *w.2* wound 2/176.

sārig *adj.* sad 13/60.

sārigferð *adj.* sad at heart 11/636.

sārlic *adj.* sad 7/5.

sārnes *f.* grief 7/30.

sārslege *m.* painful blow 13/230.

sārwracu *f.* misery 19/54.

(*ge*)sāwe *see* **(*ge*)sēon**.

sāwol, sāwul *f.* soul, life 11/593, 12/177, 10/114, **sāwl** 8/75, 15/120; **sāule** *often in oblique cases, e.g.* 3/89, 8/14, 9/63.

sāwollēas *adj.* lifeless 11/197.

(*ge*)sāwon *see* (*ge*)sēon.

sāwuldrīor *m. or n.* life-blood 11/466.

sǣ *f.* sea 2/177, 101, 109.

sæcc *f.* fighting, battle 11/359, 385, 432.

sǣd *n.* seed 19/135.

sæd *adj. with gen.* satiated, wearied with 11/496.

sǣde *see* secgan.

sǣdēor *n.* sea-beast 11/251.

sǣdon *see* secgan.

sǣdraca *m.* sea-serpent 11/217.

sǣflota *m.* ship 13/140.

sǣfōr *f.* sea-journey 17/42.

sǣgde, sǣgdon *see* secgan.

sǣgon *see* (*ge*)sēon

sǣl *m. or f.* time, season 15/80, 10/63, 11/352; 18/28 joy.

sǣlan *w.1* fasten 16/21, 11/537.

sǣlida *m.* seafarer, Viking 12/45, 286.

gesǣlig *adj.* happy, fortunate, blessed 10/99, 7/89, 10/38.

gesǣliglic *adj.* happy 4/4, 14/7.

sǣliðend *m.* seafarer 11/579.

sǣman *m.* sailor (Viking); -men *nom. pl.* 12/29, -mæn 9/106; -mannum *dat. pl.* 12/38, 278.

sǣmra *adj. comp.* weaker 11/653.

sænde *see* sendan,

sǣne *adj.* slow 11/227.

gesǣne *see* gesȳne.

sǣrima *m.* coast 2/158.

sǣrinc *m.* sea-warrior, Viking 12/134.

sæt, sǣton *see* sittan.

gesæt *see* gesittan.

(*ge*)sǣtte *see* (*ge*)settan.

scacan *6* pass, depart; sceaceð *3 sg. pres.* 11/515; sceacen *pret. p.* 11/500.

gescādan *7* decide; gescēd *3 sg. pret.* 11/296.

scamfæst *adj.* modest 7/130.

scamian *w.2* be ashamed 9/132, 139, 140.

scamu *f.* shame 9/87, 7/132; to sceame *dat. sg.* 10/8 shamefully; scome *dat. sg.* 5/21.

scanca *m.* leg 19/176.

scandlic, sceandlic *adj.* shameful 9/73, 93, 60.

gescæpene *see* (*ge*)scieppan.

gescær *see* (*ge*)sceran.

scead *n.* shadow 11/6, 19/92, 116

sceadu *f.* shadow, darkness 15/54.

sceadugenga *m.* walker in darkness 11/2.

gescēadwīsnys *f.* wisdom 10/59.

scēaf *see* scūfan.

sceaft *m.* shaft (of a spear) 12/136.

gesceaft *f.* (creation) (1) world 15/12, 11/363, 15/55; (2) creature 9/79; (3) decree (of fate) 16/107.

sceal *see* sculan.

scealc *m.* warrior 12/181.

scealt *see* sculan.

sceame *see* scamu.

sceandlic *see* scandlic.

scēap *n.* sheep 6/45.

gesceap *n.* creation, fate 5/69, 19/92.

scearp *adj.* bitter 3/1.

scēat *m.* district, region 19/3, 11/51, 15/8 n.

scēat *see* scēotan.

sceatt *m.* (coin) *in pl.* treasure, money 12/40, 56.

scēawi(g)an *w.2* look at, examine 11/517, 182, 231.

gescēawian *w.2* show 18/33.

scēawung *f.* surveying 6/33.

gescēd *see* gescādan.

scel *see* sculan.

scendan *w.1* insult 9/100, 110.

scēne *see* scȳne.

sceolde, sceoldon, sceolon *see* sculan.

gescēon *w.1 with dat.* fall upon 13/18.

(*ge*)scēop *see* (*ge*)scieppan.

scēotan *2* shoot; scēotað *3 pl. pres.* 9/75 n.; scēat *3 sg. pret.* 12/143, 270.

scēotend *m.* warrior 11/2.

(*ge*)sceran *4* cut; gescær *3 sg. pret.* 11/267.

scerian *w.1* decree 14/13; gescyred *pret. p.* 14/179.

scēð *f.* sceath 12/162.

(*ge*)sceþðan *w.1 and 6 with dat.* injure 11/265, 15/47; sceþeð *3 sg.*

214

pres. 19/39, 88; **gescōd** *3 sg. pret.* 11/243, 328, 550, **sceþede** 11/255.
(ge)scieppan *6* make; **(ge)scēop** *3 sg. pret.* 5/39, 14/6, 98, **gescōp** 19/84; **gescæpene** *pret. p.* 2/155.
scīma *m.* radiance 15/54.
scīnan *I* shine 11/258, 15/15; **scīneð** *3 sg. pres.* 11/312, 19/92, 20a/2.
scip, scyp *n.* ship 6/95, 2/4, 6/71, 72.
sciphere *m.* fleet 2/85.
scipian *w.2* ship, embark 2/3.
sciprāp *m.* ship-rope 6/35, 49, 52.
scīr *f.* division, district 6/73, 10/133; 2/39 division of the army.
scīr *adj.* bright 19/116, 12/98, 15/54.
gescōd *see* **(ge)sceþðan.**
scolde, scoldon *see* **sculan.**
scome *see* **scamu.**
scop *m.* poet 18/36.
(ge)scōp *see* **(ge)scieppan.**
scopgereord** *n.* poetic language 5/5.
scridan *w.I* clothe 3/8, 7/41.
scrīfan *I* care about 9/77.
scrīn *n.* shrine 10/124, 137.
scrīðan *I* glide, move 11/2.
scufan *2* thrust; **scēaf** *3 sg. pret.* 12/136.
sculan *irr.* must, have to, shall; **sceal** *I sg. pres.* 5/31, 11/589; **scealt** *2 sg. pres.* 11/439; **sceal(l)** *3 sg. pres.* 6/78, 122, 142, 50, **scel** 11/577; **sceolan** *I pl. pres.* 8/46, **sculon** 9/178, **sculan** 5/35; **sceolon** *3 pl. pres.* 6/129, **sceolan** 6/143; **scyle** *I sg. pres. subj.* 13/77, *3 sg. pres. subj.* 11/430, 17/74; **scylan** *I pl. pres. subj.* 9/12; **sceolde** *I sg. pret.* 16/8, 19, 17/30; **sceolde** *3 sg. pret.* 3/70, 86, 6/16, **scolde** 9/8, 11/104, 118; **sceoldon** *I pl. pret.* 4/12, 13, **sceoldan** 8/13, 14, **scoldan** 9/57; **scoldon** *3 pl. pret.* 4/11, 11/3; **scolden** *3 pl. pret. subj.* 2/28.
scūr *m.* shower 19/128, 17/17.
scyld *m.* (1) shield 11/448, 623, 12/98; (2) crest 19/174.
scyldburh *f.* wall of shields 12/242.
scyldhata *m.* evil foe; **-hetum** *dat. pl.* 13/85.

scyll *f.* (1) shell 19/116; (2) scale 19/176.
scȳne, scēne *adj.* fair, bright 19/166, 174, 14/20; **scȳnost** *supl.* 14/93.
scynscaþa *m.* hostile demon 11/6.
scyp *see* **scip.**
scypen *f.* stall 5/24.
scyppend *m.* creator (God) 5/40, 33, 13/155.
gescyred *see* **scerian.**
gescyrigan *w.2* condemn 13/85.
gescyrpla *m.* clothing 8/78.
se *def. art. Singular forms: m. nom.* **se** 1/7, 9 (*rel.*), 13; 1/21, 37 he; **þe** 7/66; *acc.* **þone** 1/3, 5, 10, **þǣne** 6/127, 9/91, 92; *gen.* **þæs** 1/9, 22, 37, **þes** 3/81; *dat.* **þām** 1/12, 33, 3/17, **þǣm** 2/50, 11/89, **ðan** 14/55, 15/122; *n. nom.* **þæt** 11/4, 15, 473, **þet** 3/20, 39, **tæt** 1/32; *acc.* **þæt** 1/13, 2/53, 64; *gen.* **þæs** 1/16, 28, 33, 14/191 (*rel.*); 11/72, 157, 249 *adv.* so, too; *dat.* **þǣm** 2/2, 10, 16, **ðan** 6/135, 139, 14/165, **ðon** 11/23, 364, 618; *instr.* **þȳ** 2/113, 116, 149, **þē** 11/120; *f. nom.* **sēo** 2/7, 95 (*rel.*), 5/60, **sīo** 2/30, 33, 36; *acc.* **þā** 1/2, 13, 17; *gen.* **þǣre** 2/84, 87, 121, **þāre** 7/18, 31, 47; *dat.* **þǣre** 1/25, 2/26, 39, **þāre** 7/20, 47. *Plural forms: nom., acc.* **þā** 1/12, 24, 26, 7/97 (*rel.*); *gen.* **þāra** 2/86, 118, 119, **þǣra** 9/23, 11/140, **þēora** 3/92; *dat.* **þām** 3/16, 17, 11/442, **þǣm** 2/26.
(ge)seah *see* **(ge)sēon.**
(ge)seald(e), sealdon *see* **(ge)syllan.**
sealm *m.* psalm 10/56.
sealtȳþ *f.* salty wave 17/35.
sēarian *w.2* wither 17/89.
searo *n.* (1) skill; **searwum** *dat. pl. adv.* skilfully 11/537, 19/151; (2) the product of skill, war-equipment 11/298, 473; (3) strata-gem, snare 8/37.
searocræft, searacræft *m.* fraud 13/109, 9/120.
searogimm *m.* precious jewel 11/522.

searolīce *adv.* cunningly 19/163.

searonet *n.* malicious web 13/64.

searonīð *m.* treacherous battle 11/511.

searoþonc, -þanc *m.* skill 11/74, 13/210.

sēaþ *m.* pit 15/75.

seax *n.* dagger 11/286.

(*ge*)sēc(e)an *w.1* (1) go to, visit 11/55, 120; *pret.* (*ge*)sōhte, sōhton 11/16, 14/87; (2) seek 2/23, 4/12, 7/72; (3) attack 2/25.

secg, sec *m.* man 11/310, 170, 636, 13/180.

(*ge*)secgan, seccgan, seccgean *w.1* say 5/50, 7/132, 8/7, 60; *pret.* (*ge*)sǣde, (*ge*)sǣgde, sǣ(g)don 2/70, 8/15, 5/54, 6/29.

sefa *m.* mind, heart 11/373, 405, 13/98.

sēfte *see* sōfte.

*ge*segen *see* (*ge*)sēon.

segl *m. or n.* sail 6/96.

segl (= sigel) *n.* sun 13/89, 50 n.

(*ge*)seglian *see* siglan, *ge*siglan.

seglrād *f.* sail-road, sea 11/220.

segn *m. or n.* banner 11/540 n, 549.

seht *f.* peace 3/84 n.

*ge*selda *m.* retainer 16/53.

sēl *see* gōd.

seldon *adv.* seldom, rarely 10/57.

sele *m.* hall 11/12, 125, 16/25.

seledrēam *m.* joy of hall 16/93.

selegyst *m.* stranger in, or visitor to, a hall 11/286.

selerǣdend *m.* hall-counsellor 11/137.

selesecg *m.* hall-companion 16/34.

sēlest(ena) *see* gōd.

seleð *see* syllan.

self *see* sylf.

sēlran, sēlla *see* gōd.

sellice *see* syllic.

sēlost *adv. supl.* best 13/170.

sēlre *see* gōd.

*ge*sēman *w.1* decide between, settle 12/60.

sendan *w.1* send 12/30, 10/35, 38; sænde *3 sg. pret.* 7/116.

*ge*sēne *see* *ge*sȳne.

sēo *see* se.

sēoc *adj.* sick, sad 11/513, 344.

seofian *w.2* sigh 17/10.

seofon, syfan *num.* seven 3/7, 13/114, 6/36, 95.

seolfor *n.* silver 3/60, 7/61, 10/124.

seolh, siolh *m.* seal 6/50, 54.

seomian *w.2* remain 19/19.

(*ge*)sēon, sīon *5* see, look 6/82, 8/1, 4/34, 13/180; gesēo *1 sg. pres.* 7/12; gesihð *3 sg. pres.* 16/46; gesēo *1 pl. pres. subj.* ? 8/66; geseah *1 sg. pret.* 4/27, 14/130; (*ge*)seah *3 sg. pret.* 11/490, 636, 5/21, 6/31; gesāwon *3 pl. pret.* 7/65, 11/138, 216, sǣgon 11/213; gesāwe *1 sg. pret. subj.* 15/4; *3 sg. pret. subj.* 7/73; gesāwon *3 pl. pret. subj.* 11/346; gesegen *pret. p.* 5/52 manifest.

seonobend *f.* sinew-bond 18/6 n.

seonu *f.* sinew 11/116.

sēoðan *2* (boil) torment; soden *pret. p.* 13/194.

seoþþan *see* siþþan.

sēowan *2* weave; sēowað *3 sg. pres.* 13/64.

sess *m. or n.* seat 11/490, 529.

set *n.* (1) camp 2/29, 31; (2) setting of sun 13/203.

*ge*set *n.* dwelling, place 13/214, 16/93.

sētan *see* sittan.

*ge*setenne *see* *ge*sittan.

setl *n.* seat 7/5, 14/166.

*ge*setnys *f.* establishment, foundation 10/62.

(*ge*)settan *w.1* place, establish 10/116, 3/19; sætte of 3/32 remove from.

sex *see* syx.

*ge*sib *adj.* related; *as noun* kinsman 9/52.

sibǣðeling *m.* related noble 11/481.

sibb *f.* (1) peace 4/6, 8/24; sybbe *acc. sg.* 13/98; (2) kinship 11/373.

sibbegedriht *f.* band of kinsmen 11/28.

sibleger *n.* incest 9/122 n.

siblic *adj.* peaceful, of peace 8/46.

sīde *f.* side 15/49.

sīde *adv.* widely 9/131, 15/81.

sīe, sīen, siendon *see* wesan.

*ge*sīene *see* *ge*sȳne.

GLOSSARY

gesīgan _1_ fall 11/432.
sige _m._ victory 2/88, 10/18.
sigebēam _m._ cross of victory 15/13, 127.
sigedryhten _m._ victorious lord 13/60.
sigeēadig _adj._ victorious 11/298.
sigehrēðig _adj._ victorious 11/338, 529.
sigehwīl _f._ time of victory 11/483.
sigelēas _adj._ without victory, of defeat 9/97, 11/86, 14/67.
sigeltorht _adj._ bright as the sun 13/201.
sigerōf _adj._ valiant 13/180.
sigewǣpen _n._ victory-weapon 11/103.
sigewong _m._ plain of glory 19/33 n.
siglan, seglian _w.1_ sail 6/21, 78, 15, 85.
gesiglan, geseglian _w.1_ reach by sailing 6/13, 76, 16, 19.
sigor _m._ victory 11/648, 13/116, 15/67.
sigorfæst _adj._ triumphant 15/150.
gesihð _see_ **gesyhþ**, **(ge)sēon**.
silf _see_ **sylf**.
sillan _see_ **syllan**.
simle _see_ **symle**.
sīn _poss. pron._ his; **sīnne** _m. acc. sg._ 11/562, 14/50; **sīnes** _m. gen. sg._ 14/155; **sīnum** _m. dat. sg._ 11/248.
sinc _n._ treasure 11/537, 356, 519.
sincaldu _f._ everlasting cold 19/17.
sincgyfa _m._ giver of treasure, benefactor 12/278.
sincþego _f._ receiving of treasure 11/657, 16/34.
singāl _adj._ continuous, continual 10/80, 15/141.
singāllīce _adv._ continually 9/110.
singan _3_ sing 5/16, 20, 28; **singeð** _3 sg. pres._ 17/54; **sang** _3 sg. pret._ 12/284, 20b/2, **song** 5/44, 69, 11/214; **sunge** _3 sg. pret. subj._ 5/55; **sing** _imp. sg._ 5/27, 31; **singende** _pres. p._ 17/22.
gesingian _w.2_ do wrong 7/21.
sinnan _3 with gen._ cease from, have respite from; **sann** _3 sg. pret._ 13/232.
sint _see_ **wesan**.

sīo _see_ **se**.
siodu _m._ morality 4/7.
sioles _see_ **seolh**.
siomian _w.2_ hang 11/540.
gesīon _see_ **(ge)sēon**.
sittan _5_ sit, stay 2/103, 14/193; **siteð** _3 sg. pres._ 14/15, 18/28, 19/90, **sit** 7/5, 9/86; **sittað** _3 pl. pres._ 9/14; **sæt** _3 sg. pret._ 2/52, 53, 11/625; **sǣton** _1 pl. pret._ 14/166; **sǣton** _3 pl. pret._ 2/10, 41, 84, **sǣtan** 10/67, **sētan** 11/343.
gesittan _5_ sit down, stay; **gesæt** _3 sg. pret._ 11/48 n sat up, 7/83, 11/215; **gesetenne** _pret. p._ 2/38 finished.
sīð _m._ (1) journey, venture 11/15, 2/3, 19/102 n.; (2) time 11/268, 320; **oðre sīðe** 2/67 on another occasion; **oðre sīðe . . . oðre sīðe** 2/29–30 once . . . again.
gesīð _m., n._ companion, company 11/405, 18/3.
sīðast _adv. supl._ last 11/483.
sīðfæt _m._ expedition 11/412, 15/150.
sīðian _w.2_ go, travel 11/19, 10/5, 57.
siþþan, syððan, seoþþan _adv., conj._ after, afterwards, when, since 2/23, 11/17, 3/5, 11/21, 8/73, 75.
slǣp _m._ sleep 16/39, 5/44, 19/56 n.
slǣpan _w.1_ sleep 5/44, 11/40, 322.
slēan _6_ (1) strike 3/42; **slōh** _3 sg. pret._ 11/306, 451, 472; 10/129 constructed; **slōge** _3 sg. pret. subj._ 12/117; **geslægene** _pret. p._ 14/138 forged; (2) slay; **slōh** _3 sg. pret._ 10/8, 11/322; **slōge** _3 sg. pret. subj._ 3/69.
slecan _5_ as delay; **slǣce** _1 sg. pres. subj._ 7/107.
slege _m._ killing, defeat 10/11, 108, 118.
slītan _1_ tear; **slāt** _3 sg. pret._ 11/40, 17/11.
sliþen _adj._ cruel 16/30.
sliðheard _adj._ severe 14/133.
smæl _adj._ narrow 6/55; **smælre** _comp._ 6/60; **smalost** _supl._ 6/62.
smēagan _w.1_ consider 8/21, 9/8, 154.
smercian _w.2_ smile 7/98.
smiþ _m._ goldsmith 19/170.
smolte _adv._ mildly 20b/8.

217

smylte (1) *adj.* serene 19/33, 20a/7;
  (2) *adv.* gently 20a/4.
snāw *m.* snow 19/14, 13/210, 16/48.
snel(l) *adj.* bold, swift 19/183, 12/29.
snīwan *w.1* snow 17/31.
snot(t)or *adj.* wise 11/125, 175, 332.
snūde *adv.* quickly 11/525.
soden *see* **sēoðan.**
sōfte *adv.* easily, gently 12/59;
  sēft(e) *comp.* 11/522, 14/188.
(ge)sōhte *see* **(ge)sēc(e)an.**
(ge)somnian, **(ge)samnian** *w.2*
  gather, assemble 5/49, 2/30, 6/129,
  19/151.
gesomnung *f.* assembly, company
  5/63–4.
somod *see* **samod.**
sōna *adv.* at once, immediately 2/12,
  102, 3/44.
sōna swā *conj.* as soon as 2/64, 7/30,
  144.
song, sang *m., n.* song 5/46, 67, 7/31,
  47.
song *see* **singan.**
songcræft *m.* poetic skill 5/13.
sorg *f.* sorrow 16/30, 11/373, 13/116;
  17/42 anxiety.
sorgcearig *adj.* sorrowful 18/28.
sorgian *w.2* sorrow, grieve 11/175,
  13/182, 14/102.
sorglufu *f.* distressing love 18/16.
sorhful *adj.* sorrowful 11/220.
sorhlēoð *n.* dirge 15/67 n.
sōð *n.* truth 9/1, 6/31, 7/129.
sōð *adj.* true 11/352, 8/24, 49.
sōðcwide *m.* truth, true saying
  20b/2.
sōðfæst *adj.* righteous 13/145,
  11/593.
sōþgied *n.* true story 17/1.
sōðlīce *adv.* truthfully, truly, certainly 7/18, 25, 36.
spanan *6, 7* entice; **spēonne** *3 sg.*
  pret. subj. 14/29.
sparian *w.2* spare 3/34.
gespæc, spǣcan, specan *see* **sprecan.**
spēd *f.* riches, wealth 4/55, 6/40,
  119.
spēdan *w.1* be prosperous 12/34.
spēdig *adj.* rich 6/40, 15/151, 19/10.
spel(l) *n.* story 5/54, 65, 73.

spere *n.* spear 12/108, 137.
spillan *w.1* destroy 12/34.
splott *m.* spot 19/162.
gespong *n.* bond, chain 14/132.
spor *n.* track 4/37.
spōwan *7 impers. with dat.* succeed;
  spēow *3 sg. pret.* 4/8, 11/627.
sprǣc *f.* speech 7/11, 19, 10/50.
(ge)sprecan, specan *5* speak, say
  15/27, 11/637; *infl. inf.* **specenne**
  9/73; **spriceð** *3 sg. pres.* 16/70;
  specað *1 pl. pres.* 3/14; **(ge)sprǣc**
  3 sg. pret. 11/391, 497, 189, **ge-
  spǣc** 14/26 **sprǣcon** *1 pl. pret.*
  2/2, 8, 12/212, *3 pl. pret.* 6/32,
  11/336, 12/200, **spǣcan** 9/7;
  sprecende *pres. p.* 5/30.
sprengan *w.1* (*tr.*) break 12/137.
springan *3* spring away, burst open;
  sprang *3 sg. pret.* 12/137, **sprong**
  11/329.
spyrigean *w.2* follow 4/35.
staca *m.* stake 10/119.
stafum *see* **stæf.**
gestāh *see* **gestīgan.**
stalu *f.* theft 9/47, 119.
stān *m.* stone 11/206, 517, 15/66.
stānboga *m.* stone arch 11/491.
stānclif *n.* cliff 17/23, 19/22.
(ge)standan, stondan *6* stand,
  stretch 10/83, 11/533, 12/19, 171;
  stent *3 sg. pres.* 6/86, **stynt** 12/51,
  standeð 6/107, 8/29, 11/153,
  stondeð 16/74; **standað** *2 pl.*
  pres. 11/639; **standað** *3 pl. pres.*
  16/76, 17/67; **stōd** *1 sg. pret.* 15/38,
  3 sg. pret. 5/25, 7/43, 10/22;
  (ge)stōdon *3 pl. pret.* 2/161, 4/29,
  12/63, 11/370; **stondendes** *pres.*
  p. 20a/8.
stānfāg *adj.* adorned with stone
  13/191 n.
stang *see* **stingan.**
stānhlið *n.* rocky slope 11/200,
  13/188, 16/101.
stapul *m.* pillar 11/491.
starian *w.2* gaze, look 11/344, 569.
staþe *see* **stæð.**
(ge)staðelian *w.2* establish, restore,
  make firm 8/47, 7/92, 13/82.
staðol *m.* position 15/71.
staðu *see* **stæþ.**

stædefæst, stedefæst *adj.* steadfast 12/127, 249.

stæf *m.* letter 5/4.

stæfne *see* stefn *f.*

gestǣlan *w.1 with dat.* accuse of 14/146.

stælhere *n.* predatory army 2/150.

stælhrān *m.* decoy-reindeer 6/43.

stælwyrðe *adj.* serviceable 2/131.

stǣr *n.* history 5/65, 70.

stǣrcedferþ *adj.* hard-hearted 13/188.

stæð *n.* shore, (river-)bank 2/82, 6/107, 12/25.

gesteal *n.* foundation 16/110.

stēam *m.* moisture 15/62.

stēap *adj.* steep 11/200, 19/22.

stearc *adj.* stern 3/16, 30, 58.

stearn *m.* tern 17/23.

stede, styde *m.* place 12/19, 14/111; steode *dat. sg.* 3/17.

stedefæst *see* stædefæst.

stefn *m.* (stem) root 15/30.

stefn, stemn *m.* period, time 2/38; nīwan stefne *dat. sg.* 11/367 again.

stefn, stæfn *f.* voice 13/92, 56, 7/48, 97.

stefna *m.* prow 13/162, 17/7.

stemnettan *w.1* stand firm 12/122.

stenc *m.* odour, fragrance 19/81, 8.

stent *see* (ge)standan.

stēorbord *n.* starboard 6/10 n, 23, 78.

steorfa *m.* pestilence 9/48.

steorra *m.* star 14/11, 20a/3, 20b/5.

steppan 6 step; stōp 3 *sg. pret.* 11/60, 192, 12/8.

stīg *f.* path 11/200.

gestīgan *1* ascend 15/34; gestāh *3 sg. pret.* 15/40.

stihtan *w.1* exhort 12/127.

stille *adj.* still, quiet 7/11, 11/603.

stilnes *f.* peace, silence 7/45, 4/54.

stingan *3* stab; stang *3 sg. pret* 12/138.

stīð *adj.* firm, strong, inexorable 3/79, 11/274, 12/301.

stīðhicgende *adj.* (*pres. p.*) resolute 12/122.

stīðlice *adv.* sternly 12/25.

stīðmōd *adj.* resolute 15/40.

(ge)stōd(on) *see* (ge)standan.

stōl *m.* throne 14/15, 28, 36.

stondan *see* (ge)standan.

stōp *see* steppan.

storm *m.* storm 13/191 (tumult), 16/101, 17/23.

stōw *f.* place 10/28, 4/33, 75.

strand *m.* shore 10/125.

strang, strong *adj.* strong 8/36, 9/98, 11/457, 19/86; strengere *comp.* 3/15; strengest *supl.* 11/88, 284.

strange *adv.* violently 20b/15.

strǣl *m.* missile? 15/62 n.

strǣt *f.* street 7/96, 126, 10/67.

strēam *m.* stream, river, current 12/68, 13/133, 17/34.

strēgan *w.1* strew, spread 17/97.

streng *m.* rope 13/133.

strenglic *adj.* strong; strenglicran *comp.* 14/28.

strengo *f.* strength 11/274.

strengþ *f.* strength 3/50.

gestrēon *n.* possessions 6/137, 8/68.

strīc *n.* ? 9/48 n.

strīð *m.* strife 14/39 n.

strong *see* strang.

stronglic *adj.* strong 14/121.

strūdung *f.* robbery 9/119.

gestrȳnan *w.1* acquire 11/571.

stund *f.* while, short time; stundum *dat. pl.* 11/214 at times; ǣfre embe stunde 12/271 every moment.

styccelmǣlum *adv.* here and there 6/4.

styde *see* stede.

stȳlecg *adj.* steel-edged 11/274.

stȳman *w.1* fume 19/95.

stynt *see* (ge)standan.

styrian *w.1* stir, stir up 11/165, 613, 13/133.

subdiacon *m.* subdeacon 8/32.

sum *adj.* one, a certain (one), some 2/43, 44, 80.

sumes *adv.* somewhat 19/124.

sumor *m.* summer 6/147, 2/117, 136.

sunbearo *m.* sunny grove, grove of the sun 19/33 n.

sund *n.* swimming, water 11/217, 227, 251.

gesund *adj.* safe, unharmed, well 7/138, 1/31, 7/67.

gesundful *adj.* sound, whole 10/74.

sundor *adv.* apart 16/111.
sunge *see* **singan.**
sunnbēam *m.* sunbeam 10/132.
sunne *f.* sun 13/203, 10/83, 19/17.
sunu *m.* (1) son 11/291, 2/59, 11/375;
(2) God the Son 8/51, 50, 15/150.
sūð *adv.* south 2/44, 46, 138.
sūðan *adv.* from the south 6/108,
20b/8; **be sūðan** *prep. with dat.*
south of 4/18; **wið sūðan** *prep.*
with acc. to the south of 6/81.
sūþanwestan *adv.* from the south-
west 20a/4.
sūþerne *adj.* southern 12/134 n.
sūðeweard *adj.* southern (part of)
6/66, 75.
sūðrima *m.* south coast 2/181.
sūþryhte *adv.* due south 6/17, 18.
sūðstæð *n.* south coast 2/150.
swā, swǣ (1) *adv.* so, very 2/124,
11/61, 4/13, 17; (2) *conj.* as 2/70,
11/172, 187; (3) *conj.* if 7/111;
(4) *conj.* although 14/146.
swā hwā swā *pron.* whoever 3/69,
14/193.
swā hwǣr swā *adv.* wherever 10/84.
swā hwæt swā *pron.* whatever 5/4,
7/23, 57.
swā hwelc swā *pron.* whoever 1/18.
swā hwider swā *adv.* wherever
10/56–7.
swā some, swǣ same *adv.* similarly 14/154, 4/47.
swā swā (1) *conj.* so that 2/107;
(2) **swā . . . swā** *with comps.* the
. . . the 6/60, 9/2, as . . . as 2/18.
swā þæt *conj.* so that 2/3, 27.
swā þēah *adv.* however 11/651.
geswāc *see* **(ge)swīcan.**
swān *m.* herdsman 1/5.
swanc *see* **swincan.**
swār *adj.* dire, heavy 19/181, 56.
swāt *m.* blood 11/466, 13/194, 230.
swātig *adj.* bloody 11/310.
swaþul *m. or n.* flame, heat 11/81.
swǣ, swǣ same *see* **swā, swā**
some.
swǣcc *m.* odour 19/96.
swǣfon *see* **swefan.**
geswǣnctest *see* **swencan.**
swǣs *adj.* beloved 16/50.
swǣsende *n.* meal 13/145.

swǣtan *w.1* bleed 15/20.
swǣð *n.* track, footprint (*fig.*) 4/35.
swealg *see* **swelgan.**
swealt *see* **sweltan.**
swearc *see* **sweorcan.**
sweart *adj.* black, dark 14/67, 100,
146.
swefan *5* sleep 11/28; **swefeð** *3 sg.*
pres. 11/519; **swǣfon** *3 pl. pret.*
11/2.
swefn *n.* sleep, dream 5/26, 50, 15/1.
swēg *m.* noise, music 11/81, 7/32, 47.
swēgcræft *m.* musical skill 7/32, 34,
37.
swegeltorht *adj.* shining in the sky
13/203.
swegl *n.* sky, sun 13/98, 19/90, 94.
swegl *adj.* bright, brilliant 11/522.
swelan *4* burn (*intr.*) 11/486.
swelc, swelce *see* **swylc, swylce.**
swelgan *3* swallow; **swealg** *3 sg.*
pret. flowed 13/231, **swealh**
11/42; **swulge** *3 sg. pret. subj.*
11/81.
swellan *3* swell 11/486.
sweltan *3* die 12/293; **swealt** *3 sg.*
pret. 3/2, 11/358, 555, **sweolt**
10/114.
(ge)swenc(e)an, swǣncan *w.1*
harass, afflict, torment 13/109,
3/57, 7/101.
sweng *m.* blow 11/261, 459, 12/118.
sweofot *m. or n.* sleep 11/322.
swēora *m.* neck 19/171.
(ge)sweorcan *3* grow dark, gloomy;
sweorceð *3 sg. pres.* 18/29; **ge-**
sweorce *3 sg. pres. subj.* 16/59;
swearc *3 sg. pret.* 13/131.
sweord, swurd, swyrd *n.* sword
11/310, 346, 12/47, 161, 11/383.
sweotol, swutol *adj.* clear, manifest
11/116, 132, 9/44, 113.
sweotule *adv.* clearly 16/11;
sweotolost *supl.* most brightly
20b/3.
swerian *6* swear; **swerige** *1 sg.*
pres. 7/90; **swōr** *1 sg. pret.* 11/511.
swēte *adj.* sweet 17/95, 19/96;
swēteste *supl.* 5/67.
swētnes *f.* sweetness 5/6, 77.
sweðrian *w.2* subside 11/475,
19/111.

(*ge*)**swīcan** *1 with dat.* fail, be false, to, betray 14/39; **swīcað** *1 pl. pres.* 13/166; **geswāc** *3 sg. pret.* 11/265, 454.

swīcdōm *m.* treason 9/120.

swīcian *w.2 with dat.* deceive 9/58.

swift, swyft *adj.* swift 19/183, 6/136; **swiftran** *comp.* 2/154; **swiftoste, swyftoste** *supl.* 6/132, 130.

swīge *f.* silence 7/45.

(*ge*)**swīgian** *w.2* be silent 7/33, 35, 137; **geswugedan** *3 pl. pret.* 9/164.

swilc, swilce *see* **swylc, swylce.**

swilce eac, swylce eac *conj.* also 3/30, 49, 72.

swimman *3* swim; **swimmað** *3 pl. pres.* 16/53.

geswinc *n.* labour, toil 3/54, 14/72.

swincan *3* toil; **swanc** *3 sg. pret.* 10/80.

geswincdagas *m. pl.* days of hardship 17/2.

swingan *3* beat; **swungen** *pret. p.* 13/201, 230.

swinsung *f.* melody 5/56.

swīð *adj.* strong 14/7.

swīþe, swȳþe *adv.* very, as greatly 1/21, 2/48, 150; **swīþor, swȳþor** *comp.* 2/140; 7/120, 9/132, 10/80 rather; **swīþost, swȳþost** *supl.* 2/141, 151; 6/139 almost.

swīþlic *adj.* great 10/71, 84.

swīþra, swȳþra *adj. comp.* right 10/74, 116, 71, 73.

swol *n.* fire 19/96, 151.

swoncor *adj.* supple 18/6.

swongor *adj.* sluggish 19/181.

swōr *see* **swerian.**

geswugedan *see* (*ge*)**swīgian.**

swulge *see* **swelgan.**

swurd *see* **sweord.**

swuster *f.* sister 12/115.

swutol *see* **sweotol.**

geswutelian *w.2* reveal 10/130, 147.

swyftoste *see* **swift.**

swylc, swilc, swelc *pron.* such 11/481, 138, 3/23, 13/25.

swylce, swilce, swelce *conj.* (1) as, like 11/56, 13/89, 15/92; (2) also 3/30, 11/129, 218; (3) as if 3/74, 4/32.

swylt *m.* death 11/227.

swyltdæg *m.* day of death 11/571.

swȳn *n.* pig 6/46.

swyrd *see* **sweord.**

swyrdgifu *f.* giving of swords 11/657.

swȳðöferhð *adj.* strong-minded, brave 11/125.

swȳðölicre *see* **swīþlic.**

swȳþran *see* **swīð.**

sȳ *see* **wesan.**

sybbe *see* **sibb.**

syfan *see* **seofon.**

gesyhþ, gesihð *f.* sight 8/22, 15/21, 41, 13/30.

sylf, silf, self *pron.* self 10/15, 53, 7/24, 48, 2/155, 4/24.

sylfren *adj.* silver 10/65, 68.

syll *f.* floor 11/74.

(*ge*)**syllan, sillan** *w.1* give, sell 10/69, 141, 7/38, 40; **seleð** *3 sg. pres.* 11/161 gives up; (*ge*)**sealde** *3 sg. pret.* 2/63, 4/22, 9/72; **gesealdon** *3 pl. pret.* 12/184 gave up; **geseald** *pret. p.* 2/17, 63, 9/37.

sȳllan 18/6 *see* **gōd.**

syllic, sellic *adj.* wonderful 15/13, 4, 11/217.

sym(b)el *n.* banquet 5/22, 16/93, 15/141.

sym(b)le, simle *adv.* always, all the time 6/60, 10/53, 14/71, 1/20, 2/27; **symles** 13/64.

sȳn *see* **wesan.**

synbyrþenn *f.* burden of sin 8/39.

synd, syndan *see* **wesan.**

synderlīce *adv.* specially 5/1.

syndolh *n.* great wound 11/116.

syndon *see* **wesan.**

syndrig *adj.* various 10/83.

gesȳne *adj.* visible, evident 9/85, 151, 11/194; **gesǽne** 9/113; **gesēne** 9/44; **gesīene** 15/46.

syngian *w.2* sin 9/139.

synlēaw *f.* stain of sin 9/143.

synlic *adj.* sinful 8/12.

synn *f.* sin 19/54, 3/90, 5/80.

synscaða *m.* malefactor 11/100.

synsnǽd *f.* huge morsel 11/42.

synt *see* **wesan.**

gesyrwed *adj.* (*pret. p.*) armed 12/159.

syðð**an** see **siðð**an.

syx, sex num. six 6/42, 39, 43, 2/157.

syxtig num. sixty 6/39, 53, 61.

tācen n. sign, feature 11/132, 8/15, 13/29.

tam adj. tame 6/41.

(ge)tǣcan w.1 teach, show 8/26, 9/141, 151; **(ge)tǣhte** 3 sg. pret. 7/93, 12/18, 13/6; **getǣht** pret. p. 7/79.

getæl n. narrative 5/64.

tǣlan w.1 censure, blame 7/35, 9/134.

tælmet n. definite number 13/113.

tǣsan w.1 cut 12/270.

tæt see **se**.

(ge)tēah see **(ge)tēon**.

tealt adj. unstable 9/51.

tēar m. tear 7/19, 13/59.

tela adv. well, properly 11/436, 510.

geteld n. tent 10/129, 131.

telga m. branch 19/76.

tellan w.1 consider 3/88; **tealde** 3 sg. pret. 11/93, 414; **teollan** inf. 3/1 assert.

tēne see **tȳn**.

getenge adj. (with dat.) close to 11/531.

teolian w.2 strive 8/61.

(ge)tēon w.1 create, appoint; **(ge)tēode** 3 sg. pret. 5/42, 13/14.

(ge)tēon 2 (1) draw, drag 13/185; **getȳhþ** 3 sg. pres. 8/41; **(ge)tēah** 3 sg. pret. 7/50, 52, 11/286; **tugon** 3 pl. pret. 2/8, 114; **togen** pret. p. 11/230; (2) educate; **tēah** 3 sg. pret. 10/55; **getogen** pret. p. 7/54.

teona m. insult 3/55.

tēð see **tōð**.

tīd f. time, season 12/104, 4/4, 5/17; 14/124 hour; 17/69 life; **sumre tīde** 5/22 on one occasion; **binnon fēawum tīdum** 7/94 after a short time.

til(l) adj. good 11/494, 16/112, 18/38.

tīma m. time 3/54, 7/105, 10/86.

timbran, tymbran w.1 build 2/152, 151, 3/20.

getimbru n. pl. building 14/31.

tintreglic adj. full of torment 5/76.

tīr, tȳr m. glory 12/104, 13/105.

tīrēadig adj. renowned 13/2.

tīrfæst adj. glorious 19/69.

tīþian w.2 with dat. grant 10/36, 38.

tō (1) prep. with dat. to, for 1/26 n., 2/30, 9/56; (2) adv. there, thereto 2/55, 159; (3) adv. too 7/13, 8/35, 36.

tō āhte adv. at all 9/18.

tō þām, tō þǣm adv. so, too, sufficiently 2/176, 12/34.

tō þæs adv. so, too 8/67, 72.

tō þæs þe conj. to the point where, when 11/13, 326.

tōberstan 3 break (intr.); **tōbærst** 3 sg. pret. 10/25, 12/136, 144.

tōbrecan 4 break in pieces 11/79; **tōbrǣcon** 3 pl. pret. 2/58, 131; **tōbrocen** pret. p. 9/85, 12/242.

tōceorfan 2 cut up 10/69.

tōclēofan 2 cleave asunder; **tōclēofeð** 3 sg. pres. 8/43.

tōcuman 4 arrive; **tōcumen** pret. p. 2/52.

tōcyme m. coming 9/3.

tōdæg adv. today 7/75, 102.

tōdǣlan w.1 divide 6/124.

tōēacan prep. with dat. beside 3/36, 6/32.

tōemnes prep. with dat. alongside 6/66, 67.

tōfaran 6 disperse; **tōfōr** 3 sg. pret. 2/136.

tōgæd(e)re adv. together 7/98, 102, 9/75, 11/403.

tōgēanes, tōgēnes (1) prep. with dat. against, towards 11/283, 17/76, 19/11, 13/45; (2) adv. opposite 11/242.

(ge)togen see **(ge)tēon**.

getoht n. battle 12/104.

tōlicgan 5 (1) separate; **tōlið** 3 sg. pres. 6/103; (2) extend; **tōlāgon** 3 pl. pret. 13/189.

tōlūcan 2 destroy 11/80.

tōmiddes prep. with dat. in the midst of 14/79.

tōniman 4 divide; **tōnumen** pret. p. 2/27.

torht adj. bright, glorious 13/105, 19/28.

torn n. affliction 11/132, 16/112.

torngenīŏla *m.* bitter enemy 13/185.

tōsomne *adv.* together 13/33.

tōtwǣman *w.1* break up 12/241.

tōþ *m.* tooth, tusk 6/34; **tēþ** *acc. pl.* 6/34.

tōgeþēodan *w.1* add 5/46.

tōweard *adj.* future 5/76.

tōweard *prep. with dat.* toward 6/132.

tōweorpan *3* destroy; **tōweorpŏ** *3 sg. pres.* 20a/6.

tredan *5* tread; **trǣd** *3 sg. pret.* 11/143.

treddian *w.2* step, go 11/24.

trēow *n.* (1) tree 19/76; (2) Cross 15/4, 14, 17.

trēow *f.* (1) treaty 2/18; (2) faith 16/112.

trēowloga *m.* traitor 11/620.

trum *adj.* strong 11/160.

(ge)trūwian *w.2* trust (in) 11/274, 14/3.

trym *m. or n.* step 12/247.

trymian, trymman *w.1* strengthen, build, order 12/17, 10/11, 12/22, 305.

trȳwlīce *adv.* honestly, loyally 9/57.

getrȳwŏ, getrēowŏ *f.* loyalty 9/52, 177, 6.

tū *see* **twēgen.**

tūcian *w.2* ill-treat 10/8.

tugon *see* **(ge)tēon.**

tūn *m.* village 6/127, 128, 135.

tunge *f.* tongue 5/15.

tungol *n.* star 13/2.

tūngerēfa *m.* bailiff 5/47.

turf *f.* turf, soil; **tyrf** *dat. sg.* 19/66.

tuwwa *adv.* twice 2/29.

getwǣfan *w.1 with acc. and gen.* deprive 11/224.

twēgen *num.* two; *m. nom., acc.* **twēgen** 2/60, 98, 6/52; *n. acc.* **tū** 2/27, 125, 153; *n. and f. nom., acc.* **twā** 2/84, 115, 125, 7/60; *gen.* **twēga** 12/207; *dat.* **twām** 2/21, 6/39, 64.

twelf *num.* twelve 2/15, 101, 9/100.

twentig *num.* twenty 6/45, 46, 7/61.

twēo *m.* doubt 14/31, 17/69.

tȳdre *adj.* weak 11/620.

getȳhŏ *see* **(ge)tēon.**

getymbrad *see* **timbran.**

tȳn *num.* ten 9/99, 100, 11/620; **tēne** *m. acc.* 14/3 n.

tȳres *see* **tīr.**

tyrf *see* **turf.**

þā *adv.* then 1/3, 10, 13.

þā *conj.* when 2/32, 39, 69.

þā *pron. see* **se.**

geþafa *m.* consenter 14/169.

þafi(g)an *w.2* consent to 13/161, 5/62.

þafung *f.* permission 9/98.

þāgīet, þāgȳt *adv.* still 6/12, 41.

ŏāh *see* **þēon.**

geþah *see* **(ge)þicg(e)an.**

þām, þan *see* **se.**

ŏanc, ŏonc *m.* thanks (*gen.* for) 2/139, 11/567, 12/120, 4/19.

geþanc *m. or n.* thought 9/138, 12/13.

(ge)þanci(g)an *w.2 with dat. and gen.* thank 14/12, 7/27, 80.

þanon *see* **þonan.**

þāra, ŏāre *see* **se.**

þāron, ŏǣron *adv.* therein 7/118, 15/67.

ŏas *see* **þes.**

þǣm, þǣne *see* **se.**

þǣnne *see* **þonne.**

þǣr *conj.* (1) where 1/25, 11/76, 150; (2) if 11/61, 96, 14/143.

þǣr, þār *adv.* there, where 1/4, 11, 6/143, 7/1; **þǣr þǣr** in the place where 2/21.

þǣra, þǣre *see* **se.**

þǣrbinnan *adv.* therein 10/97.

þǣrinne *adv.* therein, inside 1/35, 3/48, 11/358.

ŏǣron *see* **þāron.**

þǣrtō *adv.* thereto, there 1/26, 2/126.

þǣrwiŏ *adv.* in regard to it 3/68.

þæs *pron. see* **se, þes.**

þæs *adv.* (1) afterwards 2/117, 120; (2) therefore 9/41.

þæs (þe) *conj.* (1) because 14/58; (2) after 1/8, 2/15, 101; (3) according to what 9/161, 11/141, 19/179.

þæt *pron. see* **se.**

þæt, þet, ŏætte *conj.* that, so that 1/23, 28, 3/18, 23, 4/16, 19.

þe *pron. see* **se, þū.**

þe *pron. rel.* 1/3, 12, 22.

þe . . . þe *conj.* for this reason . . . because 11/411, 414.

þē lǣs (þe), þȳ lǣs *conj.* lest 7/106, 9/157, 13/77, 19/128.

þē mā þe *conj.* any more than 9/53.

þeah, þēh (1) *adv.* however 1/38, 2/97, 18, 174; (2) *conj.* although 7/11, 9/7, 2/147, 9/43, ðēah þe 11/159, 392.

þearf *f.* need 9/30, 167, 169.

þearf *see* þurfan.

þearfa *m.* poor man 10/43, 66, 68.

þearfende *adj.* (*pres. p.*) needy 8/22.

þearle *adv.* greatly 7/51, 88, 9/49.

þeaw *m.* custom, habit 6/116, 4/26, 6/142.

þeccan *w.1* cover, engulf 19/98, 131; þeahte *3 sg. pret.* 19/42.

þegengyld *n.* compensation for a thane 9/93.

þegenlīce *adv.* nobly 12/294.

þegn, þegen, þen *m.* retainer 1/24, 2/89, 9/90, 91, 2/142, 9/26; þægnas *acc. pl.* 3/33.

þegnscipe *m.* service 14/81.

þēgon, þēgun *see* (*ge*)þicg(e)an.

þēh *see* þēah.

(*ge*)þenc(e)an *w.1* (1) intend 11/276, 374, 12/258; þōhte *3 sg. pret.* 9/58, 11/38, 14/27; þōhton *3 pl. pret.* 11/99; (2) think (of), consider 4/18, 8/58, 64; geþōhte *3 sg. pret.* 16/88.

þenden *conj.* while, as long as 11/422, 14/165, 17/102.

þengel *m.* prince 11/248.

þēnian *w.2* stretch out 15/52.

þening, þenung *f.* (service) (1) mass, mass-book 4/14; (2) meal 10/65.

þēod, þīod *f.* people, country 8/6, 9/5, 10, 4/49.

geðēoda *see* geðīode.

(*ge*)þēodan *w.1* join 5/63.

þēodcyning *m.* king of the people 11/467.

þēoden, þīoden *m.* (1) lord, prince 12/120, 11/96, 11/561, 583; (2) God 12/178.

þēodenhold *adj.* loyal to one's lord 13/143.

þēodenmāðm *m.* princely treasure 14/164.

þēodland *n.* country 8/5.

geþēodnes *f.* association 5/8.

þēodsceaða *m.* ravager of the nation 11/461.

þēodscipe *m.* (1) country 9/116; (2) discipline 5/82, 8/25.

þēodwita *m.* historian 9/158.

þēon *1* prosper; ðāh *3 sg. pret.* 11/609.

ðēon = þȳwan *1* oppress 11/509.

þēora *see* se.

þēow, ðīow *m.* servant 5/64, 9/25, 27, 4/30.

ðēow *adj.* serving 7/61, 62, 70.

þēowa *m.* servant 6/114.

þēowian *w.2* serve 14/19, 23, 37 n.

geþēowian *w.2* enslave 9/38.

þes *pron. dem.* this. *Singular forms:* m. *nom.* 7/4, 9/116, 16/62, þæs 14/111; *acc.* þisne 12/32, þysne 8/43, 10/16, 12/52; *gen.* þisses 8/2, þysses 3/5; *dat.* þissum 14/163, þys(s)um 2/1, 7/8, 11/412, þysan 9/37, 50, 66; n. *nom.* þis 3/21, 6/80, 7/64, *acc.* þis 4/27, 38, 7/142; *gen.* þisses 5/63, þysses 11/89, 105; *dat.* þis(s)um 3/38, 4/60, 6/79, þysum 2/1,136, þysan 9/13, 44, þysson 15/138; *instr.* þȳs 2/15, 102, 11/186; f. *nom.* þēos 9/1, 10/72, 15/12; *acc.* þās 5/32, 8/42, 9/5; *gen.* þisse 8/15, 17, 41, þysse 5/1; *dat.* þisse 4/23, 12/221, þysse 9/31, 43, 83. *Plural forms:* nom., acc. þās 3/91, 4/33, 6/97; *gen.* þissa 4/20, 13/145, 14/135; *dat.* þis(s)um 7/90, 124, 14/137, þyssum 13/100, 14/189.

þes *def. art. see* se.

þet *see* se, þæt.

(*ge*)þicg(e)an *5* receive, partake of, consume 1/20, 11/35; þigeð *3 sg. pres.* 19/101, 141; geþah *3 sg. pret.* 18/40; þēgun *1 pl. pret.* 11/406; ðēgon *3 pl. pret.* 13/25.

þider, þyder *adv.* thither, there 1/17, 23, 6/32, 75.

þiderweard *adv.* thither 6/87.

þiderweardes *adv.* thither 2/39, 40 on his way there.

þillicon *see* þyslic.

þīn *see* þū.

þincan w.1 with dat. seem 4/50, 9/51, 116; ðūhte 3 sg. pret. 2/156, 6/31, 8/8.

geþincðo f. dignity 10/81.

þing, þin(g)c n. thing 3/31, 91, 7/63, 151; 18/9 condition (pregnancy).

geþinge n. issue, outcome 11/8.

þingian w.2 intercede 9/170.

ðīod see þēod.

geðīode, geðēode n. language 4/32, 41, 49, 44; 6/142 nation.

ðīowa see þēow.

ðīowotdōm m. service 4/10.

þis, þisan, þisse, þis(s)um see þes.

geþoht m. thought, mind 8/35, 17/34, 18/22.

þōhte, þōhton see (ge)þenc(e)an.

(ge)þolian w.2 suffer, endure 11/131, 9/109, 11/210.

þon see se.

þon mā þe conj. any more than 1/34.

þonan, þonon, þanon adv. thence 6/4, 18, 11/164, 342, 62.

þonc see ðanc.

þone see se.

þonne, þænne (1) adv. then 1/18, 2/19, 3/27, 9/4; (2) conj. when 3/37, 5/19, 11/165; (3) conj. than 1/30, 2/154, 6/45.

þorfte see þurfan.

þrāg, þrāh f. (1) time 16/95, 19/68, 13/107; (2) distress 11/656.

ðrāgmǣlum adv. incessantly 13/185.

geþrang n. throng 12/299.

þrǣl m. slave 9/91, 88, 92.

þrǣlriht n. rights of slaves 9/39.

þrēa f. affliction 13/107, 14/144.

þrēagan w.2 subdue; geþrēade pret. p. 13/150 oppressed.

þrēanȳd, -nēd f. dire need 11/131, 13/219.

þrēat n. crowd, army 13/224, 135.

þrēo(ra) see þrȳ.

þridda num. third 6/127, 11/461.

þrim see þrȳ.

geþring n. tumult 13/127.

þringan 3 throng; þrong 3 sg. pret. 11/656; geþrungen pret. p. 17/8 oppressed.

þrist adj. bold 13/219.

þriste adv. resolutely 18/2.

þrīsthȳdig adj. brave 11/583.

þrīt(t)ig num. thirty 6/61, 2/7, 10/106.

þrīwa adv. thrice 3/24.

þrohtheard adj. courageous 13/219, 161.

þrosm m. smoke 14/81.

þrōwian w.2 suffer 11/378, 330, 367.

þrōwung f. suffering, Passion 5/74.

þrȳ num. three; n. nom. and acc. þrȳ 7/96, 98, 9/106, þrīe 6/10; n. and f. nom. and acc. þrēo 2/134, 161, 166; gen. þrēora 2/162, 6/63, 7/117; dat. þrim 2/140, 142, 160, þrym 7/104.

þrȳdlic adj. mighty; þrȳdlicost supl. 11/642.

þrym m. strength 13/3, 215, 16/95.

þrymfæst adj. glorious 15/84.

þrymfull adj. glorious 13/122.

þrymlīce adv. gloriously 19/68.

þrȳð f. might, power 13/135, 16/99.

þrȳðswȳð adj. strong 11/35.

þū pers. pron. thou. Singular forms: nom. þū 5/30, 7/4, 9; acc. þē 4/20, 7/5, 26; gen. þīn 7/116, 147, 13/70 (also inflected as possessive 7/12, 13, 28); dat. þē 4/2, 20, 7/10. Plural forms: nom. gē 7/69, 99, 11/639; acc. ēow 7/106; gen. ēower 7/136, 14/182 (also inflected for possessive 1/34, 7/107, 109); dat. ēow 7/63, 71, 11/638, īow 4/51.

þūhte see þincan.

geðungen adj. (pret. p.) distinguished; geðungnestan supl. 2/148.

þurfan irr. need; þurfe 1 sg. pres. 14/45; þearf 3 sg. pres. 8/38, 11/514, 15/117; þurfe 1 pl. pres. 12/34; þurfon 3 pl. pres. 12/249; þorfte 3 sg. pret. 11/647.

þurh prep. with acc. through, on account of, by means of 4/33, 48, 7/75.

þurhbrecan 4 break through; -bræc 3 sg. pret. 11/565.

þurhdrīfan 1 pierce; -drifan 3 pl. pret. 15/46.

þurhdūfan 2 swim through; -dēaf 3 sg. pret. 11/360.

ðurhfōn 7 penetrate 11/245.

þurhscēotan 2 transfix, pierce; -scēoteð *3 sg. pres.* 8/42.

þurhslēan 6 strike through; -slyhþ *3 sg. pres.* 8/42.

þurhsmēagan *w.2* investigate 3/45–6.

þurhwadan 6 penetrate, pierce; -wōd *3 sg. pret.* 11/308, 12/296.

þus *adv.* thus, in this way 6/137, 7/62, 64.

geþwǣrnes *f.* agreement 8/24.

ðwēan 6 wash; ðwōh *3 sg. pret.* 10/136.

þȳ *pron. see* se.

þȳ *adv.* therefore 9/2, 45, 131.

þȳ lǣs *see* þē lǣs (þe).

þyder *see* þider.

þȳfþ *f.* theft 9/38.

þȳhtig *adj.* strong. firm 11/299.

geþyld *f.* patience 11/186.

geþyldig *adj.* patient 16/65.

þyncð *see* þincan.

þȳnre *see* þū.

þȳs, þysum *see* þes.

þyslic *adj.* such 8/15, 11/410; þillicon *n. dat. pl.* 7/151.

þissa, þisse *see* þes.

þȳstro *f.* darkness 14/81, 144, 15/52.

ufan, ufon *adv.* from above, down 11/241, 14/130, 61.

ufeweard *adj.* above, upper 2/161, 19/165.

ūhta *m. or* ūhte *f.* dawn 14/70, 16/8.

ūhtfloga *m.* dawn-flier, night-flier 11/533.

ūhtsang *m.* matins 10/82.

unbeboht *adj (pret. p.)* unsold 6/42.

unbefohten *adj. (pret. p.)* unopposed 12/57.

unc *see* ic.

ungecnāwen *adj. (pret. p.)* unknown 7/51.

uncoþu *f.* disease 9/48.

uncræft *m.* deceit 9/177.

uncūð *adj.* unknown, uncertain 4/73, 11/201.

ungecyn(d)elic *adj.* unnatural 8/4, 5.

undǣd *f.* crime 9/138.

under (1) *prep. with dat. or acc.* under 6/95, 11/9, 6, 119; (2) *adv.* under, below 11/207.

ungederad *adj.* (*pret. p.*) unmolested 3/41.

underfōn 7 receive 10/129, 135; underfēnge *2 sg. pret.* 7/121; underfēng *3 sg. pret.* 10/45; underfēngan *1 pl. pret.* 9/174; underfēngon *3 pl. pret.* 10/76.

undernmǣl *n.* morning 11/219.

understandan, -stondan 6 understand 7/17, 9/108–9, 178, 4/14–5; understande *3 sg. pres. subj.* 9/82, 94; understandað *imp. pl.* 9/5.

underþēodan *w.1* make subject (to, *dat.*) 3/59, 5/82, 8/30; underþǣdde *3 sg. pret.* 3/50.

unearg *adj.* undaunted 12/206.

unēðelīce *adv.* awkwardly 2/166.

unfæger *adj.* horrible 8/74, 11/26.

ungefōge *adv.* excessively 6/137.

unforbærned *adj.* (*pret. p.*) uncremated 6/117, 120, 143.

unforcūð *adj.* dauntless 12/51, 13/218.

unforht *adj.* undaunted, unafraid 15/110, 12/79.

unforwandigendlīce *adv.* without shame 7/130–1.

unforworht *adj.* innocent 9/37.

unfriþ *m.* hostility 6/21.

unfrōd *adj.* young 11/594.

ungefullod *adj.* (*pret. p.*) unbaptised 10/110.

ungylde *n.* excessive tax 9/49.

unhēanlīce *adv.* bravely 1/13.

unhēore *adj.* horrible 13/34.

unlagu *f.* violation of law, injustice 9/10, 38, 163.

unlǣd(e) *adj.* wretched 13/30.

unlēof *adj.* unloved 11/636.

ungelīc *adj.* (*with dat.*) unlike 14/111.

unlifgende, unlyfigende *adj.* dead 11/43, 180.

ungelimp *n. or m.* misfortune 9/94.

ungelimplic *adj.* unfortunate 8/6.

unlytel *adj.* great, much 9/17, 11/132, 13/192.

unmǣte *adj.* immense 13/174.

ungemet(e) *adv.* without measure, exceedingly 11/494, 501, 14/68.

(ge)unnan *irr.* (1) grant; geunne *2 sg. pres. subj.* 12/176; (ge)ūðe *3 sg. pret.* 3/18, 10/19, 11/647; **ūþon** *3 pl. pret. (subj.?) with gen.* 1/28; (2) wish; **ūðe** *3 sg. pret. subj.* 11/628.

unorne *adj.* simple 12/256 n.

unriht *n.* wrong 3/62, 8/28, 44; **on unriht** 9/35, 11/512 wrongfully.

unrihtlīce *adv.* wrongfully 9/59.

un(ge)rīm *n.* multitude, countless number 9/149, 11/397, 14/90.

unrōt *adj.* sad 7/12.

unryht *adj.* wrong, evil 1/2.

unsidu *m.* vice 9/120.

unsmēþe *adj.* rough 19/26.

unspēdig *adj.* poor 6/114.

unstille *adj.* unquiet, restless 7/81.

unstilnes *f.* disturbance 1/17.

unswīðor *adv. comp.* less strongly 11/654.

untrum *adj.* sick 10/23.

untrumnys *f.* sickness 10/139.

ungetrȳwð *f.* disloyalty 9/61.

untwēonde *adj.* unwavering 13/197.

untȳddre *adj.* unwavering 13/207.

unðanc *m.* displeasure; **hire unðances** 3/44 against her will.

unþinged *adj. (pret. p.)* unexpected 17/106.

unwāclīce *adv.* without weakening 12/308.

unwæstm *n.* failure of crops 9/50.

unwealt *adj.* steady; **unwealtran** *comp.* 2/154.

unwearnum *adv.* irresistibly 11/40, 17/63.

unweaxen *adj. (pret. p.)* not fully grown 12/152.

unweder *n.* bad weather, storm 9/50.

unwemme *adj.* inviolate 19/46.

unwrest *adj.* unstable 3/5.

ungewunelic *adj.* unusual 7/51.

unwurðlīce *adv.* unworthily 14/195.

up, upp, uppe *adv.* up, above 2/4, 36, 3/87, 13/191, 2/162.

upāstignes *f.* ascension 5/74.

upāwend *adj. (pret. p.)* upturned, upraised 10/85.

upgang *m.* rising (1) of the sun 10/83; (2) permission to come up 12/87 n.

uplang *adj.* upright 11/58.

uppon *prep. with dat. or acc.* upon 7/42; **wið uppon** above 6/58.

uprodor *m.* heaven above 17/105.

ūre *see* ic.

ūrigfeþera *adj.* dewy-winged 17/25.

ūrne *see* ic.

urnon *see* yrnan.

ūrum, ūs, ūsic, ūsses, ūssum *see* ic.

ūt *adv.* out 1/14, 2/8, 54; 4/7 abroad.

ūtan *adv.* outside, from outside 1/11, 2/36, 83.

ūtanbordes *adv.* from abroad 4/11.

ūte *adv.* out, outside, abroad 2/28, 29, 4/12.

ūtermere *m.* open sea 2/160.

ūteweard *adj.* outer 2/9, 163.

ūtgong *m.* departure 5/71.

uton (+ *inf.*) let us 8/17, 61; **utan** 9/156, 171; **wutan** 9/167; **wutun** 11/421.

ūtweard *adj.* going out, trying to escape 11/60.

(ge)ūðe, ūþon *see* unnan.

uuiþ *see* wið.

wāc *adj.* (1) weak 16/67; **wācran** *comp.* 17/87 n. inferior; (2) slender 12/43.

gewāc *see* gewīcan.

wācian *w.2* be weak 12/10.

(ge)wadan *6* go, advance 12/140, 13/226, 16/5 (*tr.* tread); **(ge)wōd** *3 sg. pret.* 11/13, 434, 12/130, 157; **wōdon** *3 pl. pret.* 12/96, 295.

wālā *excl.* alas 9/104, 105, 14/123.

wālāwā *excl.* alas 3/85.

gewalden *adj.* small 2/48.

waldend, wealdend *m.* (1) God 11/514, 648, 15/17; (2) ruler 16/78.

waldswaþu *f.* forest-path 11/194.

wan(n) *see* won.

wand *see* windan.

wandian *w.2* flinch 12/258, 268.

wanhȳdig *adj.* rash 16/67.

wanian *w.2* (*intr.*) lessen, waste away 11/348, 9/31, 19/72.

gewanian *w.2* (*tr.*) reduce 9/22, 40.

wanigean *w.2* bewail 11/86.

wann *see* winnan.

wannhāl *adj.* sick 10/141.

wari(ge)an *w.2* occupy, be the concern of 11/149, 16/32.

warnian *w.2* take warning 9/167.

waru *f.* defence 10/105.

was *see* wesan.

wāst, (*ge*)wāt *see* (*ge*)witan, gewītan.

waþem *m.* wave 16/24, 57.

wæccan *w.1* be awake 11/7, 614.

wǣde *m.* (1) garment, decoration 15/15 n., 22; (2) sail 13/134 n.

wǣdl *f.* poverty 19/55.

wǣdla *m.* poor man 10/43.

wǣfersȳn *f.* spectacle 15/31.

wǣg *m.* wave 13/132, 17/19, 19/45; wēgas *acc. pl.* 16/46.

wæg *see* wegan.

gewǣgan *w.1* distress 2/85.

wǣgbora *m.* ? 11/231 n.

wæl *n.* the dead 12/126, 279, 300.

wælblēate *adj.* deadly 11/498.

wælcyrie *f.* sorceress 9/147 n.

wælgīfre *adj.* greedy for slaughter 13/131, 226, 16/100.

wælhrēow *adj.* savage 9/38, 10/30.

wæll *see* wel(l).

wællseax *n.* battle-knife 11/476.

wǣlrāp *m.* water-fetter 11/351.

wælrǣs *m.* murderous attack 11/123.

wælrǣst *f.* death in battle 12/113.

wælrēaf *n.* corpse 19/155.

wælrēc *adj.* deadly fumes 11/434.

wælsleaht *m.* slaughter 16/7, 91.

wælspere *n.* deadly spear 12/322.

wælstōw *f.* place of slaughter, battlefield 12/95, 293.

wælwulf *m.* wolf of slaughter 12/96.

(*ge*)wǣnde, gewǣndon *see* wendan.

wǣpen *n.* weapon 12/252, 3/53, 6/138.

wǣpn*ge*wrixl *n.* conflict 9/90.

wǣr *f.* agreement, covenant 8/46.

wǣran, wǣre *see* wesan.

wǣrfæst *adj.* loyal 13/228.

wǣrlīce *adv.* carefully 9/176.

wǣrloga *m.* enemy 13/71, 108.

wǣre, wǣron, wǣrun, wæs *see* wesan.

wæst *see* west.

wæstm *m.* (1) form 14/10, 11/143, 19/119; (2) fruit 19/34, 72, 125.

wæstmian *w.2* flourish 8/11.

wǣta *m.* moisture 15/22.

(*ge*)wǣtan *w.1* wet, drench 13/134.

wæter *n.* water 2/168, 6/147, 11/564 n.

wæteregsa *m.* terrible water 13/134.

wæterfæsten *n.* river encampment 2/22.

wē *see* ic.

wēa *m.* woe 11/187, 18/4, 25.

weal, weall *m.* wall 16/98, 10/29, 11/84.

gewealc *n.* rolling 17/6, 46.

weald *m.* forest 2/8, 9, 23.

geweald *n.* power, control 3/48, 9/37, 78.

(*ge*)wealdan 7 *with gen. or dat.* control, cause, wield 12/95, 168, 272; (*ge*)wēold 3 *sg. pret.* 10/34, 106, 11/295, 368, gewealde 3 *sg. pret.* (*as weak verb*) 3/49; wēoldan 3 *pl. pret.* 9/50.

wealdend *see* waldend.

wealhstod *m.* translator, interpreter 10/49, 4/48-9.

weallan 7 surge; wēol(l) 3 *sg. pret.* 11/213, 366, 372; weallendum *pres. p.* 9/179.

wealsteal *m.* place of walls 16/88.

weard *m.* guardian 5/41, 35, 10/85.

weardian *w.2* possess, inhabit 19/85.

wearm *adj.* hot 19/18.

wearmian *w.2* become hot 19/95.

wearp *see* weorpan.

wearþ, wearþan *see* weorþan.

wēatācen *n.* sign of woe 19/51.

weax *n.* wax 7/131.

weaxan 7 grow, increase; weaxeð 3 *sg. pres.* 19/114, 116; weaxað 3 *pl. pres.* 20a/5, weaxeð 20b/9; wēoxon 3 *pl. pret.* 13/132; wexende *pres. p.* 8/10; geweaxen *pret. p.* 19/179.

webbian *w.2* contrive 8/37.

weccan *w.1* wake 19/137; wehte 3 *sg. pret.* 11/627 n.

wed *n.* pledge, vow 9/84, 176.

wedbryce *m.* breaking of a pledge 9/123-4.

weder *n.* weather, sky 19/18, 13/211, 19/57.

wedercandel *f.* candle of the sky, i.e. sun 13/131.

weg *m.* way 3/93, 6/9, 23; **on weg** away 11/62, 173, 221.

wegan 5 carry, wear; **wæg** 3 *sg. pret.* 11/477, 553; **wēgon** 3 *pl. pret.* 12/98.

wēgas 16/46 *see* **wǣg.**

wel, well *adv.* well, much 2/63, 5/6, 11/585, **wæll** 3/19; **betst** *supl.* 7/7.

wela *m.* wealth, riches 3/6, 4/34, 36.

(*ge*)**welhwǣr** *adv.* nearly everywhere 2/158, 4/74, 9/26.

gewelhwylc, -hwilc *adj.* nearly every 9/47, 96.

welig *adj.* rich 7/26, 11/380.

welwan *w.1* huddle together 9/107.

welwang *m.* field of slaughter 13/181.

welwillende *adj.* kindly, benevolent 10/43.

welwillendnes *f.* kindness 7/28.

(*ge*)**weman** *w.1* entice 10/37, 16/29.

wēn *f.* expectation 11/33, 18/25 n.

wēnan *w.1 with gen., or* **þæt,** to think, expect 8/38, 4/16, 42.

(*ge*)**wendan,** (*ge*)**wændan** *w.1* (*often reflexive*) turn; (1) go 12/316, 2/47, 69; (2) change 13/35, 14/183, 15/22; (3) translate 4/41, 46, 48.

wenian *w.2* treat kindly 16/36.

wēol(l) *see* **weallan.**

(*ge*)**wēold(an)** *see* (*ge*)**wealdan.**

wēop *see* **wēpan.**

(*ge*)**weorc, gewerc, worc** *n.* (1) deed, work 11/303, 5/37, 8/14; (2) fortification 2/65, 10, 13, 129; (3) pain 11/209, 13/232, 14/51.

geweorhte *see* (*ge*)**wyrc(e)an.**

weorod *see* **werod.**

weorpan 3 throw, sprinkle 11/564; **wearp** 3 *sg. pret.* 2/177, 11/272, 14/55.

weorð *n.* price 9/78, 80.

(*ge*)**weorðan,** (*ge*)**wurðan, wearþan** 3 be, happen, become 4/42, 8/17, 7/142, 152, 16/64; **wyrð** 3 *sg. pres.* 9/4, 42, 14/186, **weorð** 14/160, **weorþeð** 16/110, **wurðeþ** 14/185; (*ge*)**weorðe** 3 *sg. pres. subj.* 9/89, 90, 19/41; (*ge*)**wearð**

3 *sg. pret.* 1/18, 2/88, 9/80, 10/107; **wurdon** 3 *pl. pret.* 2/2, 90, 119; (*ge*)**wurde** 3 *sg. pret. subj.* 9/103, 10/45, 11/504; **geworden** *pret. p.* 7/45, 9/65, 73.

weorþian, wurðian, wyrðian *w.2* honour 5/2, 14/65, 84, 108, 10/78, 13/55, 116.

weorðlīce *see* **wurðlīce.**

weorðmynd *see* **wurðmynt.**

weorðscipe *see* **wurðscipe.**

weorðung *f.* worship, honour 9/21.

weoruda *see* **werod.**

weoruld *see* **worold.**

weoruldhād *m.* secular life 5/17, 61.

wēoxon *see* **weaxan.**

wēpan 7 weep; **wēop** 3 *sg. pret.* 15/55; **wēpende** *pres. p.* 13/59.

wer *m.* man 16/64, 7/97, 119.

gewerc *see* (*ge*)**weorc.**

werg *m.* criminal 15/31.

wergend *m.* defender 11/655.

(*ge*)**wērgian** *w.2* weary 11/625.

werian *w.1* defend 1/14, 12/82, 283.

wērig *adj.* (1) exhausted, weary (physically or mentally) 16/15, 12/303, 13/233; **wēregum** *m. dat. pl.* 13/59; (2) cursed 13/86.

wērigmōd *adj.* weary, disheartened 11/284.

werod, wered, werud, weorod, weorud *n.* troop 10/21, 1/10, 14/107, 15/124, 15/51, 69, 152, 13/62, 147.

werscipe *see* **wurðscipe.**

wesan *irr.* be 11/481, 574, 14/17; **eom** *1 sg. pres.* 7/136, 12/179, 14/127; **eart** *2 sg. pres.* 7/25, 39, 85; **is** *3 sg. pres.* 2/5, 6, 109; **syndon** *1 pl. pres.* 7/102, **synd** 14/175; **syndon** *3 pl. pres.* 8/15, 30, 14/144, **syndan** 8/55, 9/25, 32, **sindon** 16/93, **siendon** 4/74, **sint** 6/70, **synd** 6/79, 100, **synt** 13/150, 14/135, 176, **syn** 9/60, 61, 94; **sȳ** *2 sg. pres. subj.* 7/11; **sȳ** *3 sg. pres. subj.* 6/53, 7/9, 8/72, **sīe** 4/19, 6/3, 13/70, **sī** 15/144; **sȳn** *1 pl. pres. subj.* 8/22, 62; **sȳn** *3 pl. pres. subj.* 8/27, **sīen** 4/52, 56, 73; **wæs** *1 sg. pret.* 15/20, 21, 18/36; **wæs** *3 sg. pret.* 1/9, 21, 37, **was**

GLOSSARY

1/9; **wǣron** 3 pl. pret. 1/29, 35,
2/27, **wǣran** 1/20, 9/6, 175,
wǣrun 1/12, 15, 23; **wǣre** 3 sg.
pret. subj. 1/32, 2/30, 3/11; **wǣren**
1 pl. pres. subj. 4/25, 3 pl. pret.
subj. 4/75.
  Negative forms from **ne** + **wesan**: **nis** 3 sg. pres. 3/39, 8/74,
9/114, **nys** 10/139; **nearon** 3 pl.
pres. 17/82; **næs** 3 sg. pret. 3/46,
9/7, 11/316; **nǣron** 3 pl. pret.
2/154, 4/32, 11/430; **nǣre** 3 sg.
pret. subj. 1/30, 7/43; **nǣren** 3 pl.
pret. subj. 4/17.
west adv. to the west, in the west
2/47, 69, 84, 129; **wæst** 2/72.
westan adv. from the west 2/50,
20b/8; **be westan** prep. on the
west of 2/79, 80.
westanwind m. west wind 6/14.
wēste adj. deserted, desolate 16/74,
2/95, 6/4.
wēstenn n. wilderness 6/8.
westlang adv. to the west 2/6.
westweard adv. west 2/2.
wexende see **weaxan**.
wīc n. dwelling-place 11/120, 353.
gewīcan 1 fail; **gewāc** 3 sg. pret.
11/402.
wicca m. or **wicce** f. witch 9/147.
wicg n. horse 11/191, 12/240.
wicgerēfa m. bailiff 2/146.
(ge)wīcian w.2 encamp, dwell, stay
2/20, 87, 126.
wīcing m. Viking 9/89, 12/26, 73.
wīcstede m. dwelling-place 11/380.
wīd adj. (wide); **tō wīdan fēore**
13/106 for the rest of your life.
wīde adv. far, widely 9/4, 10, 28;
wīdre comp. 11/62; **wīdost** supl.
17/57.
wīdfloga m. far-flier 11/603.
gewīdre n. storm 11/166.
wīdsǣ f. open sea 6/25, 10, 88.
wiece f. week; **wucena** gen. pl.
2/83; **wucum** dat. pl. 6/64.
wīf n. woman, wife 7/115, 1/16, 2/57.
wīfcyþþ(u) f. relations with a woman
1/11.
wīg n. or m. war 11/645, 4/8, 11/402.
wiga m. warrior 11/284, 300, 12/75.
wīgbil n. battle-sword 11/348.

wīgend m. warrior 12/302.
wīgheafola m. war-head, i.e. helmet
11/434.
wīgheard adj. brave in battle 12/75.
wīghryre m. death in battle 11/360.
wīgplega m. fighting 12/268, 316.
wīgsigor m. victory in war 11/295.
wīhaga m. shield-wall 12/102.
wiht f. (creature) used in negative
clauses in the following ways:
(1) anything 11/374 n., 14/149,
19/26; (2) acc. sg. adv. at all 11/627,
630; (3) dat. sg. adv. at all 11/255,
460, 14/33; (4) **mid wihte** adv.
at all 14/136, 183.
wiht n.? weight; **wihte** dat. sg.
3/61 by weight, in bulk?
gewihte n. weight 7/60.
wilde adj. wild, desolate 6/44, 57.
wildēor n. wild beast 11/221; **wildrum** dat. pl. 6/41 n.
wilgeofa m. one who grants one's
wish, benefactor 13/62.
will n. will 3/81.
willa m. will, wish, desire 7/122,
3/17, 31.
willan irr. wish, be willing, intend;
tr. want sometimes in 7 (e.g. 7/122,
123, 130); **wille** 1 sg. pres. 4/70,
12/247, **wylle** 12/216; **wilt** 2 sg.
pres. 7/15, 90; **wile** 3 sg. pres.
12/52, 14/151, 15/107, **wille** 4/59,
76, 11/185 (or subj.?), **wylle**
11/539; **willaþ** 1 pl. pres. 12/35,
40; **willaþ** 3 pl. pres. 12/46,
wyllaþ 6/123; **wille** 2 sg. pres.
subj. 7/9, 23, 104, 3 sg. pres. subj.
7/109, 11/162; **willan** 3 pl. pres.
subj. 9/142; **wolde** 1 sg. pret. 4/74,
7/57, 129; **woldest** 2 sg. pret. 7/21;
wolde 3 sg. pret. 1/8, 3/24, 6/7;
woldon 3 pl. pret. 2/31, 32, 3/82;
wolde 1 sg. pret. subj. 11/502;
woldon 1 pl. pret. subj. 11/409;
wolden 3 pl. pret. subj. 2/23,
14/4.
  Negative forms from **ne** + **willan**: **nelle** 1 sg. pres. 12/246;
nellaþ 3 pl. pres. 9/142; **nolde**
3 sg. pret. 1/20, 11/5, 90; **noldon**
1 pl. pret. 4/37, 3 pl. pret. 1/29,
31, 4/40.

230

willsele *m.* pleasant dwelling (*lit.* hall) 19/95.

willwong *m.* delightful plain 19/89.

gewilni(g)an *w.2* wish 3/10, 7/150, 10/41.

wilnung *f.* desire 4/43.

wimman *m.* woman 3/43.

gewin *see* **gewinn**.

wind *m.* wind 11/165, 6/77, 13/132.

(ge)windan *3* (1) turn, go 11/62; (2) fly 14/173; **wand** *3 sg. pret.* 13/131; **wundon** *3 pl. pret.* 12/106; (3) (*tr.*) wind, twist; **wunden** *pret. p.* 16/32 n., 11/173 n; (4) brandish; **wand** *3 sg. pret.* 12/43.

windig *adj.* windy 11/149, 19/61.

wine *m.* friend 12/250, 11/209, 12/228.

winedrihten, -dryhten *m.* friendly lord 11/345, 495, 12/248, 263.

wineléas *adj.* friendless 16/45, 11/386.

winemǣg *m.* dear kinsman 12/306, 16/7, 17/16.

wingál *adj.* merry with wine 17/29.

gewinn, gewin *n.* strife, war 6/115, 10/13, 11/97; **winn** 14/14.

gewinna *m.* adversary 13/204.

winnan *3* fight, strive 14/33, 53, 101; **winnaŏ** *1 pl. pres.* 10/15; **wann** *3 sg. pret.* 10/107, 14/58; **wunnon** *3 pl. pret.* 11/76.

gewinnan *3* obtain, get control of, win 9/160, 12/125, 14/157; **gewunnon** *3 pl. pret.* 10/18; **gewunnen** *pret. p.* 14/56, **gewunnon** 3/53.

winreced *m.* wine-hall 11/13.

winsæl *n.* wine-hall 16/78.

winsele *m.* wine-hall 11/70.

winsumum *see* **wynsum**.

winter *m.* (1) winter 6/148, 2/93, 113; (2) (*pl.*) years 1/8, 11/506, 12/210.

winterceald *adj.* bitterly cold 13/220, 18/4 n.

wintercearig *adj* gloomy as winter 16/24.

winterscūr *m.* wintry shower 19/18.

winterstund *f.* winter hour 14/125 n.

wintergewǣde *n.* winter garment 19/132.

wintergew(e)orp *n.* winter storm 19/57; 13/211 snowdrift?

wiotan *see* **wita**.

wiotonne *see* **(ge)witan**.

wīs *adj.* wise 3/14, 4/48, 11/191.

wiscan *w.1* wish; **wyscte** *3 sg. pret.* 18/25; **wiston** *3 pl. pret.* 11/345.

wīsdōm *m.* (1) learning 4/44, 8, 11; (2) Boethius' Philosophia 20a/1, 20b/1.

wise *f.* manner, 5/83, 9/27, 62; 5/56 thing.

wise *adv.* wisely 16/88.

wishycgende *adj.* (*pres. p.*) wise in thought 11/489.

wīsian *w.2* guide 12/141, 13/140.

wīslic *adj.* certain 18/34.

gewīslīce *adv.* certainly, clearly; **gewīslīcor** *comp.* 7/17; **gewīslīcost** *supl.* 11/141.

wist *f.* food, feast 13/21, 147, 8/77.

wistfyllo *f.* fill of feasting 11/33.

wiston 11/345 *see* **wiscan**.

wita, wiota *m.* wise man, counsellor, councillor 16/65, 10/47, 1/2, 4/3.

wītan *1 with dat. and acc.* accuse 11/514.

gewītan *1* depart, go 17/52; **gewīteŏ** *3 sg. pres.* 11/151; **gewāt** *1 sg. pret.* 5/29, *3 sg. pret.* 11/342, 592; **gewitene** *pret. p.* 17/80, 86.

(ge)witan *irr.* know 7/9, 16, 21; 9/71 show (respect); 11/141 ascertain; **wāt** *1 sg. pres.* 7/148, 11/429, 14/140; **wāst** *2 sg. pres.* 7/38, 146; **wāt** *3 sg. pres.* 10/15, 11/423, 12/94; **witan** *1 pl. pres.* 9/16, 79, 114; **wite** *2 sg. pres. subj.* 7/10, 16, 131, *3 sg. pres. subj.* 11/158; **wiste** *3 sg. pret.* 11/63, 12/124, 14/141, **wisse** 6/14, 11/14, 498; **wiston** *3 pl. pret.* 4/30, 11/97; **witanne** *infl. inf.* 9/74, **gewitane** 3/10, **wiotonne** 4/52.

Negative forms from ne + witan: **nāt** *1 sg. pres.* 7/6, 8, 142; **nāst** *2 sg. pres.* 7/38; **nyste** *3 sg. pret.* 3/46, 6/30, **niste** 7/134, **nysse** 6/14, 18.

wīte *n.* punishment, torment 14/110, 5/76, 8/4.

231

wītebend *f.* tormenting bond 13/108.

wītig *adj.* wise 11/295, 18/32, 19/30.

wītodlīce *adv.* truly, certainly 3/54, 10/88.

gewitt, gewit *n.* intellect, senses 11/476, 13/35, 220; 11/655 head.

wiÞ *prep. with dat., acc. or gen.* (1) against 1/7, 2/34, 71; (2) towards 2/47, 69, 9/57; (3) from 11/32; (4) in return for 12/31, 39; (5) by, near 6/56; (6) with 11/373.

wiðcweðan *5* oppose, defy; wiðcwǣdon *3 pl. pret.* 3/17.

wiÞerlēan *n.* requital 12/116.

wiÞersæc *n.* hostility 10/46.

wiðfōn *7 with dat.* take hold of; wiðfēng *3 sg. pret.* 11/59.

wiðhabban *irr. with dat.* withstand; wiðhæfde *3 sg. pret.* 11/71.

wiðstandan, -stondan *6 with dat.* resist 10/21, 16/15.

wiðūtan *prep. with dat.* without 3/53

wlenc *f.* pride 8/77.

wlītan *1* look; wlāt *3 sg. pret.* 11/313, 12/172; wliton *3 pl. pret.* 11/333, wlitan 11/625.

wlite *m.* beauty 19/75, 20a/6, 20b/13.

wlitig *adj.* beautiful 19/7, 8/9, 13/122.

wlitigian *w.2* become beautiful 17/49.

wlonc, wlanc *adj.* proud 11/606, 16/80, 12/139, 205.

wōd, wōdon *see* wadan.

wōhbogen *adj.* coiled 11/600.

wōhdǣd *f.* crime 8/3.

wōhdōm *m.* injustice 9/163.

wōhgestrēon *n.* ill-gotten gains 9/162.

wolcen *n.* cloud (*pl.* sky) 19/61, 11/13, 165.

wolden, woldon *see* willan.

wōlic *adj.* evil 8/7.

wōlīce *adv.* wrongly 8/27.

wōma *m.* terror 16/103.

womb *f.* belly 19/173.

womm *m.* sin 8/82, 15/4.

won, wan(n) *adj.* dark 16/103, 11/165, 11/1, 15/55.

wōnes *f.* wickedness 8/3, 27.

wong *m.* plain, country, place 19/7, 11/204, 13/22.

wongstede *m.* place 11/559.

wōp *m.* weeping 11/84, 19/51.

worc *see* (ge)weorc.

geworct *see* (ge)wyrc(e)an.

word *n.* word 11/590, 4/1, 64.

wordcwyde *m.* speech 11/526.

geworden *see* (ge)weorðan.

wordhlēoðor *n.* sound of words 13/93.

wordhord *n.* store of words 20b/1.

wordriht *n.* right word, word about duty 11/404.

(ge)worht(e), worhton, worhtun *see* (ge)wyrc(e)an.

wōrian *w.2* crumble 16/78.

worldfrēond *m.* earthly friend 8/71.

worldlic *adj.* wordly 8/12.

worldrīc *adj.* powerful 8/7.

worldrīce, woruldrīce *n.* world 8/35, 16/65.

worn *m.* multitude 16/91.

worold, world, woruld *f.* world 9/1, 5/8, 8/15, 21, 4/23, 10/81, weoruld 16/107.

woroldscamu *f.* public disgrace 9/105, 108.

woroldstrūdere *m.* robber 9/148.

woruldcaru *f.* worldly care 10/40.

woruldcund *adj.* secular 4/4.

woruldgesǣlig *adj.* prosperous 12/219.

woruldgestrēon *n.* riches of the earth 19/137.

woruldÞing *n.* worldly affair 4/21.

wracu *f.* (1) revenge 14/148; (2) misery 18/4, 19/51.

wrāð *adj.* hostile 11/7, 360, 13/228.

wrāðe *adv.* grievously 11/645.

wrāðlic *adj.* grievous 14/110.

wraðu *f.* support 19/129.

wræc *n.* persecution n. 18/1.

wræcca *m.* exile, adventurer 11/386, 17/15.

wræclāst *m.* path of exile 16/32, 11/143, 16/5.

wrǣt, wrǣtt *f.* ornament 11/544, 272.

wrǣtlic *adj.* beautiful 13/93, 19/63, 173.

wrǣtlīce *adv.* spendidly 19/75, 160.

wrecan 5 (1) drive out; **wræc** 3 sg.
pret. 11/479; (2) utter 17/1.
(ge)**wrecan** 5 avenge 11/287, 12/208,
248; **wrece** 3 sg. pres. subj. 11/176;
(ge)**wræc** 3 sg. pret. 1/5, 11/648,
wrec 12/279; **wræce** 3 sg. pret.
subj. 12/257.
wridian w.2 thrive 19/27, 119.
gewrit n. written document, letter
7/127, 3/47, 4/58.
(ge)**wrītan** 1 write 13/13; **writon**
3 pl. pret. 5/69; **gewriten** pret.
p. 3/91, 7/127.
wrixlan w.1 vary; **gewrixled** pret.
p. 19/160 variegated.
gewrixlian w.2 obtain 14/90.
wrōht m. calumny 8/37.
gewrohte see (ge)**wyrc(e)an**.
wrōhtsmiŏ m. malicious foe 13/86.
wucena, wucum see **wiece.**
wudu m. wood 2/6, 5, 11/207.
wudubēam m. tree 19/75.
wudufæsten n. forest encampment
2/21.
wuduholt n. wood 19/34.
wuldor n. glory 10/148, 145, 13/55.
wuldorfæder m. glorious father
5/37.
wuldorþrymm m. glorious power
8/60–1.
wuldurcyning m. King of glory
11/568.
wulf m. wolf 16/82.
wulfhliþ n. wolf-slope 11/149.
gewuna m. custom 9/131.
wund f. wound 11/484, 498, 603.
wund adj. wounded 11/519, 526,
12/113.
wunden see (ge)**windan.**
wundenfeax adj. with plaited mane
11/191.
wundenmǣl n. sword with curved
markings 11/272.
wundian w.2 wound 1/15, 21, 38.
wundnum see (ge)**windan.**
wundon see (ge)**windan.**
wundor, wundur n. wonder, marvel 8/74, 9/114, 10/138, 11/532;
11/250 wonderful creature, monster; **wundrum** dat. pl. 11/460,
16/98, 19/63 adv. wonderfully,
very.

wundorcræft m. marvellous skill
13/13.
wundorlic adj. wonderful 11/231.
wundri(g)an w.2 with gen. marvel
(at) 4/38, 7/130, 10/133.
wunian w.2 (1) remain, continue,
dwell 8/48, 1/3, 4.
gewunian w.2 be in the habit of,
use to 5/2.
wunnon, gewunnon see **winnan,
gewinnan.**
wunung f. dwelling 7/79.
(ge)**wurde, wurdon** see (ge)**weorŏan.**
wurma m. purple 19/160.
wurman 8/1 see **wyrm.**
wurŏ, worŏ, wyrþ adj. worth,
worthy 3/47, 5/46; **wurŏran**
comp. 14/177.
(ge)**wurŏan** see (ge)**weorŏan.**
wurŏful adj. honourable, dignified
3/24; **-fulre** comp. 3/14–15.
wurŏlic adj. honourable 7/5.
wurŏlice, weorŏlice adv. honour-
ably 12/279, 15/17; **wurŏlicost**
supl. 7/77.
wurŏmynt, weorŏmynd m. or f.
glory 10/12, 22, 32, 11/300.
wurŏode see **weorþian.**
wurŏscipe, weorŏscipe m. honour
3/11, 7/80, 9/110; **werscipe**
3/52–3.
wutun, wutan see **uton.**
wyduwe f. widow 9/34.
wylfen adj. wolfish, savage 18/22.
wylla m. well 19/63.
wyllaŏ see **willan.**
wylm m. (1) surging (or water)
13/126; (2) fervour 5/83.
wyn, wynn f. joy 13/178, 11/500,
16/36, 17/27; **wynnum** dat. pl.,
adv. beautifully 15/15, joyfully
19/7.
wynlēas adj. joyless 11/120, 207.
wynlic adj. beautiful 14/10, 19/34.
wynlond n. blissful land 19/82.
wynsum, winsum adj. pleasant
19/13, 5/68, 7/31, 47.
wynsumlic adj. pleasant 8/9, 69.
(ge)**wyrc(e)an** w.1 make, work,
bring about 3/56, 5/3, 10, 14,
6/144, 12/264, 11/575, **gewyri-**

233

cean 8/41; (ge)worhte 3 sg. pret.
2/13, 116, 11/319, 485, geweorthe
5/77, gewrohte 3/48; worhton
3 pl. pret. 2/125, 129, worhtan
9/115, 10/30, worhtun 2/73;
geworht pret. p. 2/16, 53, 5/7,
geworct 2/65.

wyrd f. fate, destiny, event 11/33,
8/40, 16/5 n.

gewyrdan w.1 harm 19/19.

gewyrht n. deed 9/88.

wyrhta m. (1) worker 8/57, 55;
(2) Creator 19/9.

wyrm m. (1) serpent 11/402, 221,
442; (2) worm 19/114, 8/76;
(3) wurman ? 18/1 n.

wyrmcynn n. race of serpents
11/216.

wyrmlic n. serpentine shape
16/98 n.

wyrnan w.1 with gen. withhold
12/118.

wyrse adj. comp. worse 9/168, 14/14,
65; wyrrestan supl. 13/86.

wyrse adv. comp. worse 9/2.

wyrsian w.2 deteriorate 9/32.

wyrt f. root, plant 11/155, 19/95,
147.

wyrð see (ge)weorðan.

wyrþes see wurð.

(ge)wyrðod(e) see (ge)weorþian.

wyscte see wiscan.

yfel n. evil, crime 2/157, 3/42, 8/11.

yfel adj. evil 3/91, 7/76, 115.

yfele adv. badly 14/142.

yfelian w.2 become worse 9/4.

yfelnes f. wickedness 3/93, 10/9.

ylcan, ylce see ilca.

yldan w.1 delay 11/38.

ylde m. pl. men 11/4; ælda gen. pl.
16/85, 17/77; eldum dat. pl.
11/384.

yldo f. old age 17/70, 5/18, 10/106
age.

ylfetu f. swan 17/19.

ymb, ymbe, embe prep. with acc.
(1) around, about, concerning 1/35,
2/1, 3/14, 10/33; (2) at the end of,
after 1/8, 2/15, 101.

ymbbeorgan 3 protect (by surrounding); ymbbearh 3 sg. pret.
11/244.

ymbclyppan w.1 embrace 15/42.

ymbefōn 7 encircle, clasp; -fēng
3 sg. pret. 11/464.

ymbhwyrft m. surface 19/43.

ymbsittan 5 surround, besiege;
-sǣton 3 pl. pret. 2/45, 46.

ymb(e)sittend adj. (pres. p.) used as
noun 7/2, 43 people sitting round
at a banquet; 11/507 neighbouring
peoples.

ymbūtan adv. around (the coast)
2/44, 46.

(ge)yppan w.1 reveal 13/178.

yrfeweard m. heir 11/504.

yr(i)gan w.1 dishearten 9/97.

yrhð(u) f. cowardice, slackness
9/164, 12/6.

yrmð(u) f. misery 9/80, 19/52, 9/14.

yrnan 3 run; urnon 3 pl. pret. 1/18;
yrnende pres. p. 6/95.

yrre n. anger 9/86, 41, 87.

yrre adj. angry 11/273, 68, 316;
eorre 13/47.

yrremōd adj. angry 11/25.

yrringa adv. angrily 11/306.

ysle f. ash 19/106, 153.

ȳst f. storm 20a/7, 20b/14.

yteren adj. of otter's skin 6/52.

ȳð f. wave 11/228, 466, 13/127.

ȳþan w.1 lay waste 16/85.

ȳðgeblond, -gebland n. surging
water 11/164, 334, 361.

ȳðelice adv. easily 11/297.

ȳðfaru f. flood 19/44.

ȳðgewinn n. (wave-strife) swimming 11/225.

ȳwan w.1 show 11/607.